östberg™

Library of Design Management

Every relationship of value requires constant care and commitment. At Östberg, we are relentless in our desire to create and bring forward only the best ideas in design, architecture, interiors, and design management. Using diverse mediums of communications, including books and the Internet, we are constantly searching for thoughtful ideas that are erudite, witty, and of lasting importance to the quality of life. Inspired by the architecture of Ragnar Östberg and the best of Scandinavian design and civility, the Östberg Library of Design Management seeks to restore the passion for creativity that makes better products, spaces, and communities. The essence of Östberg can be summed up in our quality charter to you: "Communicating concepts of leadership and design excellence."

D0920016

LEADERSHIP
BY DESIGN

LEADERSHIP BY DESIGN

CREATING AN ARCHITECTURE OF TRUST

Richard N. Swett, FAIA

with Colleen M. Thornton, chief researcher

Translations of Danish texts by
Peter Wedell-Wedellsborg, MAA, and Kenneth Krabat

 Greenway Communications

 östberg

Östberg Library of Design Management

ISBN: 0-9755654-0-0

Cover design: Austin Cramer
Layout: Jennie Monahan

Published by:
Greenway Communications, LLC
A division of The Greenway Group
30 Technology Parkway South, Suite 200
Atlanta, GA 30092
800.726.8603
www.greenway.us

On the cover:
Thomas Cole (American, born England, 1801–1848), *The Architect's Dream*, 1840, oil on canvas, 53 x 84 1/16 in., Toledo Museum of Art, Purchased with funds from the Florence Scott Libbey Bequest in Memory of her Father, Maurice A. Scott, 1949.162

For Katrina, Chelsea, Shebby, Keato, Chanté, Kizi, Atty, Sunday,
and
For my parents, Ann and Philip E. Swett Sr., who taught me that
true leadership is an exercise in cooperation and love that allows everyone to participate and everyone to win whenever possible.

CONTENTS

ACKNOWLEDGMENTS

COUNTLESS INSTITUTIONS AND INDIVIDUALS have performed heroically to bring this book to fruition. I admit at the outset that it would be impossible to mention properly every single one of them. More honestly, I am certain that errors of omission ensure that some are not acknowledged here. My humble apologies are offered first and foremost to those that fall into this category.

This idea was the wellspring of my experience in politics and diplomacy, but it very quickly became a cause shared by all with whom I came in contact. Soon I discovered that others had been thinking about leadership by design in their own way and that we were able to join forces in a common cause. One of the first partnerships became one of the most important, as it resulted in the writing of this book. Colleen Thornton, my researcher extraordinaire, possessed the acumen, tenacity, and patience to deal with a sometimes distracted author and a completely disorganized and little studied body of evidence and was instrumental in collecting, organizing, and bringing to life the contents of the book. Quite literally, it would not have been done without her. My indebtedness to her is profound and my gratitude, deep.

The early financial support I received from my dear friend, James Cramer, and the Design Futures Council, combined with funding from the VELUX Foundation in Denmark and the Arnold W. Brunner Grant awarded for this research by the New York Foundation for Architecture (AIA New York Chapter of the American Institute of Architects), all provided me the wherewithal to pursue the research and begin this journey of discovery with confidence.

This book is filled with stories of leaders who have employed or currently are employing their talents in bettering our communities. Before I acknowledge the many contributors whose names appear in the following pages, I would like to make a sweeping expression of gratitude to all who gave of their time to teach me about their stories so that I might document them for others to learn from. Their generosity and friendship, as well as their examples, have inspired and nourished me throughout this journey. I must expressly thank Alex Purves, Richard Farson, Congressman Earl Blumenauer, Al Sprague, Greg Tung, Scott Simpson, Jon Bresler, Jean Phifer, Alex Garvin, Ric Bell, and Chelsea Swett for taking precious time out of their lives to read and comment on the manuscript during its formative stages.

The research has benefited greatly from the commitment and generosity of many colleagues and friends. Colleen and I would like to thank the following for their invaluable contributions to this project:

Peter Wedell-Wedellsborg, MAA, who joined our research team while still a graduate student in architecture at the Royal Danish Academy of Fine Arts in 2001, and Kenneth Krabat, well-known Danish writer and poet, who translated Alfred Råvad's 1929 masterwork, *The Mayor's Book*, from old Danish into English.

Annon Adams, independent architectural historian, of Poughkeepsie, New York, who shared her original, unpublished research on architect John A. Wood and helped us locate the original press reports on the 1892 New York architects' licensing law, along with additional information on the five architects who protested its passage.

Professor Michael J. Lewis, chair of the Art Department, Williams College, Williamstown, Massachusetts, whose book on architect Frank Furness was of great help, and who regularly provided professional assistance, advice, and support.

Dr. Cynthia Field, chair, and Sabina Dugan, architectural history specialist, of the Smithsonian Institution's Department of Architectural History and Historic Preservation, who shared their original, unpublished research on the life and work of architect Adolf Cluss.

Colleen A. Dunlavy, professor of history, University of Wisconsin, who shared her research on the development of Prussia's railroad system and directed us to original sources that might shed light on the Prussian background of architect Frederick A. Petersen.

Jay Shockley, architectural historian with the New York City Landmarks Preservation Commission, and Susan Tunick, president of the Friends of

Terra Cotta, who kindly shared their original research on Frederick A. Petersen's architectural career.

Terry Murphy, antiquarian book dealer, of Mt. Sterling, Kentucky, and Brad Carrington, bibliographer of the William T. Young Library, University of Kentucky, who went to great lengths to obtain for us original imprints of Frederick A. Petersen's Civil War pamphlets and copies of his writings, along with various 19th-century newspaper clippings about him.

J. Peter Holsman, licensed architect, of Northbrook, Illinois, shared with us the family papers of his father, John T. Holsman, architect and, most importantly, his grandfather, architect Henry K. Holsman, FAIA, as well as obtained on our behalf relevant documents from the Burnham Library of the Art Institute of Chicago. We also thank him for kindly photographing his grandfather's buildings for us.

Cooper W. Norman, of Fairfield, Iowa, who provided the background on the fight to preserve the Henry K. Holsman Historic District, and also his work to save historic transportation infrastructure through the federal ISTEA program.

Gunny Harboe, Chicago, who alerted us to the work of Danish-American architect Alfred J. Råvad and to Danish architectural historian Hans Helge Madsen, who shared his original research for his biography of Råvad.

Isabelle Gournay and Jane Loeffler, architectural historians and lecturers at the University of Maryland, who each shared their research on the political history of American architects, and have provided constant support and advice from the outset of this research project.

James Howard Kunstler, author and social commentator, who has been candid in sharing his thoughts and writings on place making, politics, and civic engagement in America.

James Dunaway, journalist, and A.D. Coleman, writer, art critic, and university lecturer, who both gave close, thoughtful readings and constructive criticisms of the text in its early drafts.

Carolyn Thornton, resident of A.T. White's Tower Buildings, Cobble Hill Historic District, Brooklyn, New York, who provided access to the buildings' interior spaces.

Lachlan Cranswick, scientist, of Melbourne, Australia, who provided Albon P. Man Jr.'s articles on the 1863 draft riots, and Nancy Cataldi, of the Richmond Hill Historical Society, New York, who contacted Man on our behalf to confirm his identity and the authenticity of his research. Man is the namesake and great-grandson of a Union League Club founder; as one of the nation's first community real estate developers, he created Richmond Hill, New York.

Carolyn Y. Yerkes, Princeton University, who provided us with Professor Robert Gutman's book, *Architectural Practice: A Critical View.*

Wallace P. Wormley, Ph.D., London, England, alumnus of Howard and Harvard Universities, who helped us gather information on African-American architects.

Linda Hopper, director of the Office of Training and Organizational Development at Georgetown University, for her invaluable insight into current leadership literature and its application to this research.

The following archivists and institutions were also instrumental in providing information and/or access to original documents:

Arthur Lawrence, librarian and archivist, Union League Club, New York City

Richard L. Baker, U.S. Army Heritage and Education Center, Carlisle, Pennsylvania

Ulla Volk, director, The Cooper Union Library, New York City

Rosalie Genevro, executive director, The Architectural League, New York City

Sarah Turner, archivist, the American Institute of Architects Archives, Washington, D.C.

Fredric Bell, executive director, AIA New York, New York City

Mary Fitch, executive director, AIA/DC, Washington, D.C.

Library of Congress, Washington, D.C.

New York Public Library, New York City

New Jersey State Archives, Trenton, New Jersey

Royal Danish Library, Copenhagen, Denmark

Royal Danish Academy of Fine Arts School of Architecture Library, Copenhagen, Denmark

Geheimen Staatsarchiv Stiftung Preußischer Kulturbesitz, Berlin, Germany

In-kind professional support for this research was provided by:
The Project for Public Spaces, Inc., New York City
The American Chamber of Commerce in Denmark, Copenhagen, Denmark
The Center for Architecture, Copenhagen, Denmark

Finally, I would like to thank the true leader in my life, my wife, Katrina, who inspires me to search for deeper meanings and gives me excellent guidance as I try to be the kind of leader my family of seven children can be proud of. I have learned more from her about leadership by design than all this book has provided and more.

FOREWORD

I FIRST BECAME ACQUAINTED WITH RICHARD SWETT, the only architect elected to the U.S. Congress in the 20th century, when I was serving as a Public Director on the national board of the American Institute of Architects. I became even more familiar with his work through our discussions as senior fellows of the Design Futures Council. But it is my enduring interest in leadership that cemented my enthusiasm for what Ambassador Swett has to say.

I'm a psychologist, not a designer, but in 1966 I was invited to speak at the International Design Conference in Aspen. There I encountered an especially distinguished group of designers—architects, graphic artists, industrial designers, landscape architects, etc.—some of whom became lifelong friends. Eventually I joined its board of directors and embarked on an affiliation with design that led to my becoming the founding dean of the School of Design at the California Institute of the Arts.

These experiences opened my eyes to the different ways that designers approach problems, and, when I coupled my understanding of the psychology of leadership with my understanding of design, I gradually came to see that problem solving through the design process is the approach most needed by all leaders to deal with the complexities and challenges of the future. But that idea has not yet taken hold among designers, let alone leaders from other disciplines. You can imagine, therefore, the excitement I felt reading the manuscript for *Leadership by Design*. With this book, Ambassador Swett drives that nail of an idea home with one swift, powerful stroke. His message is clear, compelling, and inescapable. The world is searching for a new kind of creative, inclusive leadership. This book lays out steps to achieve this and gives examples of those who have led in this fashion like no other book on the subject.

An architect and former congressman and ambassador himself, he issues nothing short of a challenge to leaders from all walks of life, including architects, to answer the call to public service and set as their goal a life of leadership and civic responsibility using the constructive creativity of the design process to build coalitions and cooperation that counter the divisive politics of our day. To support that call, he offers a fascinating history of the ways in which architects and other designers have served our society, indeed our democracy, by designing not just buildings and cities but organizations and institutions that have helped create the infrastructure of our society. More than that, he illustrates, through many case studies, the approaches architects and designers have taken to accomplish such contributions, ranging from helping communities visualize and express their values and realize their dreams to serving government agencies in designing more effective systems of management. He shows how architects, throughout history, have played major roles in the creation of our democratic way of life, from opposing slavery to eliminating slums to fostering socially and politically constructive institutions like the Union League Club, earning for themselves association with presidents and membership in high councils of decision makers. Stories abound of professional and ethical courage like that of Cass Gilbert's successful battle against the powerful alliances between New York's top corporate architects and their political representatives, perhaps a precursor to the battles to come a century later in the rebuilding of the World Trade Center. Not limiting himself to historical references, he cites many contemporary examples of such contributions.

Why are designers and people who think like them especially well equipped to be leaders? They design not only buildings and spaces but also healthy relationships and positive experiences. They design situations, and as any psychologist knows, situations are the most powerful determinants of behavior. As a result of their education, they immediately see things in a larger context, and in the sweep of history. They tend to be conversant in the arts, sciences, and humanities (as are the best leaders). They work easily in ensembles and know how to involve people in decision-making on their own behalf. They are comfortable with advanced technology yet understand its limits. They are used to dealing with complexity and multitasking. They understand budgets and schedules. They can see projects through to completion and beyond. They care about establishing higher standards of living. They are capable of a high level of creative thinking. They can appreciate and are comfortable with the aesthetic dimensions of life and leadership—for top leaders, like top athletes, combine courage, form, and grace. If only more of our nation's leaders were so endowed.

But, as Ambassador Swett makes clear, the professions of design have lost their way, and our national leaders have lost their sense of design. Too many of our leaders have let business demands rather than professional goals determine their actions. Designers have turned away from civic leadership. Today's leaders are not encouraged to speak truth to power.

This book asks leaders to take their cues from the creative examples of past designers and begin to imagine themselves as "leaders by design" of communities, governments, cultural organizations, corporations—and beyond. Indeed, people from all walks of life who are interested in leadership must recognize the crucial role that design can play in coping with the complexities and challenges of the future.

The stakes are high. The next few decades will determine the survival of our civilization. I believe we will succeed only if design becomes the organizing discipline of the future, and that will only happen when designers become leaders, leaders become designers, and the public demands of its leaders the Jeffersonian ethic that enhances our reputation, reconciles us to the rest of the world, and procures us praise.

—Richard Farson

INTRODUCTION

*Because I have confidence in the power of truth and of
the spirit, I believe in the future of mankind.*
—Albert Schweitzer

OR FOURTEEN YEARS I have had the opportunity to think long and
hard about what it means to be a leader. When I think of leadership I am automatically drawn to the arena where so-called leaders abound—the profession of politics. Like the blind man who was asked
to describe the elephant after being given the opportunity to touch only its
trunk, I came to believe that many people in leadership positions today offer
only a sliver of the understanding needed to manage and direct our complicated, fast-paced world.

It all began when I had the honor of being elected to the United
States House of Representatives in 1990. As the only architect in the 20th
century to be elected to that august body, I became painfully aware not only
of how underrepresented my profession was in the political arena but also
of how dysfunctional the political environment on Capitol Hill had become.
There was little comity between the political parties and even less desire to
cooperate during political negotiations. Worst of all, both the world of architecture and the world of politics, though inextricably intertwined, were suffering the effects of disengagement from each other in the decision-making
processes that affect both worlds.

Therefore, there is no better time than the present to reevaluate the role
of the leader or to identify what successful leadership entails as we watch
our politicians provoke each other to further extremes of ideology while
legions of special-interest groups hone their martial arts skills in the reduc-
tive power of NO.

This study, as a counterpoint to the form of leadership embodied by
professional politicians, examines an overlooked community of leaders:
architects. As a group, architects are seldom identified as leaders, although

it is understood that many talented architects possess a considerable meas-ure of social vision.

As Nicolo Machiavelli advised in 1513, "A wise man ought always to fol-low the paths beaten by great men . . . Let him act like the clever archers who . . . take aim much higher than the mark, not to reach by their strength or arrow to so great a height, but to be able with the aid of so high an aim to hit the mark they wish to reach." He also warned that "he who has not first laid his foundations may be able to lay them afterwards, but they will be laid with trouble to the architect and danger to the building."[1]

Machiavelli did not advocate divisive leadership; he simply recognized all approaches to leadership and their direct consequences and identified divisiveness as a common, but troublesome approach because of the usual negative end results. It is an unfortunate fact that inside politics, divide and conquer is standard operating procedure. Most modern theorists do not advocate this obvious approach because it is ugly and unethical, but it cer-tainly is a time-tested rule of political practice. Political strategists today, as in the past, use divisiveness as a fundamental strategic weapon in their polit-ical operations. The following example highlights this point.

In late December 1863, the editor and a journalist of the *New York World*—mouthpiece for Democratic Tammany Hall—published an anony-mous seventy-two-page pamphlet conceived as part of a dirty tricks cam-paign to whip up fear and loathing of New York's well-organized Republican Unionists. Masquerading as an abolitionist writer, the two proposed that the true and legitimate purpose of the Civil War was the amalgamation of the freed slaves with the white population, particularly with the working class. This devious political tactic was the original source of the word *miscegena-tion*, which the two imposters coined from Latin roots. The pamphlet strongly urged the Republican Party to add miscegeney to its upcoming presidential platform.[2]

This notorious pamphlet manipulated the racial issue far beyond the question of slavery and into a particularly vile partisan smear campaign, which found its way onto the floor of Congress. This, along with a slew of partisan proslavery propaganda, was met with an equal, if not greater, dis-semination of pro-Unionist, antislavery pamphlets and circulars, many of which emanated from the Union League Club, whose origins will be discussed later in this book.

Various modes of divisive social warfare continue to serve as the primary leadership models at the very top of contemporary American society. Yet the skills of strategic thinking used to direct people to destroy each other are not actually different from the skills employed to support life and to design and build society. It is the *context* and *motivation* that directly affect the outcome of the tactics we use. Thus, it is not the "strategic skills" themselves that are debated here but the actual purposes for which they are used. Build vs. destroy. Share vs. take. Win by creating vs. win by destroying. The divide-and-conquer method achieves success through the other party's great loss, not through everyone's great mutual gain. Inducing the opposition to retreat is a clever but self-serving tactic; it saves the victor from unnecessary casualties and additional expense. Voter apathy can be a strategically induced condition, and when those who have implemented tactics to this end suddenly find themselves in emergency electoral circumstances, it is very difficult to reverse that insidious effect.

This book's purpose is to strengthen the foundations of democratic society by providing examples of individual architects who were able to use their own particular brand of leadership to accomplish important work in their communities. The nature of this kind of leadership is constructive and inclusive, not divisive and adversarial, like so much of what we see in contemporary civic and social debate. These individuals had the courage to think broadly and boldly and drew upon their creativity and professional experience to fashion viable solutions, the implications of which were often not immediately apparent.

Most important, the creative processes employed allowed for participation by leaders and the public alike, with each participant making an important contribution to the development of our civic institutions along the way. How was this possible? It was possible because the relationship between the various participants was based on a foundation of mutual trust.

Today public trust is a very difficult social value to foster and maintain, particularly because it is now customary for opponents to actively endeavor to destroy public trust in those with whom they disagree. Add to these destructive human impulses a world that has become incredibly complex, and the *collective ability to trust* is further undermined. *Dis*trust has become the common denominator of a disengaged polity.

We are constantly filtering and fighting through a sea of differences— religious doctrines, ethnic cultures, divergent political philosophies, and ever-increasing layers of economic and social differentiations that isolate us from each other—as we seek our places in our communities. Added to all that is the continual bombardment of information from every direction, whether from hundreds of TV channels, movies, newspaper and print media, radio, the Internet, or new forms of digital media. Each morsel of communication, each product disseminated, has a point of view its author(s) seeks to persuade the listener to accept and is designed to place that communication in a narrow context that will, the author(s) hopes, cause the receiver to derive a favorable judgment out of it. This is an intimidating task under the best of circumstances. But when you consider how much data is out there and how little time people actually have to ingest it, much less assimilate and adequately evaluate it, it is no wonder that so many people are disaffected and distrustful of their leaders. Whom do you believe when so many incompatible versions of the same reality are being promoted?

In a society where outrageous corporate and political scandals have become mundane and private disputes, regardless of how petty, are too often resolved through callous manipulation of the legal system, it becomes very difficult to build a sufficiently healthy foundation of trust in our communities.

Why has the issue of public trust become so difficult? In part because we as citizens are no longer being asked to participate in a way that results in meaningful input into our civic processes, much less a positive impact on the eventual outcomes. The personal experience of being a good and responsible citizen can be very unpleasant at times. Just imagine being a voter in the state of Florida, where the 2000 national election ended in chaos and ongoing local manipulations have exposed a constitutional process that is still seriously flawed in both theory and in actual practice.3

Voters don't have to feel this way. A foundation of trust can be constructed in our communities that gives each of us a greater sense of belonging and a greater ability to participate in the public decision-making process. But to do this, we need leaders who are integrators, not segregators.

Trust is an intangible asset that needs space and time to grow. It must be demonstrated with consistency over time. It is built up, block by block, as an integral component of a mutually beneficial relationship. Initially trust can be freely given, but to be sustained it must be continually earned and reinforced. And if it flows in only one direction, its potential power is dissipated and eventually lost.

Communities in which people truly feel valued require leadership that is inclusive and genuinely cooperative. Expanded opportunities to participate must be met with an equally expansive vision for the community. And all those who do participate will see how the variety of contributions can be combined to improve and accomplish their shared goals.

The intellectual, technical, and creative traits we require of such an integrating vision are contained within the discipline and practice of architecture. But architects rarely, if ever, view themselves in the role of civic leaders. Unlike other well-trained, highly skilled professionals, contemporary practitioners of architecture have been disinclined to participate in the fractious politics of public service. Part I, Architects as Leaders in Civic Society, will address this basic issue.

In previous eras, architects rose to prominent roles in society's civic and social leadership and made important contributions to public life. This leadership was based not only on their personal qualities and professional training but also on a more positive, social perception of civic duty. Often these contributions have been acts of necessity precipitated by a major crisis or specifically related to a particular project on which the architects were working.

While other professions are better known for their performance of civic duty, such as the legal profession, architects also have an equally long history of political and civic engagement. Yet both architects (as a group) and the public alike are largely unaware of this fact, and, therefore, neither have been in a position to positively value and reinforce such a tradition.

The architecture profession, through its professional associations and academic institutions, has never found it necessary to maintain an organized record of these episodes of public leadership. Instead, the profession has chosen to focus almost exclusively on the history of architectural design as its vehicle for distinction in the public's—and its own—consciousness. The more comprehensive and historically relevant institutional memory that could have been, in fact should have been, passed on from generation to generation of architects has not been properly established. Thus, without a comprehensive knowledge of its own history, the public leadership initiatives taken by architects have seldom been consistently sustained or built upon by aggregating strengths over time.

From the research conducted so far, it can be concluded that from the latter half of the 19th century into the early 20th century, the architecture profession experienced a golden era of influence. And while a great deal of academic research has been devoted to examining the pervasive cultural influences of the leading European nations on all aspects of American society, particularly its architecture, I will take a look at the contributions of a more obscure but equally effective society: the influence of the Danes and their values on America's architectural and political landscape.

The power to create is a heady and intoxicating one. To exercise that power in a balanced and just manner requires great vision, discipline, and self-mastery, derived from countless hours of observation, formulation, and hard work. The architect's mastery of complex and collaborative decision-making processes holds the key to getting the job done, and done well. The power unleashed by such a combination of skills is truly transformative. It is the stuff of lasting impact that architects have within their power to deliver to society.

The design of a building, for example, requires the architect to understand a great deal more than simply how to arrange the spaces and where to place the structure on the site. An architect must know what goes on inside the walls and underneath the ground and also be in command of the technical building codes that regulate what can be built, where it can be built, and how it must be built. In addition to designing a building that looks good, the architect is also responsible for ensuring that it is built on time and within a specified budget, that it performs well in the climate, and that it withstands the test of time. Hundreds of decisions must be made about building materials, components, finishes, and the like. And if the client is more than one person—say, a community or a corporate committee or a healthcare group—design diplomacy skills are necessary to integrate everything that must be done with everyone who is involved in the project.

Architects have the necessary vision and skills to serve the complicated society in which they live. They are not leaders in the political sense because their profession has chosen not to train them with that role in mind, preferring to accentuate the formal design aspects of project management instead. This was not always so, as we will soon find out.

But it is one thing to list these attributes and quite another to demonstrate proof of their application. Part II, Examples of Effective Leadership by Architects, examines concrete examples that will help illuminate the architecture profession's hidden leadership traits and its history of civic and social leadership.

That there are not more architects participating in the public sector is unfortunate because inherent in the commitment to become an architect is the strong desire to serve society. In serving the client, the basic commitment may be realized, but that deep desire is frequently left unfulfilled and *untapped* for society's greater benefit.

Serving the public interest holds many exciting opportunities for the profession. One obvious application of leadership, embraced by so many other demanding professions, is the holding of political office. This option, among others, will be discussed in Part III, The Civic Necessity of Sustained Leadership by the Profession.

Contemporary leadership by the architecture profession and its contributions to public life must be recognized. These efforts are essential to maintaining the good standing of a profession that has seen its influence in the governance of society gradually eroded over time.

This book is just a first step in restoring the missing record of architects as leaders. These individual architects serve to inspire and direct members of a noble profession to make contributions to their communities beyond the design of buildings. In each case, the focus is on how and why these architects chose to affect influence on social and public policy.

It is my hope that the vignettes presented here will awaken the design community and inspire it to become more involved in the responsibilities of leadership in our communities. I hope that a broader audience will also find inspiration in these pages and begin to think about how the *processes* of design can enhance the quality of life in their communities.

PART I:

ARCHITECTS AS LEADERS IN CIVIC SOCIETY

I FOUR PHILOSOPHICAL CORNERSTONES OF THE ARCHITECTURE OF TRUST

OURS IS A VERY COMPLEX world that requires a tremendous amount of personal energy on a daily basis. Families depend on two wage earners or, often, only a single parent working to make ends meet. Keeping up with the changes at work, giving one's children the feeling that mom and/or dad are aware of the changes in their lives, participating in local community life, and following current events at home and abroad can be an incredibly daunting set of tasks. At the end of every day there is little energy left after all the multitasking. It is no wonder that so many people choose to drop the ball on one or more of these activities, because there simply is not enough time to do it all properly. Add to this already exhausting scenario the forces that act upon anyone who chooses to enter the public arena, and you can begin to understand why fewer and fewer people are participating in the civic processes of government, at all levels.

The decline in the public's participation in the electoral process is exacerbated by the antagonistic atmosphere that seems to permeate all aspects of public debate. Political campaigns are lubricated with special-interest monies, generating information aimed at moving the electorate with a stifling abundance of tasteless, often brainless advertising. Most people are aware that the messages presented in the ads are, at best, jingoistic oversimplifications, if not outright misrepresentations or falsehoods.4

Issues have become so overly (and intentionally) simplified that there is no longer any real attempt at nuance or depth of meaning. Every issue is reduced to a cartoonish black-or-white scenario. The introduction of elegant, fully drawn solutions is nearly impossible.

Special-interest groups must share the blame with our political parties for this situation. The purpose of organizing around a cause or an issue is

3

to draw to it greater public attention so that it exists on an equal footing with all the other causes or issues under debate. Once an issue gains prominence in the community, the goal of assimilating it into the fabric of the community can too easily get side-tracked and lost in the process. It simply becomes a means to other ends. So integrating a single agenda into the fabric of larger common causes has been a hard thing to accomplish for many of the special-interest groups; the letting go of the specialness—the uniqueness—of the cause has proven to be very difficult, indeed.

Part of this difficulty springs from the fear that in assimilating into the larger community the identity of the group, cause, or issue will be lost (as will all the jobs that were built up around it). In addition, there is a lack of confidence that the leaders of the community will uphold the good intentions of the cause. An attitude of "You're not one of us so how can we trust you to protect our interests?" feeds distrust. This has led to the over-abundance of single-issue officials currently listed on the nation's ledger of senior managers and administrators.

Those who are leading the special interests have little or no desire to connect their issues with others for fear of diluting their potential gain. In the campaign to gain and sustain power, political leaders will act in ways that undermine and may even help destroy the institutions they seek to lead. This is clearly an abdication of ethical and moral responsibility.

Newt Gingrich's campaign to take over the House of Representatives was a case in point. When C-SPAN was first introduced, he coordinated speeches from the floor that would identify individuals from the other side and criticize them as if they were present in the hall. This created such uproar that C-SPAN began showing images of the empty room from time to time just so viewers could see that no one was present. This helped stop the attacks.

Conversely, architects are trained to maintain high standards of ethical responsibility, so much so that many in the profession refrain from participating in activities that would benefit from their expertise, such as serving on local planning commissions, simply to avoid the appearance of a conflict of interest. This leaves the work to be done by conscientious, caring citizens who nonetheless have little or no training in professional planning. Also, the fact that architects are required to see their work through to completion demands a consistent, ethical approach to the task and makes architects more sensitive to these issues as well.

Architects are more inclined to think of themselves as stewards rather than leaders. Architecture is, after all, a service profession. Service denotes stewardship, involves integration and facilitation, and engenders a cooperative approach to problem solving.

The essayist and business leader Robert K. Greenleaf has identified ten traits characteristic of servant-leaders:

1. Receptive listening.
2. Empathy to accept and recognize people for their special and unique spirit.
3. Healing to transform oneself and others.
4. Awareness—especially about values and ethics.
5. Persuasion to convince others, not to coerce compliance.
6. Conceptualization to dream great dreams.
7. Foresight to understand the lessons of the past, the realities of the present, and, likely, the consequences of a future decision.
8. Stewardship to hold something in trust for another—a commitment to serve the needs of others.
9. Commitment to the growth of people.
10. Building community among those who work together.[5]

Could the pedagogy of leadership training that dominates our law schools and advanced business degree programs be the culprit responsible for turning out contemporary leaders who are unwilling to negotiate, compromise, and/or combine their efforts whenever possible? Does such a highly evolved, single-minded, self-serving focus on the bottom line produce benefits that serve the overall interests of society or just those of a select few?

Dr. J. Sterling Livingston's classic paper, "Myth of the Well-Educated Manager," originally published in the *Harvard Business Review* in January 1971, points to the lack of ethics training in our nation's most prestigious MBA programs. His concerns about the outcome of such myopic professional training can now be understood in the context of the Enron Corporation's disgraceful implosion and the collapse of other businesses of similar ilk since Livingston's article was published more than three decades ago.

The power of NO and the flagrant distortion of any opposing position has nearly eliminated the positive characteristics of trust, integrity, responsibility, creativity, vision, and courage from the platform of public debate. For example, the unwillingness of either the prochoice or the prolife movement to recognize that the majority of Americans hold a position on the subject of abortion somewhere in between the polar extremes of the issue demonstrates their respective insecurity about encouraging a more inclusive, informed public discussion on a highly sensitive and intensely personal issue.

What we get instead from our leaders are highly contrived facsimiles of the sought-for attributes of trust, integrity, responsibility, creativity, vision, and courage. Like an artist's rendering of a proposed building, what is presented to the public is a flat, illusionary image of the much more desired three-dimensional reality.

That is why the example of the architecture profession as a source of leadership for civic society is such a compelling one. Architects spend their working lives turning ideas into reality through the servant-leadership process: they listen to their clients, work with them to help visualize their dreams, and, ultimately, transform those visions into reality through the designs and plan documents they produce.

What Architects Can Bring to the Politics of Civic Engagement

Architects are masters at creating order out of chaos. Protection from the elements, security from enemies, community for living, and solitude for reflection are requisite provisions that the architect must provide to society through the simultaneous exercise of superior craft and professional service. However, the personal and professional skills required to weave this tapestry are rarely discussed in the books about architects.

Architects are generally defined by the design of their buildings, both built and unbuilt. The situations of social and political life that provide architecture with its business and integrate its functionality into the fabric of modern society are viewed through the inverted lens of aesthetics, reducing the totality of every architect's work to a separate colored thread pulled from the much larger tapestry of history. The time has come to tell other kinds of stories about architects, not just because the profession of architecture needs to hear them, which it does, but because they serve an allegorical purpose in our assessment of the nature of leadership.

To me, leadership denotes an act by an individual to provide direction to a community through the use of skills and attributes that not only reinforce the community itself but also engage its participation and allow it to take ownership of both the process and the decisions that the process produces. In times of peace, this can be a very inclusive process that touches many, if not all, the lives in the community. In times of peril, this process must draw upon the trust developed through the relationships formed by working together toward a common goal during peaceful times.

As well, the scale of the community affects the way leadership is employed. Small communities have an intimacy that allows their leaders to share more of the responsibilities with constituents. Larger communities make that delegation more difficult. But in all instances, trust is the foundation on which productive, positive leadership is built. Trust is vested in the ability of leaders to fairly determine what is best for the whole community and to prepare it for the future, regardless of whether those events are good or bad. This trust is based on a belief that members of the community have a say in their governing processes and a relationship of mutual respect with the person(s) leading them. The goal of reaching a consensus may seem more difficult to achieve in highly heterogeneous communities than it is in less diverse, more homogeneous communities—but it is equally important in both.

Ronald Heifetz, in his book *Leadership without Easy Answers*, describes the traits of leaders a little differently from those of Robert K. Greenleaf's model of servant-leadership. Heifetz says leaders possess the following attributes:

1. Leaders get out on the balcony. They step back, observe the fray, and interpret the organizational dynamics in real time.

2. Leaders know how to listen musically as well as analytically.

3. Leaders assemble confidants and allies for emotional support, as sources of information, and to draw fire on their behalf.

4. Leaders inspire others by identifying where people find meaning and by finding connections between specific tasks and organizational purpose.

5. Leaders demonstrate courage and stamina—an ability both to generate heat and take the heat.

6. Leaders demonstrate compassion and empathy. They respect the pains of change and the coping mechanisms that people use.
7. Leaders treat ripe and unripe issues differently—and, all else being equal, they tackle ripe issues first.
8. Leaders manage the timing of distress. They disturb people only when they have the time and the credibility to spend on dealing with the consequences.
9. Leaders seek opportunities for catharsis and spiritual renewal.[6]

Given the leadership qualities identified by Greenleaf and Heifetz, it seems that many of the individuals proclaimed as today's leaders do not adequately fit either model very well.

We have become convinced that only those who know how to divide and conquer can assume the mantle of leadership; however, it is time to recognize that there are those among us who possess the skills to untangle and master the jumbled mass of vital information, who can formulate priorities and strategies, and who have the capacities to mitigate the ensuing conflicts associated with shared goals and responsibilities.

Viable solutions to big problems do not have to be either/or equations. Solutions can be integrated and balanced from the best aspects of both sides of the equation, achieving a better all-round result. The ability to recognize the truth of the facts and the order contained within them and from that recognition have the ability to develop a holistic solution that is the sum, rather than the division, of all its distinct parts now seems to be a missing faculty in public life.

Integration of the Professional Polymath: Architect/Artist/Technician/Builder/Manager

Architects often succeed as leaders when they step outside of the conventional definitions they have given themselves. By the close of the 19th century, the architects' professional association in the United States, the American Institute of Architects (AIA), was publicly and loudly insisting that architects, as a profession, be considered a cadre of master artists at the head of America's cultural table.

In the process of educating the public about the value of architecture, as well as directing the profession from within, architects slowly surrendered their position as the executives of the building process. As technology advanced and new technical proficiencies were applied to building design, increasingly the authority and responsibility formerly controlled by the architect were delegated or co-opted. As a result, the status of the architect changed from that of the leader of the building team to *just* the designer on a team of building experts. Add to this a contrived and widely promoted perception of the professional architect as a European-styled artist and soon architects were involuntarily losing a substantial measure of credibility in society's broader decision-making processes.

Not only did the other creative and building professions bridle at the idea that the artist-architect incarnation was their natural superior, but this self-imposed diminishment of the intrinsic attributes of the architect—that of master builder, technician, and team manager—had a lasting negative impact. For rather than embracing and promoting the diversity of skills that place architects among society's professional polymaths, this imposition of old-world elitism by the upper echelon drove the profession away from such an empowering self-realization.

Instead, prominent representatives of the profession spent decades pursuing a self-proclaimed artistic hierarchy that envisioned the architect at the top of a great cultural pyramid. Business, politics, and whole categories of the plastic arts were relegated to inferior positions in this social model. After all, elitism is, by definition, the mechanism utilized by a minority to command entitlement over the majority. Of course, the vast number of buildings then constructed in America were not designed by the elite but by legions of the self-made who were trained on the job. Over time, the public's acceptance of this superficial stereotype of the egotistical artist-architect contributed to the profession's increasing exclusion from the "table of first decision making."

Despite these setbacks, throughout the 19th and 20th centuries, the professional architect has functioned as society's professional polymath in daily practice, meeting ever-expanding demands with new ideas, new technologies, and new solutions. The making of architecture requires the precise orchestration of hard science, advanced mathematics, technical engineering, social and economic assessment, and, now, serious environmental and sustainability issues—far more than the self-evident aspects of art that we can see and appreciate for ourselves. Just like everyone else, architects can too often be their own worst enemies.

How helpful it would be to fully employ the multifaceted skills of architects as we revitalize our blighted inner cities or attempt the rebuilding of Iraq and other decimated countries. The professional polymath's ability to understand and balance competing issues is a daily preoccupation and is a facility many leaders lack. Our leaders are further challenged by the abundant temptations and distractions that are constantly at play in the political arena. Emphasis on a disciplined, ethical approach to problem solving has always been a hallmark of the architecture profession.

This central issue of ethics has been most famously exemplified by the extremism of the Howard Roark character in Ayn Rand's 1943 novel, *The Fountainhead*. His unyielding fealty to his artistic principle compelled him to destroy his own masterpiece project after learning of the owner's willingness to compromise the exterior of his building's design.

Architects, although seldom as arrogant or destructive in the expression of their principles as Roark, do tend to shy away from any activity deemed potentially unseemly or problematic, whether serving on a local planning commission or the board of a community institution (not art museums or professional organizations) or becoming actively involved in broader political activity. Every organization, from the local planning board to the U.S. Congress, could greatly benefit from the addition of an architect—the professional polymath—to its ranks.

Visions of the Master Builder: First Define the Goals and Then Coherently Articulate Them

I was first attracted to architecture through a sixth-grade history project. I had to construct an Aztec city on a four-foot-by-eight-foot piece of plywood. Rebuilding the ruins of a great, long-lost civilization caught my imagination. Here was a world I could bring to life in miniature, re-creating all the buildings within which an ancient civilization conducted the activities of daily life. The streets and canals of their great cities connected them to each other and connected me to thoughts about where and how they created the world in which they lived.

Building is in my blood. As the son of a civil engineer who, at the time, built municipal solid and waste water treatment plants in the northeast, I was cognizant of the basic requirements served by the Aztec civilization's system of canals. My first architectural effort was rewarded when my model was displayed in the storefront window of the town barbershop.

However, it wasn't until my junior year in high school that I was exposed to the profession in a more intimate way when I served as a student representative on the local building committee overseeing the design and construction of a new high school for our New Hampshire town.

For months I attended evening meetings where I observed the give and take of the townsfolk with the project's architect. Because the town had never built a new high school, the committee wrestled with a multitude of ideas about how to plan it. This building was to be the largest public expenditure in the history of the town—a defining moment for the community. Its construction gave the community a tangible opportunity to express a common dream. Those of us on the building committee were burdened with the task of somehow conveying that abstract concept to the architect so that he could physically interpret it into an integrated architectural design.

At that young age I don't recall ever opening my mouth to comment or express an opinion. Instead I listened and observed with great interest, becoming aware of the competing interests within the community over seemingly simple matters such as location and budget. These discussions were quickly subsumed by the more complicated discussions that struggled to define the school's curriculum. Long hours of debate and discussion had to be endured between the faction that desired an open concept school and those who favored a traditional curriculum. It was a marvelous process to watch, a living tutorial in civic management for a young citizen to witness firsthand the elements of leadership, community participation, and architectural planning intersecting in a meaningful and positive way.

Although I was part of it, I am not sure that I fully appreciated what was taking place. But as I think back on that time I am struck by how, along with getting the school built, the relationships that were forged helped make the effort a success. Just like the building itself, the townsfolk and the architects needed a strong foundation of trust on which to realize their common dream. This was my first experience with what I now call the *architecture of trust*.

The second and cinching experience that led me to commit to architecture was a class I took as a junior at Yale University, taught by Professor Alec Purves, which examined the role of the architect in the community. For the course's required research project, I shadowed a young architect who was designing a senior center for the Boston Redevelopment Authority (BRA). This project was controversial because it was a mixed-use program, with the senior center located above ground-level retail space and offices. In 1978 this was not at all common. It was located in the Italian community of Boston's North End. Many concerned voices expressed doubts about what was perceived as an unholy alliance between senior citizens' residential care and commercial architecture.

The project's architect and I spent many long evenings listening to and documenting the concerns of various neighborhood groups. I continually marveled at his patience and willingness to attend every meeting, no matter how often, how late into the night they lasted, or how few the number of attendees. Although I was not yet at the stage where I understood the economics of running an architecture practice, I often wondered if he was getting paid for all the time he was investing. As it goes, the BRA's architect was not being paid for all the hours he devoted to the project, although he certainly should have been. But those sessions were materially important to the project's successful development.

By delivering a high level of personal and professional commitment, this young architect built a solid bond with the community. This dedicated outreach enabled him to address, directly and specifically, the neighborhood's concerns. And through his efforts to ensure that every voice was heard, the entire community eventually lent its support to the building of an innovative, mixed-use community development project.

In both of these cases, success was achieved by laying a foundation of trust among all the key participants. I have come to realize that the community, its leaders, and their architects were able to accomplish this by putting the skills of diplomacy to good use. When the architecture profession uses these skills, I choose to call it *design diplomacy*.

Know Thyself: Ethics, Power, and a Commitment to Serve

Leadership is often described as the action of an individual, or group of individuals, to affect broad societal change, to spearhead crisis management, or to alter the direction of a specific firm, organization, or community. On occasion, an entire community decides to take action in determining the course of its future.

In both good and bad instances, the forces that give direction to these actions arise out of the motivations and qualities inherent in those who participate. Throughout the ebb and flow of history, the need for good leadership has remained a constant. Clearly, leadership's sustainable presence relies on the consistency established in the bonds of trust built between the leaders and the community.

Unfortunately, too many stark instances spring to mind of leaders manipulating the masses with fear and confusion. The creation of crisis as the pretext for cementing power is the device of an illegitimate leader who pretends to lead through it. Saddam Hussein, a classic example, is just the latest case in point. In a more democratic order, a real crisis almost certainly will bring out the exceptional individuals who then become the leaders of a community.

America's leaders have been shaped more often by the crisis of war than by any other event. The Revolutionary War, the War of 1812, the Civil War, the Spanish-American War, World War I, World War II, the Korean War, and the Vietnam War have each left an indelible mark on the social history and cultural psyche of this nation.

And when armed conflict was quiescent, spontaneous, terrible catastrophes have also created leaders. Natural disasters like the earthquake that leveled San Francisco on April 16, 1906, or the ferocious devastation of the Great Fire that blew though Chicago on October 8, 1871, brought forth tremendous changes in how America viewed its future and how its cities should henceforth be designed and built.

In Copenhagen, Denmark, the Great Fire of 1728 likewise became an opportunity for Johan Cornelius Krieger, King Frederick IV's master builder, to institute improvements in city planning and building standards.7 Later still, after the British bombardment of Copenhagen in 1807, led by General Wellesley, Duke of Wellington, Denmark's state architect, Christian

Frederik Hansen, was appointed to lead the rebuilding process. Between 1805 and 1845, Hansen, working with serious shortages and economic hardship, was still able to significantly improve the layout of the city, incorporating important social and economic changes that benefited the populace.[8]

Each crisis creates a complex puzzle of new problems added to the existing ones. A crisis will always call upon established leadership to exert extraordinary skill in response to its civic responsibility. But many of those who rise to the challenge of leadership do so as a spontaneous response to crisis. Had no such crisis occurred, perhaps they would have continued on in obscurity, never to reach levels of creativity as significant as those that the duress of crisis challenged them to achieve.

Leadership is about gaining and then using influence. Influence is acquired through a variety of avenues. Building political organizations and/or social institutions is one modern approach that has its origins in the social clubs of yore. Creating associations within professional disciplines or through a shared ideological agenda is another process seemingly preferred by contemporary special-interest groups. But all these tactical approaches are no less foreign to architects than they are to other classes of leaders and have been used quite successfully by architects. Before, during, and after the Civil War, architects, most notably Frederick Law Olmsted, adopted various pragmatic methods to create and wield power.

Stable alliances, although difficult to maintain, are especially characteristic of influential activities in Scandinavia, where minority-led coalitions normally comprise central governments. In the United States, alliances frequently are formed between states in an attempt to influence federal government decision making. But these alliances shift like sand dunes, swept away by the fickle winds of legislators' own mutable agendas. In the European Union the new reality emerging from the EU's expansion eastward is the realignment of old alliances. What was once a process of unanimous decree will become, by necessity, a more nuanced negotiation in order to reach consensus with the many smaller nations now joined into the expanded EU.

Polemical documents and theoretical writings about social policy or on design's social potential have had a measure of influence on public policy, but this impact has either been too subtle to easily discern or, on occasion, been too heavy-handed to last. For such methods of influence to be success-ful, they need to incorporate data obtained through listening not only to one's colleagues but also to the constituents of the given community and to one's peers outside the profession. Only then can such information be crafted in a way that engenders trust and agreement. Many a passionate broadside or high-minded treatise has met an ill end because of the lack of adequately developed skills to communicate ideas in clear terms with unambivalent phrases.

Ambivalence is the Achilles heel of leadership. It validates apathy. For too many decades, behind a façade of assumed authority, ambivalence and contradiction plagued the architecture profession's leadership, its professional institutions, its practice policies, and its public policy agenda. Every forward step taken on behalf of the profession had been dogged by a pernicious foot-dragging.

As a profession, architects have occasionally emerged as leaders to address the urgent problems of society successfully. To do this, self-aware-ness and self-criticism cannot be avoided. In 1919, less than six months after the conclusion of World War I, the membership of the American Institute of Architects gathered in Nashville for its annual convention. This meet-ing would change the institutional and ideological course of the AIA and the hitherto prevailing attitudes of the profession through a profound reassess-ment of its past errors, its role in society, and its relationship to others. A long list of simple, but profound questions was asked. At the top of this list: What is leadership? After frank discussion, thoughtful answers were put on record and a slew of practical and effective initiatives were undertaken for the good of the whole profession.

Fresh from the unambiguous experience of a dreadful world war, the AIA's membership reaffirmed its commitment to the profession, to their communities, to their fellow workingmen and to their country. Their leadership identified the nature and extent of this chronic ambiva-lence and banished it. The reform program of the 1919 Post-War Com-mittee—a call for renewed dedication to purpose, for candor and fairness in all professional conduct, and a greater involvement in civic life—was overwhelmingly affirmed in an unprecedented vote by two-thirds of the majority. The profession had come to the realization, as a body, that

commitment to clear, shared, and actionable purposes is the antidote to ambiva-
lence and apathy.

The mission so effectively launched at that national convention lasted
only a short decade. The Institute's membership doubled in size during this
period, but that was not enough to sustain the inspiring ideas expressed in
Nashville. The Great Depression of the 1930s followed by World War II hin-
dered the profession's ability to fully transform itself. To do that would have
required not only the articulation of lofty ideals calling for the civic leadership of architects but also the more concrete cementing of those ideals into
the foundation of the profession's leadership structure and its institutional
memory. Before recounting the words of the inspired architects at that
momentous gathering, let's explore some of the building blocks that would
help to firm up the foundation of leadership.

2 Four Building Blocks for Building the Architecture of Trust

Order Out of Chaos: Understanding the Dynamics and Useful Functions of Association

It can be argued that, at least on some level, all progress is driven by the dynamics of association and that this is an organic function of the social human animal. Given a defined purpose, a fully formed agenda, and a mechanism to achieve a set of stated goals, this wholly natural process becomes a directional engine that propels civilization forward.

Constitutional law is institutionalized in our federal government with a triumvirate form. This particular architecture of three distinct but dependent branches of civic authority seeks judiciously to balance power on behalf of the citizens and prevent any branch of government or any clique within each branch from abusing the sacred trust of the people enshrined by the Constitution.

But the success of this formal design depends heavily upon the shared responsibility of the polity—upon the individual citizen's active association in society's civic institutions and in its regular, essential managerial function, commonly known as voting. Thus every adult in a free democratic society has, at least theoretically, an equal responsibility and an equal voice in the specifics of local, state, and federal management of civic society. The acceptance, abdication, or subversion of that inherent power is an act of free will about which every citizen makes a personal choice.

When it becomes clear that something must be done to advance the individual's interests, it is logical to seek out those whose interests are held in common and to join together to affect a greater impact than can be achieved on one's own. The exponent of the given interest thus achieves an exponential increase in the effectiveness of promoting a cause.

Every association begins with a person or a few closely associated people. The leadership and vision needed to bring other people together in a common cause is relatively rare. But once an association has been created and established, it is relied upon by those associated with it for a level of leadership that is strong and vital enough to transcend the mortality of its progenitors. This is an ongoing process that must be met with the vigilance of regularly renewed leadership.

In studying the development of association in the architecture profession, we find this truism reinforced generation after generation. Outstanding individuals who take on the responsibilities of leadership are not always the most famous, of course. But the products of their efforts stand up to the vicissitudes of time, and practitioners today continue to benefit from their willingness to invest in the power of association.

Step Up to the Plate: Taking the Initiative and Bearing the Responsibility

There are those around whom initiatives are built and those who build initiatives. The former seem to get much more attention than the latter. Let's face it—taking the initiative is often a thankless task. For most people, it is easily judged to be far more trouble than it's worth. It all depends on what one seeks to accomplish and what one's underlying motivations are.

Architecture is a field in which virtually all of society's public and private interests must be served. All life functions are, in some way, directly related to architecture. How architects react to this profound responsibility directly impacts the effectiveness of their professional practice and determines the nature and viability of their economic, artistic, and professional success. But more important, the positive actions, as well as the chronic inactions, of the profession directly affect society as a whole, regardless of either society's general awareness or its pervasive lack of awareness of the importance of architectural design to people's daily lives.

Architects know. It is their job to know. And it is their professional duty to convey that knowledge to the world. Transmitting the meaning, functions, and benefits of an architect's services cannot be left exclusively to the silent ruminations of all the inanimate bricks, mortar, steel, wood, and glass we turn into our shared environment to make this knowledge clear to people.

Nor can this transmission of knowledge be broadly delegated to media critics, high school teachers, university lecturers, and civil servants. Where will they find the insight into the making of architecture needed to do this enormous but desperately needed job? From architects, of course.

Building a Bridge of Trust: Credibility Equals Public Trust
Architects must lead the public life of their own profession. They must join their peers across professions in the forefront of social and political leadership. Understanding architecture—its values, functionalities, uses, and mechanisms of life enhancement—cannot and should not be left to others who can only see the making of it from the outside, after the fact.

If you have or know children in high school, ask them whether any teacher or guidance counselor has ever discussed the possibility of becoming an architect with them. Ask them whether architecture as a subject in itself has come up in the context of American history, economics, art, business, or social studies. Ask them if they have ever met an architect at their school's career day, or any other day for that matter. Ask whether they know who designed important buildings such as the White House, the U.S. Capitol, or the World Trade Center.

The profession cannot expect greater public trust and respect from society, much less increased commerce, until it generously delivers the necessary core knowledge on which to build appreciation and respect for the design of architecture and our environs. That responsibility starts at home, in the local community, with one's neighbors. It's no different from voting.

Creating New Value: Limitations Power the Creation of Original Solutions
In the history of architecture, major design innovations have often come out of salvaging the remnants of disaster, from adapting to technological and social development or from coping with political or economic crisis. Design is a responsive art that cannot advance if contained within a vacuum of self-reference. Creativity is not a self-contained, self-perpetuating faculty. It is a kind of receptor organ within the intellect that has the capacity to sense and exploit the potentialities in any given circumstance. When people throw their hands up and say "It can't be done!" they deny themselves the

most exciting experience of engaging their own creativity. And they lose the chance to experience the creative process and share it with others.

In terms of professional practice, architects view the project's client as either a hindrance or a sponsor of the design process. They less frequently view the client as their partner in creativity. Why? Because creativity is part of the mythology of the artist and, as such, is perceived as an exclusive attribute of those professions that market their creativity as a commodity.

It is not the purpose of this book to debate the esoteric nature of creativity. Yet, creativity is not uniquely linked to artistic or intellectual prowess. It is a stand-alone attribute that anyone can access should the need arise. Creativity is the art in the art of survival. If one is willing to look on all situations with an open mind, a *creative* attitude, then the limitations imposed by the problem become the finest incentives to exercise one's maximum ability and talent.

The late architect and teacher Samuel Mockbee comes to mind in this regard. Through his innovative teaching methods at the Rural Studio, Mockbee challenged his students with the toughest problems in design and inspired in them a level of creativity few design schools have achieved in recent years. His students were required to work with the poorest people in America as clients, use only indigenous and recycled materials, and build with their own hands the buildings they designed for the local community. Who would have anticipated students using car windshields as windows or discarded linoleum tiles to build walls in fully functional housing?

The same kind of creative response to disaster has led to the development of fireproof buildings and building components. Fire has spurred more inventive design solutions than perhaps any other form of natural disaster. And it continues to do so, as we come to understand the fire-induced structural collapse of the World Trade Center.

Limitations only limit those who accept them.

In the following chapters of Part II, we will encounter the stories of individuals who would not allow themselves to be constrained by the limitations imposed upon them. From those who acted alone, consumed by the ambition to make architecture a society-changing experience, to those who, through association, used their leadership skills to build structures of community around a common purpose, to those who moved big ideas forward for the benefit of society, we will learn of the variety and originality of creative approaches to leadership. Each offers useful lessons in the building of trust, the essential tool for a successful leadership enterprise. These demonstrations of design diplomacy incorporate the cornerstones and building blocks of the architecture of trust.

PART II:

EXAMPLES OF EFFECTIVE LEADERSHIP

3 Georg Carstensen and the New York Crystal Palace

Where were the designers of the New York Crystal Palace? ... No place was appointed for distinguished American engineers—the very men who should have held the most distinguished places—next to the President and his cabinet ...A separate platform should have been appointed for celebrated architects, engineers, and inventors ... but there was no place for the Designers of the Crystal Palace, Messers. Carstensen & Gildemeister, the engineer Mr. Detmold ...These are the kind of men whom the people should delight to honor on such occasions ... Our country is not yet republican in spirit ... such an event ... afforded a most excellent opportunity ... to pay a deserved tribute of respect to the genius and skill of our country, in the persons of some of her distinguished inventors and men of genius.[9]
—Opening of the Crystal Palace, *Scientific American*, July 23, 1853

A T THE HALFWAY MARK OF THE 19TH CENTURY, the world had never before seen such a simultaneous vitalization of all forms of science, manufacturing, engineering, transportation, and communication technologies. This moment in time, in all its glory, was celebrated in London, England, at the Crystal Palace Exhibition of 1851. The exhibition was a resounding critical and financial success. Not to be outdone, American entrepreneurs decided to take this idea and do it up as a demonstration of American know-how and democracy at its best.[10]

On March 11, 1852, the state of New York granted a charter to the Association for the Exhibition of the Industry of all Nations, and shares went up for sale in financial markets. The city granted a five-year lease on the land behind the Fifth Avenue reservoir (now Bryant Park), and the federal government granted a special customs-free designation. Then an international competition was held to design a great glass and cast-iron exhibition building.

The impressive list of architects who submitted plans included John Paxton, designer of the London Crystal Palace; respected architect Leopold Eidlitz; the architect and landscape designer A. J. Downing; and pioneering cast-iron architect James Bogardus and his partner, Hamilton Hoppin. But the winning design was submitted by two recent immigrants to New York City: Danish impresario Georg Carstensen and the German architect Carl (Charles) Gildemeister.[11] "Yet the choice of the board, after mature consideration, fell upon a sketch submitted by Messers. Carstensen and Gildemeister, and we think no one, after looking at the finished structure, will regret the selection of the committee."[12]

Georg Carstensen, the quintessential man of his time, was also way ahead of his time. Few people today realize that the New York Crystal Palace of 1853 was the brainchild of the very same man who created and laid out the renowned Tivoli Gardens in Copenhagen. That these two newcomers won the competition against well-established American architects is a forgotten tale in the legacy of place making in the Danish and American emerging modern democracies. According to Professor Martin Zerlang of the University of Copenhagen, "The Tivoli Gardens from 1843 and the New York Crystal Palace from 1853 both served as harbingers of modernity and cradles for the sophisticated lifestyles of the modern city. . . In the processes of civilization . . . the importance of such establishments . . . cannot be underestimated."[13]

A product of the Danish Golden Age, Carstensen lived in the period after the Napoleonic wars, which transformed an ancient feudal peasant kingdom into a modern parliamentary democracy. This sweeping transformation was not produced by internal political violence but by a unifying spirit of nationalism and egalitarianism. Carstensen understood that people yearned for the cultural refinements which had, until then, been exclusive to the privileged classes, and he built his career as an impresario, creating and delivering original, exciting places for the public's enjoyment.

Carstensen was born in Algiers in 1812, the son of the Danish consul general. His great imagination was fed as much by his own life's journey as it was by the dreams of an awakening world. By the time he reached North America in 1852, he had traveled extensively in Europe, Northern Africa, Asia Minor, and the Caribbean. The architectural exotica he successfully re-created in staid Copenhagen and chaotic New York City was the product of his firsthand experience.

For his visionary scheme of a public pleasure garden, Carstensen knew exactly what it should contain and how it should look. He worked in close partnership with Danish architect Harald C. Stilling to execute his orientalist theme park on the edge of Copenhagen city proper. Tivoli opened in August 1843 with a stunning fireworks display, a tradition to this day.

Called into military service during the German nationalist uprising in Slesvig-Holsten in 1848, Carstensen was away in the army when his franchise to operate Tivoli expired and he was replaced by the Board of Directors. He then left to seek his fortune in the Danish West Indies (U.S. Virgin Islands), where he met and married his second wife in 1850 and had two sons. News of the plans to build a Crystal Palace in New York City proved to be an irresistible opportunity.[14] He suddenly departed for New York, arriving in November 1852.

Carstensen again teamed up with an architect to execute his concept. This time it was Bremen-born Carl (Charles) Gildemeister, a graduate of the Berlin Bauakademie, who had arrived in the city in 1849 and was in the lithography business with another German émigré, Otto Boetticher.[15] The chief engineer was another German, Christian Edward Detmold, born in Hanover in 1810 and educated in that city's military academy. Detmold immigrated to America in 1826. An experienced civil engineer and surveyor for the U.S. War Department, Detmold had supervised the building of Fort Sumter's foundation. Detmold went into iron manufacturing and was among the leading experts in cast-iron fabrication when he constructed the Crystal Palace.[16]

Carstensen fashioned a palace quite unlike the London structure: "in the details of its construction it departs sufficiently from its prototype to make it quite a new and interesting object."[17] The designers and engineers devised innovative technical solutions to problems that had plagued the British building. The overall effect was dazzling.

Shaped like a Greek cross, the building exuded a magical atmosphere. The massive wood dome at the center was the largest built in the country, sixty-two feet above the floor, encased in tin sheathing and pierced by thirty-two windows. The glass walls were surfaced with translucent baked enamel to diffuse light and mitigate solar heat gain, rectifying a major flaw in Paxton's Hyde Park building. Around the perimeter, seventy-six-foot-high minarets contained circular service stairs. The interior was fitted with drinking fountains, and piped natural gas supplied the interior lighting for evening illumination. The iron was painted "to decorate construction rather than to construct decoration," with lead-based, buff-colored paint.[18] Detailing was gilded in bronze and gold. Decorative trim in red, blue, yellow, vermillion, garnet, blue, and orange completed the overall Moorish effect: "The result is surprisingly beautiful."[19]

"Seen at night when it is illuminated . . . it is a scene more gorgeous and graceful than the imagination of Eastern story-tellers . . . as airy and exquisite as that structure of Arabian fiction . . . a delicate coolness in the atmosphere and a light elegance in the lines . . . worthily surmounted and crowned by . . . a dome of Oriental characteristics."[20]

The floor plan was uniformly divided except for a curved space assigned to Denmark in the center of the north wing, considerably larger than would be expected for a small nation. The reason for this peculiar allotment was Denmark's unique presentation at the fair: "much spoken of by the press . . . a remarkable group of statuary by the artist [Bertil] Thorvaldsen, representing Christ and the twelve Apostles. . . . the only contribution from the Danish dominions . . . never before been exhibited either in England or here. It is to occupy a conspicuous place in a circular enclosure . . . The figures are colossal . . . twelve feet in height. . . . The reputation of the artist, and the singularity of the group, will doubtless make it an attractive . . . feature of the exhibition."[21] The *New-York Daily Times* reported that the Thorvaldsen presentation was the exhibition's show-stopper: "Many who look upon the group almost involuntarily uncover their heads, as they would in entering a sacred edifice, and stand silently gazing upon it, or quietly conversing in respect to its meaning. The contrast between this and the other portions of the buildings is very striking, even to the casual observer."[22]

A host of dignitaries joined the newly elected President, Franklin Pierce, accompanied by his cabinet, including Secretary of War Jefferson Davis, to open the exhibition on July 14, 1853. Politicians hoped in vain that championing the nation's achievements on an international stage might salve the deepening sectarian rift between North and South.

What did arise from this amazing space and the message it enveloped was a sudden awareness of the dynamic energy and resourcefulness of American talent: "the stranger who would learn the nature and value of our industry, must count the number of acres that have been redeemed from the wilderness in sixty years . . . towns are rising everywhere, as if they rose by thought and not by careful hands . . . Why should not our young mechanics . . . have similar opportunities with our young painters and sculptors . . . scholars, lawyers and divines? Surely their functions are quite as important to the progress and refinement of society, as . . . other professional men . . . we ought to extend every appliance and facility that is likely to raise the standard of excellence among those who contribute to the physical means of civilization."[23]

Unfortunately, speculators drove up the exhibition's shares, and while a few made a killing, most investors took a bath. Construction delays postponed the opening. "The great heat came and the city was deserted by all who could run away"; consequently attendance did not pick up until autumn.[24] Losses mounted and were never overcome, despite rave reviews.

Carstensen himself managed to lose a considerable personal fortune on the Crystal Palace venture. In 1854, as a testament to their belief that "architecture is the art form, which frames the social necessities of mankind,"[25] he and Gildemeister published a deluxe monograph on the building, including six large plates of floor plans, elevations, architectural details, and a reproduction of an oil painting of the building's exterior. But there was no profit in it.[26]

On October 5, 1858, the Crystal Palace burned to the ground in a spectacular fire.[27] The glittering jewel box consumed itself like a smelting furnace.[28] The building was safely evacuated and no lives were lost. But Carstensen had not lived to see his dream go up in smoke.

He returned to Copenhagen in 1855 expecting acclaim and instead was met with indifference to the exhibition of his Crystal Palace illustrations. He built one last extravaganza in the suburb of Fredericksberg to compete with Tivoli Gardens. Called Alhambra, the complex was designed in the same eclectic Moorish style as the Crystal Palace. But eight months before construction was finished, he died at age forty-four, bankrupt and alone, on January 4, 1857.

Carstensen's death was noted on the front page of the *Scientific American* on February 21, 1857, just two days before a dozen architects met in Richard Upjohn's office to form what would become the American Institute of Architects.[29] Georg Carstensen's singular achievement, which has lived on and grown with society, was the making of astonishing, joyous places for the sharing and celebration of public life.

4 Professional Leadership: Born on the Sharp Edge of the Sword

N EARLY A CENTURY AND A HALF HAS PASSED since the night of February 23, 1857, when, in the New York office of architect Richard Upjohn, a baker's dozen of America's finest architects gathered together and established the nation's oldest surviving association of professional architects: the American Institute of Architects.

Upjohn (1803–1878) was born in Shaftsbury, England, and had achieved the status of master cabinetmaker and draftsman before immigrating, at age twenty-six, to Massachusetts with his wife and baby. Joining Upjohn that night, along with his son and partner, Richard Mitchell Upjohn, and son-in-law Charles Babcock, were fellow British émigrés Jacob Wrey Mould (1825–1886), born in Chislehurst, educated at Kings College, and trained by the eminent architect Owen Jones; Henry Dudley (1813–1894); Joseph C. Wells (1814–1860), who arrived in New York City from England in 1839; and John Welch (1824–1894), a Scotsman who trained in Scotland and England and is known to have designed his first American commission, a church in Newark, New Jersey, in 1850. Also invited to the meeting were Prague-born, Vienna-trained Leopold Eidlitz (1823–1908), who had arrived in New York at the youthful age of twenty in 1843, and Prussian architect and engineer Frederick A. Petersen, a political refugee of the 1848 Revolution.

These European immigrants assembled with the American architects John Weller Priest (d.1859), the only native-born architect among the initial six approved by the American chapter of the British Ecclesiology Society; Henry W. Cleaveland (1818–1901), who pioneered mail-order house designs[30]; thirty-year-old, Paris-trained Richard Morris Hunt (1827–1895); and the respected civil engineer-architect, Edward Gardiner. Gardiner, who five years earlier had cofounded the American Society of

Civil Engineers and Architects and served as its first vice president, now lent his experience to the creation of a similar organization for what was still a shared profession.[31]

The group agreed to form an official organization with a constitution and bylaws and drew up a short list of colleagues to invite into membership at the next meeting. This expanded their number to twenty-five.

The British contingent was strengthened with the recruitment of John Notman (1810–1865), from Edinburgh, Scotland, born into a family of stonemasons and trained at the Royal Academy of Scotland, he emigrated in 1831; the architect partners Calvert Vaux (1824–1895), born and educated in London, and Frederick Clarke Withers (1828–1901), born in Somerset, England; George Snell (1820–1893), an English architect who established a practice in Boston in 1850; and Frederick Diaper (1810–1906), of Devonshire and a student of British architect Richard Smirke.

Joining the American contingent were Alexander Jackson Davis (1803–1892), a native New Yorker and one of the century's most influential architects and designers of decorative arts; John W. Ritch, a successful New York City architect; John Davis Hatch, whose Athenaeum at St. Johnsbury, Vermont, is the oldest intact art gallery in the country; Joseph Sands, who partnered with James Renwick and Alfred Janson (A.J.) Bloor; and Boston-born Edward Clarke Cabot (1818–1901), the first president of the Boston Society of Architects.

The important federal government architects Thomas Ustick Walter (1804–1887), of Philadelphia, designer of the U.S. Capitol dome and wings, and Ammi B. Young (1798–1874), of Lebanon, New Hampshire, the first supervising architect of the U.S. Department of Treasury, brought to the Institute the gravitas of their impressive civic and government portfolios and added much-needed balance to the clique of foreign-born architects.[32]

For Walter, this meeting was the realization of one of his lifetime's ambitions. Two decades earlier he had tried to create such an organization in collaboration with A.J. Davis, but neither the times nor the conditions were right. American architecture was as young as the nation itself. In 1838 Walter wrote, "If the mass of the people were generally well informed on the subject of architecture . . . nations would look to their architects and not to their arms for the means of handing down to ages yet unborn, the story of their power and greatness."33

On April 13, 1857, the Institute's bylaws were signed by the first elected officers and registered with the state of New York under the eyes of state Supreme Court Justice James A. Roosevelt. Forty-nine architects affixed their names to the incorporating document.34

Given the number of these men who were born and trained in Great Britain, it was natural for the group to look to the Royal Institute of British Architects, the leading professional institution of the day, as the prototype for the organization they intended to establish. The influence of the English Gothic Revival on American architecture, along with the spread of Anglican, Presbyterian, Unitarian, and other sects of evangelical Protestantism, ensured a steady stream of work for architects who specialized in ecclesiastical design. Reputations thus established also led to commissions for houses of worship from the swelling Roman Catholic and Jewish immigrant communities.

The predominance of this branch of practice, led by Upjohn, the most renowned Gothic Revival church architect of the period, was heavily represented in the group of twenty-five. Charles Babcock, college educated in the classics, trained in architecture by Upjohn, and ordained an Episcopal minister in 1864, became the first professor and then dean of Cornell University's architecture program, establishing the nation's first four-year architecture degree.

Along with the ecclesiastical architects, the fledgling society attracted the leading designers of residential architecture. Calvert Vaux, Alexander J. Davis, John W. Ritch, and Henry Cleaveland all had their designs for country and village homes published and widely popularized in builders' pattern books.

But equally important, if not more so, was the design of the burgeoning urban environment. Ritch designed a residential six-story building for the Association for Improving the Condition of the Poor, which, when built in 1855, was an early attempt at progressive tenement design for New York's impoverished black American community. Unfortunately, over time, the Workmen's Home, which became popularly known as the Big Flat, devolved into one of the slums of the notorious Five Points neighborhood. Despite repeated attempts by a series of investors to maintain its respectability and profitability, it was demolished in 1888.35

At the same time, Frederick A. Petersen was working on a state-of-the-art edifice that would have an enormous impact on the cultural and political life of New York City. Designed in collaboration with his client Peter Cooper, who was simultaneously manufacturing the iron girders for Thomas U. Walter's U.S. Capitol dome in his Trenton ironworks, Petersen's Cooper Institute building was one of the first constructed with wrought-iron rails, rolled beams, and columns for structural support, and it helped launch the era of urban, multistoried skyscraper architecture.

Leopold Eidlitz, remembered most often for his involvement in controversial public architecture commissions such as New York City's Tweed Courthouse and the Albany State House, would contribute mightily to the urban fabric of America and to the intellectual development of the architecture profession. The presence of Calvert Vaux and Jacob Wrey Mould, collaborators in the design of the architecture for the nation's prototype urban public space, Central Park, could not have been more fortuitous.

The energetic and enthusiastic Richard Morris Hunt, freshly repatriated from Paris, christened his stateside career with the founding of the Institute. Hunt served as the AIA's first secretary. Not long after the AIA was founded, construction was completed on Hunt's Tenth Street Studio building, which he designed for the entrepreneur businessman James Boorman Johnston. In this unique building, the first in America to be built expressly for professional artists, Hunt established his architecture practice and began his pedagogical mission to raise the design proficiency of American architecture. Modeled on the atelier system of the École des Beaux Arts, Hunt's studio played a pivotal role in shaping the educational and practice standards of American architects.

These twenty-five original founders embodied, in microcosm, the full range of the American profession's establishment. Together they reflected the collective prestige that architects had attained in the major East Coast cities of New York, Boston, Philadelphia, and Washington, D.C. The quantity, variety, and location of the churches, homes, cultural and social institutions, and public buildings designed and built by the founders of the American Institute of Architects attest to the national significance their gathering ordained.[36]

5 CREATING ARCHITECTURE'S SYSTEM OF HIGHER EDUCATION

A CADEMIC EDUCATION HAD A VERY LIMITED IMPACT on architecture practice in the American mainstream until well into the 20th century. Access to higher education was limited to the privileged minority who could afford tuition at private institutions, and study abroad was possible for only a tiny percentage of these fortunate few. Very few Americans achieved more than a secondary level of education.

In 1857 the U.S. Military Academy at West Point, New York, was the primary institution for the training of civil engineers through enlistment and training for the Army Corps of Engineers. Nearby Rensselaer Polytechnic Institute, founded in 1824 at Troy, New York, was the first private school of civil engineering in the country; its Department of Engineering and Technology was founded in 1835.

In 1854 Rensselaer was joined by the Polytechnic Institute of Brooklyn, a privately endowed school for male students ranging in age from ten years to early twenties. Architectural training was included in its engineering program, as was the norm. AIA cofounder Frederick A. Petersen designed the school's first building. Today it continues as a major science and engineering university.

In Manhattan, the Society of Mechanics and Tradesmen, founded in 1785, opened its free technical school in 1820. The Mechanics Institute provided training for the sons of its guild members in the building, manufacturing, and engineering trades. Hudson River School painter-architect Jasper Cropsey won a diploma from the Mechanics Institute in 1837 at the age of fourteen and then apprenticed in the office of architect Joseph Trench until 1842.37

Free education in the arts and sciences became available to the people of New York City with the debut of full-time evening courses at the Cooper Institute in November 1859. The innovative Cooper Institute building was also designed by Petersen. The founder, Peter Cooper, whose impoverished childhood and lack of education were overshadowed by his success as an inventor and entrepreneur, insisted that the school's idealistic goals be matched by practical, professional instruction. Its architecture drafting classes were fully enrolled from the first day. Excellent record keeping for these classes gives a detailed overview of the rapid growth rate of architecture education and its expansion across age groups, nationalities, and occupational and artistic disciplines.

New York City, with its dominance in international shipping, technology development, and heavy industry, particularly iron manufacturing, provided a natural power base for the emerging engineering, architecture, and building professions. Though architectural design was considered to be neither an autonomous nor an exclusively artistic discipline, the concentration of these schools in New York made it the center of building expertise. It was not until after the Civil War that the word *architect* was dropped from the American Society of Civil Engineers' title, demarcating the boundaries between the twinned professions of architecture and engineering.

The passage of the Morrill Act in 1862 established the federal government's long-term commitment to a national public policy for higher education. This law recognized the urgent need for an educated, highly skilled workforce in the agricultural and technical sciences. Following the Civil War, the financial means to fund the state and territorial systems of higher education were therefore in place and began to be implemented.

The first land-grant act, introduced into Congress in 1857 by Vermont Congressman Justin Smith Morrill, had passed in 1859 over Southern opposition but was vetoed by President Buchanan. Morrill reintroduced a revised bill in Congress soon after the Lincoln administration took office. The absence of the Southern states and the inclusion of military training in the bill helped secure its passage. It was signed into law by President Lincoln on July 2, 1862.

Ownership of large tracts of federal land—30,000 acres for each member of Congress—was transferred to the states for the mandated purpose of sale to finance public colleges and technical schools. Considering that outside New England fewer than 300 high schools existed nationwide, this new law reverse engineered the entire educational structure of the country.

A fortunate by-product of the Morrill Act of 1862 was the establishment of the nation's first three architecture degree programs, included as part of the act's technical and engineering agenda. The Massachusetts Institute of Technology (MIT), chartered in 1861 and funded by the land-grant act, opened in 1865 and, in 1868, launched the first college architecture program, under the tutelage of architect William R. Ware, a onetime associate in Richard Morris Hunt's atelier.

The University of Illinois, chartered in 1867, commenced the second architecture program in 1870 with Bauakademie-trained Swedish architect Harold M. Hansen as its first qualified teacher. In 1873 the school produced its first architecture graduate, who was also the nation's first, Nathan C. Ricker (1843–1924). In 1874 Ricker was appointed head of the new architecture department and in 1878 became the dean of the College of Engineering. Ricker also designed several landmark campus buildings. He was a national leader in architecture education until his retirement from teaching in 1917.[38]

The nation's third architecture degree program was instituted at land-grant-funded Cornell University, in Ithaca, New York. Established in 1871, Cornell's School of Architecture was headed by architect and academic Charles Babcock, son-in-law of Richard Upjohn. Another land-grant college, the University of Michigan at Ann Arbor, was the sixth college to offer architecture. Private colleges added architecture to their curricula in quick succession. The elite Columbia College, founded in 1754 in New York City, was the seventh to add architecture to its curriculum. William R. Ware was recruited from MIT to chair its new architecture department.

The nation's state public university systems and many of our finest educational institutions owe their existence to the farsighted vision of Justin Morrill. The importance of this public policy initiative to the education and professionalization of architects since 1862 cannot be overemphasized. The land-grant colleges graduated the nation's first women architects and African-American architects, who in turn became the vanguard of equality in the profession. For all the artistic élan claimed by the architecture programs of our elite private universities, the state universities remain the educational bedrock of the American architecture profession.[39]

6 ARCHITECT-LEADERS DURING THE CIVIL WAR ERA

A S PART OF THE BURGEONING FREE-MARKET DEMOCRACY, an indigenous American architecture profession emerged as a chaotic and spontaneous expression of the vast physical growth of a new society. Architecture practice was conducted in as entrepreneurial a fashion as each individual could manage in the plying of his trade.

The gentlemen of the AIA came together during a period racked by conflict. The group had few financial resources with which to execute its lofty goals, the first of which was to establish a proper architecture library for professionals. Just finding an office from which to administer the Institute's affairs took a full year to arrange. All efforts were voluntary, and operating expenses quickly surpassed the total amount collected from membership dues. The Institute's officers covered their own out-of-pocket expenses. In 1857 times were hard and getting harder, bringing new building to a near standstill. With the nation on the verge of civil war, New York City itself was mired in bitter political and sectarian antagonisms.

From that February night in 1857, architects were struggling to maintain their businesses under difficult economic conditions, a fortunate few managing major projects of considerable importance, while the political situation rapidly spiraled into crisis. When war finally erupted between the North and South in 1861, enormous economic, social, and political pressures were placed upon the profession.

By early 1863 the situation had deepened into such chaos that the Lincoln administration, plagued by internal squabbling between politicians and ambitious, frequently insubordinate senior military officers, found itself pitted in increasingly hostile conflict with the polity. The seams of the Union were under assault from within as well as from without.

The AIA suspended its activities for the duration of the war because it became virtually impossible to conduct any collective professional business in New York City. The office leased in the New York University building on Washington Square was relinquished and the furniture sold to pay debts. The archives were boxed-up and stored.

Until the conflict was resolved, all able-bodied men were called into service in one way or another, but this did not mean that architects were invisible or silently waiting for the smoke to clear. Throughout this extended period of divisive national conflict and unprecedented violence, members of the design profession, such as Frederick Law Olmsted, Richard Morris Hunt, Frank Furness, William Le Baron Jenney, and Frederick A. Petersen, stepped forward and courageously supported the Union. It should be understood that adamant public support of the Emancipation Proclamation came at considerable personal and professional risk.

Military men trained in building science frequently provided leadership. The Union Army's chief commander, Major-General George B. McClellan, excelled in civil engineering at West Point and was internationally renowned as a brilliant military strategist and engineer. General William S. Rosencrans, a fellow graduate of West Point and professor of engineering at the Point, entered civilian life in 1854 to practice architecture and engineering in Cincinnati before being recalled to command at the start of the Civil War.[40]

These leaders were followed by others of the building profession. AIA founder Frederick C. Withers; Frank Furness, founder of the Philadelphia chapter of the AIA; William Le Baron Jenney, Chicago's first skyscraper architect; and Dankmar Adler, another of Chicago's great architects,[41] all served as officers in the Union Army. Furness served with singular distinction.

These leading architects embraced a course of action to positively influence the ethical and political tide of civic affairs, thereby setting a remarkable precedent of enlightened and responsible citizenship for many years to come.

Frederick Law Olmsted: Journalist, Landscape Architect, Executive, Civic Leader

Frederick Law Olmsted (1822–1903) was one of the most influential individuals of the 19th century. His wide-ranging accomplishments, capabilities, and noble ambitions far exceeded the ordinary measure of a man. But for the purpose at hand, we will look at the nature of his political efforts and the methods he used to direct influence over the course of political events during America's worst civil crisis to date.

In 1861 the Union Army was not prepared for a major war; it had no plans in place or precedents to follow. The United States Sanitary Commission (USSC) was founded by citizen volunteers, initially as a ladies movement, to deliver battlefront triage, ongoing medical care, acquisition and delivery of critical supplies, and logistical support to the Union Army troops. Starting from scratch, the USSC was faced with a daunting task.

Olmsted was chief architect of Central Park when the Civil War broke out. Construction of the park was necessarily suspended, so the board of the USSC, all well-known New York professional men, had the opportunity to hire Olmsted to run the daily operations of its formidable enterprise. Olmsted took a leave of absence from his Central Park position and commenced what he thought would be a brief task. Architect Calvert Vaux, Olmsted's design partner, assumed a sort of caretaker supervisory role over the park's affairs while Olmsted was away from the city.

After eighteen months of round-the-clock labor in Washington, D.C., Olmsted, in close collaboration with the USSC board members from New York City, began organization of the Union League Club (ULC) in Manhattan. Between late fall 1862 and early winter 1863, the club's highly focused mobilization was the direct result of Olmsted's detailed strategic planning and ideological guidance.

The ULC was able to marshal significant public, material, and financial support for the Union cause at the height of the conflict, at both the local and national levels. Olmsted's foresight made it possible to restore and maintain civil order immediately following the New York City draft riots of July 12–16, 1863. The collective political efforts of the ULC effectively dominated the divisive political debate over critical national issues at the heart of the Civil War itself.

Olmsted's strategy was set down in explicit detail in correspondence with his fellow club cofounders. These letters reveal the logical thought processes and ideological bases of Olmsted's professional and civic commitments. They demonstrate his ability to create an enduring intellectual landscape from which leadership could operate with a pragmatism unpolluted by ethical compromise. Olmsted recruited into that first class of ULC charter members many of his closest friends and professional colleagues who shared his ideals as well as his political and civic concerns.

And although Olmsted left the USSC for what he mistakenly assumed was a golden opportunity to manage the Mariposa Estates in California in September 1863, he maintained his membership and public association with the ULC throughout the war. In fact, Olmsted initiated the founding of the political science magazine, *The Nation*, with several fellow club members in June 1863, in the meeting rooms of the clubhouse on Union Square.

The powerful political influence of the Union League Club endured into the next century, chiefly because it was intentionally designed to produce a lasting benefit to future generations by its cofounder, Frederick Law Olmsted and his colleagues.[42]

Richard Morris Hunt: Architect, Professional, and Civic Leader

Richard Morris Hunt (1827–1895), the son of Congressman Jonathan Hunt of Vermont, was educated in the finest European schools. This gifted, socially privileged American architect had originally intended to attend West Point to study civil engineering and serve in the Army Corps of Engineers. Hunt's change of course to architecture in his late teens probably saved his life, as well as provided a great boon to the profession.

In 1854, while both Hunt and former President Martin Van Buren were visiting Rome, Van Buren wrote a personal letter of introduction for Hunt to the respected New York architect Richard Upjohn. When he returned to the United States in 1856, Hunt formed his first architecture office and through its operation introduced France's École des Beaux Arts' atelier teaching methods to American practice. Together with Upjohn, Hunt would become a cofounder of the AIA and serve as its first secretary.

Richard M. Hunt led by example. In March 1860 Hunt, along with fellow architects James Renwick and John W. Ritch, lobbied the New York State Assembly in Albany to back pending legislation for enhanced building safety standards. Their advocacy produced positive results, including the establishment of the first New York City Buildings Department, officially titled the "Department for the survey and inspection of buildings in the City of New York." In 1862 the New York City Common Council published its revised compilation of New York state laws that related to the city. In Section 42, the AIA was charged with providing one of the three surveyors for all properties found to be unsafe by the superintendent of buildings. Section 47 of the law mandated that all officers of the Buildings Department be architects, house carpenters, or masons, and that they be appointed only after passing an examination conducted by the Examinations Committee of the AIA. In 1861 Hunt also pursued the first law case to establish the legal precedents for several fundamental professional architecture business practices.[43]

With Frederick Law Olmsted, Hunt was among the core group of organizers of the powerful Union League Club. He was an invited participant in one of the first organizational meetings in early February 1863, and helped mobilize an impressive, diverse group of New York's leading citizens in support of the Union. The club's political positions and activities earned the members the brand of radicals in the media and subjected them to vicious slurs, political scare tactics, and violent opposition. In the months before and after the New York City draft riots of July 1863, a backlash against the "radicals" was actively fomented.

Hunt and his wife, Catherine Howland Hunt, helped raise more than a million dollars for the U.S. Sanitary Commission via the Metropolitan Fair in March and April 1864. This resounding success laid the groundwork for future postwar civic efforts. Hunt designed and decorated the large temporary fair building placed in Union Square, and even the moribund AIA rose to the occasion and participated in the fair's art exhibition. The event helped to keep the AIA alive.

Richard and Catherine participated in the Union League Club's organizing, mustering in, and celebration of the first troops of New York free black men to fight in the Civil War, the 20th and 26th Colored Regiments, U.S. Infantry, in March 1864. The club's members, with their wives and children, stood defiantly in Union Square as the women presented the black American soldiers of the 20th Regiment with their regimental colors. Their provocative and potent symbolic gesture took great moral courage; it was an intentional slap in the face of widespread public sentiment against radical equality. The actions of these men and women were unreservedly political; their reputations, money, time, and talents were put on the line.

The Hunts had married on April 2, 1861. Fort Sumter was fired on ten days later. On April 15, war was officially declared. Hunt did not serve in the military, despite his initial impulse to do so, in response to his doctor's adamant objection. He had suffered through serious illnesses picked up during his travels to the Middle East in 1853 and had suffered another bout of dysentery in 1860. This left him highly vulnerable to a swift and potentially fatal relapse if exposed to the unsanitary conditions with which the military was coping.

After his doctor vetoed enlistment, Hunt paid for a substitute enlistee and proceeded on his planned honeymoon with his new bride. They left for Paris on April 27 to visit the groom's family, and Catherine soon became pregnant. Six months after their baby was born, the family safely made the return ocean voyage. The Hunts arrived home in November 1862 to a raging war that no one had anticipated would run such a virulent course. Except for summer vacations in Rhode Island, the family lived at 49 West 35th Street until 1885.

The war was omnipresent. Leavitt Hunt, Richard's beloved younger brother, served throughout the conflict as a Union Army officer and chief aide to General Heintzelman. Catherine's brother, Brigadier-General Joseph Howland, was wounded in battle and, after being brevetted out in 1863, worked closely with his brother-in-law in the political activities of the Union League Club. According to the Howland Cultural Center, originally a public library endowed by General Howland and designed by Hunt, "1862 through 1872, revolved around the turmoil of the Civil War years and its aftermath. Hunt worked actively for the Union League Club, an organization involved in supporting the war effort in financial and political ways."[44]

The founding members of the Union League Club were decidedly *not* on the periphery of the Civil War. Just as Olmsted did, Hunt recruited his closest personal friends, colleagues, and family into the first class of ULC members. His first clients, James Boorman Johnston, Dr. Eleazer Parmly, and John N.A. Griswold, and many future clients were members.

Throughout the war, Hunt served as secretary and treasurer of the ULC's Executive Committee. The club consulted with Congress on policy issues

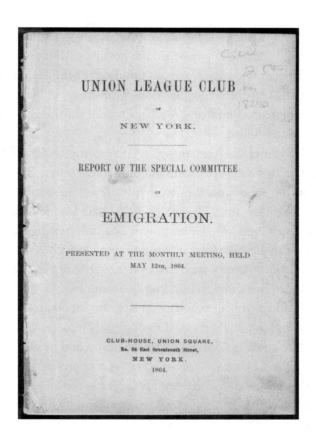

Architect Richard Morris Hunt, secretary-treasurer of the Union League Club's executive committee, is listed among the club's leadership in its widely distributed policy paper, "Report of the Special Committee on Emigration, May 12, 1864," released in the weeks leading up to the June 1864 Republican Party convention. The club's study positively influenced the party's presidential campaign platform. From the collection of Richard N. Swett

throughout the second half of the Civil War and afterward. In May 1864, just before the Republican convention in June, the club published and distributed 2,500 copies of its study of immigration policy. The report's analysis of the immigration issue influenced the inclusion of a pro-foreign immigration plank (#8) in the 1864 Republican Party presidential platform. Hunt's name on this and other club political documents inextricably tied his reputation to the group's lobbying on national public policy issues, establishing credibility for future lobbying.[45]

During Reconstruction, Hunt continued to support the club's relief efforts to rebuild the South and to aid the newly freed slave population. In 1869 he was invited to design the main building for the Hampton Normal and Agricultural Institute (now Hampton University) at Hampton Roads, Virginia, the first vocational and teachers' school for the newly freed men and women of the South.

General Samuel C. Armstrong, former commander of the Union Army's black troops and superintendent of the Freedmen's Bureau after the war, founded the school on the riverbank site of the battle between the Monitor and the Merrimac. His choice of architect was deliberate and considered, the instrument of his intention to establish "prestige and respectability" for the school.[46] Architecture was to provide shelter, inspiration, and instruction for the students, who manufactured the bricks themselves and learned skilled trades through building the campus.

Hunt's Academic Hall, completed in late 1870, stood for nine years, until it burned down. He was then asked to design its replacement, which provided better fireproofing, a less ostentatious façade, and more functions than the first building. The new Academic Hall was completed in 1881.

Hunt also designed a considerably larger second building, Virginia Hall, which provided living, dining, academic, and working quarters for female students and teachers. The plans were presented in September 1872 and accepted in January 1873. Hunt visited the campus in the spring of 1874, before the dedication on June 11. According to a school history published that year, "the brains and hands employed are all local . . . it will probably be the finest building in Virginia. The architect is Mr. Richard M. Hunt, of New York City, whose reputation is national."[47] The students raised a large portion of the costs by mounting a concert tour by the school's choir. The ULC and Henry Bellows sponsored several concerts and events for the school's benefit. Dr. Bellows even participated in the cornerstone laying ceremony for Virginia Hall.[48] These two surviving Hunt buildings on Hampton University's campus are now National Landmarks.

Booker T. Washington, born into slavery, was Hampton's most distinguished early graduate. He arrived there in 1872 and worked his way through the school as the janitor of Hunt's buildings until his graduation four years later. Washington described how the sight of Hunt's Academic Hall affected him—after he had walked hundreds of miles to enroll at Hampton: "To me it had been a long, eventful journey; but the first sight of the large, three-story; brick school building seemed to have rewarded me for all that I had undergone in order to reach the place. If the people who gave the money to provide that building could appreciate the influence the sight of it had upon me, as well as upon thousands of other youths, they would feel all the more encouraged to make such gifts. It seemed to me to be the largest and most beautiful building I had ever seen. The sight of it seemed to give me new life. I felt that a new kind of existence had now begun—that life would now have a new meaning."[49]

Washington would one day found the world-famous Tuskegee Institute for the teaching of various professional skills designed to impart self-sufficiency and self-respect to a formerly enslaved people.

Hunt also was a founder of the Metropolitan Museum of Art. At the founding meeting of the museum, held at the ULC, Hunt gave a keynote address in his dual role representing the club and the AIA. Hunt's commitment to the ULC's founding principles garnered credibility and support for the profession among his club mates.

As a cofounder, secretary, and president of the AIA, and particularly during the merger with the Western Association of Architects, Hunt provided steadfast leadership. His leadership was as important a contribution to the 1893 Chicago World's Fair architectural triumph as was his design of its Administration Building. By testifying before legislative bodies, first in 1860 to push for safe building standards in New York State and in his later appearances before Congress to persuade legislators to pass the Tarsney Act, Hunt set a high standard of civic engagement for the profession. His national reputation of personal and professional integrity came to embody the ideals of service to society. For nearly four tumultuous decades, Richard Morris Hunt brought honor, respect, and credibility to the whole profession.[50]

Frank Furness: The Architect as National Hero

Courage under fire is the mark of leadership at all times, in all theaters of engagement. Frank Furness (1839–1912) served as an officer in Rush's Lancers, the Sixth Pennsylvania Cavalry, attached to the Army of the Potomac under the initial command of fellow Philadelphian, Major-General George B. McClellan. Furness saw fierce fighting in combat, as well as service in the administration of the upper ranks. He fought at the Battle of Gettysburg and later designed one of its most evocative memorials. But it was his bravery under enemy fire on an open Virginia battlefield at Trevilian Station on June 12, 1864, that won for him the U.S. Congressional Medal of Honor. Furness is the *only* architect, to the present day, to have been so honored by our nation.

The facts of Furness's life, including his military career, are drawn primarily from the insightful biography, *Frank Furness: Architecture and the Violent Mind*, by historian Michael J. Lewis.[51]

The incident for which Furness was awarded the nation's highest honor began when Furness suddenly found himself in command of the Lancers, who were pinned down in the forward position in the middle of a field. Fifty yards away, Company C was sheltered by farm buildings, while the rest of the Lancers were behind a stone wall at the field's edge. The enemy maintained constant fire on the Lancer's positions from the safety of the farmhouse, cutting the two units off from each other. If Company C was taken out, the Confederates could break the front line and overrun the Union Army, which was regrouping after the previous night's battle to extricate General Custer's unit from its vulnerable position.

As the day progressed, the situation became critical. A soldier was ordered to crawl the length of the open field to tell Captain Furness that they were running out of ammunition. Furness had to decide what action to take, and evidently he believed that he could not ask of his men something which he himself was not willing to do.

Furness was a strapping young redhead. He picked up a box of ammunition, hefted it onto his head, and asked who would carry the other box to their comrades across the pasture. He was joined by Captain Walsh Mitchell. Together they bolted into the open range with two large cases of munitions on their heads and made it, untouched, to the farm buildings where Company C was hunkered down. Then they had to get back across the field. The previously surprised Confederates would be aiming at them with particular relish. Mitchell told Furness to run "zigzag so they can't get a bead on you."[52] Miraculously, they both made it back across the field unscathed, barely missed by a barrage of bullets. Under Furness's command, the Lancers were able to hold their battle lines until combat successfully concluded the following morning.

Furness also showed uncommon compassion under fire. Little more than a week earlier, he had crawled out from behind the barricades onto the battlefield to apply a tourniquet to the leg of a wounded Confederate soldier. He simply could not bear to watch the man bleed to death. The incident haunted him. More than four decades would pass before Furness learned what had become of the wounded Confederate. A newspaper story, placed at Furness's request, resulted in his reunion with the elderly Georgia farmer who had survived the gunshot wound, thanks to Furness's decency and selfless bravery. The reunion of the two wizened Civil War veterans in the fall of 1905 was a minor media event in Philadelphia.53

Furness's father, William Henry Furness, was a Harvard-educated Unitarian minister and leader of Philadelphia's abolitionists. The Rev. Furness was also a close friend of Charles McKim's father, another leader in the abolitionist movement. Two of Furness's brothers, Horace and William, worked for the U.S. Sanitary Commission in Washington, D.C., under Frederick Olmsted's direct supervision.

Before the war, Rev. Furness arranged a training position in Richard Morris Hunt's new Manhattan atelier for his youngest son. Furness's older brother, William, an artist, had become friendly with Hunt during his European study tour, and through this connection Frank's advanced architecture training was secured. The outbreak of war coincided with Hunt's wedding, and since business had all but dried up, the studio was shut down and the newlyweds left for their European honeymoon. Furness went home to Philadelphia and enlisted in the army.

After he was discharged in November 1864, Furness returned for a time to Hunt's studio, now as a senior employee rather than as an apprentice. On March 6, 1866, Furness, along with H.H. Richardson, was nominated and accepted into the AIA. Two days later, he was married in Philadelphia. He decided to remain in the city and establish his own practice.

In 1869 Furness was a primary founder of the Philadelphia chapter of the AIA, but soon found himself embroiled in a professional dispute that had long-term consequences. In 1871 he was hired to take over the job of

Philadelphia's renowned architect and Civil War hero, Frank Furness, still clear-eyed and dapper as a
senior citizen, is captured in this photographic portrait published in 1901 in *Philadelphia and Notable
Philadelphians* by Moses King, Blanchard Press, New York.

building a prison for the city of Philadelphia from a fellow AIA member. The
architect, James Windrim, had resigned his post midway through construction in a miscalculated attempt at forcing the client to pay a higher fee. The
city government accepted his resignation and hired Furness as its new
architect. Windrim accused Furness of stealing his client, of falsely claiming design credit (in fact, Furness significantly altered the design because
Windrim refused to turn over the plans), and of violating the Institute's code
of ethics.

This unusual situation devolved into an acrimonious battle in the
Philadelphia AIA chapter. It was played out in the press and spilled over into

the courts. Not one to be intimidated, Furness maintained that his actions in the matter were entirely aboveboard. He furiously rejected the convoluted logic used to twist the founding principles of the AIA against him for accepting a commission that a fellow member had voluntarily vacated. Philadelphia's old guard closed ranks behind Windrim and provided a sheaf of affidavits against the upstart Furness.

Windrim's gambit produced an unintended consequence in the courts: The judge not only dismissed Windrim's case as groundless but also ruled that architects' fees were not subject to any overall industry standard as promoted by the AIA. Despite this outcome, Windrim did succeed in orchestrating the censure of Furness by his Institute colleagues. For sullying his good name, which he considered to be both a professional as well as a bitter personal betrayal, Furness never again participated in the AIA.54

More than a hundred years later, in 1979, in the case of *Mardirosian v. American Institute of Architects*, the U.S. District Court for the District of Columbia struck down, among other things, Standard Nine of the AIA Code of Ethics—the very brickbat used to pummel Furness—as a violation of the Sherman Act. The code's intent was determined to be an unlawful restriction of free trade imposed on both the practitioner and the client. Furness's stand on principle, taken a century earlier, was, in effect, upheld by the courts. Federally mandated public policy on the ethics of architecture practice fully vindicated Furness.55

Frank Furness was one of the most distinctive and original of the great designers of 19th-century architecture. His passionate architectonic form with its functional, plastic dynamism found identification in the young aspiring architect, Louis Sullivan, who chose Furness as his first professional mentor. Heroic is the most apt description of the architectural mien that Furness's life and his design work embodied and upon which Sullivan so eloquently elaborated.

William Le Baron Jenney: Military Officer, Design Pioneer, Mentor, and Educator

William L.B. Jenney (1832–1907) prepared for his career from an early age, beginning at ten as a student at the Scientific and Military Academy in Unity, New Hampshire, then on to both Marlboro and Phillips Andover

Academies. He attended the Lawrence Technical School at Harvard University for one year before he transferred his engineering and architecture studies to one the finest schools of the period, L'Ècole des Artes et Manufactures, in Paris in 1854. The school's progressive curriculum included art, architecture, and city planning along with science and technology in its engineering program. Jenney and his classmates, including Gustav Eiffel, attended architecture lectures by the renowned Viollet-le-Duc. After graduation in 1856, Jenney went to Central America to work as chief engineer for the building of the Tehantepec Railroad; he returned home to Massachusetts several years later.

When war broke out, the young engineer-architect enlisted in the Union Army and served in the Engineering Corps. Appointed as assistant chief of engineers in the Army of the Tennessee, Department of Mississippi, Captain Jenney served as a staff officer to Major-General Ulysses S. Grant. Jenney was with Grant from Cairo, Illinois, in late 1861, until after the battle at Corinth, when General William Tecumseh Sherman requested Jenney's transfer to his command. Jenney was responsible for the Union Army's fortifications, serving during the battles for Shiloh, Tennessee, and for the key rail transport center at Corinth, Mississippi, in 1862.[42] Under the command of General Sherman, Jenney was engaged in the engineering preparations for the siege of Vicksburg, Mississippi, launched in May 1863. Promoted to lieutenant, then to the rank of major, Jenney was eventually appointed engineer-in-chief of the Union Army headquarters in Nashville. He resigned his army commission in May 1866.[56]

A memorial bronze portrait of Captain Jenney, created by the sculptress Theodora Alice Ruggles Kitson and dedicated in 1911, can be found at the Vicksburg National Military Park in Mississippi. Jenney also designed the park's Illinois State Memorial to honor the 36,325 Illinois Union soldiers who died in the Vicksburg campaign. Dedicated on October 26, 1906, Jenney's design is based on the Roman Parthenon; the forty-seven steps of the entrance stairway commemorate the number of days in the siege of Vicksburg.[57]

In the spring of 1863, Jenney met Frederick Law Olmsted while Olmsted was on a fact-finding tour for the U.S. Sanitary Commission. The two struck up a cordial relationship, and after the war, they both contributed to the development of Chicago's first planned commuter suburb, Riverside, Illinois.

In an April 1, 1863, letter to his father, Olmsted recorded his collegial experience with Jenney, remarking on how surprised he was to meet a man of similar interests and intellectual refinement under such circumstances. The letter recounted their discussion of the freed slaves' injuries and scars, even among the children. Jenney supposed they were prone to precocious childhood injury, but when he questioned individuals about their injuries, he could not elicit a satisfactory explanation for this phenomenon. Jenney did not conjure the awful reality of the physical abuse of the former slaves. Olmsted told his father, "[Jenney] speaks well of the Negroes as industrious, disciplinable, grateful and docile. . . . Nearly all bear the marks of injuries which they are unable to explain."[58]

Olmsted supplied his and Jenney's testimony on the freedmen as workers and potential soldiers to the American Freedmen's Special Inquiry Commission on April 22, 1863. Based on his firsthand observations, and corroborated by Jenney, Olmsted's report strongly recommended that freedmen be allowed to serve in the military. He conveyed Jenney's satisfactory experience of supervising building operations with several hundred freedmen at various locations, testimony obtained while in Jenney's company at General Sherman's camp near the port of Vicksburg, Mississippi. Olmsted repeated Jenney's statement to the commission that the freed black men who worked for him on the canal opposite Vicksburg "worked better than the whites."[59] Impressed with this evidence, the commission recommended that a Freedmen's Bureau be created to secure the civil rights of freed men and women, provide material aid, and protect them from the reimposition of slavery.[60]

In 1867 Jenney opened his architecture practice in Chicago. In the 1870s his work included city and park planning, specifically Chicago's boulevard system and Douglas, Garfield, and Humboldt parks. Jenney and his colleague, Sanford E. Loring, published a folio titled *Principles and Practice of Architecture* in 1869, one of a very few architecture books known to have been published in prefire Chicago. It contains forty-six plates of various types of buildings designed by the authors and copious text, including "an explanation and illustrations of the French system of apartment houses, and dwellings for the laboring classes."[61] A review in *Scientific American* noted "a most important chapter on modern French architecture, in which the subjects of apartment houses of Paris and workingmen's cottages are elaborately treated . . . We have not met with an architectural work more adapted to the wants of the building associations than this, and its adaptability to the wants of young architects is unquestionable."[62]

Jenney had the foresight to promote European standards for workers' housing, a timely response to the needs of the postwar era. But he could not have foreseen how quickly these design standards would find application—until October 8, 1871, when Chicago's city center was engulfed in flames. Thirty percent of the city was left in ashes; more than 17,000 buildings were destroyed, and nearly 100,000 people were left homeless. In the aftermath of the fire, the sudden, enormous demand for better fire-proofed buildings enabled Jenney to turn his exceptional training into a competitive advantage. From his first commission after the fire, Jenney's innovations in building design, which he developed by combining structural elements of iron, masonry, and terra cotta, established his reputation as the father of the skyscraper. He pioneered the load-bearing, steel skeletal frame system of multistoried architecture that made possible modern curtain-wall skyscrapers.

As one of the most important teachers of architecture and engineering practice during this crucial period of America's urban and industrial development, Jenney became the first instructor at the University of Michigan's school of architecture in 1876. For three decades, while Chicago transformed itself into the second most powerful urban center in the country, Jenney trained the best and brightest architects in town, including Daniel H. Burnham, William A. Holabird, Martin Roche, I.K. Pond, Howard Shaw, James Gamble Rodgers, and Frank Furness's young protégé, Louis Sullivan.

In 1872 Jenney was accepted into the AIA. He was elected a Fellow in 1885 and served as the Institute's vice president in 1898 and 1899. From his early commissions in the wake of the Chicago fire to his Horticulture Building for the 1893 Chicago World's Fair, Jenney was responsible for tremendous technical advances in state-of-the-art building design. Of equal importance was his key role in the education and training of young architects at the birth of modern American architecture.[63]

Though less sensational, William Le Baron Jenney's sensitivity as an army officer, the decency of his treatment of the nation's most abused people, and his honesty in reporting the truth of their condition to his colleague when he was under no obligation or expectation to do so are worthy of appreciation and emulation. This is the moral fiber of leadership.

Detlef Lienau: Design Standards Innovator

Detlef Lienau (1832–1907) was born thirty miles north of Altona, the provincial capital of the Danish Royal Duchy of Holsten, Denmark's most important and prosperous market port. Lienau grew up in direct proximity to the architecture of the great Danish architect C.F. Hansen, design star of the Danish Golden Age. Hansen was regional director of architecture of Holsten from 1785 to 1804 and was also active in the adjacent free city of Hamburg before being recalled to rebuild the burned city of Copenhagen between 1805 and 1845.[64] Neoclassical Danish and Northern German architecture influenced Lienau's early artistic development.

The technical education available outside Denmark could not be surpassed, even by the Royal Academy in Copenhagen, so students routinely traveled abroad to obtain advanced training in the arts and sciences. Lienau was typical of these ambitious provincial students. After he graduated from the Königliche Bauewerksschule in Berlin, Lienau trained with the period's cutting-edge Parisian architect, Henri Labrouste (1801–1875) in 1842. The groundbreaking Bibliothèque St. Geneviève, Labrouste's masterpiece, was being designed during Lienau's apprenticeship. It was the first building in France to use structural iron.

During this period, a Danish nationalist movement pushed for democracy in Copenhagen, while a pro-German Federation movement fomented revolt among ethnic Germans in the duchies of Slesvig-Holsten in southern Jutland. The duchies were the ancestral property of the Danish king, and since he was without an heir, the German nationalists saw a chance to finally wrest them from the Danish Crown. In 1847, just as this rebellion caught fire, Lienau won the international design competition for the Altona Municipal Hospital. He had departed Paris and returned home to design and begin construction of the hospital. But hostilities had destabilized the region and had already complicated the building's construction. The volatile situation probably led to Lienau's decision to leave Europe. His wine-merchant brother, Michael, was firmly established in Jersey City, New Jersey, so when a ship chartered by him landed in Amsterdam, Detlef seized the opportunity to pursue his career in America. He arrived in New York harbor in December 1848.

Soon after his departure, the German nationalists, with military support from Prussia, attacked the Danish army. The countryside around Lienau's childhood home became the site of major fighting. Denmark prevailed, and the German nationalists' rebellion was put down for the time being. In July 1849 the Danish monarch relinquished his absolute status and the first Danish constitution was adopted. The democratic state of Denmark became a reality. Lienau's Altona Municipal Hospital was not completed until 1861, altered and constructed by other hands.[65]

Once in America, Lienau married into a socially prominent Dutch colonial family. His first designs included modest homes and a Gothic church in Jersey City. But his excellent social connections led to commissions for sumptuous mansions and blocks of French apartments on Fifth Avenue in New York City; villas in Newport, Rhode Island; and many fine homes, apartment houses, schools, clubs, and commercial office and loft buildings in New York, New Jersey, Georgia, and Ontario, Canada, as well as in his hometown, now known as Ütersen, Germany.[66]

Although Richard M. Hunt is widely identified with the French Beaux-Arts tradition in America, he was not the first to introduce this influence. According to architectural scholar Ellen W. Kramer, "Lienau and not Hunt was the first to bring to the United States a mind and hand shaped, through contact with Labrouste, by the French Beaux-Arts tradition."[67] Lienau also had the advantage of an extensive knowledge of state-of-the-art German engineering and construction.

Robert A.M. Stern, in *New York 1880: Architecture and Urbanism in the Gilded Age*, described Lienau's importance: "Perhaps the city's most fashionable architect in the 1860s and surely one of its most gifted, Detlef Lienau frequently mixed ideas from France with those of Germany . . . he became one of the city's most prominent architects almost overnight, relying heavily on sophisticated interpretations of prevailing French taste. Lienau is credited with introducing the mansard roof to New York."[68]

He was uncompromising in his standards, whether for industrial or residential architecture. Two of his buildings still in use today demonstrate the highest international standards in design, technology, and construction, especially remarkable because these skills were not readily available, much less requisite. The F.O. Matthiessen & Wiechers Sugar Factory (1863) was recently converted to luxury condominiums on the Hudson River waterfront in Jersey City. The spectacular LeGrand Lockwood Mansion (1869), in Norwalk, Connecticut, a National Landmark and period museum, is considered to be the house that launched Gilded Age architecture.

Lienau was a founding member of the American Institute of Architects and was part of the Institute's management team, serving as a trustee from 1867 to 1871 and as treasurer of the New York chapter in 1868–1869. He was a devoted participant in Institute activities and delivered papers on subjects as diverse as "On Romantic and Classical Architecture" in 1858 and "Fireproof Construction" in 1877.

Lienau's understanding of the fusion of architectural art and science was straightforward: "With the continually changing requirements of human society, with the progress of civilization . . . architecture creates new structures, entirely adapted to the purposes for which they are intended, adapted to the climate . . . and out of materials supplied by the locality; it gives to the materials the forms most expressive of their nature and most expressive of the degree of perfection of *taste* and mechanical skill of the time; in short, structures reflecting like a mirror, the people, the country, the climate and the wants of the times for which they are erected" [Lienau's emphasis].[69]

Throughout his long career, Lienau maintained the highest technical and artistic standards in his practice and for the profession as a whole. Of the younger generation who trained in his office, Henry J. Hardenbergh and Paul J. Pelz both rose to national prominence. His many years of voluntary service on the Institute's Committee on Examinations made a vital contribution to the institutionalization of sound design practices and construction standards. Architects provided essential leadership on these critical issues at a turning point in technological and social history and, thus, inspired a heightened level of public policy advocacy. Lienau's sustained professional engagement was deeply respected, and he was held in high regard by the General Society of Mechanics and Tradesmen.[70]

Upon his death in 1887, the Institute paid tribute to one of its founders who "for many years furthered its interests . . . [and was] always a faithful and honored member . . . he always endeavored to avoid shams and to practice truth in his art . . . kind and sympathetic, ever ready to promote the best interest of the profession. . . . Having a high aim, he lived up to it . . . his influence for good was felt by those near to him in official relations; . . . his loss will be keenly felt."[71] For his peers and for generations to follow, Detlef Lienau set the bar of professional practice as high as possible.

Adolf Cluss: Washington, D.C.'s Leading Architect Was a Marxist

The failed German Revolution of 1848 caused a surge of migration to the United States. This group of refugees brought with it an unprecedented number of educated, pro-democracy intellectuals, political insurgents, and military and industrial revolution technocrats. Europe's sudden and profound loss would be America's great long-term gain.

Adolf Cluss (1825–1905) was born in the city of Heilbronn, Germany, in 1825 into a family of stonemasons and builders. His early architecture and engineering training included working as an assistant engineer on the railroad constructed between Mainz and Worms in 1845–1847. While working with laborers on the railroad, he became aware of and eventually joined the Communist League in 1847. Cluss rose to a leadership position in the radical workers' movement and helped to build the momentum that led to the violent 1848 German Revolution. In March 1848 he was elected secretary of the Arbeiterbildungsverein (The Worker's Education Association) and, later, chairman of the Mainzer Federalist Organization.[72]

Cluss had become the movement's chief propagandist in Mainz. His writing and organizational skills gained him the confidence of the two most important men of 19th-century European radical politics, Karl Marx and Friedrich Engels.

Apparently under police surveillance since April 1848 and growing increasingly frustrated with the lack of revolutionary progress, Cluss fled Mainz for America. He arrived in New York City on September 15, 1848, just three days before the failed Frankfort Uprising. He spent his first six months learning English and took the opportunity to study the city's state-of-the-art engineering and architecture. He then moved to Washington, D.C., and found work as a draftsman with the U.S. Coast and Geodetic Survey. Subsequently, in 1850, he was employed by the Navy Yard's Ordnance Laboratory, where he designed the furnaces for the casting of the Navy's new cannons.73

During his first decade in the United States, Cluss worked for various government agencies as a draftsman, including a stint in the Office of the Supervising Architect under Ammi B. Young, where, in 1855, he was promoted from draftsman to a supervisory position.74 Throughout this period, Cluss continued his political activities for the Communist cause by participating in workers' meetings. He maintained his close ties with Marx and Engels until 1855 through sporadic correspondence with the two radical leaders, keeping them informed on developments in the United States. Cluss's political writings were published in the German-American press, along with articles by Marx and other Communists sent to him from Europe, which he translated into English for publication.

He was among the many Forty-Eighters who set about organizing the German-American community. In April 1852 he cofounded the Workingmen's National Association in Washington and began publication of its mouthpiece, "The Workingmen's National Advocate." In July of that year he was involved in founding the Washington chapter of the Sozialer Turnverein, a German gymnastics society dedicated to the "cultivation of rational training, both intellectual and physical in order that the members may become energetic, patriotic citizens of the Republic." Members of the society were called the Turners.75 Cluss was elected secretary of the organization and became its chief spokesman.

Under the leadership of fellow Communist Joseph Weydemeyer, Cluss became a member of the Proletarian League founded by Weydemeyer in New York in 1853, though this organization failed to gain sufficient support and soon collapsed. Weydemeyer had hopes of establishing an American Communist League and worked hard but unsuccessfully toward this goal. He did, however, help to invigorate the American labor movement.

On June 5, 1855, Cluss became an American citizen.76 Over time, he had begun to question his affiliation with Marx and Engels and the movement they led in Europe. According to the Smithsonian Institution's architectural historians, Dr. Cynthia R. Field and Sabina Dugan, who are researching the life and work of Cluss, he was a pragmatist and an astute observer of social and political realities. The relative failure of Marxist ideology in America revealed a cultural and political situation that did not parallel Cluss's homeland experience and forced him to adapt to his new circumstances.77

Cluss traveled to Europe in April 1858. After visiting Paris, he went to London in May, where he hoped to call on Marx, even though he had not corresponded with either Marx or Engels for several years. But when he arrived at Marx's home, he found that neither of them was in London. After an awkward three-hour visit with Marx's wife, Jenny, he left, though he promised to return. Perhaps he was feeling some guilt and ambivalence about explaining the long silence that had distanced him from his former comrades. He never saw Marx or Engels or communicated with them again. The incident elicited contempt from Engels, who dismissed Cluss as a "fool" and an "ass," after having relied on his propaganda and organizing efforts for so long.78

In a letter from London to Weydemeyer in Milwaukee, dated February 1, 1859, Marx glossed over the departure of their former associate: "Mr. Cluss was over here last May. I happened to be with Engels in Manchester at the time. Cluss called upon my wife and accepted an invitation for the following day . . . He disappeared from London and never showed his face again. Instead he sent my wife a scrawl . . . Subsequently we have learned he had allied himself with Mr. Willich. This, then, also explains the mysterious discontinuation of his correspondence. If we were conceited we would feel duly chastened by the news that a fool like Willich had been able to oust us from the good graces of a shrewd chap like Cluss."79

August Willich was a former Prussian officer who had joined with Marx to fight in the 1848 German Revolution. Willich led a force of revolutionaries, known as Willich's Free Corps, that fought bravely but was defeated by William IV's army at Kandern in the Black Forest on April 20, 1848. In London, after the revolution's failure, Willich found himself in frequent conflict with Marx and Engels, and their quarrels became public confrontations in the press, continuing even after he had settled in America.

According to "A History of the 1st German, 32nd Regiment Indiana Volunteer Infantry," by Michael A. Peake, "Port authorities registered

Willich's arrival at New York on February 19, 1853, noting his proclamation of occupation as 'citizen' . . . Carpentry work sustained Willich in New York at the Brooklyn Navy Yard the first year. Traveling to Washington, he found employment with the U.S. Coast and Geodetic Survey Office, where his background in civil engineering and mathematics contributed to the coastal survey of North and South Carolina."

In 1858 Willich became editor of the *German Republican*, a German-language newspaper in Cincinnati. Along with other former revolutionary colleagues—Franz Sigel, Friedrich K.P. Hecker, Louis Blenkel, and Carl Schurz—Willich joined the Union Army at the outbreak of the Civil War. All of these comrades became generals in the Union Army. As the leader of the all-German 32ND Indiana Volunteer Infantry, Willich distinguished himself in battle and rose to the rank of major-general by the war's end.[80]

Cluss and Willich had come into contact, probably while both worked for the government and engaged in political activity in the German community. Marx's assumption that Willich influenced Cluss's estrangement was unfounded. Cluss's close friend Weydemeyer knew of his disdain for Willich and wrote to Marx to correct this misperception. Cluss's decision was, apparently, entirely his own.[81] Weydemeyer subsequently served in the Civil War as a colonel in the Union Army in command of the 40th Missouri Regiment. He died of cholera in 1866 at age forty-eight.[82]

In 1859 Cluss married Röschen (Rosa) Schmidt and was again working at the Washington Navy Yard Ordnance Laboratory. During this period, he decided to establish a private architecture practice with fellow German architect Josef von Kammerhueber who was working there as well. The two began a successful partnership by winning a school building design competition in the capital.

Cluss designed the first public schools for Washington's black American and immigrant children, which were established through the political leadership of Senator Charles Sumner, an abolitionist and founder of the Free Soil Party.[83] Cluss's eight original designs for D.C. school buildings brought acclaim at home and abroad for their innovative design and construction, winning awards at the 1872 World's Exposition in Vienna, the Philadelphia Centennial Exhibition in 1876, and the Paris Exposition in 1878. Only the Franklin School (1869), at 13th and K Streets, N.W., and the Sumner School

Adolph Cluss on the building site of the Smithsonian National Museum (today's Arts & Industries Building) with the Smithsonian's Building Committee, circa 1879–80. Pictured from left to right: consulting
engineer, General Montgomery Meigs; Smithsonian Regent and chairman of the Building Committee,
General William Tecumseh Sherman; committee member Dr. Peter Parker wearing a top hat; Smithsonian secretary Spencer Fullerton Baird; building architect Adolf Cluss in a black broad brim hat; and
clerks W.J. Rhees and Daniel Leech. Photo courtesy of the Smithsonian Institution Archives, Record
Unit 95, box 28, folder 43, Negative #78-10099

(1871–1872), at 17th and M Streets, N.W., survive. The Sumner School now
houses a museum and school archive for the District of Columbia and is a
National Landmark. As of this writing, the Franklin School, also a National
Landmark, is unoccupied and has been placed on the list of the Most
Endangered Places for 2004 by the D.C. Preservation League.[84]

Around 1860 Cluss became fully integrated into the American political scene by throwing his support behind the new Republican Party. He
proudly maintained this political affiliation for the rest of his life.[85]

During the Civil War, Cluss continued to work as a designer for the
federal government's Ordnance Department. In 1863 *Scientific American* published an article about his design for a "new tumbrel car," used to

transport gunpowder over the rails.[86]

After a devastating fire on January 24, 1865, ravaged James Renwick Jr.'s Castle, the original main building of the Smithsonian Institution, Cluss was hired to reconstruct the structure.[87] It was a difficult job, both technically and administratively, and took several years to complete.[88]

In 1867 Cluss applied for membership in the American Institute of Architects. An oblique reference to his application is recalled in *The AIA's First Hundred Years*: "A note in the Trustees' minutes of December, 1867, records receiving plans of a church from a Washington candidate for membership. These plans were 'favorably received,' and the Secretary was instructed to send the applicant a declaration form. It was not until some months later, when testimonial letters had been received from a General of the Army and a Representative from Congress, that the candidate was admitted. His prospects as a member were largely intangible."[89] The church design Cluss submitted for consideration was likely the Calvary Baptist Church, built in 1864–1865 and photographed by Matthew Brady in 1866, or the Foundry Methodist Church, built in 1864–1866. Cluss became a Fellow of the AIA in 1870.[90]

In March 1869 a scathing critique of the Treasury Department's Office of the Supervising Architect, directed by the controversial Alfred B. Mullett, was published in New York City. "Its content reflected the attitudes of the AIA, at that time centered on practitioners in New York."[91] The attack marked the beginning of a long-term campaign by the AIA to restructure the way the federal government handled the design and construction of the government's building stock.

The pamphlet, titled "The Office of the Supervising Architect: What It Was, What It Is, and What It Ought to Be," was signed by an unknown author under the pseudonym "Civis." Alfred Mullett had many bitter enemies, but there is strong forensic evidence to suggest that Cluss, with his insider knowledge, was the anonymous author. Cluss continued working with Mullett, who hired him to superintend the construction of the Washington jail in 1872.[92]

In 1869 Cluss was appointed chief of the District's Bureau of Buildings, where he "was responsible for the design and construction of almost every public building erected by the city government."[93] As the city's

chief engineer, Cluss supervised the upgrading of the capital's infrastructure and city planning during the administration of Washington's notorious mayor, Alexander R. "Boss" Shepherd. He also served as President
Grant's appointed member of the capital's Board of Works from 1872
through 1874.[94] At the same time, his architecture practice received commissions from both federal and private clients. After Kammerhueber's
death, in the 1870s Cluss was in private practice with architect Frederick
Daniel and, from 1878 until 1889, with architect Paul Schulze. By 1880
Cluss's architecture dominated the development of the capital. He designed
more than eighty buildings, including innumerable handsome row houses,
such as Phillips Row (demolished), a street of town houses now characteristic of Washington's residential neighborhoods, the opulent Stewart's
Castle (demolished), churches, civic and fraternal buildings, major government buildings, and commercial centers such as the Eastern Market, still
in use today.

Outstanding extant examples of Cluss's civic architecture include the
renovation of the grand hall in the old Patent Office's south wing; the
Alexandria City Town Hall and Market House (including its Masonic
Temple) in Alexandria, Virginia; and his most important building, the
Smithsonian Institution's first "National Museum" on the Mall, designed
and built between 1879 and 1881. Now called the Arts and Industries
Building, it is currently closed because of lack of funds for repair.[95] From
1890 to 1895 Cluss was the inspector of public buildings for the federal gov-
ernment, a position of national responsibility.[96]

He was always active in the affairs of the AIA, beginning in 1869 when
he presented his first professional paper, "Theory, Functions and Inciden-
tal Uses of Chimneys" at the annual convention in New York City.[97]
And it was the elder statesman of the capital's architects, Adolf Cluss, who,
along with Glenn Brown and several other colleagues, founded the Washington, D.C., chapter of the AIA in 1887. Cluss was elected the chapter's second president in 1888. He also served on the AIA's national board of
directors in 1890.

Throughout his career as an architect and engineer in government
service and private practice, Cluss's past as a radical political leader both in
Germany and in the United States remained largely overlooked. It was not

until the 1980s that the true nature and extent of his early political life became better known.

Adolf Cluss is slated to receive the recognition he has so long deserved with a major international exhibition titled "Adolf Cluss—From Germany to America: Shaping a Capital City Worthy of a Republic," jointly hosted by the City Museum of Washington, D.C., and the City Archives of Heilbronn, Germany.[98]

Frederick A. Petersen: Prussian Revolutionary, AIA Founder, Military Analyst, and Political Activist

Frederick A. Petersen (1808–1885), architect-engineer and one of the thirteen original founders of the American Institute of Architects, was also a Prussian colonel. What little we know of his life is gleaned from obituaries published in New York and New Jersey shortly after his death on April 20, 1885, in Orange, New Jersey. From these sketchy reports we have pieced together a profile of this architect's extraordinary life. Verifying reports of Petersen's Prussian military career is nearly impossible because all the Prussian military archives were destroyed in World War II. A check of extant documents by the Geheimes Staatsarchiv Preussischer Kulturbesitz in Berlin yielded no useful information because so little material has survived.

According to an obituary published on May 22, 1885, in the New York *Daily Graphic* newspaper, Petersen was born in an unnamed Prussian seaport on the Baltic Sea in 1808. His father held an important government office, and Petersen received a military education. He entered the Prussian army as a second lieutenant in the Engineering Corps and was posted to the staff of the commander of the Danzig District in East Prussia. He earned his first promotion for decisive action taken during a disastrous flood in Danzig (Gdansk, Poland) and the surrounding regions in early April 1829. "This had been the greatest flood tragedy in the whole history of Gdansk. During the flood, 47 villages and an area of 340 square kilometers . . . was submerged, the city's entire flood protection system (ditches, channels, pumping stations) was destroyed."[99]

Petersen was dispatched to an outlying village and determined that it was possible to save the town by cutting the dyke and releasing the overflow into the sea. His quick thinking saved the community. Despite the controversy surrounding his decision, the young officer's actions were judged "meritorious in the highest degree, both from a humane and engineering point of view."[100] He was promoted to captain at age twenty-one. He also "saw stirring service"[101] on the Prussian front during the failed November Uprising of Polish nationalists against Russia in 1830–1831.

Finding favor at the Prussian Court, his "rare reasoning powers" and "great engineering skill and knowledge" earned a promotion to lieutenant-colonel and appointment to the royal staff, affording him entrée to the upper echelons of Prussian and European society.[102]

Apparently Petersen was among those who convinced King William IV to allow the rapid development of Prussia's railroad system, though it was actually the king's father who had to be dissuaded of the fear that enemies would use the rails to defeat Prussia.[103] Only 185 kilometers of rail line existed in 1840 when William IV ascended the throne. By 1847, through a combination of government support and private investment, 1,424 kilometers of railroad lines had been laid.[104]

When Petersen was commissioned to travel to England to make "vast purchases of rails, locomotives, etc." he became acquainted with pioneering British engineers such as Stephenson and Brunel, "builder of the famous 'Great Eastern' steamer."[105] Robert Stephenson & Co. built dozens of locomotives for Prussian rail lines beginning in 1835 and continuing well into the 1840s. Two engines manufactured by Sharp, Roberts & Co. were purchased to start up the Berlin-Stettin line, completed in 1843. If Petersen did indeed conduct Prussian railroad business in England, these transactions were probably initiated near the end of William III's reign and completed before the political situation under William IV disintegrated into open rebellion.[106]

The Prussian government supervised railroad construction in the early stages, and military engineers did work closely with the managers of the newly formed railroad companies. It is possible that military engineers traveled to England in the company of high-ranking railroad officials who made frequent fact-finding trips for technical and business matters.[107]

Copies of the Prussian Royal Staff and Ministry Registers for the years 1841, 1843, and 1844 were examined at Copenhagen's Royal Library. In the 1843–1844 register, the director of the Provincial Survey Commission in Posen (Southern Prussia, now Poland) is listed as Hr. Peterson, Reg.-u. Bau-Rath I. II. III.[108] There is no indication of military rank. A rail link from the Baltic port of Stettin to Pozan, the provincial capital, was built during the 1840s.[109] So far it has been impossible to confirm, from these few resources, whether Petersen was a member of the royal staff.

In England, Petersen became impressed by parliamentary democracy, which cast a long shadow over the absolute Prussian monarchy he served. The *Daily Graphic* states that when "the movements for liberal measures began in Prussia early in 1847, Colonel Petersen joined his fortunes with the people. For a time he pursued a course so careful and so well within the lines of existing laws that he managed to evade the grip of the government."

The Prussian National Assembly met in Berlin between May 22 and December 5, 1848, to draw up a new liberal democratic constitution. William IV, a rigid absolutist, fully expected that his own draft of the constitution would be rubber-stamped. But the assembly proved to be independent; it rejected the king's draft and pursued its own version of the constitution. If Petersen was involved in the assembly or was known to support any liberal or radical faction represented in it, then the outcome of this assembly easily explains his arrest.

When it became clear that the assembly was resolute in its insubordination, the king prorogued on November 9, 1848. The electors staged a protest on the spot and continued the session. The next day, November 10, General von Wrangel and his troops imposed a state of siege on Berlin with the intention of preventing resistance and ordered the assembly to reconvene in Brandenburg on November 27. On November 11, the assembly declared the king's emissary, Count Brandenburg, a traitor, objected to von Wrangel's order to disband the city's burgher guards (local militia), and decided to refuse payment of taxes.[110]

This event was followed "on November 12th, by the bold refusal of the Burgher Guard of Berlin to obey the King and disband." With a tax strike declared as its vehicle of resistance, the assembly's last session was held on November 15. William IV dissolved the assembly on December 5, pronounced his own constitution in effect, and installed a counterrevolutionary government under Count Brandenburg. With the liberal political movement effectively quashed, the persecution and exodus of the Forty-Eighters began.[111]

It was at this turning point that Petersen's true political beliefs became known to William IV. He was arrested and imprisoned. While awaiting trial, through the intervention of friends and his wife, Petersen escaped and, "overcoming many dangers," made his way to the free port of Hamburg on the border of the Danish Duchy of Holsten. Between August 1848 and March 1849, an armistice between Denmark and Prussia was in effect, but hostilities resumed again in late March. Sometime in 1849, Petersen booked safe passage out of Hamburg on an American steamer bound for New York City. On his arrival, he immediately launched his American career.

Architectural historian Jay Shockley and Susan Tunick, president of the Friends of Terra Cotta, in researching Petersen's Cooper Union building, have turned up new evidence that "from 1853 to 1857 (the period covering most of the construction of the Cooper Union building), Petersen was associated with Richard Upjohn & Co. on a number of collaborative projects . . . . It is unclear what the exact professional relationship was between the Upjohn firm and Petersen, though since he maintained his own office, it appears that Petersen was a consultant rather than employed within the firm."[112] It is likely that this professional relationship prompted Petersen's invitation to attend the first meeting of the American Institute of Architects, held in Upjohn's office in 1857.

In 1851 the first American edition of the new German *Iconographic Encyclopedia of Science, Literature and Art* was published in New York City. The editors engaged a distinguished panel of experts to translate the German text into English, and F.A. Petersen was entrusted with the translation of the chapter on architecture.[113]

Petersen designed and/or consulted on several important buildings before and during his work on the famous Cooper Institute building (1853–1859), including Tripler's Hall (1850) on Broadway; a new Washington Market (1851; unbuilt),[114] originally located on the World Trade Center site; the Essex Market; and the Polytechnic Institute of Brooklyn (1854).[115]

Petersen's obituary notes that he knew "intimately" the internationally renowned opera star, Madame Henrietta Sontag, from their days in the

Prussian Court and that "his first important work was the drawing of the plans for a fine music hall on Broadway, where the celebrated Mme. Sontag . . . sang for the first time in the metropolis."[116] She made her American debut on September 27, 1852, at Tripler's Hall, then the largest concert hall in North America. A review of Jenny Lind's performances in the hall from the November 9, 1850, issue of *Scientific American* states that "the new hall, (splendid in design and execution) is well adapted, in every respect, to give full and legitimate effect to her voice." An engraving in the New York Public Library's picture collection shows a spare but elegant, neoclassical façade, consistent with the style of Petersen's other building designs. Jay Shockley has found reference to another architect-builder who specialized in theaters as the architect of Tripler's Hall, so the extent of Petersen's involvement in its design is still somewhat unclear.[117]

Though Tripler's Hall was also used for major public meetings, the need for a large space dedicated to civic uses was by now obvious. The hall was located very close to the site of Peter Cooper's planned institute and may have influenced his choice of architect. Cooper probably hired Petersen in late 1852 to design his Institute building with its Great Hall venue in the basement, though no information has surfaced about how they met. Perhaps because of so many calamitous fires in the city, particularly the enormous Harper & Brothers printing plant fire on December 10, 1853, that temporarily halted the building's construction,[118] Petersen designed and patented on April 3, 1855, the first fireproof "hollow burned clay tiles for floor construction ever designed," specifically for the Cooper Union building.[119] Tripler's Hall also burned to the ground on the night of January 8, 1854.[120]

Frederick A. Petersen participated in the writing of the first constitution and bylaws of the AIA.[121] His court testimony on behalf of Richard Morris Hunt for payment for the design of the Rossiter house helped to win the legal judgment for Hunt, establishing an important legal precedent in architecture practice in 1861.[122]

Between 1862 and 1863, Petersen published a series of pamphlets of his own political and military analysis which, though entirely supportive of the Union cause, were highly critical of the Lincoln administration's political and military leadership. Writing anonymously, under his own name, and possibly also using a pseudonym, Petersen's vivisection of the Union's military and political commanders provides a unique opportunity to examine the psychological nature and challenges of leadership (see chapter 7).

Petersen fully employed his practice skills through his chosen form of political engagement. He assembled an extensive amount of data from many sources on many issues in order to communicate a detailed, cohesive military analysis for a layman's consumption. This immense puzzle became the bigger picture that the reader could then see and understand. One should not forget that, in this period, European and American architects were routinely trained by the military because engineering and building science were critical components of military science. Orchestrating a multitude of disparate parts into seamless coordination was, and still is, the hallmark of an effective military leader as well as of a professional architect. Highly evolved communication skills remain critical to achieving success in both fields.

Petersen moved to Essex County, New Jersey, in 1865, though he continued to practice in Manhattan during the 1870s. He advertised his services in New York's trade directories as an architect and civil engineer using the following text: "Guarantees there will be no extras chargeable for buildings erected according to his plans and specifications."[123] He also practiced in New Jersey "and designed the Eastern District Public School, in East Orange."[124]

He was married to Lousia, a Prussian woman 25 years his junior, and had four children. According to the 1880 census, his parents were Norwegian. At the time of his death, the Petersen family lived on Steuben Street in East Orange. Petersen died of chronic kidney disease, leaving assets of less than $100, and is buried in Rosedale Cemetery near Llewellyn Park, West Orange, New Jersey, also the resting place of fellow AIA leader Charles F. McKim.[125]

The *Orange Journal* described Petersen as having "always taken an active interest in town affairs though steadily refusing to be a candidate for any office . . . He was a Democrat in politics, very outspoken in the advocacy of that party and a member of the Essex County Democratic Club."[126] And according to the New York *Daily Graphic*, "Before the war he warmly espoused the cause of the Democratic party, and to the last he was one of its most ardent supporters. . . . In his last hours his mind wandered on political matters and he would insist that the returns would come in and show that Grover Cleveland had been elected President."[127] Frederick A. Petersen's final political analysis was, of course, absolutely correct.

7 THE MILITARY AND POLITICAL WRITINGS OF FREDERICK A. PETERSEN

THE MOST EXTRAORDINARY THING that Frederick A. Petersen did during the Civil War was to publish a series of pamphlets that precisely criticized the nation's military and political situation. Petersen subjected the military strategies of the Union Army, the leadership of its senior officers, the Lincoln administration, and, in particular, the Union Army's general-in-chief, Major-General George B. McClellan (1826–1885), to the scrutiny of his professional military analysis. Original copies of Petersen's pamphlets were obtained in order to study the content of these rare Civil War political documents.

Our research has identified Petersen as the anonymous author of *Major-General George B. McClellan from August 1st, 1861 to August 1st, 1862.*[128] Confirmation of our attribution came from the U.S. Army Heritage and Education Center in Carlisle, Pennsylvania, where another original copy was found to be hand inscribed, "Rev D. Farley with his friend's, the author F.A. Petersen's compliments."[129]

This pamphlet undertakes an analysis of McClellan's strategies and his organization, from the bottom up, of more than 100,000 newly enlisted men into an army, an unprecedented challenge. Two dedications appear on the cover: "You have been taught, ere this, the value of '*one man*,' Schiller" and "To the people of the United States, Respectfully Dedicated by the Author, A Military Man Who Never Saw Gen. McClellan."

As a volunteer in the war's media battle, Petersen flaunted his professional credentials and wielded an intellectual ferocity intended to discredit all those whom he perceived to be a threat to the Union from within. Petersen's eloquence leaves no possibility of misconstruing his meaning. But his sharp remarks also reveal his own political ideology and party allegiance.

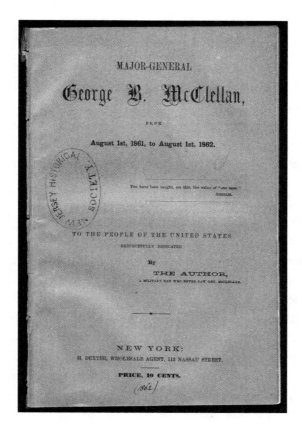

During the Civil War, architect and cofounder of the AIA, Frederick A. Petersen, entered the heated political debate over the defense of the Union with his pamphlet, "Major-General George B. McClellan from August 1, 1861 to August 1, 1862," which he published anonymously in New York City in August 1862. Petersen continued his political commentary under his own name with a series of scathing critiques of the Lincoln administration's political and military leadership, published in New York City in October 1862 and January 1863. From the collection of Richard N. Swett

Both he and George B. McClellan were stalwarts of the Democratic Party, which dominated New York City and New Jersey state politics.

Petersen launches into a critical barrage on page one. He rails against "intermeddling" politicians who "encumbered" McClellan, who was "surrounded by traitors in all branches of the government, even nearest to the veteran Commander-in-Chief." On page six, he states that "traitors in the United States offices" had been informing the enemy "of every order issued by McClellan almost as soon as the same was promulgated to his own army"; on page eight, "the authority of *several* high officials to grant passes through the lines of the army . . . made it very difficult to catch the spies." He confronts political partisanship, which he believed was the transparent motive behind scurrilous personal criticism of the Union Army's chief commander. This "system of prosecution and slander . . . of the public press" was motivated by the "alarm" of "the political wire pullers who consider *the next Presidential Election* a matter of far greater importance than the preservation of the Union and the Constitution."

Members of Congress do not escape his condemnation for their willingness to manipulate public opinion and to evade responsibility for such "disastrous results" as the defeat at Bull Run, all the while "filling their pockets with lion-share commissions on army contracts of every possible description" and expecting that McClellan should grant favors to "the Honorable Members' protégées." Petersen highlights the "hostile feeling of a certain class of Senators and Congressmen generally known as radicals," members of the Republican Party who had the confidence of Secretary of War Edwin M. Stanton. "General McClellan endured all these attacks of the radicals in silence" and remained focused on his duties "with indefatigable energy."

Secretary Stanton is the object of Petersen's most scathing criticisms. Stanton, a Pennsylvania lawyer, stepped into the war cabinet post in early January 1862, quickly assuming personal supervision of the war effort by usurping the command of the army's leadership. Stanton relieved McClellan of his post as chief commander of the Army of the United States and relegated him to command only the Army of the Potomac in the first week of March 1862. Stanton assumed direct control over all military operations.

According to Petersen, "So strictly did General McClellan live up to his duties as a citizen of the Republic, that he obeyed the order to leave the execution of his own Plans, *upon which depended the early termination of this wicked rebellion*, and . . . his reputation as a military leader, in the hands of a man notoriously incompetent, *because the order was issued in the name of the responsible Commander-in-Chief, the President of the United States.*"

"In no other country is any person ever entrusted with the direction of armies, who is not subject to the articles of war and trial by court marshal and consequently, *officers of the army alone are qualified to hold the office of*

Secretary of War." Petersen warns that having "a Lawyer and Secretary of war, (not sharing with the officers in the army the responsibilities with which the articles of war burden them)," who then "takes it upon himself to control armies in the face of the enemy" has the awful consequence of unnecessarily risking "the lives of thousands of brave men and millions of treasure." Petersen's contempt for Stanton must have had its roots in his own military and political past, having lived through the disingenuousness and treachery of William IV's rule in the face of popular demand for a constitution, a parliamentary government, and a unified Germany. This new political crisis must have revived very painful memories.

George McClellan's feat of marshaling a ragtag bunch of short-term volunteers into a disciplined army and creating the infrastructure of a modern military machine was his greatest achievement, without which the Lincoln administration would have been lost. The general had to "organize, arm, discipline and subsist an army of infantry, cavalry and artillery of 100,000 men, to create all necessary auxiliaries, . . . get rid of inefficient officers. . . . fill their places with better qualified individuals. . . . infuse in every branch . . . *esprit du* [sic] *corps;* to impress them with the conviction that their own and their comrades safety depends on the enforcement of the 'articles of war' and discipline under all circumstances."

Petersen's admiration for McClellan was positively unabashed. As he saw it, "The appointment of McClellan . . . was the signal of order, of organization, of concert of action and of redress of abuse throughout the various corps of the army." The officers were "inspired by the electrifying influence of McClellan . . . in little more than three months' time McClellan had organized an army that could move according to given orders, . . . march a certain distance in a given time, could do that under its full armament and equipment . . . [and] could be withdrawn from an engagement with the enemy at the command of its generals, . . . evidence that it possessed all the *fundamental* qualities of a *real army*." He goes on to say, "To George B. McClellan belongs the glory of having created the largest known army in the shortest time, and of having proven to the world that this can be accomplished in a Republic, without having neglected the duties of a citizen."

Perhaps for Petersen and his fellow Forty-Eighters, McClellan provided a kind of vindication of their own political movement, proof that a principled, professional military, loyal to the foundations of a democratic republic, could safely coexist with, uphold, and perform the duties of citizenship. In his polemic, Petersen was doing more than persuading the public of McClellan's superior leadership; he also seems intent on rallying the troops, particularly the Prussians, to remain loyal, attentive, and confident in their commanders: "When the outlines of the plan for the campaign of 1862 became known by degrees . . . and . . . reached Europe, they were . . . the subject of professional discussion in military circles, and . . . luminaries in the military firmament could not withhold their surprise and admiration for its magnitude, its ingenuity and practicability." He regales the reader with anecdotes of courageous and skillful leadership by Napoleon, Frederick the Great, the Duke of Wellington, General Moreau, and Prince Mentchikoff. He places McClellan on a par with these famous leaders and reminds the reader of "the immortal" George Washington's similar travails, "called a slow general without dash" who in "keeping the lasting welfare of his country constantly at heart . . . treated his calumniators in and out of Congress with contemptuous silence."

Finally, Petersen summarized the essential characteristics of leadership embodied in McClellan's conduct and demeanor, "his simple and unostentatious habits; the industrious, diligent, strict but just manner in which he attends to the regular business of his army . . . the precision of his orders, the indefatigable energy, the cool deliberate courage and self-possession with which he moves and directs operations under the hottest fire; the never failing word of encouragement and cheer in battle, and of consolation in the hospital; . . . of the eagle eye that, always calm, surveys the situation at a glance, and devises the means to become its master."

Petersen concludes that the general's "rare qualities of conspicuous gallantry, daring and professional excellence" made him worthy of the public's support as the one most fit to lead a successful prosecution of the Union's defense.

Two months later another pamphlet appeared that Petersen seems to have had a hand in. Written under the pseudonym "Antietam," and titled *McClellan and Fremont: a reply to "Fremont and McClellan, Their Political and Military Careers Reviewed,"*[130] it is an indignant rebuttal to Republican critic Van Buren Denslow's pamphlet,[131] which unfavorably compared General

McClellan to the equally controversial Major-General John C. Fremont. The cover dedication reads *Audi alter am par tem* (hear the other side).

The unknown author mentions that, "Another pamphlet has lately appeared under the title of 'Major-General George B. McClellan, from Aug. 1ST, 1861 to Aug. 1ST, 1862' written by an army officer, which discusses, in a clear and intelligible manner, the conduct of military affairs under McClellan, and while satisfactorily refuting the statements of Senator Chandler and his followers, establishes, beyond dispute, the military skill and splendid management of the Peninsula campaign."[132]

Using identical lines of logic and the literary vernacular of Petersen's earlier pamphlet, the rhetoric of defamation is refuted with a recitation of facts. "Are none but Republicans worthy to command the army of the Republic?" is asked and answered, "Ask the thousands who compose the army." The author continues, "We protest against this constant and continued attempt to foist party issues of the past upon a country struggling, with the combined strength of loyal men of all parties, to put down this gigantic rebellion."

The seriousness of Fremont's misconduct is cited: "Insubordination is mutiny, and strikes at the root of discipline, without which there can be no army. . . .Our enemy trusts nothing to civilians; he manages his army through the educated science of West Point. *Fas est ab hoste doceri.*" (It is right to learn even from the enemy, Ovidius.)

The inappropriateness of civilian management of the military, "to elevate, in the place of a well-educated system of scientific warfare, the dangerous insubordinations of haughty civilians," surfaces here as well. The author concludes, "McClellan is the representative of that respect for constitutional authority which secures the only freedom society ever acquires, and which is the chief boast and glory of the United States!" This pamphlet, dated September 30, 1862, was published shortly after the Battle of Antietam on September 17.

One month later, Petersen published in quick succession an even more ambitious two-part document under his own name. Part I of this in-depth treatise is laboriously titled *Military Review of the Campaigns in Virginia & Maryland under Generals John C. Fremont, N.P. Banks, Irwin McDowell, Franz Sigel, John Pope, James S. Wadsworth, Wm. H. Halleck and George B. McClellan in 1862* and carries the author's dedication, "A Contribution to the

Future History of The United States" and a quote from Shakespeare, "He that is truly dedicated to war hath no self-love; nor he that loves himself hath not essentially, but by circumstances, the name of valor."[133]

The two pamphlets comprise a 124-page document and provide a blow-by-blow account of the war's progress, related in painstaking factual detail. Petersen reviewed the Union Army's military operations with incisive military analysis and cutting political critique right up to the dates of publication, October 25, 1862, and January 18, 1863.

Part I begins Petersen's deconstruction of the relentless machinations of the Union Army's senior officers and their counterparts in Lincoln's administration. Praise is heaped on the noble General Ambrose Burnside, General N.P. Banks, and fellow Forty-Eighter General Franz Sigel, credited with "the rare gift of military genius, unsurpassed bravery, energy, and bull-dog tenacity." Harsh criticism is directed at the unmanageable General John C. Fremont, General James S. Wadsworth, and General Irwin McDowell, who Petersen found to be "entirely wanting in the fundamental principles of military foresight, and organizing qualities, as well as due consideration of his responsibilities and duties as a commanding general, violating the very rudiments of strategy."

Petersen's denunciation of Secretary Stanton's destructive meddling, which was contributing to Lincoln's vacillation, is harsher still. Using Stanton's letter to the *New York Tribune*, Petersen hoisted the secretary of war on his own petard: "However he might try to conceal it . . . Mr. Stanton's letter is nothing more . . . than a continuous slur, at military science and military leaders in general . . . and at General McClellan in particular."

Petersen reprinted certain "General Orders" issued by the president and the War Department, orders and reports to and from the commanders and various letters published in the press, as a forensic trail supporting his analysis of the Lincoln administration's abysmal management of the war. Considerable space is given to the problems caused by Fremont's conduct. Petersen refutes false claims that McClellan was responsible for Fremont's loss of command, with Van Buren Denslow's pamphlet, *Fremont and McClellan*, footnoted.

General John Pope is censured for "open contradiction to the very principles of strategy in general and to the revised army regulations of 1861 in particular." And after careful review of Pope's unimpressive performance, he points out: "The more intelligent rank and file of an army, the more accomplished ought to be their officers. The better disciplined an army, the more it will suffer in the hands of an incompetent general. Armies experienced in actual warfare require the most precise orders from their leaders. These are well established truisms."

Petersen is scrupulous about conduct unbecoming an officer. No one is exempt from reprimand: "We regret that General Sigel has thought it proper, in time of war, on one or more occasions to make a political speech." McClellan's honorable refusal to retaliate against personal attacks and his discretion in withholding his political opinions were much admired by the older Prussian. In his surreptitious strategy of persuasion, Petersen does not hesitate to "refer our readers to read a pamphlet published by H. Dexter, . . . entitled, 'Major-General George B. McClellan, from August 1st, 1862 to August 1st, 1863,' which gives a lucid history of the services General McClellan has rendered to the country."

The value of Petersen's analysis, aside from its legalistic thoroughness, is his intimate understanding of the burdens of leadership, reflecting not only his excellent Prussian education but also his mastery of sophisticated military science and a comprehensive knowledge of American and European political history. Petersen drove his points home through an elaboration of various examples of past and recent strategic planning, logistics, military engineering, infrastructure management, and battle tactics. He connected these elements to the strategic architecture of military science, repeatedly stressing the critical importance of issuing clearly defined, accurate orders. He articulated how orders should be constructed and delineated their relationship to the nuances of protocol in the chain of command, and showed their direct impact on military discipline. Likewise, he pointed out their indispensability to the respect of the soldiers for their leaders, and the consequential success such precision provided in the follow-through of those orders. This last aspect, the follow-through, was, in Petersen's opinion, being fatally thwarted by internal power struggles in the Lincoln administration, in Congress, and among competing senior officers.

But it is in the last three pages of Part I that Petersen takes up the most sensitive and controversial issue: the Emancipation Proclamation and General McClellan's response to its enactment. On this subject, Petersen makes his own feelings known, for this is "a subject of so immeasurable importance for good or for evil to the civilized world."

Petersen reprinted General Order-No. 163, dated October 7, 1862, letting McClellan speak for himself. The general, knowing that the Emancipation Proclamation might create dissension within the ranks, reminded those under his command that "a proclamation of such grave moment to the nation" must be upheld, regardless of the individual's personal opinion. "Discussion by officers and soldiers concerning public measures determined and declared by the Government, when carried at all beyond the ordinary temperate and respectful expression of opinion, tend greatly to impair and destroy the discipline and efficiency of troops by substituting the spirit of political faction for the firm, steady, and earnest support of the authority of the Government which is the highest duty of the American soldier. . . .The remedy for political errors, if any are committed, is to be found only in the action of the people at the polls. . . . In carrying out all measures of public policy this army will, of course, be guided by the same rules of mercy and Christianity that have ever controlled its conduct towards the defenseless."

Part II was written after Lincoln had called McClellan back to resume command of the Army of the Potomac in defense of Washington, D.C., on September 2, only to be relieved of command without explanation or disciplinary charges on November 7, 1862. Petersen was utterly disgusted by this turn of events and could not restrain his contempt for the administration's "imbecile management" of the war, its hypocritical treatment of General McClellan, or the dismal performances of his replacement, General William H. Halleck and the detested General John Pope.

Petersen included the text of the Emancipation Proclamation, enacted just eighteen days before his own document's publication. The inherent contradiction of the policy—that the twenty-eight counties of West Virginia and the counties of Virginia and Louisiana loyal to the Union were exempt from the emancipation policy—was impossible for Petersen to ignore: "The Commander-in Chief of the Army of the United States surrounds the territory wherein his war order sets free all the slaves, with a circle of slave States distinctly exempt from the operation thereof, and so makes it impossible for himself to enforce his order."

The prosecution of the war from that point on would be brutal, but the fact remained that were it not for McClellan's organizing leadership, no possibility of matching the honed military skill of the Confederacy's leaders, chiefly General Robert E. Lee, would have existed.

In 1864, *The Life, Campaigns and Public Services of General McClellan, the Hero of Western Virginia! South Mountain! and Antietam!* was published in McClellan's hometown of Philadelphia.[134] It is typical of 19th-century presidential campaign propaganda. The author is unidentified, but the publisher, T.B. Peterson & Brothers, was doing a brisk business providing the Union troops with popular dime novels and other reading matter. In this longer biography of McClellan, Petersen's first anonymous pamphlet is again quoted in corroboration of the unknown author's glowing assessment of McClellan's leadership. The use of the quote fits a pattern that points to Petersen's continued influence, if not directly, then certainly indirectly.

In each of these political tracts, factual comparisons are made to Europe's military leaders and to incidents from past and recent European theaters of war, with special mention of the Napoleonic Wars and Prussia's various military engagements and leaders. Regardless of whether comparisons of McClellan with Napoleon and other military heroes were novel when Petersen made them, they did find particular favor with the public.

Such highly reasoned and thoroughly documented propaganda helped fuel public support for McClellan's eventual nomination as the Democratic candidate in the 1864 presidential election and contributed to a vital public discourse on the nature of leadership. From his firsthand experience as a military officer, engineer, and architect, Petersen offers up his perspective as his "contribution to the future history" of his adopted country. His words provide valuable insight into the events of a now distant past. But his bold decision to write what is, in fact, a leadership handbook demonstrates how the man's professional identity was infused with the belief that all citizens were duty-bound to serve their country to the best of *all* of their abilities. In Petersen's philosophy, professional ethics and honorable conduct always superseded coarse ambition and personal gain. Loyalty to a democratic republic was held sacrosanct.

To scholars of the Civil War, it may be useful to now know the true identity and background of the author of these political pamphlets, which were published in conflict-ridden New York City during the height of the Civil War. Without these pertinent facts, it has not been possible to place Frederick A. Petersen's political writings in an appropriate context or to fully grasp the extent of his influence on public opinion leading up to the 1864 presidential election.

Petersen's position as a respected member of New York's business and professional community, a cofounder of the AIA, and an outspoken member of the Democratic Party, along with his most recent addition to New York City's skyline, the Cooper Institute, made his political commentary impossible to miss or to dismiss. His expert opinion on contemporary politics and his analysis of the military's leadership were underlined by his status as a political refugee of the 1848 German Revolution. His extensive historical knowledge and intimate experience with executive leadership at the highest levels of the Prussian government and European military circles are evident throughout his writings. If his perspective did not carry weight with the public, then whose could?

The German-American community, particularly from New York City, had committed itself in enormous numbers to fight for the Union. Thousands of enlisted men and scores of senior officers, including Franz Sigel, Carl Schurz, August Willich, and Friedrich Hecker, were seasoned veterans of the 1848 German Revolution.[135] As a credible voice from within an intensely political and motivated immigrant community, Petersen's impassioned and articulate pamphlets initially served to support the Union's war effort and ultimately became brilliant propaganda to further the agenda of the pro-war faction in the Democratic Party. His polemical writings on military and political leadership are jewels of *free speech* and ably fulfill his intent to contribute to the future history of the United States.

General McClellan, a pro-war Democrat, became the compromise candidate of a deeply split party and was saddled with a peace platform that he could not, in good conscience, support. In his letter of acceptance of the Democratic Party's nomination for president, McClellan promptly repudiated the platform, "an act unprecedented in American political life."[136]

Lincoln won the 1864 presidential election by a comfortable margin of 400,000 votes, but McClellan, the Democratic candidate, handily won two to one in New York City, losing the state by less than one percent.[137]

He won the state of New Jersey outright. Afterward, McClellan resigned his military commission, traveled in Europe for three years where he was welcomed as a hero, particularly in Prussia, and then returned home to New Jersey. He was chief engineer for the Port of New York from 1870 to 1872 and was elected the Democratic governor of New Jersey, serving from 1878 to 1881. His son, George Jr., a Democrat, was mayor of New York City from 1903 to 1910. George B. McClellan died in Orange, New Jersey, on October 29, 1885, just six months after his local champion, Frederick A. Petersen, had passed away.

8 The Union League Club: How Architectural Thinking Created a Powerful Political Organization

WITHIN THE STORY OF THE FOUNDING and early achievement of the Union League Club (ULC) of New York City is a specific historical example of how individual architects came together with their professional peers from other walks of life to deal directly with a national political and local civic crisis. The establishment of the ULC required the hitherto-unheard-of orchestration of complex intellectual, ethical, and managerial capabilities.

The nature of the architects' contribution to the creation of a powerful civic, political, and cultural machine is worthy of analysis for two reasons: one, to understand the nature of influence and how it is achieved beyond the field of one's own vocation, and two, to reposition the architecture profession historically, freeing it from the narrow confines of art history's specialized context and bringing it onto the broader plane of American civic and political life.

During the latter half of 1862, a small circle of New York professional men began to discuss the formation of a fraternity composed of individuals with whom they shared significant concerns. Their purpose was specific and clearly stated: to act decisively as a body in support of the federal government in its war against the rebellion of the Southern states.

Shortly after the Emancipation Proclamation went into effect on January 1, 1863, this tightly knit group began recruiting members and promoting their common cause. The founders wanted to create a uniquely American institution founded on egalitarian principles combined with the best aspects of patrician leadership. It was to be a model of patriotic loyalty and responsibility, a living demonstration of American democracy.

It was designed to stand in sharp contrast to the abusive aristocracies concurrently under challenge in Europe. Thus, defining the club's membership criteria was critical to the creation of a lasting, though imperfect, American meritocracy.

The ULC was certainly not the first private social organization to take a public stand on political and social issues, but it is surely one of the most successful, mobilizing and directing with extraordinary speed many of the most influential, highly talented men and women of its generation. The Civil War provided the defining moment for the ULC's inspired leadership of a city and a nation in grave crisis.

This accomplishment can be attributed directly to the conceptual prowess of Frederick Law Olmsted, the *architect* of the club's organizational structure and strategic planning and the primary articulator of its ideological purpose. Professor Wolcott Gibbs, who was "the first to suggest the idea" of the Union League Club, "chose Mr. Frederick Law Olmsted as the first person to be consulted and advised with."[138]

The founders had first come together as organizers of the U.S. Sanitary Commission (USSC), which played a vital role in the Union's successful prosecution of the war. They were the Rev. Dr. Henry Whitney Bellows (1814–1882), pastor of All Souls Unitarian Church and USSC president; George Templeton Strong (1820–1875), respected lawyer and USSC treasurer; Dr. Oliver Wolcott Gibbs (1822–1908), renowned scientist and scholar; Dr. Cornelius R. Agnew (1830–1888), leading ophthalmologist; and Frederick Law Olmsted (1822–1903), writer, farmer, administrator, and America's foremost landscape architect.

Except for Olmsted, who was employed as the USSC general secretary, all were members of the USSC Executive Committee. They were at the bulkhead of a huge operation, established in New York City, which quickly spread its volunteer network throughout the cities, states, and territories loyal to the Union. The USSC was created in June 1861, two months after the Civil War began.[139]

In less than a year, Olmsted pulled the disparate local committees together, building the USSC into an organization that eventually oversaw the Union Army's medical care and sanitary provisions and managed the formidable logistical, financial, and political problems involved. Olmsted was personally responsible for the daily administration of this critical operation from June 20, 1861, to September 1, 1863.

The USSC founders knew how precarious the climate of their city had become, its social fabric bursting at the seams. If the looming crisis was not adequately dealt with, the Union might be mortally wounded from within. The need for a unifying force awakened an idea in them.

At no time did these gentlemen equivocate about the ethical issues at the heart of the conflict. Loyalty to the Union was beyond compromise. States' rights could never be held superior to the ultimate authority of the federal government. The sanctity of the Constitution, the sacred vehicle with which to achieve the rights and ideals embodied in the Declaration of Independence, remained paramount. Slavery was an affront to any civilized, Christian society. Its existence was destroying the very premise of American democracy. War had become a catastrophic, but unavoidable, remedy.[140]

From the 1830s on, corrosive ideological disputes slowly split apart both political parties: the pros and cons of free trade, federal versus states' rights, the rights of natives versus the rights claimed by immigrants, and whether slavery was a God-given prerogative or an abomination. Long before Abraham Lincoln was sworn in, the political divisions within New York's middle and upper classes had spilled out of the drawing rooms and into the public sphere. The issue of slavery was fiercely debated in the media, from church pulpits and in saloons and meeting halls.

In 1854 the old Whig Party, exhausted and outdated, gave way to the new Republican Party, whose second presidential candidate, Abraham Lincoln, was the standard bearer of the party's radical agenda in 1860. The Democrats had come to represent the cultural values of the South and the most cynical of free-market, labor-exploiting Northern business interests.

One of America's most extraordinary men, the inventor and entrepreneur Peter Cooper (1791–1883), was at the vanguard of the abolitionist cause and an ardent supporter of Lincoln from the earliest days of his candidacy. In 1853 Cooper had used his fortune to establish the Cooper Union for the Advancement of Science and Art, which became the center of progressive thought and public debate after it opened its doors in November 1859. In addition to providing free education, regardless of class, gender, or circumstances, Cooper Union also served as a platform for abolitionists, women's suffrage and civil rights activists, and civic reform movements.[141] On February 27, 1860, Peter Cooper gave over the building's Great Hall for Lincoln's "Right Makes Might" speech, which marked the turning point in his presidential campaign.[142]

Responding to Lincoln's election victory, South Carolina seceded from the Union on December 20, 1860, instigating a chain of secessions by Southern states. By January 1861, the lines were sharply drawn. Lincoln was inaugurated on March 4, still hoping to avoid war with the South, but five weeks later, on April 12, shots were fired on Fort Sumter by Confederate troops from Charleston, South Carolina. The Civil War had begun.

On April 29, 1861, because nursing and support services were so desperately needed, a group of socially respectable women published a public call to action in newspapers sympathetic to the Union.[143] The tremendous public response produced a grassroots movement of ad-hoc relief committees. The women's organizing efforts were soon formalized into the USSC. At least two dozen of the movement's organizers were the wives and daughters of founding members of the ULC. These women created a solid structure on which to build a broader reform agenda. The ULC's future leadership could also be found among members of the Union Defense Committee of the Citizens of New York, organized in the spring and summer of 1861 to galvanize the city's support of the Union.[144]

As the Union staggered into its third year of the Civil War, New York was a city in turmoil. Many Northerners were opposed to the war itself, some were openly sympathetic to the South, many Democrats were simply opposed to any action of the Republican administration, and still others disagreed with the way the administration was conducting the war.

By 1860 New York City's population was twenty-five percent Irish, most of whom had fled the infamous Potato Famine, a natural calamity compounded by the political contrivance of British rule. Irish Catholics arrived on distant shores only to discover the same religious and ethnic prejudices entrenched in American society. Impoverished but full of aspirations, the Irish community was easily influenced by business and political profiteers. What set them apart from other immigrants was a deep reservoir of pent-up anger against the instruments of Protestant authority. This rage would splay out onto the city streets in the summer of 1863.

The incessant animosity between Protestants and Catholics attached itself to the disputes over the abolition of slavery, political party affiliation, and labor issues. Religious, ethnic, and political rivalries were hopelessly entangled, producing such contradictory rationalizations that publishing them defied common sense because it only added fuel to the fire.

In early 1863 the Loyal Publication Society was organized to generate Union propaganda. Several ULC members initiated and held office in the society: Frances Lieber, an esteemed German political scientist, was named president; Christian E. Detmold, engineer and builder of the New York Crystal Palace, was chairman; and James A. Roosevelt was treasurer. Scholars Henry Drisler and Charles King and civic reformer Peter Cooper wrote for the society. The society published some 90 pamphlets and distributed hundreds of thousands of free copies in New York, New England, and the Midwest. The propaganda was intended to engender patriotic feelings within the immigrant communities by fostering pride in a shared American heritage.[145]

While the founders of the Union League Club were mobilizing their network, those who opposed the Republican administration and the abolitionist cause closed ranks and marshaled their forces to influence public opinion against the administration's policies. Opposition came not only from the predictable places—the gutter press and the self-interested political bosses of Tammany Hall—but also from individuals of significant reputation and wide influence. Christian theology was used to justify both sides of the slavery debate.

Samuel F.B. Morse, famed artist and inventor, presided over the Society for the Diffusion of Political Knowledge; his writings rationalized slavery based on biblical precedent. Powerful politicians such as Samuel Tilden and George Tickner Curtis also wrote for Morse's society, feeding the fears of the upper classes as well as the working classes.[146]

Leading up to the fateful second week of July 1863, some in the Catholic secular press openly encouraged sedition by the Irish immigrant community as the appropriate response to conscription. These divisive elements acted in synchrony with the Democratic Party's fiercest editorial outlets, such as the *New York Herald*, *The Daily News*, and proslavery rags like the *New York Weekly Caucasian*.[147]

The recently unionized Irish longshoremen also had a bone to pick with their employers, who repeatedly hired strike-breaking black workers to replace them. Frequent violence against black workers over local labor disputes preceded the introduction of conscription in July 1863. All of this served to ratchet up the hostility of New York's enormous immigrant population.[148]

In November 1862, Democrat Horatio Seymour, a politician unsympathetic to the abolitionist cause who advocated compromise with the South, was elected governor of New York.[149] Just before the election, Professor Gibbs wrote to Olmsted at the USSC office in Washington, D.C., urgently requesting his help in forming a specifically political organization. Gibbs knew that, of all his colleagues, it was Olmsted who could best provide the intellectual and practical framework needed to build this countermeasure. Dr. Bellows explained, "Those who know the capacity, the thoughtfulness, the statesman-like qualities of Mr. F.L. Olmsted, will not wonder that Dr. Gibbs found him readiest and ripest for the plans he had in view and the best able to suggest the method by which it was to be carried out."[150]

Olmsted replied to Gibbs's letter on November 5, 1862, at great length and in considerable detail. He stated at the outset that "the method must be built up from the motive."[151] For Olmsted this motive meant far more than a statement of loyalty to the Union: "We sympathize with what has been a prevailing sentiment with the highest quality of men . . . who formed our country and gave it our keeping. . . . We wish also to establish the fact that there is an 'aristocratic class' in New York, which in this respect is not European; which shall not be felt by an English gentleman to be the mere ape and parrot of a European gentry."[152]

The notion of a legally privileged class aping European aristocracy was anathema to Olmsted. He viewed the native elite as an untapped asset, the basis of a legitimate American meritocracy. These men could lay down a firm foundation with a distinctly American tradition. Through their colonial lineages, the ideological aims of the group would be directly linked to the founders of the Republic, to those who had fought to create and preserve the nation's independence from the decadence of European aristocracy.

More than a symbolic gesture, this tactic was deliberate tradition building aimed at activating the collective cultural power of New York's blue-blood toward a socially beneficial end. Gibbs was explicitly instructed to invite, with the utmost discretion, fifteen to thirty of the "elite of the elite" to participate in the club's formation. Underlining the significance of this situation, historian Iver Bernstein writes: "Character—moral and personal—was the adhesive that bound New York's early nineteenth-century commerce and politics. . . . By mid-century, this patrician class . . . confronted an expanded and impersonal society that seemed to ignore questions of character altogether."[153]

In this first stage of the club's development, Olmsted directed that a second round of membership recruitment be instigated. Olmsted warned, "Let in . . . no man who does not burn with the sacred flame. . . . Select them, one by one with great caution." The potential member's motivation for joining must necessarily be to "aid its purpose." None could be proposed or accepted without first having his loyalty to the Union fully vetted and assured.[154] Once the test question of loyalty was met, prospective members should be classified according to their "particular genius, knowledge and habits of judgment—into committees to consider different questions of organization. . . . First, men of substance and high position socially . . . of good stock or of notably high character, of legal reputation . . . also men of established repute in letters and science . . . those of old colonial names well brought down. . . . Second, clever men, especially of letters, wits and arts who have made their mark. Third, promising young men—quite young men who should be sought for . . . and nourished with care . . . especially those rich young men . . . who don't understand what their place can be in American society . . . a society which has no place 'for men of leisure.'. . . The older and abler established men ought to fraternize with them, to welcome them and hold every true man of them in fraternity—so soon they may govern us if they will!"[155]

By recruiting across three generations, Olmsted seeded the club's immediate crisis management objectives with an internalized long-term purpose. In the interest of its own survival and in service to its external mission, the club ought to provide an environment of high ethical standards and exemplary moral conduct to younger members, especially the rich ones. As Olmsted succinctly put it, "they are greatly tempted to go over to the devil."[156] This club could be a means of curtailing the pernicious indolence that often accompanies inherited wealth and mentoring the succeeding generation into maturity graced with excellence and enlightened leadership.

Olmsted asked a basic rhetorical question, "What shall be offered [to] each of these classes and what shall be asked of them?" From the colonial elite, "everything must be asked" in exchange for "the satisfaction of a patriotic and Christian purpose." The principle of noblesse oblige was invoked: with position comes social responsibility.[157]

This exchange of values had to be balanced with the dictates of the potential members' circumstances: "all men who must live on their pay and who must live carefully and feel every dollar . . . they ought to come in easily; for once in, they will be the best working members. The fee should not be too high then." Last, for the sons of wealth, "good rooms with something to do is alone essential."[158] When a sufficient number of men had been identified who would "in loyal spirit join it heart and soul," the club would commence to function. Officers could then be designated and squads of new recruits rapidly brought in.

Olmsted's analytical abilities were essential in clarifying the next operational step, the organization of an efficient vetting process. To prevent disingenuous persons from infiltrating the inner sanctum, a means of testing personal integrity, moral rectitude, and unwavering loyalty to the Union was devised. Olmsted's advice on how to do this was deceptively simple.

In his November 5, 1862, letter to Gibbs, he stated, "Such assurance, by the by, could be best obtained negatively, by the question, 'Don't you just hate such and so?' rather than 'Don't you just love such and so?' It is easier to profess true hate than true love."[159] Olmsted drew a straight line to the heart of veracity. What appears to be a manipulative use of semantics was, in fact, a pragmatic application of design assessment—a stress test, if you will. Gibbs now had a sharp tool with which he could swiftly separate the wheat from the chaff.

After much consultation between November 1862 and January 1863, a series of invitation-only organizational meetings were called. The first was held on January 30, at the home of Dr. Gibbs, and the second on February 6, at the house of George Templeton Strong. Though Olmsted was intimately involved and in constant communication with his fellow cofounders, his name did not appear on the invitations because he was "tied to Washington by his incessant and responsible duties as Secretary and chief executive officer of the Sanitary Commission."[160] Olmsted wrote to Gibbs on January 31, 1863, before the second meeting, and again emphasized the critical purpose of the event: "On what terms would you take peace? That is what we want to know of men we are to associate with."[161]

The group's potential to emerge from its nucleus as a fully functioning, powerful leadership body was predetermined by its coherent design. Gibbs and Bellows followed Olmsted's plan precisely. It was Olmsted's carefully delineated strategy, with its crystalline logic and fully evolved ideology, that gave his fellow cofounders the advantage of focusing their efforts and time efficiently, ensuring that the all-important membership recruitment and vetting process was neither delayed nor diffused by unclear communication or overlooked opportunities.

Following on the heels of the Emancipation Proclamation, the founders launched the recruitment process in early February 1863. On March 20, 1863, the founding charter listed sixty-six members. Membership grew so rapidly—over 300 by May—that the splendid Daniel Parish mansion, possibly designed by Frederick Diaper, and located on Union Square's north side, was leased. The clubhouse opened on May 12, 1863.[162] By the end of the first year, club membership had reached 528.[163]

In assessing the impact of the Union League Club's early years, it is crucial to know who these people were and what they meant not only to New York City but also to national life, as well. The importance of the founders explains the club's longevity in New York's ever-changing political and social milieu. These gentlemen brought established professional networks, powerful personal allies, and ancestral prestige that enhanced the credibility of their collaborative venture.

From the seeds of Olmsted's careful planning, the club's roots quickly fanned out, taking firm hold in New York's upper echelons. The plan worked organically, germinating its seed naturally. The composition of the Union League Club's membership reflected the most liberal and reformist elements of the Protestant community and both political parties. Most denominations were represented, notably the Unitarians. The first squad included descendants of colonial settlers, the framers of the Constitution, patriots who had served in the first U.S. government, as well as heroes of the American Revolution and the War of 1812. Many held considerable fortunes amassed over generations.

The up-and-coming architect Richard Morris Hunt, son and grandson of respected Whig politicians and descended from wealthy colonial settlers on both sides, fell within this first category. Hunt was among the sixty-six charter members, as was his closest friend, William Jones Hoppin, who was elected the club's first treasurer. Hunt's brothers-in-law, Brigadier-General Joseph Howland and merchant Alexander van Rensselaer; Hamilton Hoppin, the former partner of architect James Bogardus; and Henry Chauncey were added to the membership list. Hunt's colleagues from the Tenth Street Studio also joined: the painters Albert Bierstadt and John Kensett, art critic Henry Tuckerman, and James Boorman Johnston, builder and owner of the building. Hunt's frequent collaborator, sculptor John Quincy Adams Ward, joined. Hunt's many friends, colleagues, and future clients would continue to swell the club's ranks within the first year and thereafter.

The complexity of personal ties between members was not limited to male relatives. Maternal ancestries and marriage were important bonds holding the fraternity together, and women played a vital, highly visible role.

The second squad represented a significant cross-section of successful businessmen and intellectually accomplished men. The city's merchant shippers, bankers, retail proprietors, and purveyors of commercial services were joined by entrepreneurs in heavy industry and professionals in engineering, railroad and real-estate development, and the embryonic telecommunications industries. Many among them were self-made men who had earned their way to the top of the American financial heap.

Politicians and social reformers from all walks of life and from a wide range of professional disciplines are found on the club's founding membership list. The educated professions were represented by a slate of top-ranking lawyers, doctors, scientists, educators, and clergy; the literati by writers, poets, critics, philosophers, and publishers; and the fine arts by painters, sculptors, architects, and composers.

Olmsted's Network of ULC Associates

Frederick Law Olmsted had become the quintessential self-made man, shaped by a confluence of circumstances onto a career path that he could never have prepared for in any school of the day. Through his extensive travels and journalistic investigations, Olmsted realized that clinging to old systems would inevitably lead to failure. His thought processes and design abilities evolved as the natural consequence of his thoughtful confrontation with the most difficult questions of his day. Over time, in the pursuit of solving so many different kinds of problems, his solutions encompassed a wide body of empirical knowledge, open and honest public discourse, and a lifetime of building upon diverse professional collaborations.[164] He perceived the application of that experience and knowledge as transmutable: "I feel . . . as if our machinery for spreading sanitary ideas through the country ought to be made use of for strengthening the Union . . . as this could be done at no cost."[165]

Olmsted was now in a unique position to maximize all his experiences and relationships and bring them together into a new form. He shepherded his most trusted friends, colleagues, and reformist allies into the first squads of the new club's recruits.

Olmsted's partner in the design of Central Park, architect Calvert Vaux, and Alfred W. Craven, chief engineer of the Croton Aqueduct, founder of the American Society of Civil Engineers and builder of the Central Park Reservoir, were inducted into the club. Former New York City mayor, Ambrose Kingsland, who successfully championed the establishment of a great urban park and won legislative approval in 1853 for its creation,[166] and Central Park Commissioners John F. Butterworth and Moses Hicks Grinnell were recruited along with city planning commissioner Issac P. Martin, who worked with Olmsted and Vaux on the layout of upper Manhattan.

Olmsted's closest associates in the literary and political realms were strong among the club's leadership, including William Cullen Bryant, famed poet, leading abolitionist, and the editor of the *New York Post* who called for the creation of a central city park as early as 1844 in his editorials; Jonathan Sturges, president of the Chamber of Commerce and confidant of both Olmsted and Bryant; Parke Godwin, influential writer and editor who nominated Olmsted for the park's superintendent position; and Henry Jarvis Raymond, cofounder of the *New York Times*, who had commissioned Olmsted to write his brilliant analysis of the Southern slave economy. Olmsted's reputation as a social scientist was established by this investigative reporting.

Friedrich Kapp, "who knows more and talks better upon the vital chords of American history than any man I know," was named by Olmsted as an ideal member in his November 5, 1862, letter to Wolcott Gibbs. Kapp was one of the Forty-Eighters, a Prussian émigré lawyer and writer who dedicated his book, *A History of Slavery in the United States* (1861, Berlin), to his friend Olmsted. George William Curtis and his father-in-law, Francis George Shaw, had been involved in Olmsted's publishing ventures. Shaw, Kapp, Bellows, and Strong were instrumental in hiring Olmsted for the USSC position. Major-General John Adams Dix, former Democratic senator for New York from 1845 to 1849 and secretary of the treasury in 1861, had been a leader of the Free-Soil Movement, which both Olmsted and Bryant were involved in.

Associated with Olmsted on USSC relief operations was the club's first president, Robert Bowne Minturn, named along with John Jay, grandson of the nation's first chief justice, for membership in Olmsted's letter, and members Samuel Bulkey Ruggles, William Henry Aspinwall, James William Beekman, Thomas Hall Faile Jr., Charles Collins, and James Morrison MacKay, who was appointed to the American Freedmen's Inquiry in March 1863. Olmsted's Staten Island friend, Edwin James Dunning, and his personal physician, Dr. Willard Parker, were also among the founders.[167]

On August 10, 1863, six months after successfully establishing the ULC, Olmsted was offered the position of superintendent of the Mariposa Estate, a vast mining and real estate enterprise in California, which had been sold to a consortium of investors by General John C. Fremont. Utterly exhausted from two years of enormous stress and compulsive overwork and in dire financial straits, Olmsted resigned from his position with the USSC and sailed to California on September 14, 1863.[168] Though absent from New York City, he remained a member of the ULC for the duration of the war, his name and reputation fixed to its mission.

The Draft Riots: Monday, July 13–Thursday, July 16, 1863

*"The assiduous fanning of every malignant passion by a portion of our public press,
and by platform demagogues, has at last resulted in
an open outbreak ..."*[169]

Casualties mounted during the first two years of the war. The administration's policy of short-term voluntary enlistments was failing to replenish the ranks. President Lincoln was compelled to enact, on March 3, 1863, the Enrollment Act of Conscription, a lottery to call up 300,000 men between the ages of twenty and forty-five. This legislation provided a blatantly unfair opt-out clause for those who had the financial resources to pay a $300 commutation fee or could provide a personal substitute for enlistment. The majority of poor men in the city, destined for inevitable conscription, were infuriated at the preferential treatment afforded to the affluent.

The conscription law went into effect on Saturday, July 11, 1863. On that weekend, people gathered in the tenements and saloons to plot with the longshoremen and the local gang leaders, particularly the Five Points gangs. They made plans to resist the draft—and to settle old scores.

The lottery was to commence at 9:00 AM on Monday. An angry crowd gathered at the provost marshal's office, and officials, sensing danger at the door, summoned the police. The lottery began at 10:00 AM, and within twenty minutes the situation exploded into violence. The mob destroyed the building's contents and set it on fire, flames engulfing the entire block. Civil and military authorities, caught off guard, were unable to halt the mob's vengeful momentum. New York City careened into bloody chaos.

The Armory at 2nd Avenue and 21st Street was looted of approximately 1,000 weapons and then burned. The few regiments still stationed in the city, their numbers depleted by reassignments to the front, were called out to put down the disturbances. Vastly outnumbered, the soldiers were quickly routed and forced to seek cover. On the west side of town, the mob tore up the train tracks and chopped down the telegraph poles. Gun shops, retail businesses, and residential buildings were attacked, looted, and set afire.

Emboldened by the apparent lack of civil defense, the rioters turned on the city's black citizens in acts of random, murderous violence. Gangs

This contemporary illustration of the start of the Draft Riots in New York City on Monday, July 13 1863, is captioned, "The riots in New York: the mob burning the Provost Marshal's office" and was published in the *Illustrated London News* (dated August 8, 1863). Courtesy of the Picture Collection, The Branch Libraries, The New York Public Library, Astor, Lenox and Tilden Foundations

sought out those who provided shelter and moral support to the "colored" community. Mob leaders targeted Mayor George Opdyke's house, along with the homes and businesses of other well known Republicans. "Some shouted, 'Now for the Fifth Avenue Hotel—there's where the Union Leaguers meet.'"170

The outspoken leaders of the abolitionist movement were singled out. Horace Greeley, editor of the pro-abolitionist *New York Tribune*, was fortunate to be absent when the mob arrived at the newspaper office with homicidal intentions. The Colored Orphans Asylum on Fifth Avenue at 43rd Street, home to 300 children, was stripped of everything the looters could carry. Within hours the orphanage was a heap of smoldering ashes.

On Tuesday, at the urging of the governor, the draft was suspended. But this did nothing to quell the violence. The rampage continued unchecked. As news of the riot spread, smaller riots broke out in surrounding communities in Brooklyn, Staten Island, and New Jersey.

Throughout the first and second days, a flurry of telegrams pleading for help was sent to Secretary of War Stanton, prompting him to order all available military personnel to immediately proceed to New York City. By Wednesday, New York's famous 7th Regiment, which had just survived the gruesome Battle of Gettysburg on July 1, arrived. On Thursday morning the city's munitions factories were posted with military guards armed with howitzers. The crowds, at some points numbering upward of 4,000, were pushed back with lethal force.

Thursday night and again on Friday, the army located large quantities of stolen guns and ammunition stockpiled within the first forty-eight hours of the rampage. Barrels of cobblestones were found buried in the garbage heaps and dark recesses of Manhattan's tenements and shanty towns. On Friday afternoon, the Catholic Archbishop John Hughes made an impassioned public appeal to bring the conflict to an end. Thousands gathered beneath the balcony of the prelate's residence as the archbishop argued, "this country is a foundation not to be destroyed . . . We have the right to approve or disapprove the acts of our rulers, but not to override them, but let us preserve the foundation, and let the American people rebuild the superstructure every four years."[171] As an Irish immigrant who had been a laborer himself, his words were cheered and were met with acquiescence.

That same day, July 18, Edward S. Sanford, of the U.S. Military Telegraph Service, sent this message to Secretary Stanton: "SIR: The plunder rioting is suppressed for the present, but there are strong indications of a formidable and widespread organization to resist the taking away of conscripts under the draft. This organization assumes a party aspect, and extends to the military of the city that are subject to draft."[172] Dix assumed command of the army's regiments in the city on that same day and firmly maintained law and order throughout the remaining summer.

Eyewitness accounts still shock in their graphic descriptions of the stunning cruelty directed at innocent bystanders and the wanton physical destruction of the city. More than 100 buildings were incinerated. The city's infrastructure, including rail lines, bridges, and telegraph cables, was severely damaged or destroyed. Damage was estimated in the millions of dollars.

New York's black citizens were brutally attacked, some murdered in their homes or in the streets. At least eighteen people were lynched. The true number of casualties suffered during the four-day riot will never be known. Countless were wounded and mass graves were filled on 11th Avenue. The Police Department estimated between 1,200 and 1,500 rioters died.[173]

Exactly two months after renting their Union Square headquarters, this was the grim reality ULC members grappled with. The municipal government, nearly helpless under siege by its population, was badly humiliated, and many of the state's antiwar politicians, including the governor, were politically discredited.

In the aftermath of the draft riots, the club's leadership organized rapid relief efforts to provide compensation and protection to the traumatized black community. During the riots, while helping the police rescue victims and sheltering the wounded inside the clubhouse, "unnamed" club members decided to "defy public sentiment" and raise a regiment of black troops.[174]

On November 20, 1863, the ULC took the bold step of adopting a resolution to recruit and equip New York state's first regiment of free black soldiers. In May 1863, before the club's decision, the New York Association for Colored Volunteers had launched an effort to gain permission for a regiment of free black soldiers but was met with strong resistance from Governor Seymour; even the White House deferred to the governor. The club sent notification of its intent to Seymour on November 22, requesting his consent as required by the secretary of war. He declined. Nevertheless, the club proceeded and obtained approval from the Adjutant-General's office in December. Again, Seymour was petitioned for his authorization. He simply ignored the request.[175]

But the biggest problem came from the War Department itself. Compensation normally provided to recruiters was withheld from the club, and "colored" recruits were to be paid less than half of white soldiers' pay. Club members raised $18,000 within the first few weeks and were able to overcome the financial limitations imposed on their initiative.

The ULC alerted Major-General Dix to reports that trickery and other abuses were being used by unauthorized individuals to recruit black men, such as swindling recruits out of their enlistment bounty or even drugging men before enlistment, and he promptly made arrests. The club fought hard to overcome the unfair treatment of its "colored" regiment. Their soldiers were not provided with adequate equipment, and the club had to provide floors and stoves for the regiment's tents. The ULC also funded the building of a hospital for treating the black regiments' wounded.

Significantly, the club mandated that officers chosen to lead the regiment must be of the highest caliber, not merely adequately trained, and be fully committed to the men. Thus the club guaranteed that its regiment was led by able, honorable men who treated the black soldiers fairly and professionally.[176] "The Union League Club during the Civil War always stood firmly and boldly for equal rights of American citizens, regardless of color."[177]

A full complement of 1,200 black soldiers, trained on Riker's Island, became the 20th U.S. Colored Regiment, U.S. Infantry. An additional 600 men were trained for a second regiment, which became the 26th U.S. Colored Regiment, U.S. Infantry. The ULC went on to recruit two more regiments of black American soldiers.

On March 5, 1864, the day of the 20th Colored Infantry's departure for active service, the ULC publicly feted the regiment. With great pomp, club members and their wives gathered in front of the clubhouse to bestow the regimental colors on the 20th Infantry. One hundred thousand spectators filled Union Square. Charles King, president of Columbia College, officiated. The women of the club provided the stand of regimental flags at their own expense. A warmly sympathetic address signed by 189 socially prominent women was published. After the ceremony, about 250 club members marched down Broadway singing "John Brown's Body" alongside the soldiers and their families to the point of embarkation on the Hudson River. Mr. and Mrs. Richard Morris Hunt were among the participants in this grand event and were signatories to its published proceedings.[178]

This extravagant ceremony was more than a potent symbolic gesture; it was also a brave one, especially for the women of the Union League Club. To publicly honor black soldiers in such a way was extremely controversial, if not downright provocative. Predictably, charges of promoting miscegenation were hurled in the press by the club's enemies.[179]

The ULC's unique response in the aftermath of the riots is explained by historian Iver Bernstein: "The men and women of the Union League Club saw themselves reclaiming the public spaces of the city from the draft rioters and their treacherous upper-class allies, and instead associating the urban landscape with elite culture, loyal nationalism, and paternalistic protection of the black community." The 20th Regiment's gala send-off and parade down Broadway "highlighted a political transformation that had occurred between the last years of the Civil War and the first years of the next decade."[180]

As the backbone of support for the U.S. Sanitary Commission, the club was deeply involved in the Metropolitan Fair of March-April 1864, the largest of the national fundraising events held to pay the costs of the USSC's field operations. Catherine Hunt's concession of French gloves and accessories, sent from Paris by Richard's brother, raised the largest single amount of all the women's concessions. The overwhelming success of the fair and the public's enthusiasm for the artworks exhibited sowed the seeds for the club's future cultural agenda.[181]

The club was deeply involved in the management of the National Freedman's Relief Association of New York and provided clothing, tools, orphan homes, schoolbooks, and schools, including financial support of the teachers in the field.[182] After President Lincoln's assassination, when his funeral entourage was to pass through Manhattan, the club flexed its political muscles to prevent the city's black citizens from being excluded from the memorial procession.

From January 1865 onward, the club became involved in the drafting of legislation. The club's Executive Committee lobbied the state assembly to "secure an improved and efficient sanitary system" for the city to be administered by a board of health "free from political influence and directed by adequate scientific skill and executive ability."[183]

Olmsted's friend, Dr. Willard Parker, whose efforts turned the city almshouse into the modern Bellevue Hospital, and surgeon Dr. John Ostood Stone, a fellow ULC member, were among the originators and first members of the Metropolitan Board of Health. Both worked tirelessly for the improvement of healthcare services and sanitary conditions of housing in New York City.[184]

During Reconstruction, the club stoked public sentiment in support of the Constitutional Amendments and Civil Rights Bill of April 1866. It threw its full support behind the 13th Amendment to the U.S. Constitution and resolved to influence government to grant suffrage to all free men, "which shall be equal and just to all, without distinction of color."[185]

Between 1866 and 1872, the club turned its collective energy toward cleaning up corruption and urged state investigation of the condition of New York City's municipal government. It also worked for much-needed improvements in public services such as the creation of a paid municipal fire department.

The club's executive committee expanded the scope of the club's initial agenda by promoting efficiency in the civil service and independence of the judiciary: "It shall be the duty of the club to resist and expose corruption and promote reform in our national, state and municipal affairs and to elevate the idea of American citizenship."[186] An eleven-member Political Reform Committee was formed, chaired by legal expert Dorman B. Eaton, with a mandate to recommend measures "best adapted to remedy such abuses and secure to the City honest and efficient municipal government."[187] Eaton drafted the laws that created the Metropolitan Board of Health in 1865, the city's police courts, and, as a member of President Grant's Civil Service Commission, the National Civil Service Act. Run in close cooperation with the Citizen's Association, led by Peter Cooper, the ULC was instrumental in bringing to an end Boss William Tweed's reign of flagrant political corruption and municipal graft.

No less important, the Union League Club pursued an enlightened program of cultural enrichment. A committee on the arts was formed in May 1865, with the leadership of architect Richard Morris Hunt, artist-architect Jasper F. Cropsey, landscape painter John Frederick Kensett, publisher George P. Putnam, and William T. Blodgett, a cofounder of *The Nation*. This committee was instrumental in founding the Metropolitan Museum of Art.

In the fall of 1870, a colossal, eleven-foot-high bronze statue of President Lincoln was unveiled in Union Square. This memorial, paid for by one-dollar donations organized by the Union League Club, was part of the club's ongoing campaign to keep alive the memory of the nation's great struggle and its leader.[188] Through a highly visible cultural gesture, the club reaffirmed its ideals and its obligation to maintain those ideals during the difficult and economically strained years of Reconstruction.

The technical and regulatory aspects of creating the city's infrastructure, housing, and commercial building stock were dealt with largely in a case-by-case manner, often in response to fires or building collapse. These circumstances not only kindled the reformist instincts of ULC members, but had earlier engendered the will to organize by a handful of New York's leading architects.

While these professional men were organizing to meet the crisis of 1863, it was not insignificant that two of the founders of the American Institute of Architects were invited to join the Union League Club at its inception. Although the AIA was in its infancy and had many years of struggle ahead, its importance was acknowledged professionally and supported financially by the ULC. In 1867, when the AIA resumed activity in postwar New York City life, it found itself in the good graces of this club, now the most powerful civic, political, and business fellowship in the city.

The contributions of Olmsted, Hunt, and Vaux to the work of the ULC had engendered a new level of respect for the profession. The work of other members, such as Cropsey, who would design the 6th Avenue elevated train stations, and sculptor John Q.A. Ward, a member of the AIA and Hunt's frequent collaborator, also created a positive image of the profession.

When the ULC decided to erect its first wholly owned building in 1879, it followed the Institute's preferred method of conducting a limited architecture competition. With customary integrity, and without favoritism, Hunt's design was not chosen. The commission was awarded to Peabody & Stearns. And all twelve entries were subsequently published in the AIA journal, *American Architect*.[189]

The Institute's first public fundraising campaign began on May 17, 1868, with the distribution of a circular requesting subscriptions to underwrite an architecture library for practicing architects and students.[190] In a letter to the editor of *The Manufacturer and Builder* in August 1869, an AIA architect described the long-term benefits of such a library: "I would call the attention of capitalists, real estate owners, and businessmen to the subject of establishing and sustaining architectural schools, libraries and museums—of which no city of equal magnitude is as deficient as New York."[191] ULC members were among the first and most generous contributors to the Institute's library fund.

In recognition of their generosity and professional support, these
founding ULC members were awarded honorary lifetime membership in the
AIA: William T. Blodgett, William E. Dodge, Henry Chauncey, Robert
Lenox Kennedy, George Cabot Ward, Ernest Tuckerman, William H.
Aspinwall, Alexander van Rensselaer, and James Wallace Pinchot. Honorary
AIA membership was also awarded to Samuel P. Avery, Peter Cooper, Parke
Godwin, William J. Hoppin, and, of course, Frederick Law Olmsted.[192]

* * *

Nineteenth-century concepts of leadership were not based on intangible
abstractions. Clear-cut role models of the Founding Fathers and the democratic processes they established were not so distant historical antecedents.
What had changed by the time the Civil War unfolded was a broader desire
among common folk for access to political power and for expanded opportunities to achieve social and economic success.

The need to fulfill the demands of industrial society, to provide the
infrastructure for transcontinental transportation, to incorporate new communication technologies, and to design and build the housing stock and civic
structures needed to meet the phenomenal growth of America's population
placed architects in an unprecedented position alongside their colleagues in
business and public service. Claimed by those who defined the post–Civil
War age were new avenues of commerce, professional recognition, and political influence. While personal relationships, nurtured among peers through
memberships in private clubs and public fraternities, resulted in architecture commissions for private homes and commercial buildings, this social
intercourse also paved the way for architects to affect the formation of public policy in tandem with designing the public structures that framed the
delivery of commercial, religious, educational, health, cultural, and civic services to the whole community.

Through the professionalization of architecture practice in New York
City and the individual and collective commitments to civic associations and
cultural institutions, architects were able to influence the city's civic and

social management and its physical development. These early associations can be seen as prototypes of today's politically active nongovernmental organizations, or NGOs, and trade industry lobbies. In fact, the particular clout of the ULC was vested in its broad assembly of talents, backgrounds, and professions, united through a shared civic and social agenda. The club's ensemble succeeded in part because it included the various disciplines associated with the built environment, each one essential to its mission of civic and social reform and to a democratic society's overall advancement. This approach allowed the reciprocation of compatible values and useful processes.

The synthesis of principled collaboration achieved by the ULC provides a vital example of what can be accomplished when personal differences of opinion and vested self-interests are put aside in mutual service to the common good. The aristocratic tradition of noblesse oblige was transformed into a workable system for a new kind of civic meritocracy—a system shaped by American democratic principles with a healthy dose of pragmatism and designed so that it could easily be replicated in both form and spirit, adaptable for myriad future purposes.

In the epilogue to his book on the New York City draft riots, Iver Bernstein states: "If Olmsted had had his way, a standard of 'democratic excellence' enforced by an active government would have been established . . . But such a thoroughgoing centralization of the nation's political and cultural life flew in the face of New York's local interests . . . Nonetheless the 'best men' who emerged triumphant from the draft riots had an immediate and lasting influence in national affairs . . . The New York gentry would not have another comparable opportunity to centralize and expand the American state until the turn of the century, when Theodore Roosevelt and Elihu Root took up the task."[193]

In the year he won the Nobel Peace Prize (1906), President Theodore Roosevelt wrote, "There are large numbers of handsome social clubs . . . and many others of a politico-social character, the most noted of them, alike for its architecture, political influence, and its important past history, being the Union League Club."[194]

Frederick Law Olmsted's high-mindedness left little room for compromise. His great ambitions regularly delivered deep disappointments. He struggled mightily to make the world in which he lived a finer, more just, more uplifting place. And yet the sheer array and creativity of his restless mind's accomplishments—both minor and major—continue to have a profound impact on American society. That a landscape architect held such a key role in this power play should not go unremarked nor should the leadership provided by the architects, artists, engineers, builders, and real estate developers within this power structure. Their share in the Union League Club's legacy of civic leadership in 19th-century America should be recognized. In the sincere judgment of the Rev. Dr. Henry W. Bellows, "Mr. Olmsted has, perhaps, rendered greater public services with less reward and less appreciation from those who have most profited by them, than any citizen of New York."[195]

9 Architectural Leadership during the Progressive Era

T HE NATION PASSED FROM THE Civil War Reconstruction period into a pressure-cooker era of social, economic, and political change. These pressures bore down on all levels of society. The astronomical growth in America's population overburdened the urban centers. Migration from the coastal states to the hinterlands hastened the transcontinental expansion of the nation's rail networks and of regional commerce, which, in turn, spurred the growth of existing communities and the building of new towns and cities.

The growth of state education systems greatly enhanced the accessibility and application of secondary and higher education for ordinary folk. Through necessity, the nation's methods of agricultural production and husbandry were professionalized, concurrent with all fields of scientific, engineering, and technical training. Professionalization became the key word in refashioning a post-slavery Republic. America had to find a new identity for itself in relationship to its colonial past, its emerging international role, and its leadership potential in a new technological age. The machines of mass communication—physically and philosophically—realigned all relationships of the polity to its governing structures.

Foremost in this swift and contentious societal upgrade was how certain fundamental human rights issues were addressed in both political and social terms. Seen through the development of the built environment, students of history, political science, and art cannot avoid the critical importance of architecture and the various public and private agendas that used it for promotion or the serious problems that were ameliorated by architecture during the Gilded Age.

Development of New York City's infrastructure and support services had begun during the Civil War. In 1862, after being lobbied by the AIA, the state authorized the creation of an executive-level city department with the power to pass upon "any question relative to the mode, manner of construction or materials used in the erection, alteration or repair of any building in the city of New York." The legislature further mandated that the department super-intendent and his officers be "either practical architects, house carpenters or masons and before their appointment shall each pass an examination before a committee . . . appointed by the American Institute of Architects . . . and shall furnish a certificate of such examination, signed by said committee, cer-tifying to their knowledge and competency to perform all the duties of such office . . . the superintendent, in addition . . . shall also have been engaged in conducting or carrying on business as an architect, house carpenter, or mason, at least seven years, of which he shall make oath before the mayor." The AIA was also appointed to assist in the survey of all buildings in violation of the fire and building safety codes and to render written evaluations for judgment by the courts.[196] Building code enforcement and owner compliance would prove to be the front line of reform efforts for decades to come.

In 1867 the state enacted its first Tenement House Law, which required landlords to install one toilet and a fire ladder for every twenty tenants. Plumbing had to be connected to the sewer system, and ventilation was required in every sleeping room. The law was enacted five years after the city's building inspection department had been established. It is important to note that inadequate or negligent architectural design was not confined to slums but was endemic and directly related to a lack of understanding of the connections between proper engineering for sanitation, fire safety, and the imperatives of structurally sound building design.

In 1879 a design competition for model tenements was mounted by the publisher of *Plumber and Sanitation Engineer*. The competition called for an economically designed tenement on a standard 25-by-100-foot city lot. The competition attracted 209 submissions but produced little in the way of improvement. According to the *New York Times* of March 16, 1879, "If the prize plans are the best offered—which we can hardly believe—they sim-ply demonstrate that the problem is insoluble . . . if one of our crowded wards were built up after any one of these three prize designs, the evils of our present tenement-house system would be increased ten-fold."

The *Times* pointed out that "the Waterlow houses of London and White's houses of Brooklyn" had, by combining lots and building properly planned structures, successfully dealt with the problem and noted that "if such public spirited citizens as those who have led this recent movement would form a company, they could put up such houses in New York and show that a good tenement is a fair investment. It would be a pity to have all this popular interest end in nothing."[197]

Architect James Ware's winning "dumbbell tenement" introduced interior air shafts and maximum coverage of the lot—and it did indeed have the unintended effect of exacerbating the problems of overcrowding, high fire risk, and spread of communicable disease. The *Times*'s fatalistic prediction was borne out by a huge increase in slum housing of the dumbbell type, sanctioned by the 1879 Tenement House Law.

To many historians, the culmination of the era is epitomized by the 1893 World's Columbian Exposition in Chicago. Its long-term influence on city planning and civic architecture is heavily documented, particularly the McMillan Plan for the capital's Mall.

But this particular episode in American cultural history does not provide a truly balanced picture of the subtle, but profound effect that designers of the built environment have had on the way our civic, political, and social infrastructures have evolved. The following examples of socially purposeful professional practice are cited as counterpoints to the more commonly lauded aspects of architectural artistic accomplishment.

Alfred Tredway White: A Civil Engineer Who Developed Model Homes for the Working Poor

Can one person, through personal initiative, dramatically upgrade society's understanding of what is an acceptable, socially responsible minimum standard of living? The answer is yes. And can that standard of living be defined through the design of private residential and public space designated for use by average citizens of modest or limited means? Again, the answer is yes. Can an education in the science of building prove instrumental to the implementation of such an enormous civic endeavor? Yes.

The life and work of Alfred Tredway White (1846–1921)—housing reformer, real-estate developer, city public works commissioner, and one of the period's most effective philanthropists—prove the point. White, a Brooklyn-born civil engineer, was educated at Brooklyn's Polytechnic Institute as a boy and went on to earn his civil engineering degree from the Rensselaer Polytechnic Institute at age nineteen. In 1865 his education in the building sciences was the very best available. As was expected of him, immediately upon graduation, he entered his father's prosperous mercantile firm on Wall Street.

A deeply religious Unitarian churchman, White had begun teaching in his parish's settlement school in 1867. In 1869 he was appointed supervisor of the First Unitarian Church of Brooklyn's settlement school, a post he held until his death. Through his settlement work the young engineer was able to identify the design and construction flaws that exacerbated the horrific living conditions and high mortality rates of Brooklyn's slums. Through his firsthand knowledge of the deleterious living conditions, White discovered his natural mission in life: "Well it is to build hospitals for the cure of disease, but better to build homes which will prevent it."[198]

White tackled the issue of affordable housing design and development by researching what other cities had done to ameliorate the problems created by slums. He traveled to England in 1875 to personally examine the latest innovations in working-class housing spearheaded by Sir Sydney H. Waterlow, London's Lord Mayor from 1872 to 1873. Sir Sydney, also a Unitarian, had worked his way up from apprenticeship in a government printing shop to ownership of a major printing and stationery business. Waterlow utilized his self-made fortune in the private development of workers' housing in London, having accumulated sufficient political clout during several terms in the House of Commons and then as London's mayor.

Waterlow founded the Improved Industrial Dwellings Company as a profitable enterprise that built low-rent, sanitary, well-designed housing for thousands of London's working-class families. His business was preceded by the workers' housing built by the Peabody Trust, founded by Massachusetts merchant banker and practical philanthropist, George Peabody. Born in 1795 in Danvers, Massachusetts, Peabody moved to London in 1837 to establish his firm there. The Peabody Trust had introduced proper toilets, laundry facilities, and playgrounds to workers' housing.[199]

White gained inspiration from the latest British approaches, as he intended to build high-quality, financially viable housing for the working poor in his own Brooklyn neighborhood. The goal was a healthy community environment that would sustain itself, inspire social and civic responsibility, and provide the stability needed for generational upward mobility. By the age of twenty-nine, White was ready to dedicate his education and wealth to his true vocation. Dealing head-on with the housing problems plaguing the city, White combined the best design principles with superior business practice and a philanthropic philosophy of supporting people's self-sufficiency.

Begun in 1876 and completed in 1877, White's first model tenement project, the Home Buildings, was financed with his own funds and with the help of his family. The two apartment buildings occupy a prime piece of former farmland at the corner of Hicks and Baltic Streets, on the heights above Brooklyn's harbor. White hired a local Brooklyn architecture firm, William Field and Sons, to execute his design specifications.

Economy of form is reflective of the purpose behind a novel housing concept. The balanced massing gives these model tenements an architectonic cohesiveness undiluted by extraneous decoration. Every unit has a private entrance on its wrought-iron balcony, floored with blue slate; open spiral staircases centered at the front of each building provide access and a stupendous harbor view.

Windows in every room ensure good cross-ventilation and abundant natural light. All apartments were fitted with a kitchen, a ventilated closet, an ash chute, and a private toilet. Fireproof brick construction and the elimination of long, dark hallways and dangerous interior air shafts resulted in the first American tenement housing designed for security, privacy, and healthy, sanitary living conditions. Courtyard windows opened on to wrought-iron fire escape platforms with stairs to the ground. Roofs were equipped with laundry lines for drying clothes. Because White firmly believed that daily contact with nature was necessary for human well-being, he included a sunny private garden, walled on two sides, for the tenants' pleasure.

The Home Buildings were immediately followed with an even more ambitious group of buildings, located just across the street. Built between 1878 and 1879, this much larger complex was named the Tower Buildings for the medieval, fortress-like appearance of the exterior spiral stairwells. A turret at the top of each stairwell provides a grand vista of New York's harbor along with access to the laundry drying area on the roof.

Amenities included bathing facilities in the basement of each building. The same spare Romanesque Revival style of the Home Buildings was used, but now stone pointing accentuated the geometry of the portals, charming window-box balconies were added to the street-front facades, and bay windows flooded corner apartments with extra light. The entrance balconies were embellished with decorative iron support columns and sheet-metal guardrails with various punch-cut motifs. Elegant neoclassical ironwork grilles embellished the roofline and stairwell towers. In total, 226 apartments rented for an average $7 per month, rates commensurate with the miserable slum dwellings in Manhattan.

Behind the U-shaped block of six-story apartment houses, White simultaneously built a mews of twenty-six row houses that enclosed the Towers' inner yard. The Workingmen's Cottages on Warren Place consist of small (11.5 feet wide by 32 feet deep), two-story houses. Each has a basement floor with a kitchen, dining room, and coal closet and separate toilet at the back. The row houses face each other on a courtyard walkway wide enough for a lush garden spanning the length of the block. Fancy brickwork frames the entrances, and the front windows are set off with wrought-iron balconies. It all creates a wonderfully harmonious community atmosphere.[200]

White became a partner in the family mercantile firm while pursuing an increasingly diverse array of civic, philanthropic, and business interests. In the 1880s, he publicly enlisted in Brooklyn's faction of the Independent Republicans, progressive reformers led by Carl Schurz, former Civil War general, U.S. secretary of state, and a Forty-Eighter. Taking a stand against local political corruption, corporate monopolies, and protectionist trade policies, these Mugwumps supported the Democratic New York governor, Grover Cleveland, for president.[201]

At the end of the 1880s, White built his crowning achievement, the Riverside Apartments, on the lower plain of Brooklyn Heights. Working with his architects, he modified the plans to include nine large buildings surrounding an enormous open space with a modern bathhouse, a proper

Alfred Tredway White's Workingmen's Cottages (1879), now privately owned townhouses called the Warren Mews, serve as the western-perimeter of his Tower Buildings affordable housing complex in the Cobble Hill Historic District of Brooklyn, New York. Photo: © Colleen M. Thornton.

playground, and a rustic music pavilion. Drying racks were neatly arranged around the perimeter of the common's landscaped lawn. The architecture itself occupied less than sixty percent of the lot, an unprecedented allocation when completed in 1890.

According to the *New York Times* report on the state's Tenement House Commission inspection in 1901, the development's tenants were predominately immigrants, many of whom were longshoremen's families because of the proximity of the docks. The largest contingent was Scandinavian, followed by the Irish and British, and the remainder a diverse mix of nationalities. The buildings delivered an annual return of five percent, even after returning annual rebates, about one month's rent, to all tenants with unblemished records of payment.

White's successful demonstration of high standards in design and construction combined with sound financial planning proved beyond any doubt that investment in decent housing for the working poor was not only a humane solution to overcrowded tenements, but also an economically viable, morally defensible business. It was clearly not necessary to treat the problems created by poverty, and thereby limit long-term solutions to its consequences, exclusively as a matter of voluntary or institutional charity.

From the opening of the Homes Buildings in 1877 to his death in 1921, White provided social and design leadership that yielded consistently positive, profitable results. Around his very public and pragmatic demonstration of civic, social, business, and design principles, the tenement reform movement slowly coalesced.

When Danish immigrant Jacob Riis, an investigative journalist and photographer, published his best-selling exposé on poverty in New York City, *How the Other Half Lives*, in 1890, he named White as the ideal builder of decent housing for the poor. Riis described White's design innovations and his business formula for model tenements and included illustrations of the Riverside Apartments' lot scheme and floor plan. For Riis, the example of White's socially responsible and profitable real estate development was proof that an easily replicable solution was already in hand. Riis knew that if enlightened social consciousness, in combination with design excellence and professional business management, became widely accepted, it had the potential to positively influence tens of thousands of lives and greatly enhance the quality of life of the city. By championing White's private efforts along with those of the Improved Dwellings Association and the Tenement-house Building Company in Manhattan, Riis helped to galvanize public support for the struggling housing reform movement.[202]

White held public office only once in his life. In 1894 the new Republican mayor of Brooklyn, Charles A. Schieren, found the financial and administrative affairs of his city in a mess. To help put things right, he appointed White as the city's commissioner of public works. White immediately upset the political patronage system by dismissing dozens of "useless supernumeraries" from the previous administration. White's statement to the press in answer to the uproar over the firings is revealing: "I fail to find anything in the law which permits me to carry men on the payrolls when there is no work for them to do. That would be a misdemeanor. I have been identified with works of charity and my sympathy for the poor has not changed since I assumed office. While I may be liberal with my own private funds, I do not think that I have the right to be liberal with other people's money."[203]

During the two years he ran Brooklyn's Public Works Department, White oversaw major roadwork, five new city parks, and construction of eighty-one miles of sewer system. He saved the taxpayers a considerable sum by his efficient and honest management of the department.[204]

When Mayor Schieren declined to run for reelection, there were public calls for White to run for mayor as the Republican candidate.[205] The party instead ran its own machine candidate, F.W. Wurster, who won the election. An entertaining incident of political payback followed. Naturally, in the face of such strong public sentiment for a potential rival, Mayor Wurster did *not* reappoint the independent Republican to the commissioner's post. White left office with no regrets but apparently with some unfinished business.

On June 17, 1896, White posted a check for $12,800 to the mayor, an amount in excess of his salary for the two years he served in office. The cash gift was stipulated to pay the entire cost of the office building and clock tower of the Wallabout Market, White's last major unfinished project as commissioner. Mayor Wurster, "after reading the letter several times," formally accepted the gift and called it a "fitting memorial of the excellent work" White had accomplished as the city's public works chief. The Wallabout Market, Brooklyn's largest wholesale farmers' market, and its clock tower stood until World War II, when the neighboring Brooklyn Navy Yards had to be expanded.[206]

After his stint in municipal government, White returned to housing with a broader approach. He was among the forward-thinking investors who, in July 1896, formed the City and Suburban Homes Company of New York to develop affordable housing of various types. Several of the directors were also shareholders of the Improved Dwellings Association, which had completed its first model tenements on First and Second Avenues between 71st and 72nd Streets in 1882.

This new company expanded White's business model by offering stock to small investors at $10 a share, with a promised annual return of five percent, a return equal to or better than a savings account. Aware of philanthropy's limitations, the directors chose a business model aimed at the very wage earners likely to live in the housing. They reasoned that "the larger the circle of people financially as well as morally interested in practical housing reform, the larger will be its development."[207] By June 1898, the firm had increased its capitalization to $2 million.[208]

The company's first project came about through the exchange of a large parcel of land on Amsterdam Avenue and 68th Street for company shares by Mrs. Alfred Corning Clark, the industrialist's widow. A design competition was held under the auspices of the Improved Housing Council's Committee on Model Apartments, an organization chaired by the activist-editor of *The Century Magazine*, Richard Watson Gilder. Twenty-eight architects submitted plans with the requirement to "eliminate the existing evils of tenement construction," while still ensuring a five percent dividend. Plans by architects James E. Ware and Ernest Flagg were selected for a large-scale development that included full bathrooms, built-in cabinetry, modern utilities, and washing facilities. Brooklyn-born Ernest Flagg had lately entered the housing debate with a stinging critique of the state of tenement housing, published in *Scribner's Magazine* in July 1894.[209] Flagg, trained at the École des Beaux Arts, aggressively promoted the scientific approach interpreted through his apartment house plans.

Of note was the submission by a young architect, Isaac Newton Phelps Stokes, then a student at the École des Beaux Arts. Phelps Stokes would devote his architecture career to housing reform and civic and cultural improvement, becoming a steadfast leader of the tenement house reform movement. With his partner John Meade Howells, he designed the nation's first social settlement, the University Settlement House, on the Lower East Side in 1899. Today he is best remembered for *The Iconography of Manhattan Island (1498–1909)*, his seminal, six-volume study charting the history of New York City, illustrated with his extraordinary print collection, the gift of which he made to the New York Public Library in 1930.[210]

Between 1898 and 1915, the City and Suburban Homes Company completed the largest urban, low-income housing developments in the country and branched out into provision of building and management services to investors in the city's affordable housing.

By the 1890s, important individuals joined White in his life's mission. In 1898 the Tenement House Committee of the New York Charity Organization Society issued a detailed report of the difficulties in gaining support from city officials for incorporating improvements into the existing building code. The committee consisted of a cross-section of professionals, several of whom were partners with White in the low-income, limited-profit housing business. The committee included Frederick W. Holls, secretary of the U.S. delegation to the 1899 International Peace Conference at The Hague; Professor Felix Adler, founder of the Ethical Culture Society; industrialist Andrew Carnegie; Jacob Riis, investigative journalist and reformer; Richard Watson Gilder, literary editor, poet, and activist; Robert W. De Forest, attorney, philanthropist, and president of the Charity Organization Society; Dr. Elgin R.L. Gould, sociologist; Dr. Edward T. Devine, social reformer; and prominent architects George B. Post, AIA president in 1898; I.N. Phelps Stokes; and Ernest Flagg.[211]

In response to the report, in 1900, Governor Theodore Roosevelt appointed a state commission to examine tenement house conditions. He chose the reform lawyers Paul D. Cravath, William A. Douglas, and Robert W. De Forest; labor leader William J. O'Brien; housing expert Dr. Elgin R.L. Gould; Hugh Bonner, former chief of the New York City Fire Department; Dr. George B. Fowler, former New York City health commissioner; and James B. Reynolds, head worker of the University Settlement. Representing the building and design professions were the architects Raymond F. Almirall, of the Brooklyn firm Ingle & Almirall; William Lansing of Buffalo; and I.N. Phelps Stokes of New York City; retired builder Myles Tierney, whose firm built the Washington Bridge over the Harlem River; builder Otto M. Eidlitz, of Mark Eidlitz & Son, nephew of Leopold Eidlitz; and Alfred T. White. Lawrence Veiller, the young social worker turned housing activist, was appointed secretary of the commission and would parlay this position into a high-profile career as a national housing policy advocate.

In announcing his appointments in the *New York Times* on April 17, 1900, Governor Roosevelt made clear his thinking on the importance of the commission: "This Tenement House Commission is the most important commission I have had to deal with . . . for it deals with one of the fundamental factors in the most difficult and most complex of the social and industrial problems of the day . . . to get all the different sides of the problem properly considered . . . for instance, I wanted builders and architects . . . lawyers who had made special study of the matter . . . I wanted [those] who had been in public life in administration . . . [those] who could speak for wage earners and . . . [those] who had devoted much of their lives to intelligent philanthropic work . . . I wanted Mr. Alfred T. White because he has had expert knowledge of the subject from many different sides."[212]

The commission inspected tenements in neighborhoods all over the newly consolidated city of New York. All of White's buildings were inspected and stood in shocking contrast to the abhorrent conditions encountered at most of the other sites.[213]

The Tenement Commission's final report, released to the legislature on February 25, 1901, was damning. Building design was actually the least difficult aspect to resolve. The biggest problem was the inability (or lack of will) of the city and state governments to enforce existing building codes. The commission recommended that the process be changed from after-the-fact violation inspections followed by a court hearing and imposition of fines to a preoccupancy inspection system that would issue a certificate of code compliance. This new supervision and compliance system would be administered by an autonomous city tenement house department. Interestingly, neither mandatory fireproof construction nor baths were included in its revisions to the tenement house building code. Acceptance of economic considerations allowed the commission to leave adoption of these building standards to the marketplace.[214]

The commission drafted the Tenement House Law of 1901. Chairman De Forrest, architect Phelp Stokes, and secretary Veiller were instrumental in framing the legislation, which revised the tenement building code and created the New York City Tenement House Department. Mayor Seth Low appointed De Forrest as the department's first commissioner. He in turn appointed Veiller and, on the recommendation of White, Wesley C. Bush as the first two deputy commissioners.[215]

Because of the historic work of the Tenement House Commission, primary municipal services and building code standards for housing were irrevocably linked to the overriding issue of human rights. The commission members and their secretary spearheaded a movement that took these issues to the forefront of national life. De Forrest and Veiller established the National Housing Association in 1910, and Frederick Law Olmsted Jr., Alfred T. White, and Jane Addams served on its board.[216] White's buildings remained the gold standard of socially responsible real estate development.

All of White's tenement buildings were fully occupied, maintained, and profitably managed throughout his lifetime and then afterward by his heirs. The Riverside Apartments lost a section to Robert Moses' Brooklyn-Queens Expressway but have recently been restored and refurbished. The restored Home and Tower buildings and the landmarked Warren Mews are the centerpieces of Brooklyn's Cobble Hill Historic District.

White, embracing life to the last, drowned on the evening of January 21, 1921, in an ice-skating accident. A multimillionaire, he was a major benefactor of the Tuskegee Institute and Hampton College. He was a founder of the Brooklyn Botanical Gardens, endowed a chair in social ethics at Harvard University, and was an original trustee of the Russell Sage Foundation. During his lifetime he created trust funds for the many organizations and charities he supported and left more than $1 million in confidential bequests.[217]

Alfred Tredway White delivered to his community a host of healthy, livable, enduring places. He fostered strong civic and social services using the combined resources of the business, philanthropic, and political sectors. His long career of public service and selfless philanthropy was—and still is—the epitome of virtuous civic leadership.

William J. Fryer Jr.: Iron Architect-Engineer and Framer of New York's City and State Building Codes

The contributions of William J. Fryer Jr. (1842–1907) to the practice of architecture and to New York City's civic life are all but forgotten. If contemporary historians know of him at all, it is through his writings on architectural iron engineering and manufacturing and the guide books to New York City's building code laws, which he edited for *The Real Estate Record and Building Guide* from 1885 to 1903.

Fryer was born in 1842 into one of New York's most respected colonial families, a direct descendant of Philip Livingston, a signer of the Declaration of Independence. His father was "the leading merchant in Albany." Fryer was educated in architecture and engineering and first practiced in his hometown.[218] In 1864, at age twenty-two, he filed a patent for a fireproof, hollow clay chimney flue tube. Fireproofing of building materials and in building construction became a primary concern for the balance of his career.[219] Fryer also filed a patent for a new kind of railroad car wheel in 1866 and another for a building in 1869.[220]

In 1865 Fryer left Albany to take a position with iron architect and manufacturer James L. Jackson in New York City. Soon Jackson was utilizing Fryer's ideas for iron products as well as his skill in writing about them. With the Jackson brothers, Fryer wrote an article, "Iron Store Fronts," in 1869 for the *Architectural Review and American Builder's Journal*, giving a glowing review of A.T. Stewart's "immense dry goods store" on Broadway. He advised readers to stand at the corner of the building to see it stretch down two street fronts. From that vantage point, the aesthetic and physical qualities unique to iron architecture could be appreciated. The columns and molded arches had "too much lightness and grace for anything but iron," and the "expansive elevations are beautiful, too, being in iron."[221]

By 1876, when he published his major tome on the manufacture of architectural iron and iron foundry management, *Architectural Iron Work . . .* , Fryer was regarded as one of the nation's leading experts in the field of iron architecture and its manufacture.[222] Cast-iron architecture historians Margot and Carol Gayle state that "Fryer's half-century of intimate involvement with the iron business in New York—as architect, engineer, and business executive—make him one of the most reliable sources on the early industry."[223] In 1879 Fryer even tried his hand at city planning by publishing a five-page proposal with a map titled "A proposed new city park for the extreme eastern portion of New York."[224]

By 1880 Fryer was a managing partner of the Etna Iron Works, located at 104 Goerck Street, near the East River. Etna produced everything from cast-iron buildings to machine engines and the "structural material for the Third Avenue Elevated Road."[225] The company's building was subsequently leased to Thomas A. Edison from 1881 to 1887 for the Edison Machine Works.[226]

In 1880, "much to the astonishment of the architects and builders of the city,"[227] the city's Department of Buildings was absorbed into the New York City Fire Department. The newly subsumed agency was renamed the Bureau of Buildings, and William P. Esterbrook became the inspector of buildings under the supervision of the city's fire chief.[228]

Esterbrook told *American Architect and Building News* that the dissolution of the Buildings Department was as an act of personal vengeance by a state senator whose brother had been discharged from the department's employ because of an insufficient staffing appropriation by the city's aldermen. He bemoaned the fact that it "suited the purposes of politicians to continue it and . . . [it is] likely to last until some legislator can benefit himself or a friend, or injure an enemy, by having it change."[229]

In July 1880 Fryer, Charles Mettam, an architect and holder of "several key patents in cast iron construction design,"[230] and Matthias Bloodgood, a successful mason builder who had served as president of the Mechanics and Traders' Society,[231] approached Esterbrook with a proposition and request for his help. The three men had voluntarily undertaken a complete revision of the existing building law. With Esterbrook they "began, voluntarily and with no organization behind them, to consult together with the view of framing a new law. They worked unaided for about three years, when associations of underwriters, architects, iron workers, and real estate men endorsed them and became interested in the undertaking. In 1885, the first remedial legislation was secured."[232]

Their work was a major step in the creation of the first comprehensive, modern building code for an American city. The framers addressed the state of building technology and the wider consideration of the uses made of the city's building stock. This remedial code included mandatory fireproofing as the construction standard for all buildings with elevators and for hotels, theaters, and all public amusement facilities. It also required total fireproof construction of all buildings exceeding a set height.

In 1885 Esterbrook was succeeded by the architect Albert F. D'Oench as superintendent of buildings. D'Oench was a college-educated architect, born in St. Louis, who had studied architecture in Stuttgart, Germany, for three years and had apprenticed in the offices of Leopold Eidlitz and Richard M. Hunt. D'Oench and his partner, Joseph Yost, are known for their addition of nine stories to Hunt's New York Tribune Building (1903–1905). D'Oench was succeeded by Thomas J. Brady between late 1888 and mid-1889.[233]

This was a period of intense political action by reformists in both major political parties. Fryer and his family were deeply involved in local and national political life. This intimate relationship is evident in the guest list of his sister's wedding to New York state Democratic Party leader, Daniel Manning, in 1884. Former New York governor and the president-elect, Grover Cleveland, and the state's future Democratic governor, Roswell P. Flower, were among the many influential attendees.[234] Fryer's new brother-in-law was appointed U.S. secretary of the treasury in 1885 and served for two years in the first Cleveland administration. Daniel Manning would begin the policy work to lower customs duties before ill health forced him to resign.[235]

In 1884 Fryer was appointed superintendent of repairs for federal government buildings in New York City, a job in the Office of the Supervising Architect of the Treasury. On February 8, 1888, he delivered to the supervising architect, Colonel Will A. Freret, a fellow Democrat, his report titled "U.S. Public buildings in the city of New York," which advocated the grouped siting of key federal buildings, including a new Custom House, Sub-Treasury building, and Post Office, at Bowling Green.[236]

Fryer's report called for a civic core in Lower Manhattan. He believed that a cohesive, well-planned physical presence for the federal government at the heart of the city's municipal and financial district would benefit the city's economy and enhance the prestige and efficiency of the government's operations: "The welfare of the city of New York ought to be the pride of every American citizen, no matter where he hails from, for New York belongs to the whole country, and the business transacted in the Government buildings in New York affects the whole country."[237]

This was not an unprecedented suggestion. As far back as 1872, the city's merchant community had voiced enthusiastic support to both houses of Congress regarding a similar recommendation made by Supervising Architect of the Treasury Alfred B. Mullet. But Mullet had already caused considerable controversy with his handling of the design and siting of the enormous Federal Post Office and Courthouse in front of City Hall. A new

Custom House was to be long in coming.[238]

With Fryer's reintroduction of this idea, the discussion of the federal government's chronic, unsolved office problems reinvigorated civic debate on the issue. Fryer presented his report to the New York Chamber of Commerce on November 1, 1888. Soon afterward, the chamber published its own report on where to build the new Custom House and included Fryer's report in full.[239]

In the spring of 1890, with Fryer's continued lobbying, the state assembly moved to facilitate the federal government's purchase of land in order to build in Lower Manhattan.[240] But matters soon got bogged down in competing business and political interests regarding where to locate each one of the necessary federal buildings.[241] After many years of wrangling and indecision, a national design competition for a new Custom House on Bowling Green was conducted. Cass Gilbert's magnificent design for the building won out in 1899. According to Fryer's obituary, his suggestion for a group plan of government buildings was, at the time of his death, being adopted in other cities.[242]

But the biggest task for Fryer still remained the articulation of a modern building code. The reestablishment of an autonomous, professionally managed city buildings department would be the natural outgrowth of a revised, effective building code.

The Board of Examiners was created by the 1880 decision to fold the Buildings Department into the Fire Department. The board was the final jury of appeal for building plans that failed to receive any one of the many necessary approvals from several different city departments. The bureaucracy for obtaining a building permit was an unwieldy, time-consuming, and expensive burden on architects who were required to provide a complete set of plans to each city department involved in the process. Architects and builders wanted to streamline the process, which logically belonged in a consolidated buildings department. Until that could be achieved, the Board of Examiners arbitrated the convoluted building permit process.

The board, chaired by the superintendent of buildings, initially comprised representatives of the major professional associations of the building business: the Society of Architectural Iron Manufacturers, the Real Estate Owners' and Builders' Association, the American Institute of

Architects, the Mechanics' and Trades' Exchange, and the New York Board of Fire Underwriters. By 1892, representatives from the New York City Fire Department and the Real Estate Exchange Limited were added.[243]

Fryer represented the Architectural Iron Manufacturers on the Board of Examiners. In this role, he gained a deeper understanding of the many obstacles that prevented adequate building design and construction standards from being met. With him on the board was the AIA's representative, Napoleon LeBrun (1821–1901), who also happened to be the Fire Department's architect. LeBrun, son of French Catholic immigrants, was born in Philadelphia. He trained in Thomas U. Walter's office, leaving in 1841 to work on his own. He designed the Cathedral of Saints Peter and Paul and co-designed the Philadelphia Academy of Music before moving to New York City at the time of the Civil War. Beginning in 1879 and continuing over the next fifteen years, LeBrun's firm designed more than forty buildings for the Fire Department, including its landmark, Romanesque Revival headquarters on East 67th Street, built between 1884 and 1886.[244]

Architect-builder Cornelius O'Reilly represented the Real Estate Owners' and Builders' Association, and Edwin Dobbs was one of the two representatives of the Mechanics' and Trades' Exchange. These gentlemen sat on the Board of Examiners throughout the period in which the first major revision of the entire building code was underway.[245]

In 1889 the various professional associations interested in advancing the development of the city's building codes formed the Committee on the Revision of the Building Laws. Fryer again represented the interests of the Association of Architectural Iron Manufacturers; LeBrun represented the New York chapter of the AIA; architect Warren A. Conover[246] and Edwin Dobbs, the Mechanics and Trades' Exchange; builder-architect Cornelius O'Reilly, the Real Estate Owners' and Builders' Association; and John W. Murray, the New York Board of Fire Underwriters. Thomas J. Brady, superintendent of buildings, represented the municipal government.

The professional, business, and political communities struggled for many years with the challenge of formulating a standard building code. The effort proved too tiresome and meddling for some in the architecture profession, as the former Superintendent of Buildings Albert D'Oench discovered when he found himself in the embarrassing position of presenting to the Revision Committee the minority report of the Architectural League's own committee on building code revision.

After working through the League's majority report, which endeavored not so much to change the law as to painstakingly "make its phraseology clearer and more effective," D'Oench then read the minority report, in which the League's former president, architect John Beverly Johnson, stated: "I beg to differ with the conclusions of the majority of the committee, for I regard all building laws as an abridgment of the liberty of the citizen and I regard it as the duty of an architect to evade the law on every possible occasion in the interests of his client."[247]

This sarcastic statement was immediately printed in the *New York Times*. Coming from a leader of the upper echelons of the profession, such an opinion could not have inspired public confidence in the civic leadership abilities of the profession. But architects did continue to contribute to the process in other ways. On April 3, 1891, representatives from the AIA, the National Association of Builders, the National Board of Underwriters, the National Association of Building Inspectors, and the National Association of Fire Engineers met in New York City to find common ground on the question of building law. Although no general building law was endorsed, the group jointly adopted and published a slate of recommendations for distribution to state legislatures around the country for their future consideration.[248]

For three years, the Committee on the Revision of the Building Laws worked harmoniously to frame a technically advanced building code. Upon completion of the code revision, some members proposed that it include an amendment establishing an autonomous New York City Buildings Department. The AIA had even sponsored and circulated a petition, signed by two-thirds of the membership, urging the formation of a buildings department. But the AIA's own representative on the committee, Napoleon LeBrun, refused to support the proposal on "personal grounds," preferring to protect his private business interests with the Fire Department rather than represent the interests of the AIA, which was his professional duty. John Murray, representing the Fire Underwriters, also withheld his support on similar grounds.[249]

A stalemate resulted between the committee and the Fire Department and held things up until it was agreed to let the bill go forward to

Albany as it was, leaving the issue of a buildings department to be worked out in legislative committee. On February 15, 1892, the new building law, a huge document, was presented to the New York State Assembly. Fresh in everyone's minds was the devastating fire at the Hotel Royal, which had claimed twenty-eight lives just the week before in New York City.[250]

The state assembly began public hearings on Assembly Bill No. 788 in the first week of March. The biggest area of contention was the issue of fire-proofing. The law stipulated the fireproofing of all elevator shafts and stair-wells. Fireproof construction was required for every hotel, theater, asylum, school, or place of public instruction exceeding thirty-five feet in height and all buildings exceeding eighty-five feet in height. Theaters were to be entirely fireproof in both technical design and construction. High standards of fireproof construction were required for the basement and first floor of all dwellings of four stories above a basement, and of five stories or more.[251]

Predictably, objections were raised by many in the real estate sector, especially hotel owners. The legislature was warned against "a species of socialism which would provide a paternal protectorate over the people."[252] But oddly enough, the New York Board of Education also objected. The *New York Times* found the board's "objections to advanced methods ... par-ticularly obnoxious, coming as it does at a moment when other departments of the city government are working in conjunction with the leading archi-tectural and building associations of the city, and in conformity with pub-lic opinion to improve building methods and practices and insure protection against unsafe and unsanitary structures."[253] Unfortunately, the assembly bowed to pressure from hotel owners and exempted them from fire-proofing existing stairwells as being too costly and likely to be overturned in the courts.[254]

Meanwhile, Mayor Hugh Grant was being aggressively lobbied to support an additional measure to reconstitute the former buildings depart-ment. Around March 12, Mayor Grant formed a subcommittee of Fryer, O'Reilly, and Conover to handle his response to this issue. With the majority of the city's architects, builders, and trades backing the idea, Mayor Grant's support was obtained before the legislature had completed its public hearings.[255]

LeBrun's self-serving actions to protect his conflict of interest damaged the credibility of the Institute before the state legislature. The AIA found itself in an odd position: It had a seat on the revision committee but no official voice in its deliberations.[256] This gave legislators the false impression that the AIA either disapproved of or was utterly indifferent to the proposal for a buildings department.

It became necessary for supporters within the Institute to bypass LeBrun to set the record straight. An anonymous letter was published in the *Real Estate Record and Building Guide* on March 26: "Mr. LeBrun, an officer of the Institute, has expressed himself as opposed to any change, and, not desiring to antagonize him, I (a well known architect and AIA member) have refrained from expressing myself of late. Mr. LeBrun, a member of the Board of Survey which surveys buildings in cases in which charges are made against the stability of buildings . . . earns about $5,000 in fees annually." This statement was followed by a list of the architects who supported the formation of a New York City Buildings Department.[257]

In that last week of March, the state Senate's Committee on Cities held a public hearing on the building law at which a new amendment to create the Buildings Department was presented by representatives of the building trades. As only three weeks remained in the legislative session, the amendment was expeditiously dropped into the new building bill under consideration and promptly voted on.

Though the Revision Committee had done its best to create a building law free from politics, it was impossible to propose the idea of a new city department without engaging the political machinery. But on this occasion, the only strenuous objections came from the chief of the Fire Department and "men who see a transfer of power and patronage from themselves and others, or a possible loss of places which they themselves are holding."[258] The amended bill sailed through the legislature, in what the *New York Times* described as "a happy accident . . . before it was possible for substantial changes to be made, both houses had passed it."

The revised code, Chapter 275 of the Laws of 1892, was written with logic and clarity so that it would be easily understood by all parties to the building process: "the law deals with the subject of building as a builder puts up a structure."[259] Governor Roswell P. Flower signed the bill on April 9, 1892, and it went into effect immediately.[260]

The new Buildings Department hit the ground running and began the inspection of tenement houses pursuant to the new rules of fireproof construction for the lower floors. This was of particular concern to Fryer, who sought to control the spread of fire from basement coal bins upward through tenement houses. The finer points of fire safety incorporated into the law, including the details of construction and building materials to be used, were written under Fryer's guidance. The added costs of building tenement houses to meet the code were well worth the investment, both in saving lives and in the value of the architecture itself.

According to the *New York Times* of May 29, 1892, Fryer had been "actively interested in building reform since that subject was first agitated." When asked to respond to builders' objections to the new code, he answered, "It is true that some builders have abandoned their plans in consequence of these provisions of the new law. I happen to know that there are other builders who believe as we do that the changes are good."[261] Also of great importance in the building code revisions were new specifications dealing with the latest innovations in building engineering, such as the technical distinctions between steel-cage construction and skeleton construction. This was the first code to officially recognize and determine the dimensions, foundation, framing, load, and wind specifications of curtain-wall construction for high-rise buildings.[262] New regulatory departments and stricter inspection measures were created, such as the Bureau of Fire Alarm, Telegraph and Electrical Appliances, a factory inspection act, and a revised mechanics lien law.[263] Revision was continual, producing a Tenement House Law in 1895.

And as he had done in 1885 and 1887, Fryer edited a hefty tome, *Laws Relating to Buildings, in the City of New York . . .* , covering all aspects of the new code. In response to subsequent code revisions, Fryer edited updated editions in 1895, 1897, and 1900. These publications, illustrated with colored engravings, have the added value of containing "a complete directory of architects in New York City, Brooklyn, Jersey City, Newark and Yonkers."[264] In 1902 Fryer edited *The Tenement House Law and the Lodging House Law of the city of New York*, which was followed in 1903 by *The New York Laws relating to apartment and tenement houses.*[265]

Contemporaneous with the enactment of the revised New York City building law and the reinstatement of the Buildings Department, another bill to create a three-member commission to draw up a statewide building code "in grades applicable to all cities in the State, except New York and Brooklyn,"[266] was working its way through the Senate and Assembly. The *Real Estate Record & Building Guide* reported on April 9, 1892, that "the commissioners will serve without pay and . . . complete their work within one year . . . Fortunately competent men stand ready to do the work, pay or no pay. For the past twelve years a few public-spirited men have worked continuously on the New York City building law without moneyed compensation whatever, and a similar gratuitous work of equal or greater importance will have to be undertaken for this State, in reality for the United States."[267]

This bill was swiftly passed and signed into law. On June 11, 1892, Governor Flower announced his appointments to the New York State Building Law Commission: Fryer was named chair, along with O' Reilly and Leon Stern, an architect from Rochester. Allan Beach, former lieutenant governor of New York, was appointed legal counsel.[268]

Fryer's credibility in the political sphere made it possible for him to consistently push forward greater and greater civil jurisdiction over the design and construction of safe buildings in New York City and the state. How the built environment should be managed was a major political issue in 1892, but it was not the only issue around which reform advocates rallied. The Democratic Party in New York was split between those who supported the machine politics and the Progressives, who fought to stem the spread of corruption. Grover Cleveland was the leader of the Progressive Democrats, and Fryer was firmly aligned with this faction of the party.[269]

In September 1894 Fryer became chairman of a newly organized anti-Tammany association, the Municipal Organization of the City of New York. Conover and O'Reilly were also members. The organization put forward Samuel McMillan for mayor. McMillan, an Irish immigrant who first worked as a carpenter and studied architecture at night school, owned a successful construction firm. He served twelve years on the Board of Examiners as the representative of the Real Estate Exchange.[270]

In 1895 the "fusion" candidate, William L. Strong, a Republican who ran on a ticket with Democrat John W. Goff, was elected mayor of New York

City on a reform platform.[271] Strong appointed McMillan as the city's parks commissioner and Theodore Roosevelt as police commissioner. McMillan was later elected to Congress as a Republican in 1906.

In 1899 a new city commission was charged with drawing up revisions to the 1892 building code, and again Fryer was a key member of the panel. In the same year, the new Republican administration of Governor Theodore Roosevelt pursued a major corruption investigation of Tammany Hall and its "boss," Richard Crocker, who had regained a lock-hold on city government aided by his crony, Mayor Robert A. Van Wyck. The "Special Committee of the Assembly for the Investigation of offices in the City of New York," under the chairmanship of Robert Mazet, became known as the Mazet Commission.[272]

Fryer, though not officially under suspicion for any wrongdoing, came under intense scrutiny as chair of the city's Building Code Commission and as a long-time member of the Board of Examiners. The investigators hoped that, by discrediting the Buildings Department and its officials, they could convince the legislature to dissolve the Board of Examiners and replace the city building code commission with a new state building code commission. Housing reformers sought to gain control of the pending revisions to the building code and to limit the authority of the principal framers of the existing building code. According to the *New York Times*, "the examination of William J. Fryer of the Building Code Commission, which consumed most of the day, was conducted with minute detail and brought out a tremendous volume of dry facts."[273]

During the investigation, the corruption and incompetence of some officials and subordinates within the department were brought to light. Since the centralization of power in the Buildings Department and the Board of Examiners would be increased under the latest revisions, this was branded an autocratic abuse of power by reform critics and the Mazet Commission.

The final report of the Mazet Commission was a meticulous vivisection of New York City's municipal operations. In exposing a chronic lack of enforcement of the building code and the ability for certain politically connected violators to gain exemptions, the commission recommended the "prompt abolition of the Board of Examiners" and that the appeals process be suspended "pending the construction and enactment of a decent building code."[274]

Fryer willingly testified before the committee, answering all questions without evasion. Despite the hostile aspersions on his character, he was forthright and unapologetic and admitted that mistakes had been made in certain rulings. Because Fryer had for years openly advertised his services as a consulting architect to those seeking to meet the building code, particularly if plans had been rejected, the investigator implied that Fryer was, in effect, influence peddling. But Fryer had always excused himself from any decisions on plans he had consulted on, and made sure this fact was entered into the official records. He further explained that, although architects did not advertise as a practice, his advertisement was primarily aimed at those who routinely sought his expertise gratis.[275]

The Mazet Commission provided an effective platform for tenement house reformers to tackle the city's poor enforcement of the building codes. Reform leaders Veiller and Flagg testified about the unsatisfactory conditions that the building code had failed to redress and the failure of municipal management. Veiller sharply criticized Fryer and the Board of Examiners, particularly since board members had written the building code.[276] The motivation for the Republican campaign against the city's Buildings Department was the reformers' fear that the 1895 Tenement House Law would be nullified in the building code revisions written by a Tammany commission. This turned out to be baseless.

Cornelius O'Reilly, speaking for the commission, said, "As I understand it, nothing that we can do can affect the provisions of the tenement house law of 1895. The Charter Commission put that law bodily into the charter and we have been advised by our counsel that we must confine our codification to matters concerning buildings other than tenement and lodging houses. That is just what we are doing."[277] Fryer had served as chairman of the 1895 State Building Law Commission.[278]

The call to abolish the city's Board of Examiners and its building code commission had no chance of picking up traction in Albany. Instead, the 1900 New York State Charter Revision Commission clarified the Board of Examiners' statutory powers.[279]

Fryer's professional and personal reputation emerged intact from the

Mazet investigation, despite Veiller's harsh testimony against him, and he continued as chairman of the Building Code Commission. He and his colleagues resumed work on revising the building code, seeing it through to passage by the legislature.

Though the code revisions did not satisfy the aims of the tenement house reformers, the new building codes modernized and expanded building standards and fire regulations for all types of buildings. Except for the extraordinary circumstance of the Tenement House Law of 1901, which considered tenement housing distinct in its code requirements from all other types of buildings and thus required its own department, Fryer's 1899 building code stood until 1907, when it again underwent major revision.[280] On technical matters, his authority remained unquestioned. In 1898 he published two new papers on the development of structural iron and ornamental ironwork.[281]

On June 2, 1907, William J. Fryer Jr. died at the age of sixty-five in his home in New Providence, New Jersey. "During a long period of years, within which occurred the most wonderful transition in building methods that American history has marked, or the mind can conceive of for the future, Mr. Fryer was in the very forefront of events . . . He was . . . a man of high intellectual power, of a forceful nature and a very useful citizen."[282]

10 Political Defeat That Could Have Been Avoided: The Real Story of the Defeat of the 1892 New York Architects' Licensing Law

I F YOU THINK OF THE NEW YORK CITY BUILDING LAW of 1892 as the main attraction in the center of a legislative three-ring circus, consider that the two smaller rings were occupied by the Buildings Department amendment and Assembly Bill, No. 451, "An Act to Regulate the Practice of Architecture." Simultaneously the three proposals, having critical importance to the future business and practice of architecture, were vying for the attention and approval of New York state legislators. Of the three, only two became law.

On April 4, 1892, a letter was submitted to New York's newly elected Democratic governor, Roswell Pettibone Flower, from five respected New York City architects. They objected to the architects' licensing law, which, having already been passed by the state Senate and Assembly, rested on his desk awaiting his signature. The letter took issue with the legislation point by point. The legal flaws framed into the language of the law were concisely discussed, along with a cogent analysis of both the intended and unintended potential consequences of various provisions drawn up by those with a vested interest in its passage.

So persuasive was the letter that it convinced Governor Flower not to sign the bill. He returned it to committee and asked that the objections be addressed. Two years of lobbying by two New York state chapters of the AIA, aided by the Architectural League and the New York City AIA chapter, were thus stymied, though not at that moment summarily defeated.

How did just five architects gain sufficient influence to sway what appeared to be a strongly supported public policy decision? Why did they

try to defeat the first state architects' licensing law to reach any U.S. governor's desk? What other special interests were connected to the passage of
this first licensing law? What were the consequences of the development
of public policy on the practice of architecture?

Architects led the fight both for and against the licensing law. Architects drafted the law. Architects effectively lobbied the state assembly to pass
the law. But this is only the surface of the story. Many public and hidden
agendas were in play. The Buffalo and Western New York chapters of the
AIA, which had initiated and pushed the bill through the legislative process,
clearly underestimated the exact nature and extent of the opposition to its
licensing bill.

This political defeat, which is exactly what it was, must be understood in the context of the political life of a place and its leaders, and their
relationship to the pressing issues of the day. Interpretation of this event via
the self-referential context of architectural history would preclude a deeper
consideration of how the precedent of law operates upon the body politic,
of how a proposed law's singular power to effect wider economic and social
development affects its chances of coming into legal force. It also illustrates
how real power is or can be wielded.

The idea of licensing the practice of architecture was not a response to
demands from civil authorities or from business leaders or even marketplace
forces. It came from within the profession itself and was motivated by a
legitimate need to create and maintain professional standards of practice.
As such, it was a valid goal. In creating a legal mechanism to both define
and regulate a critical profession's practice, the overriding interests of society regarding such a mechanism must be adequately balanced against the
self-interests of a profession, achieved solely at the public's expense.

The legislative inexperience of the architect-proponents may have
been a contributing factor in the bill's failure. But since two years were spent
working with legislators on the nuts and bolts of framing the legislation,
other factors must have contributed to its failure to be signed into law. This
is where the politics of law making and the political process converge. In
the case of the 1892 Act to Regulate the Practice of Architecture, neither the
politics of the issue nor the political process was adequately anticipated or
astutely addressed.

There were many players in this drama of earnest ambitions and missed opportunities. Let's start with the governor:

Roswell Pettibone Flower (1835–1899) was a man of integrity and great political skill. He was a leader at the national level, having served three terms in Congress, two of which immediately preceded his first term as governor of New York. He had been a member of the House Ways and Means Committee and the congressional committee on the pending 1893 World's Fair, which he had fought very hard to win for his state.

Flower chaired the Democratic Congressional Campaign Committee in 1882 and again in 1890, running a spectacularly successful campaign that achieved the largest Democratic congressional majority to that date. As a result, he was considered for the 1892 Democratic presidential nomination. It went to the former president, Grover Cleveland. As a congressman, he had the reputation of being the most thoroughly informed and prepared of his committee colleagues.

Flower, an upstate man from Watertown, New York, had a deep regard for rural life, though he went south to New York City to make his fortune in banking and brokerage. He also happened to be an expert on the city's infrastructure, having been appointed by the previous governor, David Hill, to serve on the commission overseeing the construction of the new "subway" utility tunnels under Sixth Avenue. For this task, he traveled to several major American cities on a fact-finding mission to determine the technical requirements of installing electrical, telephone, and telegraph cables under the city's streets.[283]

Flower obtained and weighed all the facts before he made a decision and was not someone who could be easily manipulated or crudely intimidated. Without a doubt, he understood precisely the wider implications of the precedent-setting bill he was expected to sign.

Among the five architects who urged Governor Flower not to sign the licensing bill was the influential iron architect-engineer and building code expert William J. Fryer Jr. Fryer was the man of the moment, with his revisions to New York City's Building Law and possible appointment to a new State Building Law Commission pending before the legislature. The considerable force of his credibility was amplified by his close political and personal links to Governor Flower. It is thus easy to presume that he was the ring leader and likely author of the letter, particularly as it states in the first of its ten points: "The need of the times is good building laws. It is the ignorance of construction of building that the state needs to guard against. Architects must be compelled by suitable building laws to plan buildings safely . . . and the truth is that the overwhelming majority of architects do not know how to build safely and well, no matter how competent they may be to draw pretty pictures or answer correctly on the five orders of architecture."[284]

Fryer's signature was followed by that of his fellow Building Law Revisions Committee and Board of Examiners member, architect-builder Cornelius O'Reilly (1835–1903).

At the moment that this dispute was taking place, New York was preparing for the cornerstone-laying ceremony for President Ulysses S. Grant's Tomb, which took place on April 27, 1892, on the late president's 70th birthday. Ground had been broken a year earlier on the same day. O'Reilly was the chairman of the Grant's Tomb Building Committee and was responsible for overseeing its construction. His position at the top of the building and construction business was not open to question.[285]

Since the 1860s, Cornelius O'Reilly & Brothers had been one of New York City's leading building firms, contractors for top architects and real-estate developers. O'Reilly, with his brother Michael, also built and owned various types of buildings for themselves. In 1876 the brothers opened the Lexington Central Storage Warehouse in a large, five-story facility on East 44th Street near Grand Central Station.

O'Reilly practiced as an architect from at least 1880. In 1890 he designed, built, and operated another much larger, nine-story storage warehouse, O'Reilly Storage, on 123rd Street and St. Nicolas Avenue in West Harlem. The words *Fire Proof* were emblazoned in bold letters under the company name on its façade.

While superintending the final stage of Our Lady of Lourdes Church, which he had designed and was building on 142nd Street between Convent and Amsterdam Avenues, O'Reilly fell from the scaffolding and died of a fractured skull on April 29, 1903. This church was built with salvaged elements recovered from the demolition of Peter Wight's Academy of Design, parts of a chapel from James Rewick's St. Patrick's Cathedral, and John

Kellum's famed marble mansion for A.T. Stewart on Fifth Avenue.[286]

The widowed father of nine children, O'Reilly was a devout Catholic and a generous patron of the church and various charities. He served on several boards, including a bank, hospital, and college, and was an anti-Tammany Democrat. According to his obituary in *American Architect and Building News*, "O'Reilly was one of the most respected of the sturdy immigrants who have made their way in New York, not by political corruption, but by integrity and industry, to responsibility and wealth."[287]

The next signature on the letter was that of the architect-builder Thomas Graham, who had, after "a liberal education and training in the offices of one of the most prominent New York architects," joined his father's firm.[288] Charles Graham & Sons designed and built residential, hotel, and commercial architecture in Manhattan. Charles Graham started his practice in 1852 on West Houston Street and is known today for the Greek Revival Northampton County Courthouse (1860–1861), perched atop a steep hill in Easton, Pennsylvania. The Graham firm also practiced in northern New Jersey, with several lovely churches to its credit.

In 1885 the firm's office and its fully equipped woodworking factory were located on East 43rd Street. By 1892 Thomas Graham had formed a joint partnership with his father and took over management of the firm. At the time of the letter, Graham was completing the Graham Hotel at 89th Street and Madison Avenue and actively developing the Upper East Side of Manhattan.[289] Graham was also an anti-Tammany Democrat and a member of the Municipal Organization of the City of New York, along with Fryer and O'Reilly.[290]

John A. Wood (1837–1910) was the next signatory to the protest letter. A popular and talented Poughkeepsie architect, Wood was born and raised in Bethel, New York. He started his career in Poughkeepsie around 1863, before moving his practice to New York City. Wood was self-employed and practiced extensively in the Catskills region and in New York City from 1871 to 1910. He was a prolific designer, much in demand at the height of his career, and known for his luxury resort hotels, churches, residential and commercial buildings, factories, and public buildings, including theaters, almshouses, armories, railroad terminals, courthouses, schools, and libraries. In addition to designing many of the buildings that constitute the

commercial centers of Poughkeepsie and Kingston, New York, and Hones-
dale, Pennsylvania, he was also active in Georgia, South Carolina, Florida,
and, possibly, also in Havana, Cuba.

Wood's clients were the leading industrialists and businessmen of the
region, including brewery owner and founder of Vassar College for Women,
Matthew Vassar, and his nephews, Harvey Eastman, founder and owner of
the Eastman Business College, and the influential Thomas Cornell, owner
of steamships and railroads and a U.S. congressman.

Wood preferred to handle virtually all the aspects of a building project
personally. He practiced in a highly entrepreneurial manner and was often
hands-on regarding all details, from financing and land acquisition to con-
tracting, materials purchase, and daily on-site supervision. Occasionally he
engaged in real estate and banking ventures.

One of Wood's important early commissions, completed in 1866, was
Vassar College's Riding School and Calisthenium, designed to house the
first collegiate physical education program for women. All that remains of
this building is its eclectic, arched Victorian façade, which has been incorporated into Cesar Pelli's postmodern Vassar Center for Drama and Film,
which opened in 2003.[291]

Architectural historian Annon Adams of Poughkeepsie has identified
Wood as the architect of the Ponckhockie Union Chapel, built in 1870, in
the Roundout section of Kingston, New York. This church is the earliest
known example in the United States of construction using concrete reinforced with iron and is listed on the National Register of Historic Places.[292]
Today John A. Wood is barely remembered as the architect of the Tampa
Bay Hotel, an extravagant Moorish Revival winter resort built by railroad
and shipping tycoon Henry B. Plant. This grand hotel, which covers six
acres, opened to great public fanfare on February 5, 1891. It had 511 rooms
and cost $2.5 million to build and $500,000 to furnish. The hotel was fitted with private baths, electric lights, and telephones. It was built using steel
reinforced, poured concrete and advertised as fireproof.

Throughout the Spanish-American War, the Tampa Bay Hotel was the
headquarters for the U.S. Army and housed the officers of Teddy Roosevelt's
Rough Riders. Now called Plant Hall, the hotel is the home of the University of Tampa. The building has survived remarkably intact; one original

wing of the hotel is maintained as the Henry B. Plant Museum. The building has been designated a National Landmark.[293]

Francis Hatch Kimball (1845–1919), the last to sign the protest letter, remains the architect with the highest profile and most professional acclaim of the five. A native of Kennebunk, Maine, Kimball served in the Civil War and afterward trained in architecture in Boston with Louis P. Rogers. His work in the firm took him to Hartford, Connecticut, where he stayed on to practice on his own. In the mid-1870s, Kimball traveled to London to work with renowned British architect William Burges, as his superintendent of building for Burges's design of the campus of Trinity College in Hartford. In 1879 Kimball opened his office in Manhattan and partnered with Gothic Revivalist architect Thomas Wisedell for five years.

Kimball was already one of New York City's preeminent architects when the letter was written, having designed several major Broadway theaters, along with churches, residences, and commercial and corporate structures, including the 1889 nine-story, terra-cotta embellished Corbin Building on Johns Street in Lower Manhattan. In 1892, having just completed his beautiful, Venetian Gothic Montauk Club, a prestigious private gentlemen's club near Prospect Park in Brooklyn, Kimball's career was poised to take a quantum leap. Before forming his new architecture partnership with George Kramer Thompson in 1892, "According to Fryer, Kimball had used ordinary caisson foundations for his Fifth Avenue Theater on West 28th Street (1891–92; demolished), possibly the first in the city to employ that technology."[294]

By winning the design competition for the Manhattan Life Insurance Company building that year, Kimball and Thompson became pioneering designers of New York's first skyscrapers. Located at 64-66 Broadway and begun in September 1893, this 348-foot-tall building was the tallest building in the world when completed in 1895. The architects had to convince the authorities in the Department of Buildings that their new design for the foundation was going to do the job safely and permanently.[295] Kimball and Thompson's development of deep concrete pneumatic-caisson foundations revolutionized high-rise building construction and solved a host of technical and construction problems inherent to building in Manhattan. Francis H. Kimball's remaining early New York City skyscrapers are now important architectural landmarks.[296]

These architect-authors of the protest letter were connected through the building permit process that brought them to the Board of Examiners. But they were also linked by their advanced use of iron, steel, and concrete in framing multistoried buildings. For instance, even Wood, the eclectic Victorian designer, used steel girders for floor support and a cast-iron façade on the dry-goods emporium he designed at 691 Broadway in 1884 for iron merchant Albert Tower. He designed the adjoining building in 1887 to match its twin. Both are in full commercial use today.[297]

In their letter, these five architects objected to the licensing act on the grounds that the bill was poorly worded and intentionally vague in key passages, and that it overstepped its primary regulatory purpose. The main point of objection was that the state should not be in the business of regulating aesthetic matters; rather, its primary responsibility was to ensure the public's safety. While no laws yet existed in any country to license architects, every major city, on an international basis, regulated building to conserve the public interest.

The bill's intention to exclude out-of-state architects from practicing in New York, except in special design competitions (Sec. 14, line 6), was deemed "a restriction on trade, and is therefore against public policy. It is against a class of laws the United States Courts have brushed away." This objection could also be read as a veiled reference to the Sherman Anti-Trust Act of 1890, which Roswell P. Flower had recently voted on as a New York congressman. Restriction of trade was a political "hot button," and it appeared to the protesters that the AIA's licensing bill *intended* to do just that.

The obvious dilemma of restricting the right to practice in the state was that it could backfire on the framers of the bill. The letter pointed out that New York architects were routinely working all over the country. But by shutting out nonresident architects from competing in New York state, the law could result in punitive reprisals. If the bill was signed into law, other states might follow New York's lead and enact similar restrictions on practice. "Shall architects in this state cut off their brethren in other states and not expect to be cut off from practice in return?" This objection drew sharp attention to the negative political and economic repercussions at a national level. A pragmatic solution to this complicated aspect of licensing the practice of architecture would take decades to resolve.

The law made no distinction between the urban architect and the country builder who normally utilized reputable architects' pattern books. Nor was it "in the interest of residents in small towns and agricultural portions of this state that builders should be prohibited from preparing plans and practicing as architects as well as builders . . . Many capable architects are former carpenters or masons." Further, provincial architects and big-city designers "are put on the same plane, and must show themselves equally capable, as a licensee can practice anywhere in the state after he receives his parchment." The obvious fear was that high-powered city architects would clear from the field of competition most small town architects and builders.

The bill also failed "to make an architect responsible to an owner for the safety of his building." Since all architects' plans were extensively examined by civil authorities, it seemed "somewhat superfluous to examine the architect . . . as well. A candidate might know much about 'architecture' and very little about construction."

The signatories objected to other bad features of the bill. A license could be revoked for "gross negligence and recklessness" (Sec. 11. line 3) but not, in the author's words, for "gross ignorance." Dishonest practices would also result in the loss of one's license, though what exactly this meant was undefined, leaving open the possibility that issues unrelated to the practice of architecture could be used to disbar a practitioner. And in order to administer disbarment, the bill would create "an architectural court, with the power to issue subpoenas and to compel the attendance and testimony of witnesses (Sec. 13)." This meant any builder or designer who used the title architect without first being granted a license would "be deemed guilty of a misdemeanor!"

The attempt to criminalize the practice of architecture under the pretense of licensing its practice was a step too far for the protesting architects: "These propositions are ridiculous. Our country is too new, and the demand for ability in men as builders and architects too great to restrict the action of individuals within proper lines of enterprise by any such law."

Since all the signers would be grandfathered a license under the proposed law, accusations of sour grapes did not hold; their sole purpose was to make known the ill effects of the bill, which many who supported it did not fully understand: "Only one side of the question was heard by the Assembly and the Senate. We respectfully ask you to veto the bill."[298]

The idea of creating a regulatory system for licensing New York's architects got rolling in the spring of 1888, when architect Albert F. D'Oench, superintendent of the Fire Department's Bureau of Buildings, made an impassioned speech on the subject at an Architectural League dinner. In attendance, along with architect John Beverly Johnson, president of the Architectural League, were the AIA chapter president, Edward Kendall; AIA national and local secretary, A.J. Bloor; and the Fire Department's architect and AIA officer, Napoleon LeBrun.

In his speech, D'Oench said that, in his three years on the Board of Examiners, fully seventy-five percent of the 12,921 plans put forward were rejected. Mistakes in drawings could be easily rectified, but the more troubling problem was the frequency of defective design in construction. D'Oench felt that this unacceptably high rate of rejection was "due to the fact that there was no legal restriction upon anyone calling himself an architect who wanted to." He stated his belief that "the days are past when the rendering of a drawing is all that is required of an architect. We are of an era in which buildings are erected, the intricacy of which in former times no one dreamed of. The most economic use of materials is demanded and the strains to which they may be subjected are carried to the utmost limit. It is my idea that laws should be passed aiming at the control of this dangerous liberty—in short, the licensing of architects . . . Responsibility ought to certainly be centered somewhere, and the architect as the designer is the one who should be held to account if an accident occurs."[299]

This central idea, expressed by Superintendent D'Oench, of architects' accountability for safe building design—and their liability for its failure—was one of the elements missing from the licensing bill, which the 1892 protest letter took issue with. D'Oench's speech met with general agreement from the nearly 100 architects present; it was agreed that a licensing law was needed and should be presented to the legislature "at its next session."[300]

Two and a half years later, in November 1890, the Western New York chapter of the AIA unanimously decided to press forward a bill that would provide "for a State Board of Examiners for students in architecture and the granting of licenses to the qualified, the same as in the case of lawyers and doctors."[301] This began a long, concerted campaign to get a licensing bill

framed and approved by the assembly. It required the total devotion of financial resources and lobbying efforts by the leadership and members of the
Western New York and Albany chapters. The proponents were highly
optimistic that the bill would be passed into law.

According to the 1892 annual report of the Western New York AIA, the
licensing bill was submitted to the state legislature for a second time on January 28, 1892, and scheduled for public hearings before the Committee on
General Laws on February 4. On January 9, the AIA Board of Directors
resolved a motion to support the efforts of architecture societies nationwide
to "place the practice of the profession of architecture on a footing similar
to that enjoyed by the professions of medicine, pharmacy, and the law, and
that the various Chapters of the Institute be requested to do all in their
power to further the passage of the legislative enactments to that effect."[302]

The Western New York chapter president, W.W. Carlin, attended the
very next meeting of the Architectural League to recruit more allies in the
lobbying effort. Russell Sturgis, president of the League, appointed a committee of five, including architect William Burnet Tuthill (1855–1929), to
speak in Albany. Tuthill doubled as the representative from the New York
City chapter of the AIA. Carlin said at the meeting "that the bill had been
lost last year because the Legislature believed that the architects of New York
were opposed to it, and this seemed to be emphasized through their not taking any concerted action in the matter."[303]

It seemed somewhat expedient for the New York chapter to send "one
of the younger members of the chapter" (as described by A.J. Bloor in the
1892 annual report) to represent its interests. Tuthill was thirty-seven years
old, relatively unknown, and had, with the assistance of Richard M. Hunt
and Dankmar Adler, just completed the major work of his career, Carnegie
Hall.[304]

Why did the most influential chapter in the state not send one or more
of its well-known, senior members to Albany to correct any mistaken
impressions held by the legislature? Perhaps Napoleon LeBrun could have
answered that question, since he and Tuthill composed the chapter's executive Committee. LeBrun was also chairman of the chapter's Committee
on Examinations.[305]

There had been strong opposition to the bill in both houses of the legislature, and Carlin was required to invest a great deal of effort to "reconcile the real and fancied opposition" of legislators. The bill was finally passed, in early April, on its second presentation without additional objections and was forwarded to the governor's office for his signature, only to be confronted by Governor Flower's unanticipated reservations about several of the bill's provisions.

This item appeared on April 9, 1892, in the *Real-Estate Record and Building Guide*: "Only one side of the question was heard by the Committees on General Laws of the Assembly and Senate. The opponents of the measure are taking their innings now in the shape of submitting to the Governor reasons why the profession would not be benefited, and the public, including many New York City architects and country builders quite generally would be greatly injured by such a law being placed on the statute books."

The protest letter, dated April 4, and the legislation must have arrived on the governor's desk at about the same time. The bill's architects hastily met with the governor and his secretary and "developed some of his reasons for being opposed to the measure." A compromise was reached, and the bill was recalled "to meet as far as possible the objections which had been raised . . . without destroying the salient features of the measure."[306] All was not lost—yet.

On April 16, 1892, the *Real-Estate Record and Building Guide* reported that the architects' licensing act had been recalled and was being amended to meet the objections raised by Governor Flower. The same issue reported that the governor had signed the new building law and that progress continued on the bill to create a State Commission on Building Law.

According to the article on the licensing act, "One of the changes will probably be to confine the operations of the bill to cities and to place the licensing power in the local authorities. Unless the bill had been withdrawn it would have been vetoed. As it is, there is but a slim chance of its passage during the few remaining days of the session."[307] But the bill was quickly amended and rushed through both houses in the closing days of the session and was returned once again to the desk of Governor Flower for his signature.

Despite the testimony by architects representing various cities and towns across the state and a variety of architecture associations, a letter and

telegraph campaign to legislators and the governor, and a petition supporting the bill signed by seventy-seven New York City architects and presented
by the New York City chapter of the AIA, Governor Flower was not per-
suaded of the bill's overriding merit.308

It seems that, while legislators were attempting to address the modi-
fications that the governor had requested, a new amendment had been
added to the bill. According to the *Real-Estate Record and Building Guide*,
"One of the amendments provides that the American Institute of Architects shall appoint the seven persons to constitute the State Board of
Architects *instead* of the appointments being given to the Regents of the
University of this State. Whether the Governor will now sign or veto the
bill is open to question."309

Regardless of any other concessions that might have been made to
address the governor's specific objections, this last-ditch move to comman-
deer the regulatory power of the state by taking total control of the State
Board of Architects, thus usurping the governor's power to make the
appointments, showed the AIA architects to be ludicrously naïve or, worse,
arrogant and disingenuous. If Fryer and his four colleagues only suspected
a hidden agenda in the language of the bill to restrict the trade of architects,
the governor was handed direct evidence of it by the bill's own authors. As
an unaccountable, by invitation only, private fraternal organization that represented but a fraction of the practicing architects in the state of New York,
the Institute had written a state law that would deliver to itself exclusive control over an essential profession. In other words, a monopoly.

At noon on May 21, 1892, bills not yet signed by the governor would not
become law. Four hundred forty-seven bills were awaiting his signature; all
but ninety-six were signed. Forty-four of those were rejected with a mem-
oranda of disapproval, and the balance left to die without comment. Assembly Bill, No. 451, An Act to Regulate the Practice of Architecture, was put
to rest in silence, judged as "defective in form or matter, opposed by local
authorities, or rendered unnecessary by the enactment of other bills."310 The
New York Times duly noted the bill's failure in light of the fact that its sponsor, Mr. Guenther, was a Democrat from Erie County.

According to statistics published in 1954 by the AIA, in 1890 more than
1,500 architects were practicing in New York state. By 1898, thirty-seven

percent of the 362 students enrolled in accredited schools of architecture nationwide attended schools in New York state.[311] Clearly, any legislation passed in New York regarding the practice or building of architecture would—indeed did—affect American society as a whole.

The humiliating defeat of the 1892 Act to License the Practice of Architecture in New York was deeply felt by those who had worked hard to bring higher standards of professional practice to architecture. When Edward H. Kendall, of New York, assumed the presidency of the AIA that same year, he made these recent events a topic of his keynote address to the annual convention in Chicago.

In his remarks, he tied the issue of building law to that of licensing, drawing the conclusion that opposition to the New York licensing act was based in the "false idea that it is the hope and intention of its professional advocates that the license shall gradually precede and eventually annul the building laws." This assertion was preceded by his lengthy praise for the Boston Society of Architects' recent participation in the process to frame building law in its city, a sentiment prefaced by, "While the New York Chapter has more duties and greater authority under the building law than the Boston Society has under its law . . ."[312]

The 1892 report of the board of directors of the AIA also dealt with the law's defeat in somewhat contemptuous tones: "No one believed that a man as enlightened and as capable as Governor Flower would fail to note the value to the people of his state of the enactment of such a law. And we fear that among the most potent factors which prevented the governor from signing the bill . . . were the inexplicably narrow-minded objections and utterly unwarranted assertions placed before him by Messers. William J. Fryer, Cornelius O'Reilly, Thomas Graham, J.A. Wood and Francis H. Kimball, persons calling themselves architects. It is especially to be regretted that among these are several who have shown by executed work that the assumption by them of the title 'architect' is not unwarranted."[313] (Didn't all American architects assume the title in 1892?)

The Western New York chapter reported that the "significant fact in connection with this is the first two names signed to the opposition report were those first mentioned by the governor as members of a commission to formulate a uniform building law for all the cities in the state."[314] Both the

Western and Buffalo chapters had emptied their treasuries, and their members were out-of-pocket in covering the cost of a two-year lobbying effort to pass this first licensing law. The New York City chapter wasn't so inconvenienced.

The AIA did not address any number of issues surrounding the bill's defeat: the substance of Governor Flower's objections to the bill; the highly conflicted relationship of its civic representative, Napoleon LeBrun; and LeBrun's intimate involvement in New York's two major legislative bills directly affecting the practice of architecture in the state. The fact that the expert opinions of architects were, indeed, respected by politicians was openly regretted by President Kendall when the AIA's conception of public policy was openly questioned through the democratic process.

Nevertheless, the architecture profession's positive impact on public policy in the year 1892 was indeed profound. Those architects who understood how to write a law, argue and defend its merits, and debate the fine points of legal precedent and whose veracity and judgments were respected got laws passed.

Fryer and O'Reilly were joined by three upstanding designers typical of the practitioners for whom the licensing law was intended. Each gentleman represented a sector of the building business that could have been adversely affected by various sections of the bill as originally written. Each brought to the protest his network of associates, clients, and political allies. All put their reputations on the line, inviting controversy and criticism from colleagues.

Belated Lessons to Be Learned

This case, in which five dissenting voices formed an alliance powerful enough to drown out the din of 110 members of the AIA, sheds light on several fundamental political principles:

1. Knowing how to write a *good* law is an essential skill which, if not learned, can have serious consequences. Responsible policy makers know that, more often than not, killing a poorly conceived and/or badly written law is preferable to passing it.
2. Know all the players in the game, including all interested parties (pro and con) and all the lawmakers and their policy stances. Understand

the scope of related existing laws and know the territory and prevailing attitudes where a new law will take effect—do the homework. Roswell P. Flower and William J. Fryer did theirs, while the leadership of the AIA did not.

3. Don't put all your eggs into one basket. Attempt to form alliances with all the stakeholders, rather than view all other interests and opinions as merely opposing.

4. Any failure to get legislation passed into law is an opportunity to learn from the specifics of what went wrong and to hone policy formation, legislative lobbying, and people skills. To miss the critical value of self-analysis by blaming the opposition for your failure only sets you up for the next defeat. From the defeat of the 1892 licensing bill, it took another twenty-three years for New York state to license architects.

5. If at first you don't succeed, try, and try again! Getting a law passed on the first few rounds is nothing short of miraculous, so surrendering to expediency provides no advantage in either the short or long run. After all, it took twelve years of continuous work and incremental revisions to get the comprehensive 1892 New York City Building Law written and on the books.

11 | Architectural Leadership at the End of the Gilded Age

I N THE CLOSING YEARS OF THE 1880s, New York state's business community and its political representatives at the local, state, and national levels battled ferociously against Illinois to convince Congress to hold the World's Columbian Exposition in New York City. But Chicago and its dynamic business leaders and architects won out. The loss—and the gain—of that political plum had unforeseen consequences for the profession and the nation.

In the aftermath of Chicago's Great Fire in 1871, the city was able to attract a bumper crop of talented architects from home and abroad who contributed to its rebirth. The consequences of the Great Fire were manifold. Technical innovation flourished in response to the relentless demand for new buildings, thus pushing construction and engineering standards higher than ever before.

The New York City–based American Institute of Architects' emulation of British-style exclusivity resulted in a small but elite membership. Consequently, the Institute's membership grew in inverse proportion to the exponential growth of the profession itself; "during the 1880s alone, the number of architects multiplied 2.4 times."[315] The Institute's sphere of influence beyond its affluent patrons was as limited as its membership numbers. This uncomfortable fact must have been driven home between 1885 and 1900 as the AIA's repeated attempts to initiate public policy changes met with minimal success.

Meanwhile, Chicago's profession rushed full steam ahead and formed its own professional association, the Western Association of Architects (WAA), in 1884. Regional professional organizations in midwestern and southern states, such as the Texas Society of Architects, founded in 1886, joined in affiliation with the WAA. Within four short years, membership in the WAA equaled that of the older East Coast organization, which had taken nearly three decades to gain its number. As well, in 1885, the WAA made the groundbreaking decision, in a unanimous vote, to induct America's first female professional architect, Louise Blanchard Bethune, of Buffalo, New York, into its ranks. She had opened her office in 1881 and cofounded the Buffalo Society of Architects in 1886, which became an AIA chapter in 1891.[316]

In 1886, when AIA President Thomas U. Walter's convention address "cited the formation of twelve new western architectural societies" and suggested the possibility of a "national confederation of architects,"[317] the Institute realized its future hegemony might be threatened. In view of these developments, the Institute sought a merger with its chief competitor in 1887. The Institute negotiated with the WAA, and the merger took place in Cincinnati in November 1889. As part of the deal, all WAA members retained the title of Fellow in the newly merged organization. Louise Bethune, who was the first woman accepted into the Institute in 1888, thus became its first female Fellow in 1889.

The merger cannily anticipated the coming world's fair. With the reincarnation of the Institute, now doubled in size to 465 members, came the enhanced prestige to firmly grasp the reins of a unique opportunity and to orchestrate it into an achievement with astounding impact on the national stage.[318]

The AIA had good cause to celebrate when it convened its annual convention at the Chicago World's Fair on July 31, 1893. The fair itself was a massive triumph, and five months earlier Congress had passed the Tarsney Act, finally opening the door for the federal government to contract with architects in the private sector. At the convention, and during the World's Congress of Architects held concurrently at the fair, the issue of creating a legal mechanism for licensing the practice of architecture continued to collide with the municipality- and state-based movements to develop building codes. The inadequacy of building standards was universally acknowledged, but there was little agreement on whether the licensing of practitioners or the creation of legally enforceable standards of safe construction was the better solution.

W.W. Carlin, president of the Western New York chapter, returned to the licensing issue to defend the components of the bill his chapter had failed to get passed into law the previous year. He dismissed "as too puerile to demand refutation" claims that licensing smacked of "trade-unionism" or that it would restrict trade between states or raise qualifications to a prohibitive level. He used an unattributed quote from the letter to Governor Roswell P. Flower by the protesting architects to make his point but misrepresented the statement by saying it was made by "people who believe that an architect is only a picture maker and decorator."[319]

Carlin conceded that no legal definition of architect yet existed and that "a system of examination" and a "standard of minimum qualifications necessary to the granting of a license" had not yet been constructed, but these were "problems which we believe are worthy of the most careful consideration and combined efforts of the brightest minds in our profession both at home and abroad."[320]

C.H. Blackall of Boston spoke on the "Influence of Building Laws on Architecture" and made the case that "if the practice of architecture could be so regulated that it would be as impossible for an incompetent architect to put up a building . . . then we could well afford to dispense with nine-tenths of our building regulation . . . our architecture today would be better and more substantial had such things as our building laws never been conceived."[321] Blackall argued that the title of architect should be "a high honor" echoing past "glories of Rome and of the Italian Renaissance" and that architects be accorded society's respect as "creators."[322]

But while Blackall called for society to accord architects the highest respect, he had nothing but contempt for the legislators who enacted the country's building laws, accusing them of knowing little at all about science, much less art. He also characterized those who administrated the laws, with few exceptions, as "ex-mechanics" about whom "the most that could be charitably said is that they are sometimes good-natured."[323] It takes a stunning lack of common sense and diplomacy to call for society's highest respect for architects while simultaneously insulting those with the power to deliver a good measure of that respect.

All this was background noise to the coming brouhaha over the implementation of the Tarsney Act. The bill had been marshaled through

Congress with the concerted lobbying of the Institute's most respected representatives and with the support of previous Supervising Architects of the Treasury William A. Potter, James G. Hill, and James Windrim, all AIA members. The outgoing supervising architect, W.J. Edbrooke, also an AIA man, expressed reservations about the act but supported it based on the recognition of the executive authority of the secretary of the treasury. The House of Representatives passed the bill in the summer of 1892, and the Senate, after hearing invited testimony from the architecture profession on January 10, 1893, amended and passed the Tarsney Act.[324]

The Institute's effort to open up federal building to the private sector had been going on for two decades. Beginning with fierce criticism of the monomaniacal supervising architect, Alfred B. Mullett, a long, drawn out, and unsuccessful campaign by the Institute to convince Congress to create a Bureau of Architecture was conducted from the 1870s onward, while the country's physical and economic expansion put enormous regional pressure on the government to provide civic buildings across the nation by the 1880s.

A bill was presented to Congress in 1884 to help relieve this problem by allowing private architects to compete for federal buildings with construction budgets over $50,000. As is always the case, the devil was in the details. Disagreements quickly arose. The AIA countered by submitting its own version of the bill. Treasury officials argued to maintain the existing system, since it had been organized to provide exacting service to meet "essential elements peculiar to public works as distinct from private works."[325]

It wasn't until a loyal AIA man, James Windrim, assumed the post of supervising architect that the Institute figured out how to pursue its aims with Congress. This time the effort was well coordinated and focused. Instead of trying to overhaul the whole government building department, the Institute simply created a legislative option allowing the secretary of the treasury to tender design of federal buildings to the private sector through architectural competitions. The bill was signed into law by outgoing Republican President Benjamin Harrison and went into effect under the second Democratic administration of Grover Cleveland.

On March 6, 1893, AIA Secretary Alfred Stone distributed copies of the new law to the membership, stating in his cover letter, "It is believed that . . . the best architects of the country will gladly participate in some of the competitions which it is hoped will result from the power placed in the hands of the Secretary of the Treasury by this bill."[326]

Though the federal government could now turn to the private sector for design services, it was not mandated to do so; rather, implementation of the Tarsney Act was under the complete discretionary control of the secretary of the treasury. "Unless there is some radical defect in the law," the AIA's board fully expected that the law would be "faithfully carried out."[327] But the Tarsney Act was a toothless law and soon turned into a hollow victory for the profession.

On March 22, 1893, the new secretary of the treasury, John G. Carlisle, called a meeting with the executive leadership of the AIA. Carlisle had served as Speaker of the House for three terms before becoming a senator from Kentucky. He resigned from the Senate to take up his cabinet post. The Tarsney Act, amended and passed while on his watch in the Senate, was now his to implement. Perhaps he recalled that his predecessor, Charles Foster, had warned the Senate at its hearings on the Tarsney Act that any change in the system operated by the supervising architect's office should be taken under serious advisement.[328]

Carlisle requested a written statement from the Institute detailing the specifics of its recommendations for implementing the new law. Instead of sending Carlisle a set of guidelines for establishing a broad national competition scheme, the Institute called for what appeared to be a self-serving cartel arrangement, in which no more than five well-known architects would be invited to compete in a national design commission, judged by the supervising architect and two outside architects appointed by the treasury secretary on the advice of the Institute.

The winning architect would not only be guaranteed the job, but he and his deputies would be employed by the government to produce all drawings and to superintend all construction at the same fees and rates of pay they would receive in private practice. The Institute also expressed the hope that the next session of Congress would amend the act to include payment of competition expenses to the selected competitors and for "such professional advice as the Secretary . . . may require in preparing the necessary instructions and in selecting the best submitted plan." The Institute offered to assist the treasury secretary by nominating architects for competitions and volunteering its members as competition jurors; that is, "until the bill can be amended, members of the Institute would make no charges for services, whether as advisors or jurors."[329]

By the end of July 1893, when President Cleveland's newly appointed supervising architect, Jeremiah O'Rourke, gave his talk, "On Architectural Practice of the United States Government," to the World's Congress of Architects, no action or official response to the Institute's proposal regarding the Tarsney Act had been received from the secretary of the treasury.

O'Rourke, a Fellow of the Institute, was an accomplished architect. Born in Dublin, Ireland, in 1833, he was educated at Dublin's Government School of Design and upon graduation in 1850, immigrated to America, where he established his office in Newark, New Jersey, and specialized in ecclesiastical architecture. Before his appointment as supervising architect, he had been the Treasury Department's superintendent for the Custom House and Post Office in Newark.[330]

O'Rourke took the opportunity of this major gathering of his peers to give a thorough briefing on the operations of his office. It is clear from his remarks that he was refuting each one of the complaints regularly leveled by the AIA at the Office of the Supervising Architect's design and management of federal architecture. O'Rourke pointed out that his office's total service "never exceeds five percent on the cost of the buildings erected," and that the professional services rendered by the supervising architect "would easily net $100,000 a year" in the private sector. For his service to the nation, the supervising architect received "the munificent salary of $4,500."[331]

O'Rourke strenuously objected to the AIA's tactic of denigrating the Treasury Department and the quality of its architectural work. He also deeply resented its assault on the professionalism and authority of his office. But without O'Rourke's willing promotion of the Tarsney Act to his superiors, the AIA could not hope to gain influence over the commissioning of federal architecture.

This internal professional conflict soon erupted over the design of a federal building in Buffalo. Correspondence between O'Rourke and Alfred Stone, secretary of the AIA, was printed in the press and then the gloves came off. AIA President Daniel Burnham wrote to Secretary Carlisle, threatening to go to Congress to introduce a mandatory enactment clause in the Tarsney Act. Big mistake.

On March 19, 1894, the *New York Times* reported the controversy surrounding the commissioning of public buildings: "Treasury officials say there is one phase of the controversy between Secretary Carlisle and the American Institute of Architects that has not figured in the recent acrid correspondence as made public. . . . the American Institute of Architects aims to compete in designs for all public buildings built by the United States. . . . this nice little plum in the shape of commissions can reasonably be supposed to have quite as much weight with the architects as their patriotic desire to improve the character and style of public buildings."

The article quoted an unnamed Treasury official who predicted that the government would find itself adjudicating competition between architects who "would indulge in a free fight to have their own design selected . . . political influence would be brought to bear on the Secretary of the Treasury and . . . his time would be taken up in settling architectural rivalries . . . In no event can the Government agree to shoulder responsibility for public buildings designed and built by parties over whom it has no control. This is aside from the extra cost involved, which, with the scheme of President Burnham, would exceed by 85 per cent, the present cost in commissions alone."[332]

The AIA attempted a compromise with the Treasury in the spring of 1894 and was able to frame a new piece of legislation to amend the Tarsney Act. The McKaig Bill submitted to Congress that June was accompanied by an Institute report that again cast the Office of the Supervising Architect in a particularly unfavorable light. At the same time, attacks on the Office of the Supervising Architect by Institute partisans, particularly Washington, D.C., architect Glenn Brown, were increasingly shrill, leaping from waspish hyperbole into seriously antagonistic territory. Brown's public relations campaign accused the government of wasting the taxpayers' money and charged that its architecture "shall debase public taste." Injected into this vitriol was the suggestion that the AIA needed a stronger presence in the capital.[333]

The McKaig Bill died in committee in March 1895. O'Rourke, who resigned after eighteen months of relentless public bickering over the issue, blamed the amendment's failure on the deliberate misrepresentation of the facts proffered in support of the legislation. Apparently, by inference, these statements reflected poorly on "the common sense and intelligence of the members of the Committee on Public Buildings and Grounds."334 Necessary support was lost from both political parties.

Amendment of the Tarsney Act was revived by the end of the year with the introduction of the Aldrich Bill, a clone of the McKaig Bill, which traveled slowly through the system and was still sitting in the Senate at the end of 1896. These amendment bills were actually conceived as intermediate steps in the Institute's campaign to create a Bureau of Architecture to replace the existing system and over which it intended to exercise artistic and professional control.335

With the changeover to the Republican McKinley administration in 1897 and the subsequent appointment of Chicago banker Lyman Gage as secretary of the treasury in March of that year, all the controversy and lobbying over the Tarsney Act was rendered moot. Secretary Gage was the business leader most responsible for the huge success of the 1893 Chicago World's Fair. Moreover, he was an honorary member of the AIA and a close friend of Burnham. Comprehensive implementation of the Tarsney Act now seemed ensured.

The reorganization of the Office of the Supervising Architect helped cool tempers and redirect attention to getting business done. For the first time, the candidate for the top job in the department would have to pass a special civil service exam formulated for the position. The job went to a staff member, James Knox Taylor, who had the distinct advantage of several years of experience in the system.

The first major federal architectural competition for New York City's Custom House, which should have been the imprimatur on the Tarsney Act, instead bore out that unnamed Treasury official's cynical prediction made to the *New York Times* in 1894.

Cass Gilbert vs. Carrère & Hastings: The Ethical Battle over the U.S. Custom House

The AIA was single-minded in its assertion of the professional architect's dominant role in the nation's cultural hierarchy, and this assertion was a key element of all the public policy initiatives the AIA presented to its civic and professional counterparts. While the intelligentsia lionized the architect's place in society, many people did not accede to their version of the profession's status, perhaps because the conflicted self-image of the architect always seemed to bubble up to the surface when it was time to decide who was going to build an important building.

The case of *Cass Gilbert vs. Carrère & Hastings* over the New York City federal Custom House illustrates the collision of ethics with politics at the turn of the century. When the young midwestern architect Cass Gilbert was invited to participate in a national competition to design the new Custom House, his expectations were realistic. He knew he was up against some of the most talented and powerful of his peers. He knew his chance was a long shot. But Gilbert was a determined man. When his design was chosen, he was pleasantly surprised but not overly so. He had done his best and his best was superb.

But when he went to Washington, D.C., for what was supposed to be the formal award of the commission, he became embroiled in an intrigue of influence peddling, backstabbing, and straightforward intimidation, all aimed at wrenching the commission from him and handing it over to the runners-up, John Merven Carrère (1858–1911) and his partner, Thomas Hastings (1860–1929), principals of one of New York's most prestigious firms.

They met while attending the École des Beaux Arts. Carrère found employment with McKim, Mead & White just months after Cass Gilbert had left the firm. Hastings also worked for the firm, and together the two young architects had decided in 1885 to establish their own firm. Shortly before the Custom House competition, in a much larger field of competitors, Carrère & Hastings had won the competition for the newly endowed New York Public Library. McKim, Mead & White was among the three top finalists. The commission for the new federal Custom House would have been an enormous professional coup for the partners, coming on the heels of the much coveted library job.[336]

Gilbert's fight to maintain his fairly won commission was conducted with quiet dignity and unwavering principle. The story is recounted in Gilbert's frank letters to his wife, Julia, over many weeks of stressful negotiations. This power struggle between colleagues is an object lesson in professional ethics and conduct.

In preface to the tale, it must be noted that the profession's elite Beaux Arts establishment viewed the Tarsney Act as the means to a specific self-professed end, "of making an open distinction between the real leaders of the profession and the rank and file."337 The high-minded artistic motives used to justify this end could not conceal the bare-knuckled tactics employed to achieve it.

Cass Gilbert opened his office in New York City in early 1899 to oversee the construction of the Broadway Chambers Building. At the same time, the new Custom House was going to be tendered out to a nominally national, but highly selective, architectural competition. Months before, Gilbert had traveled to Washington, D.C., and made a personal request to Secretary Gage that his name be included on the list of architects eligible to compete for major federal building projects under the new invitation-only competitions program.

The Custom House competition was announced on May 11, 1899, and Gilbert's firm was among the sixteen New York firms invited, with another two from Boston and two from Chicago. His former employer, McKim, Mead & White, was on the list, as well as several of the Institute's regional and national leaders, including past presidents Daniel H. Burnham and George B. Post. It was clear that the recipient of this prized commission would achieve or cement the kind of high-profile leadership position that all the participants craved.

It wasn't until Gilbert was actually chosen by the jury that his right to compete at all was suddenly challenged. Did Cass Gilbert deserve the job based on the superiority of his design, or was he merely an ambitious arriviste from the rank and file who had manipulated the competition unfairly to his advantage? James Knox Taylor, the supervising architect of the Treasury, was, after all, his former partner. Gilbert stood accused by a clique of the losing New York competitors of unethical and unprofessional conduct—in short, of cheating. They also pointed a finger at the three jury members, accusing them of fixing the outcome.

The issue of leadership was at the heart of the controversy. At a moment when his best work had been seen, judged, and chosen, Gilbert was

called "an interloping opportunist" by his peers.338 They publicly assassi-
nated his character and defamed his good name, in a letter to the president
of the United States. Gilbert didn't just have to produce the best design of
the twenty competitors; he also had to prove he was the best man of them
all. Was he capable of leading the profession? Could he take the heat?

Gilbert came from a family with a strong political history. He was born
in Zanesville, Ohio, in 1859 and was named for his great-uncle, Lewis
Cass, U.S. secretary of war under Andrew Jackson. Lewis Cass was the
Democratic candidate for president in the 1848 election, won by the Whig
party candidate, Zachary Taylor. His grandfather, a Yale-educated lawyer,
was one of Zaneville's first mayors. Gilbert's father, Samuel, was a surveyor
for the U.S. Coast Survey before the outbreak of the Civil War. During the
war, he served with valor and was promoted to the rank of brigadier-general of the 44th Ohio infantry. Samuel Gilbert's health was seriously weak-
ened by his war service and his subsequent work in Central America. He
died of tuberculosis in 1868.

The austere Presbyterian, Quaker, and Puritan values of Cass Gilbert's
upbringing were imparted amidst the boundless surroundings of America's
vast, open plains. His early career was devoted to building a new Midwest
metropolis, St. Paul, Minnesota, after study at MIT in Boston, a study tour
in Europe, and an apprenticeship in New York City. His time as assistant
to Stanford White put him in contact with many talented, creative people
in the arts. He was a cofounder of the Architectural League while working
in New York City. He took all this experience back home to the plains and
went to work.339

Gilbert's career path brought him back to Manhattan for a major
commission, the Broadway Chambers Building at 277 Broadway, on the corner across from A.T. Stewart's elegant Italianate department store. Gilbert's
building, with brightly colored terra-cotta and bronze ornamentation, was
designed to be the most exclusive commercial office space available in
town. While preparing and superintending construction, which began in
May 1899, Gilbert was also overseeing the firm's projects in the Midwest,
including the completion of the Minnesota State House. He did all this
while also designing the Alexander Hamilton Custom House to fit into a
city, and a site, rich in history. Its lyrical facade narrated the story of global

commerce and its monumental mass supported the delivery of vital services to the people. If Gilbert's true intentions were corrupted by blind
ambition, as his opposition claimed, it is significant that not one of them
attempted to find fault with the design itself.[340]

On September 20, 1899, Gilbert wrote to Julia that he had heard
through the grapevine that the competition jury was coming to New York
City to confer with Carrère and Hastings. He wrote that he wished he "had
a lobby" as they did, but "a sense of delicacy toward J.K.T. [Taylor, his former partner and the supervising architect] prevents my doing anything in
that direction and besides *I want to win on the merits of the thing* if at all"
[Gilbert's emphasis].[341]

Gilbert told her that he felt the whole competition system itself was
"wrong," because it placed the architect in an untenable position of financial and professional risk and "then to have to work by political methods to
hold what you may have won fairly by merit." He could not understand why
"McKim and other men of equal standing submit to it."[342] But Gilbert
placed his faith in the work itself and would not be discouraged.

On September 24, the finalists were announced to the press: Carrère &
Hastings and Cass Gilbert. The *New York Times* reported, "The Secretary
of the Treasury has written each of the firms suggesting certain modifica-
tions in the designs submitted . . . it is understood here that for business reasons one of the above firms may withdraw from the contest, in which case
the order will go to the other. Senator Platt of New York talked today with
the President about the new Custom House building at New York, and said
that he was only interested in getting the contract awarded to the best architects in the country."[343]

That same day Gilbert wrote home again and tried to explain the new
turn of events to his wife. He told of being summoned to meet with the jury
and the other finalists in the Murray Hill Hotel. After so much anxiety over
the outcome, he went there "always holding fast to myself the thought of
God's strength behind and above and through all. Excited but calm—
fearing nothing; . . . having absolute self control."[344] The jury had already
asked the two finalists to consider partnering on the project, and Gilbert had
"steadily declined," but juror Frank Miles Day asked them again to consider
whether they could "combine" before the jury delivered its final decision.

Gilbert described the moment: "I waited for Carrère to answer. He answered in a low voice—hoarse—so hoarse that I, sitting beside him, could scarcely hear what he said—that he would have to consult with Hastings, that Hastings was out of town and it would require until tomorrow to answer. Day looked at me for my reply. I said that this idea had originated with Hastings, that at first I was indisposed toward it but there were no men whom I more highly honored and would be more willing to work with. That I was willing to combine if the jury wished it and Mr. Carrère could answer immediately; but for *me*—rather than pass another such a day I would take their answer *now!* And win or lose by myself alone" [Gilbert's emphasis].345

Day looked to Carrère for an answer and got none. The verdict was then read. Cass Gilbert had been chosen. "Dead silence followed. Then Carrère turned heavily to me and offered congratulations. Rising, I put my arm around his shoulder to comfort him while overcome, not by exultation, but profound sympathy. . . ."346

Before leaving the meeting, the architects were asked not to discuss the outcome until it had been confirmed by the Treasury Department, "as otherwise the political leaders might attempt to upset it," and therefore he cautioned his wife not to celebrate just yet. But at the end of the letter, after describing the preparations taking place in Manhattan for the grand naval parade for Admiral Dewey, he couldn't resist telling Julia what this commission would mean to their lives: "We are rich. This fee alone will be over $130,000 and perhaps $200,000 . . . tell the children my ship has really come in just ahead of Admiral Dewey's."347

Samuel Gilbert wrote to his brother on September 25 from Washington, D.C., to pass on word from Jim Taylor that Senator Thomas Collier Platt, boss of New York state's Republican party machine, had met with President McKinley about the competition result and urged Cass "not to think of withdrawing and to make no move in that direction . . . [Taylor] has already argued with the Assistant Secretary that if this jury is not supported, and if their verdict is reversed, it will make it impossible for the government to get any gentleman of standing . . . to serve on any future juries . . . it will make it impossible to get any first-class man to enter competitions in the future, and that it will be an extremely bad precedent for the Department . . . if they allow politicians to interfere." Because of his conversation with Platt, the president sent word to the assistant secretary of the treasury to hold the decision until Secretary Gage's return.[348]

Cass wrote to Julia on September 27 that he had just learned that Taylor had, in fact, removed himself from the jury's deliberations after the elimination round, and the competition had moved to the finalist stage without his vote. And now Senator Platt would use the time he had gained by delaying the award to lay the groundwork for a "fight for a New York man. Now comes the political play."[349]

Cass decided to go to Washington to defend the decision. "I am not going to ask political help except as a protective measure. . . . there is no use of my backing out now, and I am not going into the fight unprepared . . . *I'd rather be friends than enemies with these men—but not at the price of honor"* [Gilbert's emphasis].[350] His friends and business colleagues in the Midwest and in New York City rallied to his defense and sent testimonies on his behalf to the secretary of the treasury.

On September 28, the decision of the jury was publicly announced, along with the news that Senator Platt had simultaneously requested that the decision be held up until Secretary Gage returned to the capital from his journey out west.[351] Things heated up in the weeks while Gage was away, giving plenty of time for Platt and his favored architects to marshal their political and professional flanks behind closed doors. Gilbert wrote almost daily to his wife about the escalation of the campaign to overturn the jury's decision.

On October 4, he recounted the machinations of his colleagues in the city, noting that Mr. Berg, principal of the firm Cady, Berg & See, who had been cut before the final round, was agitating for revoking the prize. Gilbert said, "I think he is only a 'cats-paw' of some bigger man."[352] He described an unctuous letter he had just received from Carrère and Hastings inviting him to their office to discuss the situation. He considered this overture as childish as it was disingenuous, for it was accompanied by a copy of the letter addressed to President McKinley protesting his selection.

He was heartened by the loyalty of William Rutherford Mead (1846–1928), his former employer, and by the congratulations from peers such as Bruce Price and Arnold Brunner. But the scuttlebutt that he and Jim Taylor had "some deal" had to be countered. Since he had been assured by juror Frank Miles Day that the project "was won on a close study of the plans," Gilbert showed Day the correspondence from Carrère and Hastings, which called the jury incompetent. Gilbert's fight was now full on, not only for his own rights in the matter but for the jury's as well: "I am going about it in a thorough, quiet, strong way . . . A little tired but always cool and dignified . . . I can only be upset by gross political pressure at Washington that would become a scandal . . . I have no fear of the result."353

In each letter Julia Gilbert was again told that her husband could not come home, and under the circumstances, she and the children must postpone coming East to settle. Gilbert's letter of October 8 disclosed the actual terms of the deal for combining, which Carrère and Hastings had put to him in the days leading up to the jury's final selection. Carrère and Hastings were, he said, "acting like spoiled children" and "talking in the clubs and among their friends doing all they can to upset the award." William Mead kept Gilbert informed of what was being said behind his back. He was infuriated by the losing firm's claims that he had begged them for a partnership on the Custom House commission. This was too much, and he told Mead to "say that's a lie direct!"354

Gilbert recounted that Thomas Hastings pushed on him the idea of their firms partnering from the beginning of the final round of the competition. Gilbert had only grudgingly considered a partnership on the final day because the jury seemed to be deadlocked and needed a way out. What Carrère & Hastings actually meant by an equally shared partnership for the Custom House was a three-way split: They wanted two-thirds of the commission and one-third for Gilbert. Gilbert said, "No! I mean half for my firm and half for yours . . . I am on an even basis with you now! *My office* against *your office* and I believe I've got the best design or you would not want to make such a bargain. I am willing to take my chance against you for the whole thing or nothing" [Gilbert's emphasis].353

Hastings countered with another offer: "equal division on the fee for the sketches (i.e. on 1/5 of the total fee) and . . . after that we divide the expenses" and after deducting expenses from the profits, "divide the balance into thirds." At that point Gilbert tersely ended the conversation, stating that he preferred to leave the partnership option and its terms up to the jury if it determined that such a solution was optimum. With a half dozen witnesses to this discussion, he felt confident he could refute the malicious gossip about his conduct in the matter. Gilbert was losing patience with all this and told Julia that if it continued, he might have to "prefer charges against them in the American Institute of Architects for unprofessional conduct."[356]

On October 23 Senator Platt, in pursuit of annulling the jury's decision, met with Lyman Gage, who agreed to "hold the matter in abeyance" until November 1.[357] The following day, Gilbert met with Secretary Gage and Assistant Secretary Taylor to make his case for upholding the jury's decision: "I saw Sec'y Gage . . . and was as much as told that he would confirm my appointment no matter what Platt does. The Secretary reviewed Platt's protest with a keen irony in every sentence, and as he talked I could see he was framing the thing in his mind, for his reply to Platt, or to a higher authority if called on to do so. . . . Still it isn't over yet. I am up against the most powerful 'machine' organization, and the most wily politicians in this country—and one can never be safe until the final action is taken. Even after the whole thing is over they are practically sure to bring it up in Congress this winter and fight it all over again."[358]

While Gilbert was writing to his wife on the Congressional Express train back to Manhattan, he was interrupted by questions from a *New York Times* reporter. The following morning the *Times* reported on the apparent outcome of the meetings with Secretary Gage. "Architect Gilbert Does Not Fear Senator Platt's Opposition" was the subhead of the article. The article stated that the Treasury Department was likely to maintain Gilbert's award, despite Platt's contention that because Gilbert "had only recently arrived from Minnesota and is not a member of the Republican organization of the City and County of New York," he should not be allowed to design the Custom House. On reaching his hotel that evening, Gilbert told the press, "I am a believer in the old saying that courageous confidence in the intelligence of the community is a sure sign of leadership and success."[359]

He was then asked point blank, "What are your politics, Mr. Gilbert?" to which he replied, "I have not been asked except by members of the press as to my political affiliations and I do not believe that the Treasury Department will be influenced by such considerations. . . . As to the attitude of the other architects who were in competition for the Custom House plans, I am assured the large majority of them cordially acquiesce in the verdict of the expert jury. . . . It is hardly to be supposed that in this, the first of the great competitions for the new Government buildings, the men who have been foremost in urging this reform will now attempt to defeat its practical operation."[360]

Platt, on the other hand, was desperately searching for more reasons to block Gilbert's appointment. He closeted himself with party leaders—former New York Republican Congressman Lemuel E. Quigg and New York's custom collector, George R. Bidwell—to plot their next move. Quigg emerged from their meeting and told reporters that "it looks like a Chicago scheme," claiming that, in addition to the supposed competition fix by a prejudiced jury, now a contractor from Chicago would be getting the building contract as part of the conspiracy to rob New York architects and builders of valuable work. According to Quigg, "If Mr. Gilbert's plans are executed we will have another specimen of architecture as hideous as the 'Post Office.'"[361] The contradictory context of this statement is almost comical.

The protest letter Carrère and Hastings taunted Gilbert with was indeed sent to President McKinley in the last week of October and was printed in the *New York Times* in its entirety on November 2, 1899. Nine of the sixteen competing New York firms were signatories. Clinton & Russell retracted its endorsement of the protest, stating that the firm had never agreed to sign the letter. Bruce Price, who had offered his congratulations to Gilbert, signed the protest, as did Francis H. Kimball, who had signed the notorious protest letter against licensing in 1892.

The protestors challenged the qualifications of Omaha, Nebraska, architect Thomas R. Kimball (1862–1934) to serve on the jury. He was too young, "about thirty-two years of age" (he was in fact thirty-seven), not a "prominent" architect, not a member of the AIA, and was understood to have worked for Gilbert and Taylor's firm back in St. Paul. Kimball, who had recently served as the chief architect of the 1898 Trans-Mississippi Exposition, had studied architecture at MIT, attended the Cowles Art School in Boston, and studied in Paris with the famous Barbizon painter Henri Harpignies.[362]

A preexisting relationship between Gilbert and two of the jury members was the core of the complaint. Unethical conduct was automatically assumed based solely upon this coincidental fact. There was no actual evidence of misconduct by anyone.

Kimball was selected as a juror through a nomination process in which each of the twenty invited contestants was asked to nominate a potential juror. It was impossible to determine exactly who nominated the two independent jurors without breaching the confidentiality of the nominating process. The disgruntled losers asserted that Gilbert must have nominated Kimball, although no one could prove it—much less dispute his right to nominate anyone of his choosing, as everyone else had done.

They objected to the supervising architect's decision to accept Kimball as a juror and to Taylor's abstention from the final round of judgment. This meant that there was no tie-breaker in a jury of three. It did not seem to cross anyone's mind that if Taylor and Kimball were in cahoots, a vote of two against one would have prevented any stalemate and secured the fix. Frank Miles Day's integrity was ultimately in question but was not mentioned at all.

That Cass Gilbert's design was the worthiest, most appropriate solution to the Treasury Department's brief was, apparently, beside the point. That it actually may have won on its architectural merits was the last thing that the protestors wanted to debate.

Their letter asked the president of the United States personally to "investigate these matters before the making of the award, and if, in your judgment, the proceedings have not been entirely regular, that you will cause the appointment of a new committee, upon whose judgment, on merit only, the competitors and all other persons may rely. It is with the greatest reluctance that we bring this matter to your attention, and we only do so believing that we are justly dissatisfied, and your interposition is necessary."[363]

Back in Manhattan, the New York chapter of the AIA gathered in a secret general meeting to deal with this potentially disastrous situation. After thirty years of prodding and lobbying to obtain this federal policy initiative, it was about to blow up in their faces. A vote was taken, and the membership immediately sent a confidential resolution to Secretary Gage, urging him to uphold Gilbert's appointment. The Philadelphia chapter did the same. Gage received the petitions on November 2; the decision was to be made on November 3.

Backpedaling as fast as they could, Carrère and Hastings publicly affirmed the award, as did Charles Berg, whose firm signed the protest letter. To the *New York Times*, Berg spoke remorsefully on behalf of the letter signers, realizing that they had "done a very foolish thing." Berg said, "It is a gross insult to Secretary Gage ... after all he has done for the architectural profession, it seems absurd to try to have his authority overruled."[364]

The *Times* reported that Republican Senators Thomas Platt and Chauncey Depew were still bringing pressure to bear on President McKinley to appoint a new jury and set aside the award, and they still believed that their mission would be successful.

Lyman Gage's situation required the wisdom of Solomon. In response to pressure from all sides, the Treasury Department asked the competition's twenty firms whether the jury's decision should stand. Only the eight firms who opposed the award rejected the decision. The Chicago and Boston firms sided with the jury. Six New York firms supported the jury and two did not respond.

Three days before the final decision was handed down, Gilbert and his attorney, George Squires, traveled to Washington at the invitation of Secretary Gage. They were shown the lengthy brief filed by Platt and Quigg attacking Gilbert's integrity and that of the jury. Gage told them he would hear their response the following day, and Squires prepared a brief in answer to the accusations. The next morning, they arrived at the Treasury Department and presented their brief, and Gage told them he would have an answer for them within a day. The following morning, they received word that Secretary Gage would bring up the matter at the day's cabinet meeting and a decision would be forthcoming shortly. President McKinley, in receipt of the protest letter, turned the matter over to Secretary Gage to handle. Supervising Architect James Knox Taylor informed Gilbert later that day that the award would stand, and he was to be the designer of the new Custom House.[365]

A "well known architect" who wished to remain nameless told the *New York Times*: "Had the jury's verdict been set aside it is difficult to see how any architect could have grumbled in future if the Federal authorities chose to ignore the competitive system altogether. Of course, a good many architects do not believe in that system at all, and the American Institute of

Architects has officially declared that the direct appointment of architects is to be preferred . . . However that is not the question, and so far as public buildings are concerned, I personally believe in having competitions."[366]

The plans for the Custom House were published a few weeks after the decision came down. Gilbert, on the offensive, took a preemptive measure in anticipation of further obstruction in the next session of Congress. The local political machine had failed to discredit him professionally, so he knew exactly what they would do next, and he was ready.

On December 1, 1899, the *New York Times* reported Gilbert's warning to the custom collector, George R. Bidwell, who had worked so feverishly against him with Boss Platt. The building would be built with an appropriation of $2,750,000, and in confronting Bidwell, "It is said in political circles that Mr. Gilbert went even further, and told Mr. Bidwell that in the event of an application for an additional appropriation, those making it would get no aid from him, and that he intended that the new structure should be adequate in all respects and should not cost more than the sum available."[367] No quarter given, no quarter taken.

The two beleaguered judges, Frank Miles Day and Thomas R. Kimball, would both be elected president of the AIA, Day in 1906–1907 and Kimball in 1918–1920. Succeeding Day as president of the AIA in 1908 and reelected in 1909, Cass Gilbert provided the critical leadership needed to preserve and enrich the architectural legacy of the nation's capital.[368]

After the Custom House debacle, the Tarsney Act proved not to be the breakthrough so long anticipated by the profession. Only thirty-one new federal buildings, out of more than 400 built, were tendered to the private sector through the design competition process, a mere eight percent of the Treasury's total building production throughout the lifetime of a public policy framed in the professional interests of the AIA. According to historian Antoinette J. Lee, "The benefits of the Tarsney Act reached only a small, elite group of architectural firms."[369] The Tarsney Act was revoked by Congress in 1912.

Cass Gilbert rose to the occasion of the Custom House scandal and withstood its public test of his character and integrity; he proved himself not only a great architect but also a born leader of both his generation and his profession. He stood up to a domineering clique and forced the profession's leadership and the nation's senior politicians to deal with him as an equal. He fought the good fight, but he fought to win. And most important, he was not afraid of losing.

12 Seeking Power: An Unvarnished View of the Golden Era of Influence

Because Sir Isaac Newton was superior to others in understanding,
he was not therefore lord of the person or property of others.[370]
—Thomas Jefferson to Henri Gregoire, 1809

ANKMAR ADLER SPOKE IN 1887 to the Illinois State Association of Architects and said, "Our architecture will never be the expression of the conditions or wants and desires of any small class, but of the American people as a whole."[371] Richard Morris Hunt, in his presidential address at the 1890 AIA convention, stated, "We should be most conscientious in our endeavors to faithfully serve the interest of our clients to the best of our ability; to do so even should it at times be necessary to sacrifice some of our artistic preferences."[372]

Adler and Hunt acknowledged the two fundamental truths of architecture practice in America: that the country's pluralist democracy itself was reflected in the cultural expression of architecture and that the practice of building design was a business contract formed to meet the client's intentions, first and foremost.

But it was Daniel H. Burnham who zeroed in on the power-filled potential of federal government architecture in 1887 when he staked a claim to its design on behalf of the public, which had "a right to the talent of its greatest architects," and the profession, which had "a right to the work."[373]

In pursuit of greater professional authority, political influence, and social recognition, on January 1, 1899, the national office of the AIA relocated from New York City to Washington, D.C. At the suggestion of one of Washington's leading architect-activists, Glenn Brown, cofounder in 1887 of the D.C. chapter, the AIA moved into the Octagon building, designed in 1799 by

William Thornton. With the generosity of Charles F. McKim, among others, it was later purchased to become the Institute's permanent home.

Though the move to Washington did bring a range of issues to the front door of the federal government's house, this first era of modern political lobbying can claim only a few major successes, primarily connected to the architectural development and planning of the nation's capital. These accomplishments were shared with the AIA by many patriotic citizens from all walks of life—presidents, members of Congress, design professionals from all disciplines, business leaders, and ordinary voters who were impressed and excited by the City Beautiful ideal displayed at the 1893 World's Columbian Exposition in Chicago. At the turn of the 19th century, Pierre L'Enfant's original vision for the new nation's capital city needed only to be brought to light again and effectively presented to the nation's decision makers. The Institute was the ideal platform around which to coalesce such a civic design movement.

Glenn Brown, the Institute's secretary-treasurer and chief functionary from 1899 through 1913, saw in L'Enfant's plan a great design solution that also presented a great opportunity and quickly seized upon it. As an example of the symbolic power of architecture, this could not have been more appropriate or timely.

Ultimately Brown's inability to translate this cultural phenomenon into a deeply rooted power base or a more sophisticated means of advancing issues pertinent to architecture practice for either the government or the profession itself had a self-defeating long-term effect. Under Brown's tenure, the Institute would continue its hostile turf and style wars with the Office of the Supervising Architect and Congress. Though the great civic buildings have survived Washington's notorious temperature changes, the profession's tenuous political influence evaporated like the clouds of hot air that regularly vacate the capital's political atmosphere.

According to an article about Theodore Roosevelt's support of architecture published in the journal of the White House Historical Association, "there would never again be such a time, or such a relationship, between the architects and a president."374 This telling statement reveals more by what it does not express than by what it chooses to say about the period. It may be possible to understand why the first decade of the 20th century was both the beginning and the end of the profession's overt political influence on the national stage by dispensing with the rose-colored glasses of nostalgia.

At the turn of the century, membership in the Institute was restricted to an exceptionally small minority of practicing architects. Membership was predicated upon acceptance of a classical European aesthetic, an academic methodology, an elitist social ideology, and an adherence to a rather inflexible set of business rules. The Institute asserted itself as the national voice of an entire profession largely by default, since, with the Institute's incorporation of the Western Association of Architects, an alternative voice no longer existed. The Institute's superficially glorious but deeply conservative definition of the term architect was coupled with a profoundly discriminatory and circumspect concept of practice. The Institute's strategy was to establish its supremacy via a contrived national cultural identity and to facilitate the control of that identity by its leading members. Missing from the Institute's propaganda was an objective consideration of the fiscal and pragmatic realities inherent in the production of government architecture, the related political issues being weighed in tandem with the interests sacred to the AIA, and the inescapable complexity of legislative politics and governmental operations.

The inextricable role that architecture plays in the growth of the nation's economy, its implicit responsibilities to both client and labor, and the fiscal nuances of supply and demand were barely addressed, if at all. Architecture as a topic, with all its attendant practicalities, was presented as detached from such banalities in order to focus all eyes on architecture's singular power to create symbolic cultural iconography.

This strategy was adopted in order to elevate the social status of the architect in the public's mind by divorcing the art of architectural design from its essential technical sciences, the skilled trades of building, and the sordid motivation of profit. Art's power of edification was disconnected from architecture's inherent sources of power: that of shelter and sanctuary, material productivity, functionality, adaptability, place making, and social responsibility. These attributes were de-emphasized as secondary values in the process of sculpting a grander societal status for academically trained architects.

By emphatically aggrandizing the architect-as-artist into a social mythology, the profession inadvertently surrendered all but the artistic aspects of building to the control of others. Convincing politicians and the public alike that architects should be considered fine artists first and foremost meant dispensing with the traditional perception of architects as master builders. But what the profession failed to anticipate was that such an altered perception might not actually produce a greater material or political advantage in terms of either business development or elevated social status.

Subjective debates on the nature and civic import of art in architecture and assertions of architecture's inherent superiority over other artistic disciplines, particularly the related applied arts within building, conveniently obscured the hard facts of the building business, such as the key issues of who rightfully could use the title architect, who should rightfully manage the building process, and how compensation for an architect's services should be calculated. For the profession's privileged elite, validation from the federal government could and would be utilized to enforce its own top-down domination of a diverse, widely dispersed profession. Management of the building business and control over access to the marketplace still underlay each issue, including the art of it all.

Early on, the Institute foolishly chose a political pressure strategy that employed the negative tactics of personal politics, in which the abilities and judgments of important decision makers were questioned, ridiculed, or castigated in an attempt to discredit federal policies. Those professionals responsible for handling the federal building stock, including the Congress itself, were cast in this contrived tableau as untalented, intellectually limited, financially wasteful, public-trust-abusing incompetents. A black-and-white scenario was delineated to highlight the Institute's preferable policies in contrast to what it considered to be the horrendous federal policies in architectural matters. This scenario was intended to demonstrate the appropriateness of having favored Institute members solve the purported aesthetic dilemma and to deliver to the electorate greater fiscal prudence than the government could possibly heretofore manage.

Concurrence by the majority of the nation's architects with this narrowly defined agenda was not remotely possible, but it also was of no great concern to those pursuing influence over federal design matters. By presuming to speak for all legitimate practitioners, the Institute's highly paternalistic posture toward its own constituents also presumed the gross ignorance of most Americans on all architectural and artistic matters. Therefore, the role of the professional architect was projected into the public arena as a kind of artistic pedagogue, a noble missionary sent to cure the hunger for real art of a culturally deprived, artistically misguided people.

This attitude did not sit well with the many intelligent and capable men who served as secretary of the treasury or in the Treasury Department's Office of the Supervising Architect. Nor did scores of congressional leaders appreciate the Institute's repeated attempts to wrest from Congress its constitutional right and moral obligation to direct oversight and fiscal control of the legislative proposals brought before it by the AIA-led lobby.

The Institute had a few powerful political allies in the Senate, but far fewer in the House of Representatives. Ardent support from Senators James McMillan, Republican from Michigan (who died in 1902); Francis G. Newlands, Democrat from Nevada; and Elihu Root, Republican from New York and former secretary of war under McKinley and secretary of state under Roosevelt proved enormously helpful on a series of measures introduced to secure adoption and implementation of the L'Enfant plan. Despite their persuasive efforts, there was no wellspring of support among their political colleagues or among the many functionaries of government whose careers paralleled those of the profession's advocates, for building a durable relationship between the federal government and the Institute.

Perhaps the forging of such an alliance was never an Institute objective in the first place. The AIA's proposals consistently included a transferal of statutory power from Congress to itself, conveyed in a one-way transmission of trust. In other words, Congress was to unconditionally trust the judgment of a select few members of an essential profession *because* they believed it unwise to trust Congress in matters related not only to building design but also to all artistic issues over which legislators governed.

Such a transfer of responsibility ideally included, along with total control of all architectural matters, the selection of "furniture, lighting fixtures, and decorations, painting, statuary, and other objects of art purchased or presented to the Government."375 (The diplomatic implications of subjecting all gifts to the nation to official artistic censorship are mind-boggling.) The impossibility of convincing the majority of legislators and government department heads of the proposal's logic did not seem to deter Institute lobbyists from relentlessly pursuing this objective, year in and year out. Even as late as 1913, a bill to create a Bureau of Buildings and Grounds, presented to the AIA convention, required only the Senate's advice and the president's power of appointment, and entirely eliminated the House of Representatives from the equation. Was congressional apoplexy the real goal?

The unprecedented extent of artistic superintendence over the discretionary power of Congress and the cabinet was demanded by what was essentially a self-appointed special interest that did not have an industry-wide mandate to represent those interests. Without substantial architectural constituencies working to influence public policy at the state level, there was little hope of mustering support in Washington. This made support of the AIA's agenda a matter of personal preference of the individual legislator and placed that agenda in direct conflict with far more powerful, well organized home-court interests with preexisting, firmly established political influence.

The unanticipated good fortune of having a sitting president, Theodore Roosevelt, with a major home-court constituency of proactive architects, both inside and outside the AIA, cannot be overstated. Had he lived, would President McKinley have given such personal and generous attention to the Institute's interests? Not likely, since Daniel Burnham's close ties with Lyman Gage, McKinley's secretary of the treasury, did not produce more than a placable utilization of the options available under the Tarsney Act.

The "wild swings in editorial opinion on the part of private architects"[376] undermined the veracity of the altruistic motives claimed by the architecture profession's lobby. Treasury Department officials were either demonized or lavishly praised by the Institute, depending on whether work was delivered to "one of their own."[377]

The AIA's professional goals were dampened down by its overbearing dictation of artistic standards and its intransigence on basic practice and policy issues. Glenn Brown's omnipresent, obsessive personality and his narrowly focused artistic preoccupations during fifteen years as chief executive of the AIA resulted in the artist-architect persona becoming a stereotype in the minds of those he was hoping to persuade. While this identification served Brown's chief passion, the design of Washington, D.C., it stymied progress on a number of fundamental practice issues.

Under Brown's direction, the AIA attempted to assume a supra-identity as the nation's self-appointed curator, insisting that it should orchestrate all aspects of the capital's and, ultimately, the nation's architecture, fine arts, and city planning. Brown routinely presented the government with AIA-exclusive decision-making proposals, in which Institute members outnumbered all the other artistic professions combined by two to one, and often three to one. Non-artists were almost always excluded from these proposals.

The concerns of the AIA's rank and file were often disregarded in pursuit of these high-minded affairs; day-to-day practice issues played second fiddle to Brown's all-encompassing campaign to create a national aesthetics program, showcased by the McMillan Plan, which he envisioned would be controlled by hand-picked members of the Institute, including, of course, himself.

Beginning in 1909, the Institute raised its members' minimum professional fee from five to six percent of construction costs. This rate increase was followed by a move to substantially raise the annual dues. The cost of running the national office, including personnel, operating expenses, membership services, and publication costs, came out of membership dues. Brown's desire to restore and refurbish the Octagon, along with the increased costs of lobbying, was the justification for a dues increase. A circular sent out that summer to canvass members' reaction to the proposed increase elicited some spirited objections.

The Institute's "overconservative admissions policy"[378] had unduly restricted membership growth, and any increase in dues added to this problem, as well as to the existing burden on the membership. From A.B. Jennings in New York City came the suggestion that the Institute set up a legal bureau to provide a service that would attract members and, in regard to the dues increase, "will not such an advance in dues tend to still further curtail the membership—already so small a fraction of the number of our practicing architects?"[379]

John M. Harris, of the firm Wilson, Harris & Richards of Philadelphia, was less polite: "I think . . . those having the matter in charge should

consider carefully the case of architects who are not as successful as some
of us . . . If the Institution does its work, it does it by helping along the rank
and file as well as the more successful members and if the change of dues
means hardship for these fellows, it seems to me that no amount of satisfaction in having an elegant club house at Washington would justify raising the dues."[380]

Robert W. Gibson of New York City bluntly rejected the idea and provided three pages of facts to support his belief that "it would be most inju-
rious to the Institute to follow this course . . . the proportionately small
number of architects within the Institute are in danger of being out-
weighed by the influence of the larger number outside it . . . these practicing architects are not merely abstainers from Institute influence, they are
opponents. They are doing a great deal of work. The profession is growing
enormously and the Institute is not keeping pace with it . . . The Institute
should now . . . broaden its influence, even if it has to relinquish some of the
luxuries which they cultivate . . . a little more attention to self-supporting
features will be better than the one proposed . . . P.S. I will send this letter
to a professional publication after time has elapsed for you to read it."[381]

Henry Lord Gay of San Diego wrote to Brown to caution him. He
recalled his experience of the sudden loss of half of the Chicago chapter in
1875, when dues were similarly increased. He also pointed out that "reference to higher dues of European associations . . . is not well taken . . . the
American Institute of Architects should cover its halo over the smallest and
least important member of the profession as well as its greatest ones. And
it has a territory to enfold, of which there is no comparison with local or
European associations of a similar character . . . my vote is against the
raise."[382]

The Institute had virtually no fiscal management procedures or other
means of revenue generation in place after a decade of Brown's tenure as
treasurer. Expenditures under Brown's direct control continuously exceeded
income. When Cass Gilbert assumed the presidency, he took matters in hand
and instituted the first formal budgetary and contingency planning.[383] But
the dire state of Institute finances forced a dues increase in 1911.

In 1900 Brown estimated that, if properly evaluated to meet his deter-
mination of professional standards, 2,000 architects nationwide would

be eligible for acceptance into the Institute. "Brown was behind the establishment of a system of examination for membership instituted in 1902."[384] In 1901 AIA membership stood at approximately 750.[385] Between 1900 and 1910, more than 6,000 new practitioners had been added to the profession nationwide, and the total exceeded 16,500 in 1910. During the same period, enrollment in architecture degree programs had increased by 400 percent.[386]

Yet during a period of exponential growth, the percentage of architects who were accepted into the Institute remained static, between six and eight percent of all practitioners.[387] Even if Brown had been able to meet his membership target in 1900, the AIA would still have excluded at least eighty percent of the practicing architects in the country. Moreover, by the end of 1914, after years of intensive political activity in the nation's capital, the Institute had only 1,191 members.[388] The AIA's high profile issue-specific influence had not increased its representative share of the profession's ranks. Thus, when all was said and done, as a lobby it could not impress upon legislators the clout of critical mass within its own industry sector.

If the ultimate goal was to gain control of the profession through compliance with AIA-created regulation, then control over federal building practices must have appeared the preferable, perhaps expedient, option over opening up membership to a widely inclusive, grassroots constituency. By securing government compliance with AIA policies, the Institute's much-touted artistic goals and its domination over professional practice could be spread downward to the local marketplace from the power-base of the federal platform.

Brown directed all of his efforts and the Institute's limited financial resources to the battle with officials over the design of the capital and his cherished dream of creating an autonomous federal bureau to control fine art on a national scale. The Institute was thus slow, if not openly reluctant, to address its own policies to meet the ever-increasing demands of architecture practice. This stagnation maintained Brown's singular position in Washington and kept a hierarchy of connected interests entrenched for a long time. But as the old-boy network became increasingly outmoded, this stagnation began to sap the profession's field of influence, strained the

Institute's financial stability, and stalled the modernization of the only association with the possibility of representing the profession nationwide.

Brown's network of symbiotic, locally established civic arts organizations, most of which he cofounded, was housed within a few feet of his desk in the Octagon. His control of satellite organizations evolved into an increasingly myopic and misguided concept of what real political influence actually consisted of, and how it should be effectively expanded and maintained. Policy and strategy decisions affecting the whole profession were made by a handful of chums in the confidential comfort of the Octagon or Washington's ultra-exclusive Cosmos Club.

Beginning in 1898 through 1915, the AIA's annual convention was held in the capital twelve times. Brown conducted his lobbying campaigns around the convention with the skill of an impresario entertaining the troops. He orchestrated impressive art and architecture exhibitions, promotional programs, and gala dinners and receptions, all scripted to sway the sentiments of key politicians, influential individuals, and Institute members.

After the Tarsney Act was implemented, Brown directed his full attention to the capital's beautification and any ancillary fine art activities that could be used to promote his dream for a Federal Bureau of Fine Art. He generated a steady stream of skillfully crafted propaganda and monopolized the Institute's public relations and professional publications with his critical editorials and scholarly writings on artistic concerns for the capital and the nation.

President Theodore Roosevelt arrived in the White House in 1901 with a keen, exceptionally well developed understanding of the built environment. His ascendancy to the presidency, through the tragedy of presidential assassination, brought to the architecture profession a natural ally who could not have been more open to useful, well-considered ideas regarding public policy on architecture, preservation of the nation's natural resources, and the quality of life for all citizens the office is sworn to protect.

Before being placed on the Republican ticket as vice president in 1900, Teddy Roosevelt, the Spanish-American War hero, had been elected governor of New York in 1898. During his term, the Mazet Commission investigated political corruption in New York City, with special attention to the management of the Buildings Department and its failure to enforce the city's building code, while another state commission revised the building code laws. During his term, the tenement reform movement garnered widespread support and political clout.

In 1895, as New York City's police commissioner, Roosevelt joined forces with crusading Danish-American journalist and tenement reformer Jacob Riis. For two years Roosevelt accompanied Riis on his nocturnal rounds of the slums of Lower Manhattan. Together they worked ceaselessly to push through political and social reforms at the municipal level. As Roosevelt's career progressed, he and Riis were joined in their reform efforts by architects, social workers, real estate developers, and wealthy philanthropists. The two remained lifelong friends.

In 1899 Governor Roosevelt did nothing to assist his political nemesis, Senator Thomas C. Platt, in subverting the selection of Cass Gilbert as architect for the New York Custom House. Boss Platt found the independent and unintimidated Roosevelt such a thorn in his side that he engineered Roosevelt's nomination as vice president just to remove him from his field of influence over New York state politics.

Teddy Roosevelt grew up in Manhattan during the Civil War. His father and several of his uncles were cofounders and leaders of the Union League Club. Theodore Sr. was an ardent reformer who devoted himself and his wealth to addressing poverty, injustice, and political corruption. Riis wrote that Theodore Roosevelt Sr. "pleaded, even on his death-bed . . . for a farm where the boys in the House of Refuge might be fitted for healthy country life; for responsible management of the State's Orphan Asylums, for decent care of vagrants, for improved tenements."[389]

In 1873, when Teddy was fifteen, his father built a new home for the family at 6 West 57th Street. The well-known New York architect Russell Sturgis designed the building and the young Philadelphia architect Frank Furness designed the exuberant interiors and custom-made furniture.[390] In 1884, Teddy Roosevelt hired Charles Lamb and Hugh Rich to design Sagamore Hill, his family home in Oyster Bay, New York, and so gained the experience of collaborating on a major architecture project as the directing client.

Roosevelt was also a member of the Union League Club and, along with many prominent architects, the Century Club, the city's hub of fine arts.

In these private clubs he encountered and came to know personally many of the profession's leading lights.391

When the large Roosevelt family moved into the White House, its accommodations were found wanting. Glenn Brown described the state of the White House décor in withering terms: The State Dining Room was "like our better-class boarding house," the East Room was a "saloon on a Long Island Sound Palace Steamer," the Red Room was a "Pullman Palace car," and the entrance hall with it's stained glass screen and "arabesque walls" looked like a "typical bar room of the period."392

In 1882 Associated Artists, led by Louis Comfort Tiffany, was commissioned by President Chester A. Arthur to decorate the public rooms of the White House with a congressional appropriation of $30,000. Tiffany's signature piece was the entrance hall's floor-to-ceiling screen of opalescent glass decorated with a motif of brilliantly colored national emblems. During the Harrison and McKinley administrations, interior designer Edgar S. Yergason refurbished the White House and introduced Colonial Revival to the décor.393

President and Mrs. Roosevelt decided to overhaul the whole building and hired AIA President Charles McKim to redesign the plant and restore the public rooms to their original colonial splendor. Work began in June 1902 and was completed in less than six months. Brown superintended the architectural work, conveniently walking over to the White House from his office in the nearby Octagon. Roosevelt specifically ordered McKim to "break up in small pieces that Tiffany screen."394

Roosevelt's public support for the McMillan Plan, his decision to restore the White House to historical accuracy, his administration's limited implementation of the Tarsney Act, and his parting gesture of authorizing a Presidential Council on Fine Arts were political acts that set high standards for the next administration and others to follow.

In his brief remarks at the 1905 annual AIA convention dinner, President Roosevelt made clear his understanding of the key issues underlying the McMillan Plan and the government's role in the matter: "I would say that the best thing that any elective legislative body can do in these matters is to surrender itself within reasonable limits to the guidance of those who really do know what they are talking about . . . What I have said does not mean that we shall go, here in Washington for instance, into immediate and extravagant expenditures on public buildings. All it means is that whenever . . . a public building is provided for and erected, it should be erected in accordance with a carefully thought-out plan adopted long before, and that it should not only be beautiful in itself, but fitting in its relations to the whole scheme of the public buildings, the parks and the drives of the District."[395]

Roosevelt's use of the phrases "reasonable limits" and "extravagant expenditures" should have resonated with the profession's lobbyists, for in these terms is the crux of all the policy battles they fought with those entrusted with the public purse. In addition, Roosevelt's grasp of the importance of architecture was as much a consequence of his own ethical beliefs, political priorities, and relevant personal experience as it was of any enlightening influence of the AIA.

During the Roosevelt presidency, architects of substantial national repute—McKim, Burnham, and Gilbert—carried the banner of the Institute. Each was able to parlay his business and personal relationships to a distinct political advantage on behalf of the Institute. McKim's wisdom tempered the more aggressive tendencies of Brown's rhetoric and his confrontational impulses. McKim's diplomatic skills were subtle and proved effective, culminating in the glittering 1905 celebratory fundraising dinner he orchestrated for his cherished project, the American Academy in Rome. "Charles McKim's leadership had brought the AIA to a position of professional leadership and political respect."[396]

Dissatisfaction with the management of Institute affairs began to surface among its leadership around this time. In 1906 and 1907, AIA President Frank Miles Day tried in vain to set up an administrative system in Brown's office that could provide oversight and accountability to the board. "What Day intended to alter was Brown's personal control over the AIA's administrative machinery."[397]

Brown's obsessive control of all aspects of the Institute's endeavors and his stage-management of public support for various capital-specific issues backfired in the context of a profession struggling to survive in a competitive, free-market economy. The regulation of the built environment was swiftly moving forward, with or without Institute leadership on the ground.

There was little if any consultation with the rank and file beyond the choreographed annual convention, the site of which was no longer shared among cities in key regional centers. Resentment grew in the hinterlands as well as among the more involved members who served on various committees.

In the final years of Brown's administration, he and the Institute's senior leadership were consumed by the campaign to establish a supervisory fine arts commission and the battle over the form and location of a memorial for President Lincoln. When Burnham went head to head with Brown over the monument's location, the conflict became public in a flurry of negative publicity.

Burnham had previously objected to how Washington's development was being handled when he attempted to resign from the Senate Park Commission in 1907: "What we need in Washington is a system . . . if this amicus curiae method—or lack of method—goes on, serious trouble will arise to our discredit, and what is more, to that of the work we have at heart."[398]

President Roosevelt's executive order creating a Council of Fine Arts on January 19, 1909, was issued in direct defiance of Congress. Roosevelt had no illusions about its statutory viability. On January 22, 1909, the *New York Tribune* reported the outrage of the House of Representatives at what it considered a "direct violation of a federal statute . . . which prohibited the Chief Executive from employing such an advisory commission or even from accepting its services gratuitously." The House leadership took umbrage at the rejection of Congress's judgment on architectural and artistic matters of federal import and "the taking from Congress of functions which it has always enjoyed and perfectly performed."[399] According to a member of Congress quoted in the *New York Sun* on January 22, "That order is designed to have the force and direction of a law . . . as it stands it would constitute an abridgement of the power of Congress to legislate . . . a sort of right of legislative repeal vested in a commission of thirty having no legislative status."[400]

Roosevelt's "Memorandum to Accompany Sundry Civil Bill, 1909," which he signed into law on March 4, 1909, reveals the true extent of the power struggle between the executive and legislative branches and places the Council of Fine Arts in a wider context. In this bill, Congress attempted to curtail certain presidential initiatives by banning the funding of all presidential commissions or boards it did not specifically authorize. Roosevelt believed that the congressional restrictions already in place and this new prohibition on funding for presidential committees and advisory boards were aimed primarily at his Conservation Commission and Country Life Commission. He made only cursory mention of the arts council.[401]

Sections 1 and 9 of the Sundry Civil Bill specifically forbade appropriations for any aspect of the Council of Fine Arts or the use of any government employee to support its activities. Furthermore, an act passed in 1906 also forbade the acceptance of voluntary services "in excess of that authorized by law," which was the consequence of earlier Institute skirmishes over government building and memorial sitings.[402]

Brown should not have been surprised when President William Taft terminated, immediately, Roosevelt's order. But he was. "This action surprised and shocked Brown, who had underestimated the powerful animosity House members harbored toward Roosevelt's order."[403] The House was seething with anger over the president's stunt, which had summarily preempted its consideration of the "Bill for a Bureau and Council of Arts," presented by Senator Francis Newlands to the Senate, on behalf of the AIA, on the very same day Roosevelt issued his executive order.[404]

Taft, one of America's finest legal minds, knew the danger to his administration of sustaining Roosevelt's order. Taft revoked the order on May 21, 1909, shortly after taking office. The issue was then placed in the capable hands of Republican Senator George Peabody Wetmore of Rhode Island and the Senate's Committee on the Library.[405]

Brown had little awareness of the bigger picture, of the implications of countermeasures framed into legislation over several years in response to his lobbying efforts, or of the depth of Congress's fury at attempts by a special interest, or by the president himself, to usurp its constitutional power. This is indicative of why Brown came to be perceived by the rank and file as a political liability to the Institute. Even as he was presenting his list of thirty advisers (twenty-one architects, eight fine artists, and one landscape architect), with himself in the executive role, for President Roosevelt to appoint to the Council of Fine Arts, he could not resist going after the supervising architect once again: "We venture to recommend that the appointment of any future Supervising Architect should be made on the advice and nomination of the American Institute of Architects."[406]

The Taft administration, through Senator Elihu Root (an honorary AIA member), told Brown in no uncertain terms that it wanted no more talk of a Bureau of Fine Arts but that the administration would carry on with plans for the formation of a congressionally approved Fine Arts Commission. After a year of consultations with various cultural and professional organizations, a bill to create a federal Commission of Fine Arts was sent to Capitol Hill.

On the House floor, Brown's involvement in any future commission was the topic of heated debate. That Brown should gain control of the commission through his appointment as its secretary, his well-known modus operandi, was objected to in the strongest of terms. Illinois Representative James R. Mann, a Republican who opposed the bill, asked, "Does the gentleman really think that if Mr. Glenn Brown was appointed secretary to this art commission he would really need any of the members to ever come to Washington?"[407]

Mann was sure that Brown's motives were not only inappropriately ambitious for himself, but more importantly, that "his purpose is to secure extravagant appropriations for new works of art in Washington."[408] Mann had gained his early experience in public service in Chicago, where he was the legal counsel for Hyde Park and the South Park Commission, chartered to develop Chicago's park system, and had served as a city councilman during the 1893 World's Fair.[409]

Despite opposition, the bill creating a seven-member Fine Arts Commission, written in more conciliatory, widely inclusive terms than previous incarnations that demonstratively favored architects, was passed on May 17, 1910.

But it was Daniel Burnham's advice to Senator Wetmore on how to go about his task of short-listing nominees to the commission, given on May 19, 1910, that is most revealing: "I am aware that many of the professional class are exceedingly anxious to 'get on this commission,' and that they desire to do so because it will give them personal distinction. This is not a high motive; it is unworthy of the important office to be filled. No man who asks for a place should be considered . . . the men who serve should be above

jealousy and envy. They are to create the 'tone' which the country needs."
Burnham put forward several names for the panel, and added "one word
more. By far the best man for secretary is F.D. Millet."[410]

Charles Moore, former secretary to Senator James McMillan and a
close personal ally of Glenn Brown, got the job of secretary, and Taft
appointed Burnham and the respected painter and muralist Frank D.
Millet, former director of decoration for the Chicago World's Fair
buildings.[411]

The success of establishing an arts commission was immediately followed by a vicious political fight over the Lincoln Memorial. Brown, in his
usual way, mounted a massive campaign to secure adherence to the McMillan Plan. This pitted him against his sworn enemies, namely Speaker of the
House Joseph G. Cannon, a Republican from Illinois, and Representative
William P. Borland, a Democrat from Missouri.

Critical help came from Senator Root who advised Brown to hook up
with the Washington Chamber of Commerce, a novel move that greatly
enhanced the chances of success.[412] Brown prevailed in this, his last pro-
tracted battle against Congress. He got his concept, site, and designer,
Henry Bacon, for the Lincoln Memorial, but "it is fair to say that the AIA
. . . won the Washington battle but lost the war against the government."[413]

Between 1909 and 1913, when Brown was politely but firmly removed
from office, the board of directors and the membership slowly clawed back
control of the Institute. After the minimum professional fee was raised from
five to six percent in December 1908 and some semblance of fiscal planning
initiated in 1909, a national Committee on Public Information was established in 1911.[414] The new, three-member committee took over editorial control of the Institute's publications. Brown lost sole editorial direction and
profoundly differed with fellow committee members, Philadelphia architects David Knickerbacker Boyd and Frank C. Baldwin, on broadening the
Institute's program to include more chapter input.

Brown's oversight of all committee work and correspondence had been
increasingly neglected as lobbying consumed most of the secretary's time.
This lack of attentiveness to the membership's investment in Institute
work engendered growing dissatisfaction with his job performance,
particularly as decision making had become chronically drawn out. These

responsibilities were transferred from the Octagon back to the committee members. Brown became embittered over what he saw as encroachment on his hitherto unchallenged authority.[415]

The fact was that the national association had, under the direction of a local AIA chapter leader, devolved into a glorified extension of that local chapter in its single-minded pursuit of its own geographically centered interests. Brown tailored the policies and operations of the Institute to suit his ideological and professional priorities as well as his own personal artistic and career objectives. The pronounced elitism of the Institute's agenda at the turn of the 19th century was embodied by the organization's front man whose outward demeanor of a mild-mannered southern gentleman masked a shrewd and manipulative character. Within Glenn Brown's makeup lay the seeds of his success and also of his downfall.

Brown was the grandson of Senator Bedford Brown of North Carolina. Both sides of his family were among the southern colonial elite. Brown's grandfather owned the Rose Hill plantation, which included a mansion house built in 1800 and 1,000 acres of farmland worked by 100 slaves. Starting in 1830, Senator Brown, a Jacksonian Democrat, served on the powerful Committee on Agriculture and was its chair from 1833 through 1837. He was a vehement opponent of secession, though he remained a staunch supporter of states' rights. The senator did not voluntarily relinquish ownership of his slaves, despite remaining loyal to the Union.[416]

His father, Dr. Bedford Brown Jr., served as a military surgeon and then as medical director of the Confederate Army.[417] The Confederacy's defeat brought financial ruin to the Brown family but did not result in a loss of respect in the halls of power. After the Civil War, as part of the Reconstruction reconciliation effort, Senator Brown was granted a full pardon by his former Tennessee colleague, President Andrew Johnson.[418]

An early childhood spent playing with his powerful grandfather's slave children on the family's ancestral plantation must have contributed to Brown's sense of superiority and entitlement. In later years he did not fail to use his prestigious family history to sell his leadership agenda to southern architects.

As Brown's reputation slowly became inseparable from the public's perception of the Institute, his desire for personal authority and artistic recognition began to infiltrate the policy initiatives he ostensibly fashioned on behalf of the profession. As each lobbying campaign became increasingly contentious, an undisguised tone of condescension or contempt tainted much of Brown's communications. He seemed to thrive on exacerbating hostile relations with his opponents, which hampered the mature development and institutional self-awareness that the AIA sorely needed to meet the many challenges it faced.

As the eminent architects upon whom Brown relied for direct engagement with the nation's political leadership disengaged themselves, retired, or passed away, he lost the benefit of their diplomatic and mediation skills, professional reputations, and invaluable personal relationships. This generational change left him unshielded from the accumulated consequences of having made more enemies—in government and in the profession—than he was apparently aware of and contributed to his forced retirement as the Institute's de facto executive director.[419]

As the second decade of the 20th century began, the membership, now advancing into corporate structures of their own and dealing with far more complex technological, legal, and business practice issues, expected modern, appropriately systematic management practices in place at the national level in order to meet their professional needs and practice concerns.

Glenn Brown's personal fiefdom was overthrown by a checkmate engineered by the younger generation. The New York architects, led by Robert D. Kohn, presented a motion at the 1913 convention to implement major changes in the Institute's bylaws that would prohibit the offices of secretary and treasurer from being converged into one office and held by one person. The membership passed the motion and enacted immediate implementation, despite Brown's long-winded plea to maintain the status quo. So instead of standing again for the combined office as he had become accustomed, Brown had to choose which office to compete for. He decided to run for the office of secretary, under the assumption that he could retain his former position with most of its authority. Brown lost the election.

The new bylaws also created the position of executive secretary, an employee who would not be a board member or even an Institute member. Brown's detailed litany of the administrative work he performed came back to haunt him when his services were replaced by those of an experienced business manager accountable to the board through the Institute's newly elected secretary, David Knickerbacker Boyd. For the next few years the main priority of the new management regime was to put the Institute's house in order.[420]

The final stroke that sealed Brown's fate was the repeal of the Tarsney Act. After decades of petty squabbling, high-handed tactics, and some rather regrettable instances of unsavory conduct concerning commissions awarded to private architects, the act was repealed by Congress on August 24, 1912, in a particularly cutting rebuke to the Institute's management, its senior members, and board of directors.

This hard-won legislation should have been the precedent for an era of progressive management of the government's building portfolio, efficient investment of federal resources, and the introduction of best design principles for the public interest. Instead the opportunity was squandered by a few protagonists whose actions in the name of the profession poorly served its interests. The repeated assertions made by the representatives of the profession that the Office of the Supervising Architect was a nest of mediocrity and incompetence undermined any chance for a sustained partnership between the AIA and the government. The straw that broke the camel's back came when the Institute raised its minimum fee to six percent and insisted that the Treasury Department accept this increase.

According to the *Congressional Record*: "The Government maintains a well-organized architect's office costing upward of $1,000,000 a year. In the judgment of three of the committees of the House there was no sound reason for the employment of outside talent under such conditions imposed by the architects by which they charged the United States twenty percent more than they received from other clients. While the service of the best architectural talent at times is required by Government, it should, and as experience has shown, can be had upon reasonable terms both fair to the government and attractive to architects."[421]

Even the architecture press acknowledged the profession's blunder: " . . . at the present time the American Institute, or its representatives, has antagonized departmental heads and government officials generally by unbusinesslike, untactful, or obviously biased presentations of their demands . . . An argument . . . must be placed before them in a businesslike manner and must indicate a due realization of and regard for practical considerations . . . considered from a point of view from which these officials themselves have to confront the question."[422]

On a number of fronts, the repeal of the Tarsney Act reflected Congress's pent-up anger at and resentment of AIA dictates. Because the AIA's refusal to recognize the Office of the Supervising Architect as the legitimate manager of federal building design was ongoing, and since the bulk of the nation's architects did not conform to the AIA's new fee schedule, the final blow was the arbitrary fee increase, which appeared to favor only *some* architects' remuneration. Nor had the AIA bothered to broker an agreement with lawmakers before increasing the Treasury's cost of doing business with private architects. The personal animosity of members of Congress and key government officials toward Glenn Brown and the Institute carried over into their negative attitude toward architects in private practice.

Soon after this setback, global events redirected America's attention to more pressing concerns than those promoted by the architectural elite at the turn of the century. The Beaux-Arts vision, exemplified in Chicago in 1893 and trumpeted for more than two decades by Institute spokesmen, had calcified into an outdated civic design orthodoxy before the situation created by the repeal of the Tarsney Act could be effectively redressed by the profession.

World War I served to amplify the emptiness of winning the style war with the federal government: "The prejudice which restricted employment for architects during the war was so great that a plan to make available the services of AIA membership to the War Department was never adopted . . . even though similar programs involving the engineering societies had been welcomed."[423]

Rather than conveying to the nation's political leadership the great value of the architecture profession to national life, the AIA's foray into amassing political influence succeeded in convincing Capitol Hill that these artists were far more trouble and expense than they were worth. At a moment of national crisis and absolute need for architects' skills, the Institute's offer of service to the nation was not valued.[424]

But the damage was not wholesale. Many architects contributed to the war effort by working for local, state, and federal governments throughout the conflict. Precedents in design and in new housing policies were influenced by architects working for the government during the war, many of whom were AIA members. And of course, architects served in the armed forces and saw action in the war.

On Armistice Day, November 11, 1918, World War I ended. Less than six months later, on April 30, 1919, the American Institute of Architects held its annual convention, took candid stock of itself, and faced up to its collective past. The membership, under new leadership and with renewed idealism, began planning its future.

13 THE 1919 AIA CONVENTION: POSTWAR REFORM FOR THE 20TH CENTURY

The last convention was held in the midst of the turmoil of a great war. This is being held amid the turmoil, almost as great, of the readjustment. A great tide of change is sweeping over all the accustomed landmarks, and those that are not firmly bedded in wisdom and justice will surely be uprooted and swept away. It is our duty to seek, humbly but with all earnestness, to discern those elements of our profession that are sound and secure on which to build the great future of the practice of architecture.
—Report of the Board of Directors, Fifty-Second Annual Convention of
The American Institute of Architects, 1919

EVERY THERAPIST WORTH HIS OR HER SALT will tell you that a catharsis is good for the psyche. World War I was just such a catharsis for an unlikely group: the architecture profession.

In post–World War I Germany, the Bauhaus school revolutionized modern architecture, literally and intellectually. In the United States, the membership of the AIA spontaneously embarked on a grassroots reformation and dealt decisively with the unfinished business of prewar professional practice, public policy setbacks, and society's changed conditions. This process began with the formation of the Post-War Committee at the 52nd AIA convention, held April 30–May 2, 1919, in Nashville, Tennessee.

The younger practitioners, routinely held in check by successive generations of the profession's elders, assumed leadership and shouldered the task of confronting institutional rot and a host of damaging, anachronistic prejudices commonly associated with the profession, particularly by the indispensable engineering profession and allied building trades. While pitching in with other workingmen in the trenches and the factories, these architects discovered the depth of resentment wrought by so many decades of the profession's aloof, superior attitudes and its suspicious, disrespectful treatment of skilled labor. This new generation of leadership no longer looked to the past for guidance, but to each other. Elitism had served no useful purpose during the "war to end all wars." Elitism did not help build ships and airplanes, barracks and landings. Nor could elitism rebuild the smoking ruins afterward.

The "Proceedings of the 1919 AIA Convention" is an inspirational document that every student of architecture should be required to read, cover to cover, as a leadership tutorial and model of professional self-governance. The following excerpts from the proceedings provide an understanding of the reform imperative of the 1919 Post-War Committee:

> It seems to me that the trouble with the architect is that he does not get right down to the small things in his immediate neighborhood. . . . If all the architects of the United States, in all of these small communities, would enter into this phase of development, not only as an architect, but as a citizen, to a certain extent get into politics . . . so far that we will be able to carry through our ideas and ideals; if all the architects of the United States would agree among themselves to perform this obligation free of expense . . . there is no doubt the work of the architect professionally would be felt within the very next few years.[425]
>
> —George Washington Maher, Chicago Prairie School architect and city planner

> . . . if the architects as bodies and as individuals would take an interest in public affairs, would lend their talents . . . to the problems of society in their immediate neighborhoods, the people would soon . . . bring them problems to solve that the architects never thought of solving and they would extend their services. . . . There would be a great extension of the architectural field if we would take more interest in public affairs and urban affairs. . . .[426]
>
> —Henry K. Holsman, architect, automotive engineer, entrepreneur, and president of the Chicago Architectural Club

. . . the public had confidence in us because we demonstrated we were unselfish. . . . The Mayor said . . . when he started the [WWI] memorial organization, that "We want you . . . to lead us in this way and we want you to make the same kind of collaborative effort as you did for us in the housing". . . One other lesson we learned from this experiment was the great strength of unionism.[427]

—Ellis Fuller Lawrence, dean of the School of Architecture at the University of Oregon, Eugene, describieing the successful efforts by architects on the board of a municipal housing corporation in Oregon to design and build 2,000 houses under war conditions.

. . . the first way for anyone to become a citizen is to accept the responsibility of citizenship . . . Every architect should be familiar with the names and positions of those who are the governing officials in his city and his state and furthermore, his own representatives in the House and the Senate of the United States . . . there are very few architects here present who have a copy of the Congressional Directory . . . each one of us should be supplied with a copy so that we might . . . get in touch with [those] that we, as citizens, elected to represent us in the national capital . . . we should . . . keep in touch with all civic associations and other civic bodies, all chambers of commerce . . . we should affiliate with engineering bodies and builders' exchange . . . we should keep in touch with educational institutions, with home and school associations . . . with building and loan societies . . . responsible for the financing of the homes of the people . . . we should keep in touch with the local insurance rating organizations . . . with the local organizations in the building trades . . . who . . . are, after all, interested in the safety of those engaged in building construction and in better workmanship and in the improvement of materials.[428]

—David Knickerbacker Boyd, 1914 AIA secretary, 1915 vice president, Philadelphia

The purpose of architecture is to promote and support rational living; the great mass of architecture in our urban centers does not. For this condition the responsibility is general. In it the architect shares, for the profession as a whole has accepted the conditions and the program for buildings which are now developed by industrialism and capitalism . . . the larger social purpose, which should appear as the aims of the profession, have been lost sight of, while the possibility of really effective collaborative effort among closely associated vocational groups has been completely defeated . . . Over the total mass of our architectural environment . . . the profession has exercised almost no control . . . our education, both general and vocational, has failed to accomplish what should be its major purpose . . . it appears to the student that the practice of architecture is a cultural activity completely removed from the affairs which concern the mass of people. This introduction to professional activity, and the scale of values thereby established, very largely explains why the majority of the "educated" profession take but slight interest in offering advice on community or political action which has nothing directly to do with commissions. It follows . . . that the public and Government officials do not ask advice . . . The almost universal practice of teaching design without any contact whatever with the world of reality, and of imposing purely academic judgments upon the work accomplished by the student, develops a set of utterly false values with respect to architecture and the function of the profession in the community . . . the student thus engaged is never afforded the opportunity of actually testing his ideas by application . . . Responsibility of thinking is thus completely suppressed by these false and artificial methods of rating and appraisal . . . not one of these educational experiences takes place in the world of reality where the architect must gain an honest livelihood . . . opportunity should be afforded in a school of research for the architectural student, in collaboration with others, to study architecture and art, industry and government, and the complex

forces with which we must contend in directing the growth of
our environment.[429]
—Frederick Lee Ackerman, chief of the Housing and Planning Department, U.S. Shipping Board

. . . the Architect's standing . . . is in great measure made by that
great mass of men who are not members of the American Institute of Architects. . . . We must concern ourselves with what every
other architect is doing. Unless we find ways . . . to get in touch
with all the men competent to practice the profession, and test the
validity of our standards in light of their experiences, and in
light of their needs, we are not sure that we are right.[430]
—Robert D. Kohn, chief of production at the U.S. Shipping
Board and 1931–1932 AIA president

What is the remedy? I think it is to go back and recover our lost
traditions . . . master the building problem absolutely, and not be
so dependent on others . . . these limitations . . . have been largely
self-imposed. Such a recovery would automatically bring about an
extension of the field of the architect. . . . and make the architect
what he once was—the master-builder.[431]
—Emil Lorch, chair of the Department of Engineering,
University of Michigan, Ann Arbor

The experience and social activism of such architects as Henry K.
Holsman, innovative developer of mutual-ownership housing and 1919
president of the AIA Chicago chapter, and Frederick Lee Ackerman and
Robert D. Kohn, of New York City, influential leaders in housing design
and public policy, inspired the profession's idealism and creativity.

Ackerman was a leading architect, educator, town planner, writer, and
thinker on the role of architects, design, and technology in American society at the beginning of the modern technological age. Educated at Cornell
University and in Europe, Ackerman partnered with Alexander B. Trow-
bridge until 1920. During World War I, he was appointed chief of the
Housing and Planning Department of the U.S. Shipping Board and was

responsible for the design of housing for wartime workers. Ackerman collaborated with Henry Wright and Clarence S. Stein on the design of the planned suburban community of Radburn, New Jersey, where he first introduced detached and semidetached garages into residential housing. Ackerman was technical director of the New York City Housing Authority and taught architecture at Cornell and Columbia universities. He was a member of the New York State Board for Registration of Architects.

Robert D. Kohn, president of the New York City AIA chapter in 1913, went on to become president of the AIA in 1931 and again in 1932. A graduate of New York City College and Columbia University, Kohn also studied at the École des Beaux Arts in Paris and was a design partner of Clarence Stein and Charles Butler. During World War I, he was chief of production for the U.S. Shipping Board. In 1921 Kohn led the founding of the New York Building Congress: "We started out with the idea that the only hope for effective improvement in the industry was to render through cooperation of all of its elements some measure of service which the public had the right to demand of us."[432]

Kohn's specialization in the design of low-cost housing led to his appointment as director of the Housing Division of the Public Works Administration in 1933–1934. Kohn later bacame vice president of the 1939 New York World's Fair. He designed many important buildings, including the New York Ethical Culture Society Auditorium, the Evening Post building, Mt. Sinai Hospital, and R.H. Macy's Department Store. Kohn was also a president of the American Ethical Union.

Ackerman and Kohn were involved in the founding of the Regional Planning Association of America in 1923 along with Wright, Stein, and Lewis Mumford. They were also among the sixteen original leaders of the Technical Alliance (1918–1921), a multidiscipline think tank.[433]

The National Council of Architectural Registration Boards (NCARB), the federation of state architectural licensing and registration boards, was born at the 1919 Nashville meeting. Fifteen architects from across the country decided to form an organization to address the long-standing problem of how to create a nationally viable, uniform process for the states to license the practice of architecture. NCARB's founding officers were its chairman, Professor Emil Lorch, chair of the Department of Engineering

at the University of Michigan, Ann Arbor, and Chicago architect Emery
Stanford Hall, its first secretary. On May 6, 1920, Lorch and Hall were
joined on the NCARB board by official representatives of the AIA and the
American Association of Engineers. NCARB was incorporated as a nonprofit
organization in the state of Illinois in 1921 and initially operated out of
Emery Hall's Chicago office. He remained NCARB's secretary-treasurer
until his death in 1939.

Under Hall's leadership, NCARB created the standards and guidelines for
architects' licensing examinations and reciprocal state licensing and registration. In 1940 NCARB was instrumental in forming the National Architectural Accrediting Board (NAAB), which evaluates national accreditation
standards for architecture education. NCARB's ongoing work is crucial to the
practice of architecture and to the protection of the public's interest. The
sustained leadership of architects working in all fifty states for the advancement of professional standards through NCARB has effectively influenced the
framing of progressive laws to govern the practice of architecture and to
"achieve the enviable goal of a reciprocity system among the states that is
unequaled by any other profession in the United States."434

Another influential development that received invaluable support during the 1919 convention was the Architects' Small House Bureau (ASHB), a
concept presented to the convention by its Committee on Small Houses.
Four Minneapolis architects—Carl A. Gage, Beaver Wade Day, Frederick
Mann, and Roy Childs Jones—initiated the bureau to "improve the architecture of the small house, to eliminate waste in the building thereof, and
to insure good, safe, and at the same time economical building."435

The ASHB was a limited dividend corporation that operated as a design
cooperative and was administrated by thirteen regional service bureaus. It
produced for sale to the public handsome, functional, and economical
designs for small homes of up to six rooms, along with the complete elevations and working blueprints. The bureau offered sound advice to potential homeowners on all issues associated with building and owning a home.

The ASHB was publicly endorsed and enthusiastically supported by
the AIA, as well as by the U.S. Department of Commerce under Secretary
of Commerce Herbert Hoover. Beginning in 1922, the organization began
publishing its housing designs in a monthly journal, *The Small Home.* In 1923

the bureau produced *Your Future Home*, a portfolio of nearly seventy home plans in a wide variety of popular styles, including Colonial Revival, Cape Cod, Spanish, Bungalow, and "Modern American," which incorporated some elements of the Prairie and Modernist design trends. In existence until 1942, the ASHB never became a profitable business, though its positive, constructive message of the benefit of an architect's services did reach millions of average Americans in the residential market and helped to raise the public's appreciation and demand for quality architectural design.

This activist movement benefited other architect-led organizations, such as the New York Society of Architects (NYSA), founded in 1906. James Riely Gordon led the NYSA throughout the postwar period, from 1916 to 1929; through his leadership, the NYSA established a close working relationship with city and state government. Gordon helped to rewrite the city's building codes to meet modern conditions and developed better institutional management of the built environment. His distinguished career took off at the 1893 Chicago World's Fair as the designer of the Texas state building. He worked for the Office of the Supervising Architect of the U.S. Treasury and designed several landmark courthouses in Texas. He moved to New York City in 1902 and briefly went into partnership with Evarts Tracy and Egerton Swartwout. Gordon's dedicated civic activism made him a leader in all of New York's professional architects' associations, and he served under several New York City mayors on municipal committees governing housing, planning, and building codes.[436]

The 1919 watershed convention created a ripple effect at the grassroots level, resulting in a marked increase in the membership of the Institute. After six decades of slow, incremental growth, suddenly the AIA's membership doubled between 1920 and 1925 and continued to climb at a steady pace until 1930, when the stock market crash on Black Tuesday, October 29, 1929, staggered the economy. The nation suffered immense hardship for the next decade. Of all the professions, architects were particularly hard hit as the economic conditions that provide the profession's lifeblood collapsed with Wall Street. The AIA stood by its members, some eighty-five percent of whom were out of work for long periods. The durability of the AIA, unified and supportive of its reorganized priorities, made it possible to weather the crisis of the Depression. The initial sharp decline in membership was short-lived and was soon restored to the previous level of growth and continued to escalate until the outbreak of World War II.[437]

A keener social consciousness, manifested in the federal Works Progress Administration projects during the Depression, also infiltrated the profession. Progressive ideas were being translated into design in new, exciting ways. While dark forces gathered in Berlin and drove many of Europe's best and brightest minds into exile abroad, the United States became the lucky recipient of much of that cultural diaspora. Scientists, writers, performers, and the brilliant artists and architects of the Bauhaus School became Americans during this period.

In 1939 the New York World's Fair showcased the World of the Future and projected onto the public's imagination a world of state-of-the-art architecture and design, raising to new heights the expectation that modern design would provide a higher standard of living for ordinary Americans. Modernism had arrived, and the bright future it announced temporarily bleached out the clouds of catastrophe hovering on the horizon.

14 Leadership through the Great Depression: Henry K. Holsman and Mutual-Ownership Housing in Chicago

The character of a profession depends upon the character of its individuals. The repu-tation of a profession depends upon its organization and the participation of all in its welfare ... Architecture is a social phenomenon, not an individual phenomenon.
—Henry K. Holsman, President, Illinois Chapter,
The American Institute of Architects, Inaugural Address, June 10, 1919

SOON AFTER HE ATTENDED the momentous 1919 AIA convention, Henry Kerchner Holsman (1866–1963), was elected president of the Illinois chapter of the Institute. His career began in a traditional fash-ion. Born right after the Civil War in 1866, in Dale, Iowa, and orphaned at age eleven, Holsman went to work to support his siblings but continued with his schooling. After graduation from high school in 1884, he taught grammar school for three years before enrolling in college in 1887.

His first experience with architecture came when he solved a building problem for a neighbor. In a rural area with no local architects, the homeowner wanted to double the size of his one-story house. Holsman came up with the unusual solution of raising the house up on stilts and building a new ground floor beneath it, with all the much-needed modern amenities added.[438]

Holsman gained an instant reputation as a clever designer and prob-lem solver, and his architecture career was launched. Through his remod-eling work, he saved enough money for tuition at Iowa College (now Grinnell College), founded in 1846 by New England Congregationalist social reformers. The Civil War had decimated its enrollment, but during Reconstruction the school slowly began to grow again. Women were admit-ted and the curriculum broadened to include the natural sciences and a department of political science, one of the first in the nation. "Grinnell became known as the center of the Social Gospel reform movement."[439] It was in this environment that Holsman found his design vocation influenced by a distinctly ethical consciousness and social commitment. During summer vacations, he worked in architecture offices and graduated from Iowa College in 1891.[440]

In 1892 he moved to Chicago and worked as a building superintendent for high-rise buildings. He then formed a partnership with William H. Brainerd, a fellow alumnus of Iowa College.[441] They designed two gymnasiums for their alma mater in 1897 and 1899. By 1900 he had his own practice in Chicago.[442]

Holsman became known for the academic facilities he designed for the University of Nebraska (Lincoln); Parsons College (Fairfield, Iowa), listed as a National Historic District in 1983 and subsequently demolished by the nominating owner between 2000 and 2002;[443] Ripon College (Wisconsin); University of Danville (Illinois); and the University of Chicago's Ricketts Laboratories and Disciples Divinity House.

In 1896 he married his artistic collaborator, Elizabeth Tuttle, one of the first graduates of the Art Institute of Chicago. The couple's three sons eventually worked for their father. Tuttle created the sculptural elements incorporated into much of Holsman's residential architecture.

Holsman's gift for mechanics and technical refinements led him to pursue innovations in architectural design and construction as well as in industrial design. This bent also prompted him to develop unique business concepts to implement his ideas.

Simultaneous with his architecture career, Holsman went into automotive design after buying his first vehicle and finding it problematic. By 1901 he had completed the prototype of the Holsman high-wheeler automobile, which was designed to safely navigate the harsh conditions of the midwestern farmlands. Holsman and his younger brother, J. Arthur Holsman, started the Holsman Automobile Company and introduced one of America's first mass produced motor vehicles, the Holsman High-Wheeler, in 1902.

Within ten years, Henry had secured more than twenty patents in automotive engineering, his goal being a reliable and affordable vehicle for working people. The savings in manufacturing costs realized through his development of the engineering and design enhancements were passed on to consumers. The high-wheeler's ability to climb hills and negotiate rough terrain led to competition from other manufacturers, but Holsman remained the industry leader from 1904 through 1909. It was this success, however, which led to the firm's dissolution.

With the company's 1910 order book full and its loan note due, the bank refused to extend additional credit for building the normal seasonal inventory. With no financial alternative, the Holsmans closed their plant. The patents were sold to the Independent Harvester Company, and Holsman was hired to oversee the auto's production under new ownership. He stayed on only two years. The high-wheeler motor carriage had had its day and was about to be replaced by a newer city-going automobile, the Ford Model T.444 It was a good time to return to architecture.

In the first decades of the 20th century, Holsman designed churches, colleges, banks, schools, and commercial buildings. He also designed many impressive private homes, including Prairie Style and Arts and Crafts houses in the Oak Park and Beverly Hills suburbs of Chicago, nestled comfortably among the houses of Frank Lloyd Wright, Walter Burley Griffin, and George Maher.445 Holsman remained focused on housing throughout his career and concentrated on efficiencies in planning, technologies, and materials.

Before World War I, Holsman began experimenting with new formats for apartment house design. Aesthetics reflected mainstream tastes and demands, while the technical originality of his programmatic planning and execution contributed to the safety, livability, and cost-effectiveness of the buildings. His designs eliminated waste by integrating more open space with fewer corridors and much larger windows. Landscape design, learned during his 1908–1909 stint as a Chicago park commissioner, became an indispensable element in his formula. He developed safer, cost-effective wall partitions made of two-inch-thick plaster, which were not only fire resistant and vermin-free but also significantly cheaper than traditional lathing and plaster wall construction.

Around the time America entered World War I, Holsman was asked by a group of artists to design and build a residential studio building they intended to own by forming a corporation of private stockholders. But the

artists were unable to raise the necessary funding because of wartime mortgage restrictions, and the project fell through. This attempt at occupant
ownership sparked an idea in Holsman's mind, though it had to wait until
the war's end.[446]

The issue of housing loomed large as the profession grappled with post-
war conditions at the 1919 AIA convention. Despite the success of individual and charitable housing projects undertaken in the previous century, few
developers were yet inclined to build decent, affordable housing for the lower
middle and working classes, much less for the urban poor.

Holsman knew he needed to find a new financial model if he was going
to introduce affordable housing in a manner that would not be driven by
short-term financial gain. If he could integrate state-of-the-art building and
modern design with a secure means of ownership, the possibility of building his designs would be within reach for many potential homeowners.

He came up with a new business model called *mutual ownership,* which
made apartment dwellers the beneficiaries of a mutual trust corporation that
owned the buildings in which they lived. For a modest investment, owners
purchased certificates in the trust and received a renewable, low-cost lease
on an apartment. As their families grew, the trust members could trade up
to larger apartments and sell their shares at market value. The new owner
would assume occupancy and leasehold of the apartment.

As both an executive trustee and the architect, Holsman maximized
efficiencies in the cost of design, construction, and materials. These efficiencies, combined with nonspeculative fiduciary management, made it possible for trust beneficiaries to pay monthly rents well below market rates and
to redeem a potential profit on their initial investment in the trust.

Near the end of his life, Holsman wrote about the success of his
mutual-ownership model: "I designed a Mutual Home Ownership Trustee
Plan and had it printed. Milwaukee's Mayor sent a man to Chicago to see
it just as the pamphlets arrived from the printer. Thence he took back the
whole edition for the price of printing. Therefore my first large Mutual
Owner project was built in Milwaukee, Wis. as promoted by the City
Plan Commission."[447]

The Garden Homes project, built in Milwaukee in the early 1920s, thus
became the "nation's first experiment in municipal public housing."[448]

A 2004 exhibition at the National Building Museum, "Affordable Housing: Designing an American Asset," described the benefits of allowing the city to own stock in cooperative companies: "For like-minded wage earners, limited-equity co-operatives present an attractive alternative to capitalistic ventures. As self-governing non-profit corporations, they pool their members' resources and hold a single mortgage. Since the price of shares is not tied to that of the property, and their resale value is strictly controlled, limited-equity co-operatives preserve long-term affordability."449

In 1922 Holsman formalized his concept with the founding of the Community Development Trust (CDT). CDT rode out the Depression without a single default and survived into the 1950s, before hitting insurmountable business difficulties unrelated to the fundamental soundness of the trust business model.

Initially, Holsman had to take all the risk personally. The Chicago Trust Company loaned him the money to buy land on University Avenue in Hyde Park, near the University of Chicago. Construction of his first sixteen-unit building began in 1923. After the first floor was completed, Holsman sent a letter to area residents, describing his mutual ownership scheme. The building was soon fully subscribed.

This apartment house was quickly followed by five more moderate-income mutual-ownership buildings in Hyde Park containing between sixteen and sixty units. A seventh building, erected in 1929, was designed for upper-income owners; it was the only trust building negatively affected by the Depression.

In 1925 Holsman's eldest son, Henry T., with the help of his father, started a realty firm specializing in cooperative apartment management. In 1931 the firm merged with another to form the Parker-Holsman Company, which successfully managed the Holsmans' trust buildings throughout the Depression. It is still in business today under different owners.450

Henry K. Holsman's standing in the community was indeed high. He served as president of the Chicago Architectural Club in 1903, was elected president of the Illinois chapter of the AIA in 1919, was a cofounder and director of the Association of Arts and Industries, and helped found the Museum of Science and Industry, which saved the 1893 Chicago World's Fair Palace of Fine Arts as its home. Holsman was a member and director

Henry K. Holsman's affordable mutual ownership apartment buildings constructed in the 1920s include these classic Tudor-style garden apartments at 7855 South Shore Drive, Chicago, Illinois, erected in 1925. Photo: © J. Peter Holsman

of the Association of Illinois Architects, the Architects Club of Chicago, and of the Municipal Art League. He also was a member and officer of the famous Cliff Dwellers Club, one of Louis Sullivan's favorite haunts.[451] In 1927 Holsman was elevated to the AIA College of Fellows.[452]

As the nation's economic conditions worsened with the Depression, Holsman immersed himself in the problem of "blighted cities." He contributed an article titled "Thoughts on Cooperative Apartments" to *Living Architecture: A Discussion of Present Day Problems*, published in 1930 by AIA Illinois and edited by Arthur Woltersdorf. In 1931–1932, he chaired the

Architects Club of Chicago's Committee on Blighted Area Housing and wrote its final report, "Rehabilitating Blighted Areas." The report examined the operational methods of mutual home ownership and asserted that such housing trusts provided social stability and could regenerate Chicago's blighted areas.

Citing the President's Conference on Home Building and Home Ownership and data gathered by the Economic Research Department at Northwestern University and the Social Science Department at the University of Chicago, the report's conclusion is a forceful call to action: "there are sufficient surveys and reports available to warrant the organization of a group of responsible business, professional, and civic minded citizens to begin the assembling of funds and properties and to start the actual building of low cost housing in blighted areas under a comprehensive physical and financial plan."[453]

Holsman pursued a vigorous personal campaign to raise awareness of the viability of his mutual-ownership concept. On November 22, 1931, the *New York Times* reported that profits from resales in Holsman's eight cooperative apartment buildings ranged from "25 to 105 per cent." And as of May 1, 1931, all the buildings "were 100 per cent occupied . . . and had treasury surpluses larger than those reported for 1929."[454]

Interviewed on a broadcast of the Armour Institute Radio Program in May 1933, Holsman spoke about the topic of urban blight and stressed that "no vast schemes of public works for the employment of surplus artisans and labor can surpass the beneficence to be derived from rehabilitating our blighted areas with decent homes for families of low income. It is directly in line with the ideals and aims of the constitutional spirit of the nation; it is a test case for democratic leadership."[455]

The *New York Times*, on October 22, 1933, in an article titled "Rebuilding Slum Areas, Low Cost Construction at Low Ebb, Says Architect," reported Holsman's concerns over the dire housing situation for most Americans. He cited alarming statistics on the socioeconomic consequences of urban poverty: "the building industry, while employing nearly one-third of wage earners . . . built no homes within the rent range of two-thirds of all American families . . . Chicago has thirty-six square miles . . . of blighted area where ordinary municipal services . . . cost more than two and a half times the revenue levied thereon. Much of that section has been reduced to slums."[456]

Holsman was also invited to design a model home of the future for Chicago's 1933–1934 Century of Progress exhibition. His Country Home Model Farm House was constructed with his latest innovation of load-bearing, one-story high, four-inch-thick, reinforced brick slab walls.[457]

In the early 1930s, Holsman's twin sons joined his firm. John worked as an architect, and William became the firm's administrator. They were both graduates of Cornell University's School of Architecture. The firm survived the Depression, despite the scarcity of work, by concentrating on residential design of various types, particularly low-rise garden apartments and private homes.

According to architect Edo J. Belli (1918–2003), hired as a junior draftsman in 1936, the firm consisted of Holsman, his two sons, a daughter-in-law, and himself. When things were slow, "from time to time they'd loan me out to various offices." Holsman paid Belli's fees for two years of night courses at the Armour Institute (now Illinois Institute of Technology) in preparation for the licensing exam.

While John Holsman was "the delineator, the designer, the dreamer," Bill Holsman was "the construction man." The firm developed new methods of doing prefab housing and designed two-bedroom homes with an average cost of $3,000. Belli described the Holsmans as "innovators in almost every field that you could imagine . . . it was a good German firm." The senior Holsman "didn't tolerate a lot of nonsense. No mistakes."[458]

In the late 1930s Holsman participated in a consortium of architects, Associated Architects–South Park Gardens, that served as consultants to the newly established Chicago Housing Authority on the early stages of public housing projects, such as the Ida B. Wells Homes. In 1941 Holsman was chair of the group.[459]

As World War II approached, the Holsman firm, now well established as leading housing experts, designed private developments such as the River Forest Garden Apartments (1939)[460] and the Princeton Park Gardens (1944–1946), a large-scale development of 908 row houses "for Negros" funded by a Federal Housing Authority (FHA) mortgage in what is now the Auburn Park neighborhood of Chicago's South Side (just north of

Roseland).[461] This project proved problematic for its investors, which included the architect Lawrence Bradford Perkins (1907–1997), of Perkins & Will, who acknowledged serious difficulties with contractors.[462]

To meet the demands of another postwar housing boom, the firm grew very rapidly, from about thirty people in 1945 to more than double that number in 1952.[463] With the addition of two new partners, architects Benard Klekamp and D. Coder Taylor, the firm changed its name to Holsman, Holsman, Klekamp & Taylor.

Between 1945 and 1951 the firm built more than 3,000 mutual-ownership apartment units for the Community Development Trust. Each trust prospectus included a no-speculative-profits statement: "Mutual owners pay no speculative profits. They pay for land, labor, and materials at cost and necessary services at not to exceed regular, established fees."[464]

The firm's major mutual housing project of the era was the Parkway Garden Apartments; the complex consisted of 694 two- and three-bedroom units in thirty-five buildings, built on a fifteen-acre site formerly occupied by the White City amusement park. The Dining Car Employees Union initiated the project in 1945, and the apartments were intended for ownership by union members and the local African-American community. This development was beset by difficulties from the start.

According to Holsman's account, written on January 11, 1954, securing ownership of the land was complicated by insinuations that the mutual-ownership scheme, which provided no "middle-man profits," was concocted by "Communists." The land was acquired, but the local brokers' association demanded "untenable agreements." Since no local mortgage could be obtained (in large part because of "Negro tenant owners"), the firm turned to the FHA for the mortgage but met more obstacles intended to prevent the project from moving forward.[465] Architect Charles Booher Genther (1907–1987), a CDT trustee in the late 1940s and the founder of PACE Associates, later noted that the Holsmans "were very persistent," despite having "every roadblock . . . thrown in their way."[466]

According to D. Coder Taylor, dealing with the FHA was "a very difficult thing . . . I think the real secret of getting it approved was to try to familiarize the [FHA] staff, who was not familiar with innovative methods, that the merit of the design . . . was in effect a cost-saving device. They couldn't argue about that point, but it took a long time to convince them."[467]

The firm hired Bryant Hammond, a local community leader, to represent the firm to the bureaucrats in Washington, D.C. Taylor recalled that "one of the top people at the FHA came over to me . . . and he said, 'you know Mr. Taylor, Bryant Hammond is certainly an exceptional representative for your firm," and he was right. He was highly respected by our firm, in Washington and in the black community. I think the fact that we hired him to assist in the project was an innovation."[468]

The Holsman firm was pressured, despite its serious objections, to hire a contractor designated by the FHA's representative. It is important to note here that Congress investigated the FHA in 1954 for corrupt business practices: "Unscrupulous builders, aided by corrupt FHA officials, had reaped enormous profits at the taxpayers' expense."[469] The contractor failed to complete one-third of the project by the contract deadline, resulting in "a worse default than the architects feared at the time of their objection."[470] The firm negotiated a complex deal with subcontractors and had to sell off the northwest corner of the property in order to cover the financial shortfall.[471] Nevertheless, the housing complex was completed and dedicated in September 1950.

In the 1970s, the Parkway Garden complex was one of the largest rehab projects undertaken by the Chicago Housing Authority. The remaining trust beneficiaries were bought out at a profit and the complex was converted, via HUD refinancing, to a nonprofit corporation with all units on a rental basis.[472]

Two high-rise apartment buildings, the Promontory (1946) and 860 Lake Shore Drive (1948), designed in collaboration with Ludwig Mies van der Rohe as the lead architect and PACE Associates as production architects, grabbed the attention of the public and the profession. Holsman, Holsman, Klekamp & Taylor, as the consulting architects, handled the integration of engineering and construction of both projects and, significantly, the structuring of the buildings' mutual-ownership plan. Real-estate promoter Henry Greenwald, who had once worked for the Holsman firm as an administrative assistant, sponsored both projects.

In a 1983 interview for the Chicago Architects Oral History Project,

Charles Genther recalled how PACE, Mies, and H, H, K & T collaborated on the project. His admiration for the Holsmans, particularly for their excellence in design at the lowest possible cost to the homeowner, was genuine. Genther said, "Oh, golly, were they ever committed to it. They were committed to doing it at a low price that everybody could afford." When the interviewer Betty Blum asked if that was to make the world better, Genther replied yes.[473]

In January 1950, *Architectural Forum* magazine published an in-depth issue on the design, construction, and financing of new housing and featured the Promontory and 860 Lake Shore Drive, both International Style apartment towers, along with various low-rise housing projects designed by the Holsman firm. According to the magazine's editors, "Pioneering Construction Ideas, ranging from reinforced brick walls to radiant heated ceiling beams, save space, time and money . . . As an apartment-building device, mutual ownership is now a major force in the Chicago area."[474]

Into his eighties, Henry continued to take "a lively and patriarchal interest in the development of more projects,"[475] and John T. Holsman became the firm's principal designer and spokesman. In John Holsman's *Architectural Forum* article on community trust as a vehicle for private enterprise, he laid out the philosophy that had guided the firm for so many decades: "The only solution to the urban housing shortage . . . must lie in some form of tenant ownership of apartments . . . If housing problems are to be solved, more of the really competent . . . must be attracted to this work. For large numbers of individual families to pool their resources, find and employ competent technical service, acquire a proper site, let sound contracts, and realize an economical and worthwhile housing development is extremely difficult, so difficult that there must be some established pattern available to them—an organization willing and able to guide and safeguard the effort. It is for this purpose that the Community Development Trust was organized."[476]

The mutual ownership scheme originating from Chicago was also used in Walter Gropius and Marcel Breuer's modernist Aluminum City Terrace apartment complex, designed for Alcoa Aluminum employees and commissioned in 1942 by the Federal Works Agency. This was "the first defense housing project to be purchased by tenants under provisions of the Mutual Ownership Plan of 1948."[477]

In 1950 the architectural press was highly optimistic about the Holsman firm's approach; it embodied a new, dynamic role for the architecture profession at the outset of America's postwar baby-boom economy. But the fate of the firm followed a sharply different course than the one predicted in January 1950.

The sudden eruption of the Korean War soon stifled the supply of materials and capital. The FHA strained to gain control of the low- and middle-income housing sector through stringent mortgage controls and building specifications that made few if any allowances for the design innovations associated with the Holsmans.[478] Harsh marketplace conditions and frequent contractor default added to the firm's difficulties and led to a series of ill-advised decisions that undermined the partnership's financial footing.

According to Taylor, "I felt that Bill Holsman, who was handling financing, was not very prudent in what he was doing. I can't say that if I were in his position I would have done anything differently."[479] Apparently, funds were being transferred between the individual building trusts to keep the various projects going as construction and financing delays mounted. Taylor recognized a bad situation and resigned in mid-1952, but stated that "There was no personal benefit to anyone in the firm or trusts. They were trying to proceed with the projects. They were being beset with problems . . . the shortage of materials, contractors, all the factors that are necessary, including shortage of funding."[480]

On July 12, 1952, the CDT's trustee bank obtained a court order that allowed it to freeze the firm's assets and seize its records. By December 31, 1952, the H, H, K & T partnership was perforce bankrupt and ceased operation. Liability insurance for architects did not yet exist, and the costs of the ongoing legal battle and the firm's financial obligations stripped the Holsman family of all its assets.

Henry and his sons regrouped as Holsman & Company and tried to carry on, but it was too late. Contractor delays and financing difficulties depleted the remaining trust funds. The Holsmans were unable to complete their last project, an extension to the Winchester Hood Garden Apartments. The reconstituted family firm was forced into bankruptcy.

In 1956 the Holsmans were charged with technical mail fraud because they had used the U.S. Postal Service to solicit and receive investments in the trust funds. No proof of intention to defraud was proffered, but because the firm had been paid for it services as the architects, and Henry and William Holsman were trustees of the Community Development Trust, they were held personally liable for the failure of the last project. Tried without a jury, ninety-year-old Henry, "in view of his fine record," was remanded to the custody of the marshal for one hour. William, the firm's financial manager, was sentenced to a short prison term.[481]

Taylor felt the court's judgment was wholly incorrect: "it was not justified . . . the expenditures were all made, in the interest of the mutual owners . . . In other defunct projects very frequently the architect is not paid . . . In this case the architect was paid, quite properly so . . . The court found . . . that they [Henry and William Holsman] were fiduciarily responsible."[482]

In 1957 Henry Holsman wrote his reflections on the closing events of his life. He described how the CDT's bank trustee, the Trust Company of Chicago, was taken over sometime in 1950 by the principals of the Southmoor Bank and Trust Company. Southmoor's chairman, Leon Marcus, brought in his own people to replace the bank's experienced trust officers. Within two years the bank sued the firm in direct violation of its trust rules on a pretext of "the liquidation of all our trusts business." The Holsman firm, already vulnerable under pinched business conditions, was blindsided.

This legal action seemed to defy any perceivable logic. Holsman could find no valid reason for the bank trustee to sabotage the very trust it was mandated to protect: "none of the . . . attorneys or officers of . . . trust companies I've dealt with thought it possible that any Trust officers could go so berserk as to violate their trust agreement . . . and cause the loss of thousands of dollars of hundreds of their trustors . . . Had . . . leading Trust Company officials thought of such a possibility, they would surely have organized a private institute to watch over and discipline any apparent unethical or illegal practice, or the negligence of public officials."[483]

Marcus was a shady Depression-era hustler in the real estate and construction businesses who moved into banking to "engage in financial manipulations." He was a crony of Orville E. Hodge, the Illinois state auditor who used the Southmoor Bank as the conduit for the theft of $1.5 million in state funds. Under federal indictment and awaiting trial for his role in the Hodge embezzlement, Marcus was found shot in the back of the head on March 31, 1957, his pockets still stuffed with cash and a highly incriminating loan receipt made out to Chicago Mafia boss Sam Giancanna.[484]

Holsman found no comfort in the fate of the embezzlers: "It's no restitution that some of the Hodge case embezzlers are in prison. Using lame laws (loop holes) for crime is worse or more dangerous than highway robbery . . . Nothing is more progressively destructive of good government . . . than baneful statutes that may insidiously or inadvertently lead or urge citizens to think unethically or act unjustly . . . If colleges start giving post-graduate education degrees in legislation (government trustees) as they did in Science 70 years ago; the results would be just as astonishing."[485]

Despite the great personal cost to himself, to the very end of his long life Holsman remained unshaken in his deep conviction that building affordable homes and livable communities was the greatest vocation of his profession.

On September 30, 1950, Holsman spoke to the future owners of Parkway Garden homes at the cornerstone ceremony; "We designed these gardens, playgrounds, walks and runways . . . knowing that if many children . . . play with . . . each other in the wonderful business of growing up—to learn to give and take, to teach and be taught, to win and to lose, to be proud and to be humble, to develop in their own natural way among trees and shrubs, grass and grounds—they will grow up to be . . . mutually cooperative citizens . . . Mutual development and ownership itself, by its very nature, selects a community of all classes with enough common interest and respect for each other to produce a balanced society."[486]

Henry K. Holsman died on May 15, 1963, shortly before his 97th birthday. His mutual-ownership model was among the very earliest prototypes for the future development of co-op apartments and condominiums. Though the business formula he created to benefit those with the greatest need and least resources can function independently of an altruistic dimension, mutual-ownership housing still works for those who share his vision of social equality and civic harmony and is once again becoming a popular vehicle for development of affordable housing.

15 20TH-CENTURY LEADERSHIP: APPRAISING THE PAST AND FUTURE PROMISE

WHEN WORLD WAR II WAS FINALLY OVER, Congress did its part and passed the GI Bill, giving veterans the unprecedented opportunity to finance a higher education. Enrollments in architecture degree programs skyrocketed, and the giants of European architecture were now American teachers.

Throughout the 1950s and into the 1960s, America enjoyed the longest sustained economic boom in its history. Architecture, as both a profession and a business, expanded with the economy. And yet influence in civic and political life, which seemed to grow exponentially for the allied trades and building industries, continued to diminish in the design profession.

On the occasion of the AIA's 100th anniversary, the Institute took stock of itself in a variety of ways. A small book was published as its commemorative history. Though written with great affection, it studiously avoided delving too deeply into any aspect of the Institute's history. The text's real value is hidden in what the author glossed over, diverted attention from, or left entirely unexplained, such as the purposes and actions of the 1919 Post-War Committee, which was blithely dismissed as a form of group neurosis.[487] The questions provoked by this peculiar description provided the clues to finding a significant bit of missing AIA history that the author did not care to recall. The commemorative narrative makes only a brief mention of the AIA's recently completed major research project, the two-volume *The Architect at Mid-Century*, which is still a quite useful resource for understanding the evolution of the practice of architecture in the United States.[488]

The centenary of the profession's institutional past is thus presented with markedly different perceptions of its reality. While one history waxes romantically over the guest list and menu of the AIA's 1905 benefit bash for the new American Academy in Rome, the other provides a densely thorough documentation of the statistics of professional education and business practice for 100 years, a literal illustration of the contradictory impulses and conflicting self-images that historically have plagued the profession.

In 1950, when the AIA's research was undertaken, there were so few women practicing architecture in this country that the study's authors decided the statistical data on women were so insignificant that there was no need to break out those figures.[489] The decision to ignore certain uncomfortable facts based on a mathematical anomaly precluded any substantive discussion of why or how these realities came to pass or what affect they might have on architecture and on the development of American society. No mention was made of architects from disadvantaged and/or minority backgrounds.

And yet this study was published in the same year, 1954, that the first African-American woman passed a state architects' licensing exam. Norma Sklarek attended Barnard College (Columbia University) shortly after the war. She competed with men who had served in the military and had already received college degrees. She passed the four-day licensing exam on her first sitting. In 1980 she became the first black woman to be elected a Fellow of the AIA.[490]

How many people today, even architects themselves, know of the accomplishments of Louise Blanchard Bethune, the first woman known to have practiced as a professional architect in America? She was also the first woman to establish and run an architecture firm. Accepted as a member of the Western Association of Architects in 1885, Bethune was elected for a term as the association's vice president. Though accepted into the AIA in 1888, her election as a Fellow of the AIA was by default, since she was grandfathered in through the merger deal between the AIA and the WAA.

Despite being invited, Bethune refused to compete for the commission of the Woman's Building for the 1893 Chicago World's Fair. She objected to the whole notion of architecture competitions, and further objected to the Chicago competition on the grounds that the meager compensation of $1,000 for female architects was insultingly discriminatory. The men were being paid $10,000 for each of their building designs, with all production costs paid by the fair committee.[491]

Instead, Sophia Hayden Bennett (1868–1953), the first woman to graduate, with honors, from MIT's architecture program in 1890, designed the Woman's Building. Her work was critically disparaged simply on the basis of her gender. That this beautiful structure, designed by a woman to display the accomplishments of women, should be devalued because it was too feminine is understood to have caused Hayden to abandon a career in architecture.[492]

The example Bethune set was not easy for women to follow, despite the earning of an architecture degree. Discrimination hampered the ambitions of many of the first few generations of female architects. But the situation did motivate some to passionately pursue political activism.

For MIT graduate Florence Hope Luscomb (1887–1985), winning the right to vote for women meant as much as, and ultimately more than, her career in architecture. While still a student, Luscomb faced the reality of discrimination when she sought an apprenticeship. Twelve firms turned her down before she found one willing to take her on.[493]

After graduation Luscomb formed a partnership with Ida Annah Ryan (1883–1960), the first woman to obtain a master's degree in architecture from MIT, in 1905. The two practiced together from 1909 to 1917. One of their buildings is the spacious, well-appointed home of Waltham, Massachusetts, industrialist B.C. Ames, designed in 1917.

World War I caused a severe building slump, and discrimination against women by the Boston Society of Architects finally convinced them to close the firm in 1917. In order to find a local chapter of the AIA that would accept her and thus provide access to membership in the national organization, Ryan moved to Orlando, Florida, in 1920. She designed buildings and homes in the Prairie Style and became one of the first female members of the Florida Board of Architects.[494]

Luscomb decided to stay in Boston and turned to full-time political activity to replace her thwarted career in architecture. An ardent suffragette who had been taken to hear Susan B. Anthony speak when she was only five, Luscomb became one of America's most effective and enduring champions of human rights. She led the women's suffrage movement as executive secretary of the Boston Equal Suffrage Association and helped to organize and run the Boston local of the United Office and Professional

The young suffragette-architect, Florence Luscomb, is seen here practicing her speechmaking on the proverbial soap-box, at the turn of the century. Courtesy of the Schlesinger Library, Radcliffe Institute, Harvard University

Workers of America. Luscomb was also an executive of the Boston League of Women Voters and the Women's International League for Peace and Freedom.

Upon her mother's death in 1933, her inheritance, a legacy handed down from her grandfather, Missouri's Unconditional Unionist Congressman Samuel Knox (38th Congress 1864–1865), gave Luscomb the financial independence to pursue her social and political goals without distraction.[495] In 1935 she joined the NAACP and served as vice president of the Boston chapter. She ran for public office four times. As the first woman to run for Boston's City Council, Luscomb came within one percent of winning in 1922. She ran for Congress in 1936 and 1950 and for governor of

Massachusetts in 1952. During the McCarthy era, in 1955, she was called to testify before the Massachusetts State Commission and promptly sued it for violating her constitutional rights.

Luscomb continued to be a thorn in the side of the establishment. Her travels to countries such as Cuba, the USSR, and China provoked the State Department to temporarily confiscate her passport in the early 1960s. She was the oldest protestor against the Vietnam War at the National March on Washington in 1965, and she continued her advocacy for world peace and human rights until her death at age ninety-eight. Luscomb was a devout Unitarian and a member of the Community Church of Boston for sixty years.

Today, in the Massachusetts State House, Florence H. Luscomb—architect turned activist—is among the six women honored for their outstanding contributions to public life. Her portrait in bronze bas-relief was designed by two faculty members of Yale University's School of Art, Shelia Levant de Bretteville and Susan Sellars.496

While the University of Illinois can claim the honor of bestowing the first degree in architecture on a woman, Mary L. Page in 1879, and Cornell the second, in 1880, to Margaret Hicks, MIT has the distinction of awarding the first architecture degree to an African-American, in 1892.

How many fledgling architects are taught about Robert Robinson Taylor (1868–1942), who twice received MIT's prestigious Loring Scholarship? His career as one of America's preeminent educators as well as the first university-educated black American architect is overshadowed by his white American colleagues. Yet his legacy to the profession continues today. Booker T. Washington recruited Taylor to head Tuskegee Institute's architecture program as well as to design and build out the campus. He designed and oversaw construction of some forty-five campus buildings.

Taylor designed the Negro Building at the 1895 Atlanta Exposition. He was the only black American to speak at MIT's 50th anniversary celebration, the Congress of Technology, held in April 1911. In 1929 he traveled to Liberia to develop and design its Booker Washington Institute, based on Tuskegee. Taylor's forty-one years at the Tuskegee Institute established the rigorous standards taught at MIT and provided the example that other black colleges, such as Howard University, would follow. Robert Robinson

Taylor died one Sunday morning while attending services in the chapel he had designed on the Tuskegee campus.[497]

How many architects today know that the Philadelphia Museum of Art, Harvard University's Widener Library, and Duke University were all designed by Julian Francis Abele (1881–1950), the first black American graduate of the University of Pennsylvania's architecture department? He spent forty-four years as the chief designer and eventually a partner in the prominent Philadelphia firm of Horace Trumbauer & Associates. This resulted in his life's work being credited to the firm's founder, Horace Trumbauer. That Abele was forbidden to visit the "whites only" campus of Duke University while his buildings were being constructed is an ugly irony. It was not until 1988 that Duke University publicly acknowledged what it had always known, that Julian Francis Abele, a black man, was its architect.[498]

In the 20th century, architectural influence became internationalized in a variety of important ways, not all of which were exclusively related to style or design issues. An unprecedented sharing of cultures across whole continents and oceans occurred, spreading new ideas, social values, and pragmatic solutions to old problems.

Every American school child learns about how a Danish immigrant, pioneering journalist, and social crusader, Jacob A. Riis (1849–1919), changed our country's built environment and our social priorities for the better. He is a real American hero. And yet Riis and the implications of what he accomplished are still largely unacknowledged in his homeland, despite the significance of how dramatically and effectively he conveyed to American society the Scandinavian perspective on democratic social values.

Riis, born in the ancient Danish town of Ribe near Jutland's Atlantic coast and the son of the local newspaper editor, was one of America's foremost social reformers. He was also the first photo-journalist, using photography as forensic evidence in his crusade for social justice. Through his photographs and investigative reporting, Riis proved, beyond any doubt, the urgent need for rehabilitation of the urban built environment.

Riis knew firsthand the suffering of New York's other half. He had spent seven hard years of living hand to mouth, sometimes sleeping on the streets or in a police lodging house, after he arrived in America in 1870. That a bit of good fortune and an agile mind allowed him to overcome his wretched circumstances was not something he could take for granted, nor could he allow society to do so either.[499]

Riis published the first of his many books, *How the Other Half Lives: Studies among the Tenements of New York*, in 1890. The bestselling book succeeded in energizing public opinion on behalf of tenement reform. The combination of thorough research, compelling prose, and Riis's unposed, starkly moving photographs made an undeniable case for the basic human rights of decent, safe housing and sanitary living conditions. Riis also championed progressive social ideas such as mandatory playgrounds for all New York City public schools and the establishment of settlement houses for community development and stability.

Riis's book made such a strong impression on the young, idealistic Teddy Roosevelt that he decided to help "Jake Riis" fight his battle for the slums. Riis described how their friendship began: "It could not have been long after I wrote 'How the Other Half Lives' that he came to the Evening Sun office one day looking for me. I was out, and he left his card, merely writing on the back of it that he had read my book and had come to help. That was all and that tells the whole story of the man. I loved him from the day I first saw him; nor in all the years that have passed has he failed of the promise made then. No one ever helped as he did."[500]

In the spring of 1895, Teddy Roosevelt became New York City's police commissioner. In the dark of the early morning hours, Riis and Roosevelt would meet on the steps of the Union League Club and make the rounds of Manhattan's notorious slums and flophouses. Riis said, "For two years we were brothers in Mulberry Street."[501] When Roosevelt saw for himself the terrible conditions of the police lodging houses, he closed them down.

During those two years of intensive work, Roosevelt relied heavily on Riis's guidance as he worked to rid both the Police Department and the Board of Health of widespread corruption and pushed through many reforms to improve the living conditions of the city's underclass. Roosevelt paid Riis the highest compliment when he wrote in his autobiography that "my whole life was influenced by my long association with Jacob Riis, whom I am tempted to call the best American I ever knew," and he recalled that "as President of the Police Board I was also a member of the

Health Board . . . I felt that with Jacob Riis's guidance I would be able to put a goodly number of his principles into actual effect. He and I looked at life and its problems from substantially the same standpoint. Our ideals and principles and purposes, and our beliefs as to the methods necessary to realize them, were alike."[502] Their friendship endured throughout Riis's life and through Roosevelt's ascent to the governorship of New York and then to the White House. His pioneering work in investigative and photo journalism had an enormous impact on the nation's housing reform movement and a profound influence on the ethical beliefs and public policies of President Theodore Roosevelt, whose administration was remarkably sympathetic to the idea of best design principles for the built environment.

The Danish-American landscape architect, conservationist, and social reformer Jens Jensen (1860–1951) is known as the father of the Chicago Park System and the dean of the Prairie School of landscape architecture. As the son of a Jutland farmer, Jensen's attachment to nature was inbred. He studied plant life and agriculture with a passion in Denmark and Germany before he immigrated to the United States in 1884. Jensen, like Riis, left Denmark for entirely personal reasons. But once he settled in Chicago in 1886, Jensen found his calling, first as a laborer and then as a foreman for the Chicago Park Department.

His first project was the American Garden in Union Park, which he designed and planted in 1888. His exceptional aptitude earned him rapid promotion to the position of general superintendent of the entire West Park System. Of the many city parks he landscaped over a thirty-year period, the most important were Humboldt, Garfield, Douglas, and Columbus parks.

In 1905 Jensen designed the Garfield Park Conservatory in consultation with Prairie School architects Schmidt, Garden and Martin and the New York engineering firm of Hitchings & Co. Jensen left city government in 1906 when graft and corruption interfered with his work, and he then set up a private practice. Jensen designed more than 350 landscapes for private residences, including the estates of such leading industrialist families as the Armours, Florsheims, and Fords. Very little of his private work survives today, though Fair Lane, Henry Ford's estate in Dearborn, Michigan, with grounds landscaped by Jensen over a six-year period, is beautifully preserved and open to the public as a National Historic Landmark.[503]

Jensen's design philosophy was based in his respect for the indigenous plant life and topography of a region. He sought to preserve the natural beauty and balance found in nature and eschewed what he considered to be the artificial, tortured machinations of European landscape design, the predominant style in America when he arrived.

Conservation of our natural resources was the essence of Jensen's personal and professional philosophy, and he worked tirelessly in that cause. He was instrumental in the early environmentalist movement throughout the Midwest, helping to create the Illinois State Park System and the Cook County Forest Preserves. In 1913 Jensen founded Friends of Our Native Landscape and helped to save the Indiana dunes.

After retirement in 1935 at age seventy-five, Jensen founded The Clearing in Ellison Bay, Wisconsin, on property he had purchased in 1919 for a summer retreat. This legendary school, on 128 acres of undisturbed land, is open not only to architects, landscape architects, and artists but to all individuals seeking "to renew their contact with the 'soil' as a basis for life values."504 The Clearing was inspired by the traditional Danish folk school that Jensen had attended as a boy. The folk-school movement, one of the greatest achievements of 19th-century Denmark, created the social and educational infrastructure for transforming an illiterate peasant population into the citizenry of a modern democratic society.

Jensen remained active in The Clearing until his death in 1951 at age ninety-one. As the nation's foremost landscape architect of the 20th century, Jens Jensen was the awakening spirit of America's modern environmentalist movement. The organizations he helped to found throughout his career and long life carry on today inspired by this Danish-American's heartfelt mission.505

In the same year that fellow Dane Jacob Riis published *How the Other Half Lives*, Danish architect, engineer, city planner, and activist writer Alfred Råvad (1848–1933) arrived in Chicago. All these Danes shared their culture's egalitarian social values, which place all people on equal footing, and all were idealists who did not hesitate to publicly fight for those values to be upheld, first and foremost, as public policy. But the accomplishment of architect Råvad's life's work is far more obscure than that of his fellow Danes.

Råvad was born just north of Copenhagen to a bricklayer-mason father. His father was interested in city planning and drew up plans for distant places such as the Suez-Canal. Råvad's artistic ability surfaced early on and his father eagerly trained him, first as a carver. Råvad started out as a craftsman making ornamentation and won a medal at the 1878 Paris Exhibition. He began practicing architecture in the 1870s and designed several important apartment buildings, particularly the Rørholm, facing Copenhagen's reservoir lakes. This building incorporated new features such as french window balconies and modern heating and ventilation systems, along with carved sculptural elements.

Little is known of Råvad's built work in America, although his distinctive Copenhagen apartment buildings and houses, constructed before 1890, still stand in testimony to the functionality of their layout and site planning. And his affinity for Louis Sullivan's work is apparent in Råvad's distinctive Nordic aesthetic treatment of structural ornamentation melded to form. Råvad was one of the first European correspondents to publish an interview with Sullivan in Europe (Copenhagen) in 1898.

Alfred Råvad was a middle-aged man when he and his family immigrated to Chicago. Despite his lack of fluency in English, he quickly found work in his profession simply because he was so talented. He first worked for the Keystone Bridge Company, owned by Andrew Carnegie, where he learned the engineering skills to build skyscrapers and designed the columns and beams for Burnham & Root's Great Northern Hotel. During this time he began formulating his own ideas for Chicago's lakefront and its future city planning.

Before long he was working for Daniel H. Burnham as a member of the engineering team that built the Chicago World's Fair. His project was the steel construction of the Manufacturers and Arts Building, the largest building in the world at the time. Råvad also won the Chicago Tribune's design competition for a city logo that would be used to symbolize the fair.

On June 9, 1894, after several years of determined effort, Råvad's design for the future development of the South Shore and Jackson Park, which connected the lakefront to the city center, was published in the *Chicago Times*. However, the full-page plan did not credit Råvad as the architect.

Råvad continued his quest to promote a master plan for Chicago and

Danish-American architect and city planner, Alfred J. Råvad, at eighty years old. This photograph was published along with the favorable review of his opus, *The Mayor's Book*, in the Danish architectural journal, "Arkitekten," in 1929.

presented his ideas to the Chicago City Club on October 20, 1908. His plan focused on the lakefront as the main attraction for residents and tourists and promoted the idea of developing the lakefront for various public recreational uses. Råvad tried to interest Burnham in his ideas, but Burnham had a different vision for Chicago's development. Råvad did not consider Burnham a particularly good city planner, though a talented architect and businessman. Of course, it was Burnham's Chicago plan that the city adopted in 1909.

After the World's Fair closed, Råvad worked for various firms designing mass transit systems, from elevated rails to moving walkways. In 1897
he worked for engineer J.A.L. Waddell on the construction of the Chicago
Loop, and from 1904 to 1906 he was the only architect on the staff of the
great bridge engineer Joseph B. Strauss. Råvad's work took him to many
cities and towns in the Midwest, and wherever he went he studied the problems developing American cities faced under natural and artificially created
conditions.[506]

Råvad was a political activist long before he moved to the United
States, having led a national citizen's movement in the 1880s to build
defensive fortifications around Copenhagen. He was also an accomplished
writer and correspondent. In 1911, writing under his Americanized name,
"Roewade," his memoir of this extraordinary Danish civic and political initiative, titled "How Copenhagen Was Fortified," was published in the U.S.
Army and Engineering Corps' journal, *Professional Memoirs*.[507] Throughout the twenty-five years he practiced in America, he wrote extensively for
professional journals and newspapers in the U.S., Canada, and Denmark.
He reported on the latest developments in architectural design, city and
town planning, building technologies, engineering, and the new science of
sociology, which he believed architects had a responsibility to help
develop.[508]

In 1908 Råvad introduced his new ideas to Denmark in a planning competition sponsored by Copenhagen's municipal government. The city purchased his plan, mainly because he advocated retaining the older villages as
local centers and encouraged the participation of architects to design public spaces that maintained and promoted community marketplaces as the
centers of local democracy.

When Råvad reached retirement age, he returned home and pursued
the completion of his life's dream: the publication of *The Mayor's Book*. He
had spent nearly three decades refining its ideas and enlarging its scope as
a practical handbook on city planning written for elected officials, civil servants, architects, and planners, as well as the public. It took him nearly ten
years to raise the funds to publish it. Råvad was more than eighty years old
when it was finally placed in his hands in 1929. He died four years later.[509]

In the publication announcement and review of *The Mayor's Book* in the leading Danish architecture journal, *Arkitekten*, critic Ivar Bentsen stated, "In an advanced age he returned from the great world with his freer view of things . . . and valuable observations from the forced big city formations, namely in America."[510]

Råvad's book lays out his visionary plan for Copenhagen's future; he called it "Copenhagen 1999." He prophesied that the Øresund region—the natural gateway between northern, western, and eastern Europe—would transform the quaint, canalled jewel of northern Europe into the hub city of a growing megalopolis. His analysis of the city's future and his ideas for developing a comprehensive mass transit plan, including infrastructure to accommodate automobiles, buses and trams, commuter trains, international shipping, and an international airport, were extraordinarily far-sighted. The new Ørestad Tunnel and Bridge between Copenhagen and Mälmo, Sweden, follows almost identically his pathway for a tunnel to connect the two cities, an idea he considered inevitable as they grew closer together in economic and urban development. In his future vision, Råvad depicted a greatly expanded commercial harbor and a city with equally expanded public amenities, including a ring of open parklands around the urban core, new museums, a zoological garden, and a marine park to preserve both land and sea environments. He cited Jens Jensen's landscape design of Humboldt Park, inspired by the flatlands of Jutland, using "beautiful and interesting plants" indigenous to the prairie, as an example of urban park design that had met with great public acclaim.[511]

One of Råvad's most interesting professional projects was his submission to the 1912 international design competition for Canberra, the purpose-built capital of Australia, which was won by the well-known Prairie architect Walter Burley Griffin. Råvad's design featured a street layout of connecting grids and a horseshoe-shaped acropolis containing the main railroad station on the southern riverside. He placed the Parliament at the northern curve of the acropolis arch. His was among the several imaginative Scandinavian entries.[512]

Many of Råvad's planning ideas have found their way into the mainstream of Denmark's city planning profession and underlie the urban planning program adopted by Copenhagen in the late 1940s. Råvad's thesis, so well thought out, articulated, and visually presented, was acknowledged after his death as the inspiration for the famous Finger Plan, Copenhagen's city planning blueprint for long-term development, a work in continuous progress.[513] Råvad believed that "every nation must shape its city building from its own conditions, and that only through a succession of such national city building overviews can we manage to procure a conclusive international overview of this urbane topic, by extracting the common threads from this, when works from the leading nations come into existence."[514]

What is so striking about Alfred J. Råvad was his willingness to share his ideas unselfishly, even though his design concepts and sociological premises were unlikely to be roundly applauded or garner for him any great measure of professional recognition. His vision was not dimmed by age or financial hardship. Råvad had the courage of his convictions and the strength of character to stay the course throughout a long, often materially unrewarded professional life.

Another Scandinavian architect-turned-activist also merits mention here, although his architecture career was very brief. Raoul Wallenberg, who saved tens of thousands of Hungarian Jews during World War II, started out his professional life as an architect. It was only the deep-rooted traditions of a powerful family and the tsunami-like forces of global war that diverted the young Swede onto the dangerous and eventually fatal path he chose. That he decided to set aside his love of architecture was a blessing to innumerable lives.

Born August 4, 1912, Wallenberg was a member of a prominent Swedish banking family, comparable to the Rockefellers in the United States. His father died before he was born, and Raoul was raised under the strong paternal influence of his grandfather, Gustav Wallenberg. A very bright student who excelled in all his subjects, Raoul's top grades were in Russian and drawing. It was his interest in drawing that led him to study architecture at the University of Michigan in Ann Arbor in 1931. He earned his B.S. in architecture in three and a half years, graduated with honors, and received a coveted medal of distinction. Professor Emil Lorch was his academic mentor.

Wallenberg enjoyed his life in America and his time at the university. He wrote frequently to his grandfather about his impressions of American life. On November 7, 1931, he wrote, "I think what you intended by sending me here was not so much to acquire the skill to build skyscrapers and

Architect-trained Swedish diplomat, Raoul Wallenberg.

movie houses but to acquire a desire to build them! In other words to catch some American spirit that lies behind their technological and economic progress."[515]

Three years later, on November 13, 1934, Wallenberg wrote about his final term design project: "I've enjoyed being here so much that I'm sad at the prospect of leaving in February . . . I'm now finishing my final course in archi-tecture . . . we've been working with so-called 'cheap housing'. The problem calls for constructing sixteen city blocks, with space for 4,500 people. The entire area—at least in my project—is designed as a park in which there are four-story laminated buildings. We are also to include two churches, a school, a childcare center, a 'community center', stores and a fire station, etc."[516]

The Depression was still making life tough for aspiring architects, and political storm clouds were forming on the European horizon. Sweden offered little opportunity for architecture practice either, so his grandfather sent him to Cape Town, South Africa, where he worked at a Swedish firm selling building materials. Six months later he was working at a Dutch bank in Haifa, Palestine (now Israel), where he came into contact with Jewish refugees who had just escaped Hitler's Germany. The horror of their personal stories affected him deeply.

After he returned home to Sweden in 1936, he was introduced by his financier cousin Jacob to a Hungarian Jew named Koloman Lauer, the director of a Swedish-based import-export company. Raoul joined the company, and his excellent language skills, engaging personality, and refined upbringing enabled him to rise quickly in its ranks. His work there also gave him the opportunity to travel widely and see firsthand the terrors of war wrought by the Nazi regime.

The "final solution of the Jewish problem" became fully evident to the Allies in May 1944, when two eyewitness reports of what was happening in Auschwitz came from escapees of the Nazi gas chambers. Nearly simultaneously, the Nazis began deporting Jews from the Hungarian countryside. Desperately, the Jewish population turned to the embassies of the neutral countries to secure provisional passes for protection.

The Swedish government successfully negotiated with the Nazi regime to allow the Swedes to give exit passes to anyone with a connection to Sweden. Soon it was apparent that the demand far exceeded the ability of the Swedish diplomats to respond, so reinforcements were called for from the foreign ministry in Stockholm. After a first choice was rejected, Wallenberg was selected, in spite of his youth, based on a recommendation by Koloman Lauer, who called attention to Wallenberg's familiarity with Hungary through his many business dealings there. He was appointed first secretary at the Swedish legation in Budapest and charged with starting a rescue operation for the Jewish population. Needless to say, Raoul was eager to undertake this important task.

His first act as leader of the new section was to write a memo demanding full authorization to do as he saw necessary without first getting approval from the ambassador. The memo was so unusual that it was referred directly to Swedish Prime Minister Per Albin Hansson, who then consulted with King Gustav V before announcing his approval.

Very quickly, Wallenberg launched a program that shocked the Swedish legation's diplomats with its audacity, but these were terrible times that required extreme actions. Wallenberg understood the German and Hungarian authorities' weakness for overly ostentatious documents decorated with emblems, crests, and titled signatures, so he designed his special pass, called a *Schutzpass*, accordingly. He used bribery and threats with equal success. Courageously, he would rush onto deportation trains and pull people off as he handed them the flashy yellow and blue protective passes, sometimes while Nazi guards were firing bullets over the heads of the crowds. Some say it was his demonstrative courage that moved the soldiers to disobey orders and not fire directly into the crowds.

The stories of Wallenberg's heroics are legendary. By the end of the war he was operating a section with more than 340 people managing more than thirty safe houses where Jews were hidden and protected. All told, 120,000 people, out of a prewar population of 700,000 Jews, were saved, in large measure because of one man's leadership.[517]

Raoul never lived to receive the gratitude of those he had saved. He was arrested, for reasons still unknown, by the Soviet military as it swept into Hungary in 1945 and later died either by execution or illness in a Soviet prison. Despite the tragic ending to a heroic life, Wallenberg's deeds single him out as one of a very few individuals in recorded history who have selflessly sacrificed their own lives in the protection of countless others. He started his life's journey with optimistic ambitions to be an architect, but his sensitivity and compassion reached a spiritual depth far greater than just the love for designing buildings.

The University of Michigan proudly honors its most famous graduate with an annual lecture series and a traveling scholarship for its architecture students, "a reminder of Wallenberg's courage and humanitarianism . . . aimed at reflecting his ideals."[518]

* * *

These are just a few of the stories of groundbreaking architects who have contended with enormous social, political, and economic barriers in pursuit of their vocations. Their leadership should not be ignored, much less devalued, by artificially ranking their artistic achievements against their better-known or more privileged peers, especially without informed and adequate acknowledgment of the complex circumstances of society or the difficult conditions of practice they struggled to overcome.

We would be well served to derive inspiration from the courage, ideals, and devotion to craft that propelled these architects forward, in the face of overwhelming odds, to professional and personal success. Before the profession can direct its energies outward to exert influence on society with greater impact, it must first visit the interior space where the dissonance of self-imposed contradictions unbalances the inner pendulum of the profession.

PART III:

THE CIVIC NECESSITY OF SUSTAINED LEADERSHIP

16 From Superstar to Star Citizen: Speaking Truth to Power

If we fail to dare, if we do not try, the next generation will harvest the fruit of our indifference: a world we did not want, a world we did not choose, but a world we could have made better by caring more for the result of our labor.
—Robert F. Kennedy

FROM THE MOMENT THE ARCHITECTURE PROFESSION began to detach from its grassroots-oriented civic responsibilities and direct the power of its collective professional focus on developing an artistic elite solely engaged in designing structural sculpture, the problem of its diminishing influence on society's governance accelerated. This ideological trend gained ground long before the idea of the architect as an egotistical, self-centered artist would be glorified by the appearance of Ayn Rand's fictional architect, Howard Roark, in the popular culture of the novel and Hollywood film.

In the 19th century, many notable architects rose to prominence in society through the respect they engendered by their performances as leaders of the community as well as by the structures they designed. Architects participated in the Industrial Revolution, supported the abolition of slavery, fought in a brutal Civil War, coped with massive immigration from abroad, contributed to continental expansion and the building of the West, helped to shape the nation's education system, integrated the first innovations in telecommunications into the function of design, negotiated and worked with newly organized labor, strove to innovate building and engineering technology, and fought for legislative and civic reforms that would protect the health, safety, and welfare of society by improving the built environment. These achievements are the foundation upon which the profession has long stood.

But by the mid-point of the 20th century, something significant had changed. In the wake of two horrific world wars, ignited in a period of less than thirty years, the ideal of the citizen architect gradually fell from prominence and was replaced by a reincarnated form of the Gilded Age's superstar architect ideal.

It was no longer held necessary to work in concert with the political establishment or cater to the concerns of ordinary folk. Fantastic designs for modern buildings and futuristic plans for cities of tomorrow could be created out of whole cloth without concern for the existing order or more mundane, pragmatic considerations. Design, as its own paragon, was to prevail in solving all of society's needs.

Ultimately 20th-century architecture's attempts at solving social problems have proven woefully inadequate. Hard-won wisdom gained by former generations was lost, while aspirations to success, be it artistic or professional, were greatly inflated. The profession's loss of acumen resulted in an increasing loss of control over how politicians, big business interests, and other clients used their design skills.

Walter Gropius, the founder of the Bauhaus school, linked his design philosophy to manufacturing industries as he sought to develop a marriage of design with technology, the product of which could be mass produced and made easily available to the masses. One of the keys to the Bauhaus philosophy was the establishment of close working relationships with the business world so that designers might eventually gain their independence by selling their designs to industry. While the Bauhaus philosophy rested on the belief that art should be responsive to the needs of the consumer in a modern industrial world, it perversely put the power of design into the hands of those least inclined to serve those needs. Although the Bauhaus emphasized functional, efficient design of objects for mass distribution, ultimately those objects were priced beyond the means of the very people for whom they originally had been intended.

Gropius, Marcel Breuer, Mies van der Rohe, innovators of what eventually became known as the International Style, and the style's other adherents turned the old view of design on its head. This new industrial aesthetic found its beauty in an austere, minimalist purism, which eliminated the luscious, classical ornamentation of the Beaux-Arts era as well as the decorative geometries of contemporary Art Deco design.

The predominance of a building's façade—so critical in earlier days in the placing and stating of a structure's purpose in a community—gave way to buildings that could only be understood by walking into, through, and around them. This insistence on the idea that no one side of a building should dominate the architectural program, the literal message of the place, helped disconnect these designs from their surrounding environs.

Before Bauhaus, a building had a face that spoke to its neighborhood and community. After Bauhaus, buildings had no elaboration on the façade—they were literally faceless—and while this equality of all sides was tacitly democratic, the orthodoxy became doctrinaire, often functioning with societal side effects bordering on the totalitarian. Modernism did not strive to serve its setting but to dominate it. As more emphasis was placed solely on the building, the context of its location in a community lost importance. So, speaking the truth of the building within the context of its placement and designated function was overrun by the power of the building's design alone, without regard for anything other than its visual and physical aura.

The idea of the building as the icon of modern corporate power became a public relations statement in itself. And from it the public might infer that corporations were not interested in being part of a larger, more diverse community. Architects enamored with making each edifice a special, self-contained, and self-expressive jewel could be relied on to focus the attention of the outside world on the paying client's pretensions to status and power. To reach these ends, such clients had many talented designers eager to do their bidding.

A panel convened at the 1992 AIA national convention, held in Boston, was asked to reread Ayn Rand's infamous 1943 novel, *The Fountainhead*. The ensuing discussion was a real surprise. The entire panel, which included architects Stanley Tigerman, Susan Maxman, and Denise Scott Brown and architectural historian Vincent Scully, agreed that Rand's novel was probably the worst thing to happen to the architecture profession in recent memory. In spite of their concurrence on the subject, the discussion remained lively and entertaining, in large part due to the strength and vibrancy of forceful personalities that, perhaps unexpectedly, found themselves in total agreement.

They were unanimous in their belief that, in all his arrogance, the character of Howard Roark had completely lost his senses when he resorted to the destruction of his creation. Roark began by stooping to deceit by using another architect's name to gain the desired commission and, in spite of the subterfuge, still demanded creative control. Roark could not see this as an ethical breach, nor could he recognize anyone but himself as the owner of the design process and its end result. Moreover, Roark did not recognize the building process as a collaborative creative possibility, neither with his peers nor the client. When his hidden identity was discovered and his stylistic intentions compromised, Roark should have spoken truth to power to preserve the building's integrity. But instead, Roark went berserk and destroyed the client's building, the object of his blind ambitions. The rationalizations for this destructive behavior, which the architect employed in defense of his artistic integrity, are, unfortunately, responsible for the simplistic stereotype that has claimed the popular imagination.

Yet the profession of architecture has nothing to do with Rand's point. It was simply a convenient literary device used to validate the tenuous premise of Rand's objectivist philosophy. Roark supposedly embodies the heroic ideal in Rand's fiction, yet the character of the architect lacks the maturity of an experienced professional or the tempered rationality necessary to handle the complex task of managing the building process.

As an architect, Roark possessed none of the skills of leadership or diplomacy—skills strongly identified with the profession historically—that would have made it possible for him to arrive at a viable solution to his predicament. The author had no need of placing a real person in the real world of architecture practice because Howard Roark is merely a superficial means to the end of demonstrating a self-centered theoretical tenet. His story is as detached from reality as any other two-hour fantasy produced in Tinseltown.

In the strictest sense, Rand's ideological purposes could only be served by reducing the architect to a professional misfit, unable to deal with utterly commonplace and predictable conditions of professional practice. Howard Roark could not rise to a rather mundane challenge to his artistic vision simply because it did not serve the author's need to contrive an intellectually pretentious and legally impossible conclusion to Roark's vainglorious story. Howard Roark did not speak truth to power because he could not speak the truth, period.

To make matters worse, this archetype is not really of Rand's creation, but is the preexisting myth of the Beaux-Arts architect-artist on which she could hang a new set of modernist clothes. The profession had already saddled itself with this phantom, and Rand had only to exploit the creature in pursuit of a mythical destiny.

The difficulty in all this is that the public has embraced a Hollywood stereotype of what an architect is without grasping Rand's ideas and without understanding that her literary and movie scenario is total artifice. Rand's archetype hero serves only her philosophical agenda and has nothing to offer to the vehicle of her message, the architect.

In similar circumstances what would a real architect, say, Cass Gilbert, have done?

* * *

Speaking Truth to Power

Speaking truth to power is a very difficult thing to do. The high and mighty are too often uninterested in addressing the truth of an issue or situation. To effectively speak truth to power—to be direct and forthright with those who wield power—it is important to define the process of creating both the atmosphere and the valued relationships essential to making the truth understood. Simply stated, there are four basic steps:

1. Identify the truth.
2. Speak the truth to oneself first and then to one's peers.
3. Then speak this truth publicly, as well as privately, to authority.
4. Be prepared to accept the consequences, whether good, bad, or indifferent.

IDENTIFY THE TRUTH. This is probably the hardest task of the four because it requires an intimate and objective understanding of what the facts actually are as well as a broader understanding of the implications of revealing the truth at hand. Only from an essentially dispassionate, self-critical, and honest assessment of the facts can the truth be discerned; from that assessment, what needs to be said will become apparent.

The eloquent speeches on leadership, civic involvement, and professional/personal responsibility delivered at the 1919 AIA national convention are examples of this basic process of understanding and self-awareness. In identifying the truth of the profession's situation in the aftermath of a deeply traumatic world war, it also became possible to revive some long-lost truths once very much a part of the profession's lifeblood.

A more recent example involved the rediscovery of an obscured truth that became broadly understood during the 1992 congressional debate in the Public Works and Transportation Committee, now the Infrastructure Committee, on the issue of life-cycle costing. In this case, the truth was that it ultimately costs less to build our nation's infrastructure if the life-cycle costs of a project are factored into the budget from the beginning. In 1992 the federal budgetary process did not consider this approach, and one committee member decided to reveal its benefits to his peers.

SPEAK THE TRUTH TO ONESELF FIRST AND THEN TO ONE'S PEERS. In the example of the 1919 AIA Post-War Committee, the convention speeches were intended not only for the attending delegates but also for the entire profession, and they were ultimately heard at that broader scale.

As a congressman from New Hampshire, I was the one who introduced the life-cycle costing approach to congressional budget-making. I am also an architect, accustomed to applying this constructive method of budgetary planning in my professional life as a building project leader. I initiated the discussion of the benefits of life-cycle costing with my peers on the committee and introduced the subsequent budget amendment for them to consider.

Life-cycle costing is the incorporation of all the expenses incurred by an infrastructure or building project—from initial construction costs to the costs of maintenance—over the entire duration of its life. Over the life span of many public projects, taxpayers are forced to expend much larger sums of their hard-earned tax dollars because Congress, in its infinite wisdom, does not take into consideration the costs that will accrue down the line. These costs are not considered because doing so would raise the initial cost of the project, even though in the long run it would be significantly less expensive.

During one evening's committee deliberations, this budgetary management concept was proposed and an amendment to incorporate life-cycle costing into the budget bill was submitted to the committee. After extensive debate, there seemed to be substantial agreement on the idea, resulting in a consensus that favored life-cycle costing as a practical, useful evaluation tool to be included in the budgetary process. It was moved that a vote on the proposed amendment to the bill be taken the following morning.

THEN SPEAK THIS TRUTH PUBLICLY, AS WELL AS PRIVATELY, TO AUTHORITY. This is where the process can get a bit sticky. It is important to know who and/or what the authority actually is. In the case of the budget amendment, the presumed authority—that is, Congress's Public Works and Transportation Committee charged with managing the nation's infrastructure—proved to be a facade for the real authority. My miscalculation of where the true authority resided led to the amendment's demise.

The committee voted on the amendment the next morning. Much to my surprise, it was resoundingly defeated. It took several weeks to find out what actually happened, but once a confession was finally obtained, the events that transpired that day suddenly made sense. The evening between the positive debate and the following morning's negative vote was filled with phone calls made by an authority never considered or included in the discussion. I simply had not identified who the authority actually was on this issue.

Apparently, the lobbyists working for the asphalt pavers industry spent a sleepless night phoning all the members of the committee, urging them to vote against the amendment. Why? Because this industry had the biggest vested interest in the issue and therefore had the most to lose from reforming the government's project management methods. Life-cycle costing clearly demonstrated that applying a new layer of asphalt every four or five years is one of the least cost-effective methods of road maintenance.

But why were these lobbyists' calls instantly heeded? Because they came from one group of campaign contributors with deep pockets that supported the careers of many of the members of the Public Works and

Transportation Committee. Those campaign contributions would have disappeared if those committee members had supported the proposed amendment.

So, the true authority in this case was not the congressional committee charged by voters with overseeing their interests but an influential industry sector whose private interests superseded the constituents' best interests. Though the authority of Congress was self-evident, the authority of vested private interests had gone unrecognized. Ultimately, the power of this industry held sway, successfully protecting its interests over all others—which brings us to the fourth consideration in this process.

BE PREPARED TO ACCEPT THE CONSEQUENCES, WHETHER GOOD, BAD, OR INDIFFERENT. Again, easier said than done, but essential if one intends to remain standing to fight another day. The result of the 1919 convention speeches was a subsequent increase in the professional membership of the AIA. In Congress, life-cycle costing was defeated because the proposal had not taken into account the business survival concerns of the largest campaign contributor to the members of the Public Works and Transportation Committee.

Not every good idea succeeds. But one thing is certain: If an idea is not pursued in the first place, it will *never* succeed. Strong, effective leadership can never be attained if fear of failure induces paralysis. If this paralysis persists, failure is inevitable.

* * *

The process of understanding these four precepts has played a transformative role in my life. My path has been one of continuously discovering truths, identifying authorities, and making earnest attempts—though not always successful—at speaking the truth, as I perceive it, to the authorities. A brief summary of my experience may serve an instructional purpose here.

When I first started working at Skidmore, Owings and Merrill's (SOM) San Francisco office, I, like most architects, viewed architecture as a means to an end: Buildings were *objets d'art* that I aspired to design. That was how I had been trained at Yale. Discussion about the use of a building and how it contributed to its surrounding community was secondary. Least important was the attention paid to the language students used to describe their work. I mention this because it became an issue later in life when I decided to run for public office.

Several wonderful experiences at SOM contributed to my professional maturation. I was fortunate to work on a design team that stayed with a major project from the preliminary design through completion of the construction documents. This was an unusual opportunity in SOM's environment. The firm typically operated as the Brooks Brothers of corporate architecture, with each department handling its own specific responsibilities (i.e., project design was handled by the designers, interior design was done by the interior design department, and construction drawings by a separate department).

But in the San Francisco office, under the watchful eye of head architect Charles Bassett, I was able to spend three years on a team that participated in every aspect of the project's development. It was a seminal experience that has stayed with me. Although I left the firm shortly after the project's completion to strike out on my own, I continue to appreciate what I learned there.

At SOM, I also realized that architects gave up control of their projects by extracting themselves from oversight of the construction phase of a project. When I left SOM I was intent on successfully creating a design-build firm that could manage the whole project from design through construction. Issues of leadership and public trust were beginning to awaken.

As I bumped along, trying to manage designers, construction crews, and subcontractors, it dawned on me that a third party had greater influence over the design of a project than the architect. This third leg of the project team was the owner or developer who had the money to buy the services I was offering. So, my professional career took yet another distinct turn. I became a project manager for a company that developed multihousing units in San Francisco.

Not long after, I returned to the East Coast to fulfill my dream of working with my father, Phil Swett Sr., to develop and construct biomass (wood-chip burning) and natural gas cogeneration facilities. With our combined professional training, his in engineering and mine in development and design, we felt we were more highly qualified to develop, design, and build these facilities than were other firms in the field. So, once again, my career altered course.

Returning to New Hampshire was one dream fulfilled with yet another to be realized. The new dream was to create a sustainable community incorporating the latest environmentally responsible design and technology with an alternative energy power plant (presumably biomass) as its center-piece.

This was too large a step to take in one stride, so I began developing projects that would first get an alternative energy plant up and operating. Then the sustainable community it supported would be pursued. It immediately became clear that developing such a project was both capital intensive and highly politicized. Complex environmental modeling required extensive engineering during the permit process, while the political process of obtaining public support required long hours of meetings with community folks, state officials, utility negotiators, and lawyers. My first real exposure to the vicissitudes of local politics was as an active participant in the local promotion of sustainable energy development.

Many enjoyable hours were spent discussing one such project proposed for Pembroke, New Hampshire. The most productive meetings were held in the local coffee shop in the early morning hours. This is where I learned how the town had, more than twenty years earlier, rejected plans to build a coal-burning power plant within its borders along the Merrimack River. Residents feared that emissions from the plant's stack might endanger the community. Considering the substantial property taxes that could have been collected to support the town's budget, this was a difficult, far-sighted decision to make in the 1960s.

But the decision to forgo the coal-burning power plant became a sore point for the community, as the consequences were harsh. Industry abandoned the community in the decades that followed. The local employment situation stagnated, and the school system suffered from a lack of funding caused by insufficient property taxes. To make matters worse, the public utility company successfully negotiated a location for a new plant in the town just across the river. Consequently, its municipal coffers were always full, local employment was healthy because of the strong economic foundation laid by the power facility, and its local school system had sufficient funds with which to attract good teachers to good facilities. The neighboring community took pride in the quality services it could provide to its citizens. Today, the prevailing winds still carry the plant's emissions downwind over Pembroke and sometimes deposit a filmy reminder of a decision made decades ago.

I soon realized that as much as I enjoyed the power of creation as an architect, the power of interpretation and persuasion that took place among architect, client, and community was just as exhilarating. Although I did not formally recognize it at the time, I was using the design process to solve problems that encompassed concerns well beyond that of physical structure or the aesthetics of the built environment. Those town meetings and presentations were an invaluable opportunity to work cooperatively with the community.

Every question, no matter how silly, had to be treated with the utmost respect and seriousness. For instance, when one resident announced, "I've heard that the vibrations made from the exhaust gases traveling up the stack will sterilize the deer population surrounding the plant," the first response was to acknowledge that a valid issue had been raised. I then proceeded to respond as completely as possible. In addition, if this, or any, response was judged unsatisfactory, I pledged to research the issue more thoroughly and get the results back to the concerned citizen in a timely fashion.

The community's comments and concerns were integrated into the program and design of the project. I had to weigh the economic impact of the community's input with the project's ability to bear the additional expense. Make no mistake: this was a complicated, difficult balancing act.

For the most part, however, I found people to be reasonable. Their demands and ideas could be negotiated and integrated in a way that generally did not negatively affect the project and often improved it. The interaction was beneficial because I was building on a foundation of trust that had been established months before, over many early morning cups of coffee. Little did I realize how useful this process of interaction and negotiation would become once I entered public service.

On occasion, when I pause to look back on my journey, I realize that I am happiest not when I am alone with my ideas at the drawing board but when I am working with people, helping them realize their own dreams, working to solve problems with them, and delivering real improvements to their lives. I learned that the most creative and productive way to design is to engage people—the users—in the design process itself. The interpretive and inclusive processes of design are greatly enhanced by the sharing of responsibility and participation.

Developing alternative energy power projects was a capital-intensive activity requiring great sums of cash for securing construction and operating permits. The time, money, and effort required in the endeavor left little time or opportunity to pursue the bigger dream of creating a community built around sustainable environmental principles. More to the point, the financial wherewithal to accomplish this goal far exceeded my financial network. I slowly came to the realization that it would be many years before I would be in a position to build such a community.

Compounding this realization was the downturn in the economy. As the business climate contracted, the demand for new power supplies dried up and the possibility of future projects went with it. Some lean years lay ahead. My wife, Katrina, and I began to talk about our options, knowing that regardless of the ultimate career decisions we would make, belt tightening would be necessary. It just so happened that 1990, when we faced this situation, was also an election year.

Through my participation in community activities, I had become increasingly involved in New Hampshire's Democratic Party. As I became more and more enthusiastic about participating in public forums and working with communities to solve economic and planning concerns, the possibility of running for public office became a topic of discussion. I was concerned about the declining participation of voters in the electoral process and could sense a destructive cynicism spreading across the land.

Since the Vietnam War, Americans have become more and more cynical. Lack of faith in the vitality and functionality of a proactive democracy had drastically diminished voter turnout. The reasons for this condition are complex and fraught with strong feelings. As a concerned private citizen I knew I could not address them all, but I had an obligation to do whatever

I could to improve the situation.

My original career decision to become an architect was in response to a "call to serve." It was my small candle to help combat the darkness of cynicism. But I came to realize that I needed to do more. The necessity of removing from office those who abused the public trust, who were breeding this destructive cynicism, had become clear.

At first I only tried to encourage others in the New Hampshire Democratic Party to run against the Republican incumbent, thinking that someone would be willing to step up and take him on. As much as we all agreed on the reasons to oppose him, everyone was convinced that he was invincible, what with his impressive legal career, articulate intellect, and take-no-prisoners attitude. Too many people had seen him successfully demolish his opponents in the courtroom and had no desire to become his next victim.

But a democracy is not a democracy without choice, and a candidate without an opponent is not a choice. Furthermore, off-presidential years, which 1990 was, are generally more favorable to candidates of the party not in power and offer a longer time frame to focus on the incumbent and the issues. Thus, I reasoned that the circumstances presented an ideal time to run for the 2nd congressional district seat in New Hampshire. At the time all I could think was, since no one else dared to run, why not me?

I addressed what I perceived to be the voters' feelings—at best, alienated, and at worst, under attack by their government. I believed that by bringing a deeper understanding of the decision-making process and giving a greater sense of ownership of that process (much as I did in my design days) to the voters, the tide of cynicism might be turned back, if only a little.

There is another book to be written about the excitement of that campaign and its *highly* improbable outcome. Suffice it to say that the *Manchester Union Leader*, one of the most conservative newspapers in the country—the paper that lays claim to making Senator Ed Muskie cry in his 1972 campaign against President Nixon—ran this headline the day after my election: THOSE SOUNDS YOU HEAR ARE THE SOUNDS OF HELL FREEZING OVER! And my career changed once again.

This time I was stepping further from my original vocation than ever before, but when I went to Washington, D.C., I felt I went as a local architect elected by my community of clients. My campaign slogan was "Every House Needs a Good Architect." Much of the campaign imagery I used to discuss the issues with voters drew upon elements of architecture. For example, in speeches I would liken decision making about the federal budget to that of homeowners making decisions about their house: Government officials shouldn't add to the federal budget without need or available funding just as individual homeowners wouldn't build an addition to their home without the need or the money to pay for it. I was only appealing to common sense, that's all.

I focused on the building of trust through relationships rather than relying exclusively on establishing agreement with voters on the issues. The public relationship I hoped to cultivate was one patterned on the open and collaborative relationship between architect and client. Issues were, of course, very important and always present in the public discussion. Good solutions must come from an open, healthy process of debate.

But issues are dynamic. They ebb and flow like the tide. The constant is how they are dealt with. Only by gaining people's trust could I hope to represent their best interests. This meant involving them in the decisions made on their behalf by their elected representative. The specifics of issues would, and could, be dealt with in a broader context of trust.

The prevailing political norm can be compared to an architect presenting only one design to a client, with no opportunity to view two or three other schemes or to say to the client, this is my idea of how your project (your congressman's position on this issue) should look. Instead it is a take-it-or-leave-it proposition. Furthermore, this fait accompli is backed up with the threat, if you disagree with my design and desire something different, I will do all in my power to destroy your effort; there is no room to incorporate your ideas into mine.

The origins of this divisive attitude are as ancient as civilization itself, but in the United States the most recent cycle is a by-product of the political and social polarization of the 1960s. The sixties gave birth to many of today's special-interest organizations, from citizens fighting to secure their basic civil rights to environmentalists fighting to preserve our natural resources, religious activists pursuing public policy initiatives on theological grounds, and corporate lobbyists seeking both protection and expansion of private-interest agendas.

All these competing and frequently clashing special interests began to plow more and more money into political campaigns in order to influence the direction of government policy. Even though much good has come from this political activism, a darker side, one that we are dealing with today, also emerged from it.

Many of these issue campaigns were organized and carried forward without a genuine willingness to listen to, consider, negotiate, or compromise with differing opinions. For many of the protagonists in the early days of these movements, the urgency of dire circumstances precluded such willingness. In many cases, what was originally established to promote equality of opportunity, integration of diversity, and stewardship of shared resources has ultimately served to prolong distinction and further ingrain separateness. The social and environmental problems remain, many of which are largely unresolved.

In his book, *Community and the Politics of Place,* Daniel Kemmis states that "one of the side effects of this polarization of politics, with its missing middle, is a mutual frustration among those on either side of the struggle."[519] "[W]e readily and regularly oppose each other at public hearings, avidly pursuing our own interests and protecting our own rights with no sense of responsibility to hear or respond to the legitimate interests of those on the 'other side' or to discover common ground. More and more often, the result is deadlock—and then frustration and withdrawal from all things public."[520]

He points out that our republican form of government was not initially established to foster a closed-minded approach to public discourse. He posits that the burgeoning regulatory bureaucracies represent "a major development in the modern project of 'keeping citizens apart'—shielding them from the necessity of direct face-to-face (republican) problem solving."[521] This may explain why fewer and fewer citizens regularly participate in elections, allowing the percentage of participants to dwindle to embarrassingly low figures at times. In Denmark, where an average of 80–90 percent of the electorate routinely vote, many citizens cannot understand why Americans are so loath to perform their basic civic duty.

Kemmis believes that place has something to do with keeping the community engaged in a cooperative fashion. He says that "in a number of settings, people who find themselves held together (perhaps against their will) in a shared place discover as well that their best possibility for realizing the potential of the place is to learn to work together. In this way places breed cooperation, and out of this ancient relationship of place to human willing, that specific activity which is rightly called 'politics' is born."522

The creative process of designing three-dimensional space is, by necessity, an inclusive and constructive one—a powerful, productive form of diplomacy that is nearly defunct in politics. By expanding the dynamics of our formal design processes beyond the subjective limits imposed by aesthetics and engineering, by broadening this dynamic to routinely incorporate community members, civic leaders, and quality of life issues, the traditional paradigm of architecture as a profession can be transformed into a discipline with substantial influence on public policy formation.

As I discovered during my early political career, the trust that is necessary to lead effectively is a fragile thing. In 1994 I took a stand on an issue that I felt was important enough to risk my reelection. I stood in favor of the Clinton administration's crime bill. One of the provisions of the bill, the ban on assault weapons, was especially controversial in my district. Initially, I had opposed the ban, a position favored by a very vocal portion of my constituency, the members of the National Rifle Association. As the vote approached, I had the opportunity to better understand the potential of the legislation; it provided funding for an additional 100,000 police officers nationwide and additional resources for crime prevention, in addition to the assault weapons ban. I knew that this legislation was beneficial. I also knew that the NRA would be furious about my change in position on the assault weapons ban. I decided, after long hours of deliberation, that the overall content of the crime bill, including the assault weapons ban, was an important step in battling the nation's rising crime statistics. In spite of the power of NO so forcefully possessed and expressed by the NRA, I knew that the right decision was to support the legislation. With very little time left before the vote in the House of Representatives, I informed my leadership that I was going to support the bill.

Ultimately, the legislation passed by one vote, my vote, as far as I and the NRA were concerned. What turned out to be perhaps the most courageous vote of my congressional service turned into the nightmare issue of my reelection campaign. I became a bull's-eye targeted by the NRA, attacked for changing my position on the assault weapons ban. No firearms were taken away from law-abiding citizens, and the legislation had a tremendously positive impact on bringing down the violent crime statistics. But these facts did not matter. My opponents realized that to defeat me they could not actually attack my record but instead had to paint a portrait of me as a vacillating, untrustworthy politician. A ferocious political slur campaign was mounted, which drove this single point home. In the end, these single-issue opponents succeeded in placing me among the ranks of fifty-one other moderate Democrats from Republican districts who were defeated by Newt Gingrich's "Contract with America" campaign.

I was forced from office by a very narrow margin. But that did not diminish the pride I felt—and still feel—for casting that vote, because the nation's citizenry has been made safer and the constitutional rights of America's gun owners have not been threatened.

17 Building Community through Community Engagement

CONTRARY TO THE HOLLYWOOD ICON of the egotistical solo-artist Howard Roark, leadership by design is not a solitary pursuit. It is a multilayered process built on coalitions, cooperation, and understanding.

For this process to succeed, it is essential to focus on contemporary issues that affect people's lives. Architects would define these issues as quality-of-life considerations, which broadly encompass everything from sustainability and environmental design to increased security needs; revitalization of the infrastructure and amenities of local communities; the impact of architecture on learning, health, and economic productivity; and more, much more.

Quality-of-life issues encompass art, science, and politics—all of which constitute the domain of the profession of architecture. Architects are, by their very nature, primary experts in dealing with these issues. And in order to realize their maximum potential, architects need to take an active role in our civic institutions. Even extraordinary events, such as the terrorist attacks of September 11, 2001, and their aftermath, are opportunities for the profession to weigh in on a host of vital national issues.

Leadership by design can make a critical contribution—a real difference—to civic society. It rang especially true when the Danish Minister of Culture, Elsebeth Gerner Nielsen, spoke about the role architects play in society: "Architects, by virtue of their training, possess [a] particular ability to look forward into the future and furnish the present accordingly. But the focus is not on ability alone—responsibility also comes into play.

"Architects are co-administrators of large sums of public funding. It's essential therefore that architects be aware of this responsibility by contributing to the public debate on how these funds can best be spent in the social context. Not just in terms of a narrow discussion on the advantages of one architectural solution compared with another, but equally, in terms of the role architecture and planning plays in society...

"Denmark has a distinguished design tradition. Danish design has its roots in an idiom that gives priority to simplicity and quality craftsmanship. Internationally, Danish companies have won huge recognition for their ability to combine form with user-friendliness, and economy of materials . . . design is also a question of quality of life—of concrete visions that will provide better living conditions for all, by means of products and surroundings designed with respect for the individual . . .

"It is important for architecture to represent something genuine and of high quality, which a policy on architecture must, of course, support. . . . It's important that architects acknowledge architecture's fundamental social and ethical dimension. Architecture can give us a common validity and hold our everyday lives together, now and in the future."[523]

The Project for Public Spaces, Inc.

An example of using the skills of architects in new and unusual ways is the New York City–based nonprofit organization, the Project for Public Spaces (PPS). Founded in 1975 by activist Fred Kent, PPS aims to revitalize and reorient lifeless, disconnected communities into vibrant, engaged communities with thriving social, cultural, and economic activities. PPS provides technical assistance, education, and research through a variety of programs, both on-site and via the Internet. The PPS Web site (www.pps.org) provides a venue for presenting and discussing the issues connected to a variety of public spaces around the world.

Kent was deeply influenced by the social analysis of his mentor, William H. Whyte, author of the bestselling book, *The Social Life of Small Urban Spaces* (1980). Whyte moved away from a highly successful career in publishing (he was an editor of *Fortune* magazine) to spend the latter half of his career studying in painstaking detail how people interact with and use public spaces.

Before he went to work for Whyte's Street Life Project in the early 1970s, Kent had worked for a major New York City bank where he came to realize that banking's real estate development sector was in large part responsible for the disintegration of communities. This realization inspired him to establish a nonprofit organization that could offer a more constructive, long-term approach to developing public spaces.

A geographer by training, Kent has become a sensitive designer of public spaces. His career has taken him all over the world, acting as a place doctor who heals sick places. Along with his team of ardent advocates and architects, Kent has visited and helped to heal more than a thousand communities in forty-four states and twelve countries. Through PPS's meticulous methods of soliciting and analyzing information from communities and through motivating them to participate in the process of changing their public spaces, citizen interaction, economic activity, and the overall quality of life in those communities have greatly improved. For three decades, PPS has seen how "the public has become genuinely interested in learning about and understanding architecture and urbanism."[524]

Kent says, "What we have done over the last several years is identify the issues that architects ought to focus on as spokespersons for the community. Building better communities through improving their public spaces is one area where architects can really add value—but only if they let the community drive the programming and design. Architects should be a resource to help communities visually express their values and their culture."[525] Building better communities by improving public spaces is one of the issues that architects should be speaking about.

For much of PPS's history, Kent steered clear of architects, believing that the profession had little interest in addressing the context of community building, preferring instead to design large-scale objects. However, he has recently developed alliances with a growing segment of the profession that is in tune with his broader community and social design mandate. Architects now make up a significant portion of his team as well as his coalition of community-builders. The gulf that once existed between PPS and the profession is now being bridged, as both parties realize that neither can succeed without the professional collaboration of the other.

> Both inside and outside the formal boundaries of architecture
> there is today a tremendous energy being devoted to rethinking

how buildings, streets, and green spaces shape our lives, our communities, our economy, our democracy, and our sense of ourselves. The distinguishing feature of this new direction in design is the subtle but significant shift from the "project" to the "place." This small recalibration in focus delivers an enormous change in results. When creating a place becomes the goal, then important questions about what happens all around and throughout the building or development move to the forefront. It's a step away from the 20th-century vision of the architect's work as an isolated triumph of aesthetic devotion (even fetishism) to a more inclusive 21st-century idea of the designer as part of a vibrant, messy, exhilarating process of creating a living, breathing community. . . .

Making this leap from project to place has profound implications for the profession. Architects lose the Howard Roark supremacy in setting out how things shall be. Ideas, decisions, and even inspiration will come from a wider assortment of sources, including people who live there, work there, or visit there. And a number of disciplines must be drawn upon to create places that meet the various needs of people using them.[526]

The process of building community requires a coordinated effort on all fronts, with a matrix of political, economic, cultural, and design elements integrated from the onset. Architects cannot, in all practicality, be outside this integrated process.

PPS's approach to information gathering is rooted in the communities it serves and the places important to them. Detailed surveys are conducted, which are then subjected to rigorous internal analysis and scrutiny in public meetings. Input-rich data produce recommendations that help the community promote the qualities that make it a good place. Kent believes that if a place provides comfort and image, sociability, safety and utility, connectivity, and linkages, then it is a place that is building its community and has a strong chance of being successful.

PPS vice president Kathleen Madden works closely with Kent and the PPS staff to produce quality publications for use by professionals and

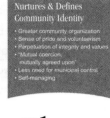

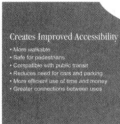

© 2003

The Benefits of Place

PPS
PROJECT *for*
PUBLIC SPACES

Project for Public Places' matrix of interconnected benefits created by successful places. Image: © Project for Public Places

community members alike. One of the organization's most useful and popular publications is *How to Turn a Place Around: A Handbook for Creating Successful Public Spaces*, now in its third printing. The text, written by Madden, provides clear explanations of and instructions for place making based on PPS case studies.

When asked who were his most reliable sources of information in the survey stage, Kent replied with conviction: "Fifth graders. They are sophisticated enough to understand when a problem exists but not politicized enough to be concerned with anything but stating the truth of their perceptions."[527]

Although fifth graders may be among its most reliable sources, PPS has developed ways to gather useful information from the other groups in a community. PPS is working with engineers at state departments of transportation. It is also developing training programs aimed at teaching designers well-tested methods of working with the public and the community's key stakeholders to design mutually satisfactory solutions.

PPS is in the process of transitioning from its long-standing strategy of working on a project-to-project basis to establishing a member-driven movement that can set up local PPS chapters in communities. This new phase of operation is intended to extend the successful principles of place making, as conceived and practiced by PPS, across the globe.

Bridges between the Project for Public Spaces, Inc., and architects, engineers, and public officials continue to be built. Fred Kent sums up his approach to leadership in the community as follows: "Our job is not to become architects. Our job is to find a way to allow architects to work better with communities by focusing on place. We are not going to replace architects because we come from a different, context-oriented perspective. Hopefully, we will help communities and architects work together to create both great places and great buildings. When you focus on place, everything changes."[528]

Freedman Tung & Bottomley

The urban design firm of Freedman Tung & Bottomley (FTB) of San Francisco is another fine example of how the practices of place making and architecture have been married. This private sector design firm addresses the difficult tasks of creating a sense of community in a California landscape divided by strip developments and freeways.

According to partner Greg Tung, the firm is "much more market oriented in our practice, saying that basically, the way you make revitalization happen is you bring a sharpening of policy tools together with capital improvements (understanding how those are tools to catalyze change) and knowledge of urban design history and practice. Then, [you] work . . . with the marketplace because cities don't have that kind of money to rebuild entire areas like urban renewal used to do."[529]

They define their work as the overlap activity of the architecture, city planning, and landscape architecture professions that focuses on the design of the public realm and the development of public policy and strategy to revitalize city neighborhoods—in short, the making and activating of places with beauty, functionality, and livability. They work almost exclusively under contract to municipal governments, along with other firms that accomplish aspects of the plan through private development work.

Many of the truly memorable urban places of the world were conceived and evolved over time under less-than-democratic circumstances (i.e., under kings and oligarchs), so attempting to craft great public places in a short-term, election-cycle driven democracy powered by a market economy is a unique challenge.

Although many conventional architecture, city planning, and landscape architecture firms engage in and advertise their practice of urban design (commonly from their own somewhat narrow professional perspectives), firms that exclusively specialize in urban design are relatively few. There are historical American precedents: In the late 19th and early 20th centuries, well-known city planner-landscape architects such as John Nolen, the Olmsted brothers, and Walter Hegemann practiced in cities and towns across the rapidly urbanizing United States. In the post–World War II period, however, physical planning became suspect; zoning, density, and other seemingly more quantifiable, scientific controls became the tools for shaping communities and their growth.

Today, America's postwar suburban expansion has reached maturation in many regions, with educated and often well-traveled electorates asking for (and sometimes demanding) more services, more community, and more quality-of-life possibilities from their physical settlements. Edge expansion continues but has hit legal and ecological limits in many areas. Many decayed city centers have been restored, while others continue to decline or languish. Within one generation, structural changes in the economy and family life have deeply changed how and where Americans choose to work, dwell, play, and shop.

Many of the conceptions of city making held by the art disciplines had been forgotten through the acceptance of conventional market-delivered models of urban settlement patterns. Placeless suburban sprawl has been the most obvious consequence. The approximately twenty-year-old New Urbanism movement has highlighted the desirable characteristics of early 20th-century towns and neighborhoods and adapted those characteristics to current needs and lifestyles. In this milieu, FTB believes that urban design is emerging again as a distinct practice.

FTB's planning process involves significant participation of community members and elected officials, similar to that of PPS. Many California communities require the involvement of these groups when changes in land use, density, and the like are proposed. The firm's belief in the participatory process thus complements local regulations, providing a good example of how the public and private sectors have both gotten it right. The firm holds workshops and charrettes with community members and works with elected officials to develop a vision and coordinated direction for each project.

Most planning processes, whether conducted by municipal staff or by the planning or design consultants they hire, include an investigation/analysis phase concerned with developing concepts and evaluating alternatives. Decisions are made based on this analysis, and the implementation phase follows, which might also include policy changes and refinements, capital improvement projects, and other measures.

What distinguishes FTB's practice from others? This is a firm of advocacy planners and designers—they love great cities and beautiful places, and the prospect of creating them is their practice motivation. They also try to select and work on projects for which there is client-side leadership interest in achieving quality results. The content of their work focuses on restructuring organizational patterns of streets, blocks, and districts and seeding them with elements of urbanism: furnishings, beautiful infrastructure, streetscapes, landmark elements, great civic buildings, and harmonious infill buildings. They design by working with the character of the local place (architecture, urbanism, and landscape), combining its indigenous features with lessons and inspiration from the history of cities. The goal is to create a memorable new synthesis.

Part of the firm's early planning process involves educating the public and elected officials on historical precedents and influences, urban design possibilities, and the development of a strategic plan to achieve the desired change. In a series of three to six workshops, held four to six weeks apart, the firm guides community members and officials through conversations focused on the presentation of analyses, design concepts and strategies, refinements, and final recommendations. Each session builds progressively on the previous session's issues and follow-up design and planning work.

Workshops include slide shows that examine the site and surrounding community as well as a presentation by the firm on how to revitalize a shopping district or how to design a successful public plaza. The groups look at examples of proposed design concepts in other communities, consider before and after views of design or planning changes, ponder supporting evidence from allied professions (real estate economics, traffic engineering, horticulture, etc.), and review strategic recommendations. The initial workshops always focus on existing conditions. These workshops are active-listening sessions, opportunities for the designers to elucidate their ideas and opinions and to vet them with city officials and key community members who can explain local perspectives.

Workshop activities include community image surveys (point score rating of slides to ratify images of designs that fit or don't fit) and roundtable sessions (small facilitated discussions of up to eight people, reporting back to the group at large). Attendees vote on proposed designs by applying pink (no) or green (yes) tags to the displays. All of these activities are designed to break patterns of audience passivity and avoid a one-way, lecturer approach to the session.

For public design and planning, FTB strongly believes in discrete workshop sessions as opposed to the charrette process, in which all decisions are made over the course of an intense work session lasting several days. By staggering the meetings, stakeholders have time to reflect and deliberate rather than make snap decisions about unfamiliar issues.

The firm strongly argues against the establishment of a steering committee or other select project constituency, apart from the general workshop process; this simply creates an empowered supragroup and two masters to serve. In the firm's experience, such groups are counterproductive to public decision making.

At the conclusion of the workshop sequence, a joint study session with the planning commission and city council ensures that these officials get to ask questions and debate the project's primary recommendations. Because the officials are under no pressure at this point to vote, the study session allows issues to be aired and responded to, eliminating most surprises *before* a public hearing. It also helps confirm the design that will be voted on, and will be the start-up for the ensuing implementation phase.

In addition to these formal instances of communication and exchange, FTB holds informal conversations and corresponds with city staff members and other stakeholder groups to ensure that everyone gets a complete picture of the design issues.

Anyone—I'm thinking particularly about young design students—who believes that participatory design or planning inherently weakens the designer's or planner's control and influence clearly has not spent time with the designers and planners at FTB. In 21st-century American communities, Greg Tung "believe[s] it to be an essential part of building community understanding and ownership for the shape of their settlement patterns—especially if their existing patterns are dysfunctional. That requires, however, a well-organized design and participation process structure that is focused on distributing information clearly and well; providing a common conceptual vocabulary (especially for inexperienced participants) so that specific design and planning issues may actually be discussed; allowing for the human need (in an information-overloaded society) to have enough time to reflect and discuss ideas; and making the craft of the professionals evident and valued so that it can be understood and bent towards the community's needs. We then work hard to complete the political design phase, and then dive into the technical work of our craft freed from most distractions. We believe this to be essential to great urban design in a democracy."530

Plan New Hampshire

Public officials, developers, and contractors all have considerable influence over what is ultimately accomplished in a community, but often their input is not registered until late in the process and rarely is it thoroughly integrated. One organization, a forerunner of sorts, was established in 1989 to change this situation by offering pro bono planning services to towns and cities unable to afford the services of a private sector firm.

Plan New Hampshire (Plan NH), the brainchild of the AIA's New Hampshire chapter, was created by a group of architects, including Jim Somes, Pat Sherman, Chris Poole, and Bill Norton, as "a 501(c)3 non-profit foundation for the purpose of supporting and preserving [New Hampshire's] quality of life . . . [It] strive[s] . . . to create a forum to improve New Hampshire's communities, through excellence in planning, design, and development. The unique aspect of Plan NH is that it is a multi-disciplinary professional organization whose members include architects, engineers, developers, historians, planners, insurance, real estate, banks, and other professionals involved in the planning, design, and development process. The diversity of [its] membership brings a variety of views and perspectives to discussions of issues concerning New Hampshire's 'built environment.'"[531]

Soon after its inception, Jeff Taylor, who previously had spent twelve years as the town planner of Berlin, New Hampshire, arrived in Concord, the state capital, to serve as the state's planning commissioner. With Taylor, the Municipal Officials Association, the Associated General Contractors, and the local engineers' association, along with support from several of the state's prominent architecture firms, Plan NH began to work in earnest to create what has proven to be one of the region's most successful pro bono planning and design operations.

Plan NH holds three to four annual design charrettes. Communities compete for a charrette by submitting proposals to Plan NH requesting assistance with everything from designing community structures to creating strategies for managing future growth. So far, twenty-four communities, each with unique, important concerns, have benefited from the program. Plan NH also sponsors various education forums and mini-charrettes. These weekend charrettes, organized by volunteers from the broad spectrum of professions involved in community development, have proven to be both efficient and effective brainstorming exercises.

An examination of a Plan NH charrette will illustrate the impact it has had on its community over time. Although I participated in a charrette in Madison, New Hampshire, in 2001, the example discussed here took place several years prior.

The first formal case undertaken by the organization was the Belmont charrette, held on January 26–27, 1996. Belmont was caught in the throes of deciding what to do with a dilapidated old mill in the center of town. Like most rural communities in New Hampshire at that time, Belmont had no available funding, and a community-splitting fight swirled around the future of the property. Half the town wished the mill to be torn down. The other half wanted to preserve it and bring in businesses and services to occupy the once stately structure. Without local redevelopment funds, the only hope was to get a Community Development Block Grant (CDBG) from the federal government. Taylor could see in the local press how quickly and publicly the town was tearing itself apart and said, "This is a project that Plan NH needs to get its hands on."[532] Its community relations plummeting, Belmont agreed to the offer of planning services.

Taylor organized a meeting at the community's volunteer fire station. Two presentation teams were formed to address both sides of the issue: one represented those who wanted to take down the whole structure, and the other represented those who wanted to take down just the outbuildings and preserve the original Federal style mill itself.

The simple goals that guided the process that weekend have remained constant over the years and have been at the foundation of every subsequent Plan NH charrette:

• Give people options to consider in solving their community's needs.
• Show several development strategies with varying budgets.
• Point the community toward the resources that can help them realize their goals.

The Belmont project took two years, but it worked. The mill was saved and reused. Matt Upton, the town attorney, went to work assembling potential tenants. The program included low-income daycare services and an affordable senior center. A restaurant and employment training center completed the occupation of the first three floors. Private offices for commercial businesses filled the fourth floor. The CDBG money split the costs and covered the low-income activities.

Taylor reflected back upon the project: "Here [was] a warring town brought back together. Here [was] a town that was in part determined to take the building that was both the historical explanation of why Belmont existed and the mill itself is the center of the town scene. . . .

"In Belmont there were two sides. What we tried to do was to validate and empower the position of both of them. And to give them sort of a framework for interaction as they move[d] forward. Cleaning up the

Jeff Taylor conducts a typical Plan NH charrette somewhere in New Hampshire on a Saturday morning. Courtesy of Plan NH

out-buildings was a good thing. Ultimately, maybe tearing the building down [was] a good thing. There was no time pressure."533

Following the Belmont charrette, Plan NH formalized the application process for communities. The organization sends a letter and two-page application to every community in the state. Three projects per year are selected.

"Plan NH has achieved remarkable success in terms of changing things," according to Taylor.534 Plan NH has the ability to bring both project boosters and project opponents together because it is not embroiled in the local controversy, which helps it build trust between all the parties involved as they craft a shared outcome.

The organization has initiated a scholarship and fellowship program to assist students who demonstrate the "greatest potential for a future career that will positively influence some aspect of the built environment in northern New England."535 Plan NH also has an annual Merit Award, "given to completed projects that have enhanced the quality of life, demonstrated vision, responsible development, creative planning, and design."536

These several examples demonstrate what writer, social commentator, and architecture critic James Howard Kunstler has written extensively about the long-term need for and the social implications of community engagement in place making. In 1996 Kunstler wrote, "Fortunately, a democratic process for making this change exits. It has the advantage of being a highly localized process, geared to individual communities. It is called the charrette. In its expanded modern meaning, a 'charrette' is a . . . professional *design workshop* held for the purpose of planning land development or redevelopment. It includes public meetings that bring together all the players in one room—the developers, the architects, the citizens, the government officials, the traffic engineers . . . , the environmentalists, and so on—so as to get all the issues on the table and settle as many of them as possible, avoiding the otherwise usual, inevitably gruesome process of conflict resolution as performed by lawyers . . . The object of the charrette is to produce results . . . not to produce verbiage."537

Samuel Mockbee

At first blush, the word leader would not seem an apt description of the architect-teacher Samuel "Sambo" Mockbee (1944–2001). Although he was a larger-than-life, bear of a man who filled every room he occupied with his expansive personality, he also believed that architects were "house pets to the rich" who had little or no concern for the needier, less affluent classes of society. His ragged clothes and ever-present baseball cap somehow matched his beloved old red pickup truck. His roots were in the Deep South where he learned and then taught architecture at Auburn University in Auburn, Alabama. Unlike many of his classmates, he remained in his home territory instead of heading for the prosperous, commission-rich cities to pursue his career. His classroom, the Rural Studio, located in the remote backwater of Newbern, Alabama, thrives today as a "tribute to his ideas."538

What makes Samuel Mockbee a great leader of his profession is certainly not the number of awards he received or the size and location of his many design projects. His projects were intentionally small and located in rural settings, far from the urban centers of the architectural elite. He received only a few accolades during his career, though in 2000, shortly before his premature death at age fifty-seven, Mockbee became a MacArthur Fellow, only the third architect to receive this coveted "genius" award.539 As well, the prestigious AIA Gold Medal was conferred on Mockbee posthumously in 2004.

His leadership derived from his deeply felt beliefs about the role architecture can play in society. Mockbee challenged the education establishment's attitudes and through his example changed the direction of architecture education from a purely theoretical exercise to one that integrates the theoretical with the practical: "For me art is a very personal endeavor, a way to reflect on what I'm trying to do as an architect. An architect, on the other hand, has to be an extrovert. You can't get anything done by yourself. You've got to have consultants, suppliers and a client who understands what you're trying to do. The connection is that art is a reflection of the best of who we are. One informs the other, and vice versa."540

The Rural Studio, established in 1993 with Mockbee's collaborator, D.K. Ruth, addresses the housing and community needs of the poor. For more than a decade, the program has sent architecture students with high ideals into nearby rural communities to work with people who would not normally have an opportunity to work with an architect. Together they have collaborated on everything from single-family dwellings to community centers and houses of worship.541

Mockbee's leadership philosophy permeates everything the students do. He "applied a light touch, cautioning students that goodness was more important than greatness, compassion more eventful than passion."542 His belief that "everyone, rich or poor, deserves a shelter for the soul"543 is similar to the Danish approach to public housing, in which the quality of design and construction often equals that of the private sector. Mockbee was a classic example of the leader as a servant of the people, one who unselfishly lends his exceptional talent to serve his community. That ideal and attitude has remained a staple of the Rural Studio.

Mockbee located his teaching studio in Hale County, Alabama's second-poorest county, because not only did the residents need help, but

A Rural Studio class in its element. Courtesy of the Rural Studio

being there would force students to test their abstract notions about poverty by "crossing over into that other world, smelling it, feeling it, experiencing it, [as] he said."544 The Rural Studio's clients have few, if any, financial resources. Discarded goods—everything from corrugated cardboard to carpet squares and automobile windshields—are often recycled for use as building materials.

This initiative would not have been successful without the establishment of a strong bond of trust between the Rural Studio and the community. Without Sambo, this might not have been possible. He identified with and cared for the lives of those the studio serves. The students learn about the region's architectural history, local cultural luminaries like William Faulkner, and the basic ethical values of responsibility, fairness, and decency.

His hands-on approach to leadership, combined by necessity at a practical level with the realities of life, was able to transcend the purely theoretical aspects of architecture education. Mockbee was less diplomatic with his phraseology, describing this integration by saying "Screw the theory; choose the more beautiful."[545] He knew his clients could be just as inspired in their participation as, say, a monarch of a bygone age was inspired by his court architect.

The Rural Studio represents a vision of architecture that connects practical architecture education with the community's social welfare, encourages the reuse of salvaged materials, and celebrates vernacular aesthetics. This, more than anything, gives residents pride in who they are and where they live.

Through Mockbee's leadership, the Rural Studio has entered its second decade as a vital, flourishing program. Thanks to the energy and ideas of its new director, Andrew Freear, Mockbee's successor, the Rural Studio has continued to evolve, its future secured by Mockbee's vision. The Rural Studio's foundation rests on the trust and commitment forged in those early days by a man who believed that leadership was service and that in that service one should always "proceed and be bold."

* * *

This chapter, so far, has focused on instances in which the client has had a very direct and involved relationship with the design leader. In many of the cases, the client has been the broader community, brought into the process and engaged at a fundamental level. This engagement is vital to the decision-making process for two reasons: first, as we have already seen, it provides useful information about the needs of the client, and second, it transforms the ultimate users of the project into its stakeholders. Without stakeholders, there is little appreciation for the outcome of the project and little desire to maintain it.

Examples abound of projects without stakeholders, and the results are usually disastrous. The public housing projects of the 1960s come readily to mind. Planned without input from or consideration of the tenants themselves and constructed of cheap materials, these monolithic, prison-like structures were so despised and abused that within ten short years many had to be torn down.

An enormously undervalued by-product of client-oriented design engagement is the strengthening of the client community itself. Greater connection, established through a bridge of trust between the architect and the users, brings about a greater feeling of self-worth in a broader social sense. A commitment to take good care of a structure is augmented by the desire to care for it as a community endeavor, not just as individuals in individual living units. When this level of commitment is engendered, communities will do things like get together to design and build playgrounds in a collective way, where everyone, from the children to the adults, has a say in the design of the playground. This is place making.

Stubbins Associates and Dynamic Team Design

There is a firm in Cambridge, Massachusetts, that is combining integrated leadership, involving everyone from the bottom up, with the demands of an accelerated schedule. I call this process dynamic team design, or DTD. At first, this concept might not look like it could work. It is easy, and not unreasonable, to assume that squeezing more information into a shorter period of time might just be a recipe for disaster.

However, Stubbins Associates' CEO, Scott Simpson, has found that there are two new assumptions that must be considered today. First, "a new model is emerging that brings together the entire team . . . This collaborative model goes beyond traditional design-build [models] in that it integrates the knowledge, expertise and innovative ideas from the beginning."[546] Second, speed is here to stay. As Simpson puts it, "we accept no excuses on issues of speed and we make speed our friend."[547]

Speed achieved through technology is here to stay. Computers have accelerated the decision-making process enormously. But the combination of technology and DTD has tremendous potential for cost savings, and it still maintains the highest quality in the decision-making process. Let me offer two examples.

Phil Bernstein, vice president of Autodesk Building Solutions, notes, "New delivery approaches involving roles and fresh technologies offer a real opportunity and create economic value."[548] Autodesk is working on technology to integrate the information produced throughout the design process in such a way that it will result in substantial savings. How? If you look at current approaches in the building industry, approximately twenty to thirty percent of construction costs could be saved if the linear approach to decision making, in which first one expert handles the project drawings before another gets involved, were to be changed to the DTD approach. Integrated technology allows information to be passed quickly between all members of the team, but it is the dynamic relationships between the team members that make the process work.

The Stubbins Associates successfully used DTD to solve a difficult problem, and its experience will serve to illustrate this point. Simpson noticed that a friend's company was about to encounter a difficult problem. The zoning regulations that controlled the use of property owned by the Amgen Corporation in Cambridge were about to be rewritten, reducing the property's allowable floor area ratio (lot size divided by the buildable area) by nearly half. The negative economic impact of this revision would be significant. Simpson calculated that it would cost Amgen nearly $31 million if a building permit to build on the property could not be obtained before the zoning change occurred in just twenty-eight days. He telephoned Amgen's CEO and shared his concerns.

Before the zoning change in the late 1990s, it usually took two years to obtain a building permit in Cambridge. How could they possibly obtain a permit in twenty-eight days? The firm assembled a team of its best leaders and decision makers, all of whom shared one common attribute—they were all team players. This team reviewed the design phase of the project, but instead of lining up chronologically to work on the project, as would be customary, they all piled into one room and worked simultaneously around a table. All of the team members had to realign their part in the process.

The architect became the group's conductor and all the participants became, to some extent, a designer. It was the architect's responsibility to ensure that the group interacted in a constructive fashion. There was no time to worry about who received credit for specific ideas incorporated into the design. Everyone worked toward the goal of producing a plan that sufficiently satisfied the building codes so that a permit could be issued in twenty-eight days.

Some of the most critical relationships formed were between the design team and the community, both in the neighborhoods and at city hall.

The city's building inspector observed the process from the beginning, so he would better understand the plans before they were submitted. In fact, he was able to offer criticism and suggestions while the plans were being drafted that helped the team better understand the requirements of the city.

In twenty-eight days the plans were submitted and approved and the value of the property had been preserved, though there was still a great deal of work to be done if the building was to be realized. After all, twenty-eight days did not provide adequate time to think through and resolve every aspect of such a building project.

Through this emergency situation, the group discovered that the Dynamic Team Design process worked extraordinarily well, so a decision was made to continue with it through the completion of the project. The building drawings did, of course, change between the permit approval date and the construction date five months later, but not significantly. And the building was completed in twenty-four months from start to finish—a year less than the time normally required to complete a comparable 400,000-square-foot facility in that area.

Through the dynamic relationships established by the DTD process, design decisions resulted in a better use of floor area (eighty-nine percent efficiency vs. the typical sixty-five percent efficiency), making the square footage costs $100 less than what this type of building would otherwise cost. Simpson calls it a "choreography of design or drawing conclusions vs. drawing the lines."

This process worked because Amgen first went to the town's leaders and said, Let us understand what you want. The process engaged publicly with every group of the project's stakeholders. Little things, like having children from the local elementary school paint pictures on the construction signs around the building site and providing public programming on the local cable station, went a long way toward establishing a bridge of trust between the community and the corporation.

It also worked because the people who took on the leadership roles all understood that the model to be followed was one of cooperation and collaboration. This architect-led approach saved the client $65 million of capital investment. The municipality of Cambridge gained a greater sense of closeness in the community, and Amgen adopted a new approach (one that is radically different from the adversarial model used before) for its future development projects. The Amgen executive who headed up this project advanced to take responsibility for the corporation's global real estate, an appropriate reward for a job well done.

Finally, it worked for the architects because, as Simpson said, "Design is sort of a sticky finger thing with architects. If it isn't my [the architect's] idea, it can't be any good. If you reverse that mentality and everybody is a designer . . . then the architect is the team leader. We chose participants based on attitude. It makes this whole design diplomacy thing available to anybody who wants to participate."549 The Stubbins Associates is a better leader in the community and in its business because it took the risk of trying a new approach to discovering design solutions.

All these designers of our built environment have developed a style of leadership that is based on sharing their power and its prerogatives with the people they serve. It is too soon to know the impact of this trend, but the evidence suggests it will be positive. For example, who would imagine that a team of architects would be called on to assist the U.S. Department of State in forming the Coalition of the Willing?

Architectural Training at the U.S. Department of State: A Design Charrette Tackles National Security Issues

On October 31, 2002, a specially arranged charrette was held at the State Department's offices in Washington, D.C., by a team of architects, computer systems designers, and senior State Department officials. I was at the helm. The task at hand was the design of an organizational system to integrate information from embassies and consulates all over the world to be used in the federal government's efforts to build a global antiterrorism coalition.

Undersecretary Marc Grossman, the director general of the Foreign Service at the time, approached me because he was impressed with the work I had done to overhaul the management structure of the U.S. embassy while I was the U.S. ambassador to Denmark. Utilizing both the architectural design skills and the management experience derived from professional practice, I had introduced a team-based structure to the embassy's staff, similar to the teams that form around projects undertaken in an architecture firm.

The substantial difference in this circumstance was that the embassy's teams were formed around issues and diplomatic dialogues rather than physical buildings. Rather than using concrete construction materials, blocks of information formed the components of the staff's daily building endeavors. Instead of designing office structures, these career diplomats and their administrative employees designed collaborative information structures in order to schedule and track complicated, interrelated diplomatic discussions. The team-based structure also lent more transparency to measurable results.

In the midst of an unprecedented crisis, the State Department wanted creative, problem-solving assistance in designing a rapidly deployable system to coordinate and manage a plethora of changing data. My approach to reorganizing the Copenhagen embassy so intrigued Undersecretary Grossman that he decided to give it a try. To do this, the undersecretary took a brave step—one outside of the conventional box. He convened a design charrette to utilize the skills of some of the nation's most highly accomplished architects.

This unusual step was not without precedent. In 1909 President Taft's secretary of the treasury, Franklin MacVeagh, called in the prestigious architecture firm York and Sawyer to do an efficiency study of the Treasury Department. The architecture firm's recommendations contributed to the first professionally conducted overhaul of the Treasury Department, from the arrangement of the offices to the modernization of building security and the elimination of redundant staff positions.[550]

Two architecture firms, NBBJ and Gensler, were ideally suited to address this emergency. In their client relationships, both firms emphasize that the design of a building's processes are as important as the design of the structure. This design approach acknowledges that the flow of information within the work environment is as important as the flow of people, goods, and materials.

NBBJ was founded more than fifty years ago by several architects in Seattle. It is now the third largest architecture design firm in the U.S. and the fifth largest in the world. Freidrich K.M. Böhm, chairman of NBBJ, represented his firm at the State Department charrette. As Böhm explores new ways to expand the firm's consultation services to offer better design of a client's business processes, such innovation will add a new dimension to architecture practice, expanding the client relationship beyond the strict parameters of building design as the foundation of the design contract.[551]

Gensler was founded in 1966. When the firm received the AIA's Architecture Firm Award in 2000, it was cited as "a model for the design professions in the 21ST century," managing twenty-five offices and 1,700 employees. Gensler's consulting arm has developed technological applications to augment its architectural design services. Representing the firm was principal and board member Diane Hoskins, an architect with an MBA. Hoskins clearly understands the benefit of applying the creative problem-solving skills of an architect to the practice of modern business management.[552]

By the end of the day, the cobwebs were cleared away from old government habits ensconced in the chain of command. The primary problems that challenged the government's management of its antiterrorism efforts were identified as a need for (1) top-down leadership action, and (2) bottom-up information capture and sharing. Practical recommendations focused on facilitating the rapid and cohesive two-directional flow of information, including the use of critical path management software. With a management team matrix that identified goals to be achieved and critical path schedules that outlined and prioritized the necessary actions to be taken, the State Department was given an implementable methodology to create an effective *new* working process as well as the tools to build a logical structure out of a huge and chaotic information database. The State Department charrette helped to conceptualize a workable information management system to support the activities of a complex network of decision makers.

Thanks to the joint effort by a team of expert architects and a group of open-minded government officials the application of architectural thinking was *creatively* utilized in the fight against international terrorism.

On October 2, 2000, Undersecretary Marc Grossman spoke at a conference on 21ST-century diplomacy. He asked, How are we going to get the right people to the right place at the right time with the right skills to lead and manage that diplomacy? In addressing the State Department's future, Grossman answered his own rhetorical question with this statement: "Leadership and management training for all supervisors must jump to the head of our list of human resource goals. Continuous training in many fields will be an essential factor in the careers of the diplomats of the future, if we are to retain the best people and arm them with the tools they need to represent our interests to the world."553

Two years later, in the face of an unprecedented national crisis, the State Department turned to architects for creative assistance and professional management expertise in order to refine a cogent response to rapidly developing security issues.

18 Issues to Lead By

I T IS THE RECOGNIZED EXPERT who most often has the opportunity to influence public policy issues—and it helps a great deal if the expert has a large sum of cash available to dispense to public officials whose support is being sought. The experts of the fossil fuel and pharmaceutical industries readily come to mind.

The next best way to obtain influence in the public arena is to be more knowledgeable than most decision makers about the subject being considered. As a freshman member of both the House Public Works and Transportation Committee and the Science, Space and Technology Committee, I understood that my lowly position would not command the respect of my powerful, senior colleagues. But I also knew that my understanding of technical and practical matters made me useful to those in a better position to move legislation forward. So when I offered my professional knowledge and experience to my peers on the framing of legislation, I had no expectation of getting equal billing, or any billing for that matter. I concentrated instead on providing my senior colleagues with as much useful information as possible so that important issues might be addressed in a timely and constructive manner. The nation's infrastructure, energy management, and environmental and technology issues dominated my political interests and my congressional efforts. In short order, it became known that the congressman from New Hampshire was particularly knowledgeable in these areas.

Many of today's critical issues have their basis in areas routinely dealt with by architects in their professional practices. The fragmentation of society, proliferation of information, environmental degradation, need for security and sustainable technology, and the rebuilding of our infrastructure are vital topics on which architects could and should assert themselves as the global experts because, at the moment, these issues are not being comprehensively addressed or coordinated by any of our current leaders.

In his remarks at the AIA's international conference, "Design Diplomacy: Public Policy and the Practice of Architecture," held in Copenhagen in 2000, former Congressman Steve Gunderson, a Republican from Wisconsin, said that "in a 1999 Frederick Schneiders Research (FSR) survey of community policy makers, respondents said that 'architects should play an important role' in dealing with housing and commercial development, in bolstering the quality of education buildings and facilities, in contending with urban sprawl and assuring the quality of government buildings and facilities. They were less clear about the urgency of architectural involvement in less building-oriented areas: parks and open spaces, traffic congestion, air and water quality, and government planning.

"What the FSR findings suggest is that the general public thinks of architects as coming to the table when we—individuals, corporations, or in this case communities—have decided what to do. But it is less clear to us that designers belong at the table during the discussion that leads to those decisions.

"This is understandable. It is also regrettable. Because the process by which our most competitive corporations and our most vexed communities determine what they should do is, in fact, a *design process* [italics added]. It is, or it should be, the methodical set of elements that in 1996 the Carnegie Foundation's president urged all America's teachers to use in enabling students to solve social problems: understanding what must be achieved, researching data, developing a core concept, detailing the solution and doing it all 'publicly.'"554

If leaders with vision could capture the public's attention and instill confidence by showing exceptional competence in all of these areas, through both their work and effective public relations campaigns that explain that work, an entirely new brand of leadership would emerge. The solutions to problems concerning loss of community, security, information overload, environmental sustainability, and rebuilding our infrastructure are all design problems and should be the clarion call to action by the architecture profession. Unfortunately, architects have yet to seize this potential. How might this be done? The issue of sustainability is an ideal case in point.

No other public policy issue is more appropriate for the architecture pro-fession to adopt as its central social theme than sustainability. It is, dare I say, a no-brainer! Though strides have been made in certain areas with edu-cation initiatives and innovative design solutions, the profession has done almost nothing to advance this issue in the halls of power. I know from first-hand experience in Congress how little interest, communication, and sup-port came from my own profession. This lack of interest in policy making became a real thorn in my side during the terms I served, especially while we marshaled the 1991 Intermodal Surface Transportation Act (ISTEA) through the legislative process.[555]

Perhaps the profession took for granted that having such an eloquent and committed advocate as Senator Daniel Patrick Moynihan was all the political stewardship it needed. His keen intellect, devotion to cause, and consummate legislative skills were indeed rare and are deeply missed.

But there are those in Congress today who are ready and willing to get behind issues and legislation directly relevant to the interests of the profes-sion. Why have these legislators gone largely unnoticed and unassisted by the profession? Oregon Congressman Earl Blumenauer is one such individual.

Congressman Blumenauer and his associate, Robert Stacey, started working on sustainable development issues with a team of like-minded col-leagues in Portland. They have pursued and maintained a consistent pub-lic policy agenda of sustainable development over a thirty-year period. Its success has depended on building community consensus through aggres-sive citizen involvement in charrettes and annual conferences.[556]

Blumenauer served as Portland's commissioner of public works from 1987 to 1996, when he was elected to Congress. Many of the professionals in Oregon's local and state government who contributed to Portland's long-term plan of sustainable development have continued to pursue these policies over the years in positions at the national level. Congressman Blu-menauer and Doug Wright, who has served as associate deputy secretary in the U.S. Department of Transportation and as deputy mayor of the City and County of San Francisco, are among them.[557]

In Blumenauer's local constituency, the AIA and other design profes-sionals are continually engaged in the management of Portland's development, because legislation requires that the city's master plan be updated every five years. On the other hand, that kind of professional engagement has been sorely lacking in Washington, D.C.

Blumenauer expressed his concern that the profession was missing an extraordinary opportunity to participate in public policy formation, especially given the close proximity of the national headquarters of the AIA to the nation's legislature. He stressed the equally critical and unmet need of legislators to have access to the design profession's skills in communicating ideas, solutions, and projects to communities.[558]

He compared the participation of the profession with that of other non-governmental organizations (NGOs): "The design profession, as a coalition, under-appreciates the role we play. We look at the power that [other] NGO's have, but the 350,000 design professionals who have the knowledge should be marching down here. The synergies are here. And it's very slow at the local level too. The AIA in DC is VERY QUIET on the [H]ill. There is no attempt to maximize any proximity. As a sitting member [of Congress], in seven years I've spoken to [the AIA] once and spoken at one event. At my instigation, we've had three 'brown bags' in seven years."[559]

Despite the congressman's apparent frustration, he still delivered sincere praise for the profession: "Designers are 'conveyers'; they can be neutral but convey ideas and projects into the community—politically, in the media and in the community. We've just scratched the surface."[560]

Just scratching the surface is not enough. The architecture profession needs to coalesce around these fundamental issues. Architects as citizens and as a profession must be willing to invest the time, expertise, and money to make these subjects their particular providence in the public's mind, so that every time the nation confronts a question of how to deal with sustainability or security or building community or rebuilding infrastructure it instinctively turns to its architects for advice and help.

Architects should be considered a primary resource in providing answers to society's vexing questions. Any organization representing the profession's interests ought to aspire to this achievable goal. Architects have the breadth of vision to balance competing interests and synthesize the desired outcome from all those interests. These unique, underutilized, and invaluable abilities are desperately needed by civic society. It is high time for those with these special gifts to step forward with commitment and resolve and take the reins of leadership to help tame this runaway society.

Nobody says it will be easy, though there is one place this kind of leadership has already taken hold. It is in the federal government's General Services Administration, the nation's agency for the design and management of all federal architecture.

Architects as Public Servants: The Reform of the General Services Administration

The work of the General Services Administration (GSA) is well known in the architecture community, though the public is largely unaware of its existence. Yet everyday the public conducts business in federal government buildings and uses its public spaces.

For more than fifty years, the federal government did not employ the services of a chief architect to manage, design, or direct the huge real estate portfolio of the GSA, the largest landlord in the United States. This lack of oversight from within meant that the guiding principles of the GSA, written by Senator Daniel Patrick Moynihan during his service as a presidential aide in the Kennedy administration, were more of a hope than a plan of action. That all changed when the Clinton administration decided to reestablish the position of chief architect of the U.S. government.

Since then, Chief Architect Edward Feiner has revitalized the inner workings of the GSA. He has revived Moynihan's visionary ideals of best design principles as the agency's internal and external program and has brought to federal architecture both the finest design skills and state-of-the-art management practices currently available in American architecture.

In Feiner's own words: "In the late 1980's the GSA developed the first 'Strategic Plan' in the agency's history. As a part of this plan, a small group of architects and program managers included the objective 'to be a leader in the real estate development community.' At that time the GSA also became aware of a huge necessary expansion of the U.S. Courts. In fact, the Courts Program included the construction of 192 new Federal Courthouses throughout the United States. It was estimated at that time that the Program would require over $5 billion in funding."561 This was the beginning of the most extensive improvement in the federal government's public building portfolio in modern times.

"In April 1993 GSA convened a panel of a group of America's leading architects, representatives from the American Institute of Architects, the National Endowment for the Arts, and GSA Officials to discuss the quality of 'our' public architecture. GSA had already in the early 1990s begun to emphasize design quality in its architect selections and had reinstituted a Design Awards Program in 1990 to recognize Design Excellence. GSA had not had a Design Awards Program for over a decade. Of course, anyone familiar with most of GSA's buildings of the 60s and 70s could understand why. The April panel included many of the Jurors who participated in the recently revived GSA Design Awards Program. They had the best 'view' of the work in progress. Ironically, Robert A. Peck, the then commissioner of the Public Buildings Service, GSA, had previously represented the AIA as senior vice president for External Affairs. Bob had much to say at that meeting, especially since he was intimately aware of GSA's history of construction as Senator Moynihan's former assistant and the author of numerous pieces of important legislation regarding design, historic preservation, and urban policy."[562]

Peck's previous experience has made him knowledgeable about design issues, and he is adroit at getting things done in the political realm. But he too was frustrated by the reluctance of architects to get involved in the political process: "Architects who can actually talk to people are rare ... [They] need to get their hands dirty and work directly with decision makers."[563] He was also amazed that many architects had no idea about how to work with the federal government. For example, he and Feiner tried to find an architect to take the lead on public art for a $3 billion transportation infrastructure project in Phoenix. According to Peck, the eligible architects themselves "were clueless as to how to get the work."[564]

The 1993 GSA panel came up with a long list of recommendations for improving the quality of public architecture. The GSA staff then consolidated those recommendations into a short list of initiatives, which have become the Design Excellence Program.

The most important of the GSA reform initiatives were concerned with improving the selection of architects. The creation of a peer review process utilizing both private sector and government professionals would now assist the GSA in the selection of architects and the review of proposed building designs. These initiatives greatly improved the mechanics of the selection process and became official GSA policy in 1994.

Feiner is proud of the agency's progress and says that, "The results have been striking, to say the least. We found that by reducing the cost and difficulty to compete for GSA work, a huge new talent pool became available to the Federal government. Firms and architects that would never consider doing 'government work' were drawn to the Program. For the first time in the nation's history, women and minority architects were designing Federal Buildings and Courthouses. Most of all, the quality of Public Architecture was on the rise."[565]

Harvey Gantt: Practicing Architect and Mayor of Charlotte, North Carolina

Harvey B. Gantt, a founding partner of the architecture firm Gantt Huberman Architects, is accustomed to taking the initiative. Gantt was the first African-American to win election to the office of mayor of Charlotte, North Carolina, in 1983. He was also the first African-American to attend Clemson University in South Carolina, in 1961, albeit under court order, and earned his degree in architecture with honors, graduating in 1965. He went on to earn his master's degree in city planning from MIT in 1970, before establishing his practice in Charlotte.[566]

Gantt began his political career on the Charlotte City Council in 1974, when he was appointed to fill a vacated seat. He ran for election in 1975 and won, serving two terms, before serving as mayor pro tem and then won two terms as mayor (1983–1987).

Subsequently, Gantt made two unsuccessful attempts to unseat Republican U.S. Senator Jesse Helms.[567] Had he won, he would have been "the state's first Black elected to the Senate since Reconstruction."[568] Gantt spoke of these two hard-fought political campaigns when he recently nominated North Carolina's Senator John Edwards as the vice-presidential candidate of the Democratic Party on July 29, 2004: "In the 90s, I ran two Senate campaigns in North Carolina that many of you may remember. My opponent ran a campaign of divisiveness. I firmly believed that an appeal to our best instincts as citizens, harnessing our hopes and aspirations, could free us from the perils of poverty, ignorance, and bigotry."[569]

In 1995 President Bill Clinton appointed Gantt to the chairmanship of the National Capital Planning Commission, the federal body responsible for the planning and development of the National Capital Region, including the District of Columbia and its surrounding counties. He served until 2000.[570]

At the AIA's Design Diplomacy conference, before an audience of architects, educators, public officials, and design professionals from around the world, Gantt described the way architecture has substantially informed and enhanced his political life. He recalled the moment when "Whitney Young, a prominent civil rights leader, in 1968 chastised us [architects] for being too silent on the raging wars taking place in the cities. His speech had a dramatic impact on the profession, and for at least a decade we started to see a heightened presence of community design centers in large cities nationwide."

Gantt's instinct following graduate school was "to work to influence people who were movers and shakers." He learned a great deal from the principal of the large, influential design firm where he worked: "The principal of that firm impressed me with how he moved the mayor, business leaders, and developers to accept his building designs—and sometimes his other ideas for city development. In 1970, I worked on a new town in rural North Carolina and watched the developer of that new town lobby both leaders in the state and federal governments."

By late 1971, Gantt had come to understand that "the way to make real changes was to influence the prime actors in the community—the leaders of business and industry—and the politicians who initiated and made public policy. I always felt that architects had a lot to offer. Our training to solve complex problems was an asset. Our orientation to assembling disparate pieces together—could be useful in understanding complex constituencies. Our visionary ability to see a physical picture—down the road—and to predict the consequences of certain actions—negative or positive—could make a difference. Clearly, we are a respected profession— but all too often pigeon-holed to provide, at best, secondary second-tier decisions . . . Architects can be far more influential simply because of what they know about physical growth and people functions . . . What I discovered in 1975, my first year as a council member, was that I had a lot to say about all of these tools of physical growth and development—and was at least, if not more, knowledgeable than my peers, who were lawyers, housewives, real estate brokers, businessmen, etc. . . .Working in the political arena was not much different than solving complex design projects. In design, architects had a site, a program, a need to understand the intangibles of the client, a budget, and a schedule—all oriented toward creating a successful, completed piece of architecture. In the policy-making arena, political leaders had a problem needing a solution, the parameters of place, a budget, varied constituencies, the intangibles of working with peers of different orientation and the need to work within time constraints. The two environments had more similarities than you could imagine."

Gantt's election campaigns always remained focused on the managed growth and infrastructure policies he believes will improve the quality of life in any city. As an advocate of better public transportation, higher density development, and downtown revitalization, Gantt emphasized policies that would produce a more equitable allocation of city resources.

The effective input and leadership by an architect, Gantt believes, contributed to the success of the many policies and programs implemented during his years in the leadership of Charlotte's municipal government. He listed the accomplishments achieved by the city during his tenure: "We built between 1975–1987, more public housing—scattered throughout the city in small, well-designed communities of 50 to 60 families . . . developed new policies for downtown development that encouraged revitalization of both housing and mixed use projects . . . initiated balanced growth policies that selectively extended utilities into areas that needed growth and development . . . effected a capital improvement program that extended public services and facilities to under-served communities . . . [and] significantly upgraded our public transportation."

Gantt offered this advice for the development of the next generation of the profession's leaders: "Perhaps, we ought to start with the profession's educational institutions—by reinforcing our already wonderful curriculum with more supplements in politics, planning, sociology, and leadership development. On the practice level, perhaps more of us ought to seek positions outside the traditional office, and apply our training to problem-solving in other areas—like education, business, and real estate development.

If we keep working at this, perhaps we will one day again be thought of as our society's master builders."57¹

Architects as Public Advocates: Architecture for Humanity and New York New Visions

There is no lack of impassioned advocacy for the support and development of high-quality design circulating in the architecture profession, but there is far less advocacy for the application of design skills to specific critical events or overriding issues of the human condition. The architecture community's response to two international public issues, AIDS and terrorism, demonstrates what can be done when a crisis is met with design ingenuity and cooperation across disciplines and communities.

Architecture for Humanity Inc. began in 1999 when a young architect was moved to address the crisis in Bosnia by mobilizing designers to create temporary housing units for refugees. Cameron Sinclair has since organized a global design competition for economically viable mobile AIDS treatment units for use in Africa, and has been mobilizing assistance for the rebuilding of the Iranian city of Bam, a World Heritage Site, in the wake of the recent earthquake.

Modeled on the famous humanitarian organization Doctors Without Borders, Architecture for Humanity has begun to provide a long overdue contribution of pro bono services to vulnerable communities. The idea sprang to life when Sinclair saw *The Valley*, a documentary about the Kosovar conflict by filmmaker Dan Reed.

Sinclair described how the film motivated him to take action: "The film provoked two realizations: First, I realized the extent to which scorched-earth tactics had destroyed the valley's homes. Then it became clear that the residents were determined to return—no matter what destruction lay ahead. Within a couple of weeks NATO and allied forces were pounding Kosovo with aerial bombardment. All we heard on CNN was 'the end game' and 'our tactical goal.' The question of how hundreds of thousands of displaced residents would return and rebuild their war-torn country seemed to come later—almost as an afterthought. It occurred to me and the group of people I was working with at the time that five-year transitional housing could be built next to the existing homes of returning refugees to provide shelter as they rebuilt their former homes. Originally, I had planned to work on the project myself, but the more I researched it, the more it became apparent that this was a global issue and that the design world could better respond collectively."572

Through his work with Architecture for Humanity, Sinclair believes more than ever that "good design can change lives . . . [D]esign often acts as a catalyst for political change. For instance in some neighborhoods something as simple as designing a bus stop or persuading the city to reroute a preexisting bus can create opportunities for residents to commute to jobs or to educational institutions that might have otherwise been inaccessible. Therefore this single act becomes an economic engine; a pathway to self-sufficiency."573

Together with his wife and Architecture for Humanity's cofounder, journalist Kate Stohr, Sinclair operates this growing nonprofit organization on a very meager budget; ninety-five percent of its funding comes from individual donors giving $30 or less. With a network of more than 8,000 architects, engineers, and designers worldwide, Architects for Humanity is already building impressive support for its activities. This growing community of concerned designers proves that, collectively, the design world has the unlimited potential to affect thousands of lives for the better.

New York New Visions, Inc. (NYNV) is a coalition of various organizations from across New York City's design community that spontaneously came together to deliver pro bono research and design services to the Lower Manhattan community in the wake of the terrorist attacks on September 11, 2001. NYNV's outstanding achievement under extraordinary and shocking conditions was the result of its highly skilled advocacy, substantive design research, and expert recommendations. Months before the terrorists destroyed the World Trade Center complex, as part of our research, we had interviewed several key individuals who subsequently became involved in the World Trade Center recovery and rebuilding process. Fredric "Ric" Bell, executive director of AIA New York; Jean Phifer, president of the Art Commission of the City of New York; and Alexander Garvin, former director of planning, design, and development for the Lower Manhattan Development Corporation (LMDC), were included in this project because of their individual approaches to professional leadership.

As AIA New York's new executive director, Bell immediately understood the magnitude of the 9/11 catastrophe and the role architecture would have to play in its aftermath. He also knew that the traumatized public would inevitably turn to the profession to cope with the destruction. Bell has been the proverbial man on a mission, coordinating the activities of the various groups involved.

It was no miracle that he knew what to do. He was trained both academically and professionally by one of the savviest architect-politicians around, New York City Planning Commissioner Alex Garvin. Bell put his political and organizational training, earned as a staff member of the New York City Planning Commission, to good use by organizing and conducting public forums, issuing press releases extolling the ideas and actions of the design professions following the attack, mobilizing the donation of financial contributions and material goods for victims of the tragedy, and marshaling all the resources these key professions could muster.

His special combination of sensitivity, personal humility, and advocacy has given New Yorkers and the world the best possible impression of how architects can provide crucial assistance in a time of crisis. He is among hundreds of design professionals who jumped into the breach to help rebuild the community, both literally and spiritually. With Bell and the representatives of many city agencies, architect Jean Phifer spearheaded the effort to improve the appearance of temporary construction shunts and scaffolding that sprang up all over Lower Manhattan through use of a consistent, dark green paint and simplification of details. They also helped to design handsome, informative signage to explain the work in progress and when it would be completed. These small steps served the important psychological function of reassuring jittery residents that progress was being made in rebuilding their stricken city. Ironically, through the efforts of New York New Visions, Bell found himself once again working in collaboration with Alexander Garvin.574

Alex Garvin was initially interviewed for this book because he is one of the rare breed of architects who has worked as a government executive, as New York City's deputy commissioner of housing and director of comprehensive planning. He continues his distinguished career in public office as an appointed member of New York City's Planning Commission. He has taught urban planning for more than three decades at Yale University's School of Architecture and is the author of several books on urban design, including the award-winning *The American City: What Works, What Doesn't* (1996).[575]

Garvin's design of the "Olympic X" plan was the linchpin for the NYC 2012 Olympic Committee's proposals. He is only the second urban planner ever employed to mastermind an international city's bid for the games.[576] His design follows the example of the 1992 Barcelona Olympiad, which vastly improved that city's infrastructure and venues: "Like Barcelona, New York is affirming the city rather than the suburb, and unfurling its edge to the water."[577] Garvin is serenely confident that New York City will benefit in a similar manner with the same kind of design leadership. But he could not have anticipated that his willingness to lead the city's Olympic bid would land him at the center of the Lower Manhattan Development Corporation's (LMDC) efforts to assemble a world-class design team to rebuild the World Trade Center site.

In early 2002 Garvin joined the Lower Manhattan Development Corporation as director of planning, design, and development. How did an architect become the supervising executive and chief catalyst for the World Trade Center's rebuilding process? Garvin likes to think it was, in part, because he "taught [himself] the language of the bureaucrat, the language of the banker, the language of the developer, the language of the designer." He was "able to walk in and out of those worlds and communicate with people on their own terms."[578]

From the Javits Center town meeting, where thousands of New Yorkers rejected outright the six original schemes, to the international competition that selected architect Daniel Libeskind's team to design the site plan for the new World Trade Center, Garvin has managed the give and take of complicated processes and volatile, often contentious groups: bereaved families, politicians, developers, the public, local business and residential communities, and various design professions.

In these difficult circumstances, Garvin knew that the complex fabric of Lower Manhattan needed to be rewoven by the local citizenry working alongside the families of the victims and supported by a nation still recoiling from the alien notion that Americans could be attacked on their own

The Javits Center in New York during the July 2002 Listening to NY town meeting for the World Trade Center rebuilding. Photo: Jacqueline Hemmerdinger

shores. Although he designed this difficult weaving process and even had a hand in selecting the threads that would be used to color the whole cloth, Garvin decided not to stay on at the LMDC to manage the rebuilding.

During the same period that the LMDC was tackling the rebuilding of the World Trade Center, New York City's 2012 Olympic Committee successfully navigated the byzantine Olympic selection process, becoming a finalist in the international competition. With Garvin's comprehensive "Olympic X" plan under development, New York City awaits the International Olympic Committee's choice to host the 2012 Summer Olympic Games.579

When asked why he left the LMDC, Garvin just smiled and, like a good politician, said his services were needed at the NYC 2012 Olympic Committee, where he is now the director of planning, design, and development. But behind that smile, one senses that Garvin may have had some ideas about how the World Trade Center project should be managed that did not mesh with the closed-door agenda of the powers that be.

Garvin's work on the original NYC 2012 Olympic bid was criticized for what some described as uninspired architectural designs for many of the competition venues.[580] However, he is quick to point out that he has a drawer full of designs for venue sites by notable architects that have not been approved by neighborhood bosses or borough presidents—yet. Garvin sees these negotiations as an ongoing process, and though many of the Olympic Committee's ideas have been criticized, such as the siting of a new Jets stadium, the proposed stadium is still a part of the overall program, an indication that "there is still something in the scheme that intrigues the opponents."[581]

Judging by how the WTC project has progressed since Garvin left the LMDC, perhaps things might have turned out a bit less conflict-ridden had this architect-leader remained at the helm. But New York City can still look forward to the opportunity to host the Olympics. If the city is chosen, Alexander Garvin will see his Olympic X plan used to overhaul the city's antiquated transportation infrastructure and reinvigorate whole neighborhoods with exciting new sports venues and beautiful new housing complexes. Only time will tell.

EPILOGUE

BACK TO THE QUESTION OF THE FUTURE: DRAW UP YOUR PERSONAL PLAN!

Our national civitas is failing, and it will not do any longer to pretend that all forms of conduct are equally okay, or that all economic choices are equally favorable, or that all products of human ingenuity are equally beneficial ... It will no longer do to say that virtue is too complex to be understood—and that, therefore, we prefer no definition of virtue to a possibly imperfect one.
—James Howard Kunstler, *Home from Nowhere*

WHEN THIS PROJECT WAS LAUNCHED in January 2001, there was no premonition of what the near future would hold. The events of September 11, 2001, have thrown the roles of architecture and architects into a sharp, new light. This awful tragedy has mobilized many people in the design and building professions to work together to address a national crisis in a variety of ways. Before 9/11, many of the individuals subsequently engaged in the rebuilding of the World Trade Center site were already part of the interview process for this book. The relevance of their input now resonates with an unanticipated significance.

From within New York's design community emerged New York New Visions, a coalition that successfully harnessed various professional associations into a collaborative organization. Creative people from a broad range of disciplines have provided pro bono expertise, research, and outreach efforts to grapple with, in concrete, practical terms, the tangle of recovery problems.

According to Jean Phifer, NYNV "was a spontaneous uprising . . . [whose] future as a coalition is quite possible. [It has no] conflict with the Arts Commission since it is not a city property . . . Because the Art Commission, the city's design review agency, does not have jurisdiction over the World Trade Center site (it is administered by the Port Authority of New York and New Jersey), this coalition of arts and design professionals has served quite effectively as an informal stimulus for public design review."582

In order to survive, NYNV realized it had to maintain an open door policy that allowed all willing members of the community to participate. This policy, along with a commitment to remain transparent in all its dealings, contributed significantly to building an architecture of trust.[583] The long-term rebuilding issues and intensive public debate surrounding the site, its immediate environs, and the future of its community have heightened the awareness, at all levels of public discourse, of the critical functions of architecture, the public role of design, and the professions vested with these responsibilities.

As a consequence of our communications in the context of the research, I was honored to be invited by the Lower Manhattan Development Corporation to serve on the jury for the World Trade Center Site Planning Competition. The research revealed surprising and edifying parallels between past national crises and our current circumstances. By connecting this history to the present, I hope to provide inspiration and practical advice for contemporary and future practitioners.

The redesign of the World Trade Center site in New York City represents a tremendous opportunity to change the way we think about creating community and our collective responsibility to participate in community stewardship; it also affords us a fresh chance to see how the architecture profession reacts to a modern-day crisis. Are we are up to this huge task?

Here is a design project—the result of ruthless, calculated violence against one of the world's most important cities and its people—that must accommodate the grief of a nation and the diverse cultural communities of a major urban center. It must replace a static and, except for its height, undistinguished monument to capitalism that barely made a profit in its thirty-year existence, and it must rebuild a mass-transit hub that serves a metropolitan region with millions of travelers. All this must be accomplished under the pressure of an exhausting urgency that plagues contemporary life in New York City.

Enlisting architects in the crafting of the solution was not supposed to be a dry, academic exercise; although the unfortunate truth is that most of the participants in the competition could only relate to the program as if it were exactly that. The competition was an invitation to participate in a design study that would have immediate application and a direct impact on society. This is quite a different process from that of a design competition. The WTC site design competition asked for qualifications to conduct a design study; it did not ask for submissions of final designs for buildings on the site. Architects who participated in the international site planning competition should have delivered a much higher degree of coordination with and input from the affected communities, taking a cue from the Listening to New York town meeting mounted by the LMDC and held at the Jacob Javits Center in July 2002. The more than 5,000 citizens who attended this open forum made their concerns clear, and though heard by the project's managers, their input went unrecognized by most who submitted proposals to the site design competition.

The site's design mandate could have—perhaps should have—been a much looser representation of the multitude of design elements to be considered in the rebuilding of the entire site. Instead of the expensive, elaborately executed, and nearly final building models that were presented, a set of comprehensive presentations based on the integration of physical design, political and economic realities, and the cultural and civic ideals of the Lower Manhattan community should have been considered the primary objective of the competing design teams.

The competition was an important opportunity for the design community to assume a leadership role in identifying the appropriate remedies for healing a bereft nation. Unfortunately, many of the architects were simply not up to this difficult task, as they failed to comprehend its very nature and could not summon the creative wisdom necessary to generate adequate solutions.

This book has documented numerous examples of powerful and compelling leadership by architects over a span of a century and a half. They have remained obscure to modern-day practitioners because there has not been sufficient academic interest in recounting their stories. It is important to remind our communities and the profession that it was the politics and relationships of many of the great architects that laid the foundations of their fantastic design accomplishments. It has always been the design leaders' involvement in the community that has created and expanded the opportunity to build a better society.

Today, the need for civic participation is greater than ever. The need for an inclusive leadership model is not limited to the profession of architecture. Every association representing every aspect of building, land-scape, and infrastructure design and construction voices this common con-cern: we need to work more closely together.

As Jerry Howard, executive director of the National Association of Home Builders, told us: "Architects are isolated in a design ghetto . . . There is a lot of back-stabbing . . . True opponents take advantage of that to the detriment of the industry. It needs pretty strong leadership to bring some pretty contentious high powered groups together . . . Architects have been out of the game so they haven't created a big enemy . . . The time is right [to build coalitions] and needed [because of] changing conditions and increased pressures . . . Creativity is on the line and needs to be protected."[584]

Bente Beedholm, the secretary general of the Danish Federation of Architects (DAL), is clear about the need for cooperation in leadership models. In Denmark, a much smaller and more intimate society, coopera-tion is much easier to accomplish. Architects have greater access to their political leaders. Education plays an important role in Denmark as well. Beedholm believes that instilling skills in teachers, not the students is the best way to ensure that good architectural design continues in perpetuity. The DAL is very involved in accomplishing this goal. This approach has two benefits: it inspires in the public a much greater appreciation for the design process and enables the juries for design competitions in Denmark to be paneled with at least fifty percent nonarchitect members.[585]

With more than ten professional organizations with differing agendas, the American engineering profession is even more fractured than is the architecture profession. Coordination is an even more important and dif-ficult task for engineers. Pat Natale, director of the National Society of Pro-fessional Engineers, simply states, "We're trying to bring people together." Education is the one issue that unites the engineering profession because there is great concern that the profession is losing young people to the high-tech industry.

Practice issues that make it difficult to thrive in today's political envi-ronment are the ever-widening reach of liability laws and the need for tort reform, Superfund issues regarding the cleaning up of contaminated land, and the difficulty of managing the increased responsibilities of the engineer in society. The profession is concerned with the basic question, Who's making the call? Natale and his colleagues are eager to get the message out that engineers improve a community's quality of life, yet this message is not coordinated with the other building professions and therefore gets lost in the cacophony of construction issues.[586] The stated hope of the representatives of the American Planning Association, Jeff Soule and Peter Hawley, is that "someday all the design professions will cooperate and start [a design council] that includes all the members' voices."[587]

When Tom Peters, leadership training guru, tells his audiences that design is one of the core competencies of their operations he is positively stating that the quality of design is perhaps the most fundamental factor affecting businesses today, encompassing the relationships between executives and their staff, clients, communities and even their competitors as well.[588]

"Perhaps never in history have the talents, skills, the broad vision and the ideals of the architecture profession been more urgently needed," a frequently cited quote from the late Dr. Ernest L. Boyer and Lee D. Mitgang's seminal study, *Building Community: A New Future for Architecture Education and Practice*, addresses the critical role the profession must fulfill in contemporary society.[589] Dr. Boyer did not promote an agenda for more elaborate tokens to architectural design, rather his research sharply focused attention on the fact that architects have the skills needed in solving problems of national import. He strongly advocated that school curriculums, from primary and high school through graduate school, highlight and utilize architects' design skills and processes for these social purposes. Even former Congressman Steve Gunderson shares Boyer's belief that "the profession could be powerfully beneficial at a time when the lives of families and entire communities have grown increasingly fragmented, when cities are in an era of decline and decay rather than limitless growth, and when the value of beauty in daily life is often belittled."[590]

Walter Gropius tried to create a mass-produced, industrial-based design formula to improve the quality of life for those who could not afford an architect, but he seems to have overshot the mark. His design agenda was co-opted by emerging corporate and political powers and never genuinely engaged those he originally set out to serve. Henry K. Holsman rejected the top down approach in favor of promoting the participation of every inhabitant in his housing designs. By incorporating the residents' financial, family, and community concerns as well as their aesthetic sensitivities, he made their homes and local places livable and sustainable.

Today the terms *New Urbanism* and *smart growth* are bandied about with increasing frequency. These movements promote theories that are thoughtful and well-intentioned but the desired results will hardly be better than what they hope to replace if they represent merely a theoretical application of integrated community design without actually engaging the community in the design process. To be effective and consistent with the philosophical approaches espoused in this book, perhaps these terms should be modified to *community-based new urbanism* and *community-based smart growth*.

* * *

The research and writing of this book has been a journey to discover how we can become better leaders who have the capacity to improve the quality of our own and our neighbor's lives. Along the way, I have identified four cornerstones of what makes a good leader:

- A good leader uses the design process as a model that allows everyone to participate and thus improves and expands the politics of civic engagement.
- A good leader has the broad reach of a polymath who accesses design and technical proficiencies to build and to manage what is being built.
- A good leader possesses the vision of the master builder by first defining what is to be done, and then by coherently articulating those defined goals to others.
- A good leader knows who she or he is; personal ethics, the understanding of power, and the desire to serve come from this wellspring of inner knowledge.

The building blocks upon which our leadership foundation can be built are also four in number:

- ORDER OUT OF CHAOS: Power is a force engendered through associating with a broad constituency.
- STEP UP TO THE PLATE: Courage is necessary to take the initiative and bear the responsibility of our decisions.
- BUILDING A BRIDGE OF TRUST: Personal and collective professional credibility makes possible the public's trust in us.
- CREATING NEW VALUE: Limitations can unleash the power of creation that leads to new and original solutions. (Make lemonade out of lemons!)

In a time when it seems that unbridled selfishness and narcissism run amok in contemporary society, the good leader should not be a superstar but rather a star citizen who speaks truth to power—first to himself, then to the community, and ultimately to those in authority. Most important, the leader should be ready and willing to accept the consequences of his or her actions. These are the elements of character in our leaders that will enable us to address the future of our communities.

To do so for yourself, begin with a personal plan, an agenda of priorities based on your most deeply held convictions and professional concerns, and identify issues or projects that can be acted upon in tangible ways within the sphere of your daily life. Don't be cramped by the superfluous activities and distractions that seem to impinge upon your time. Rather, prioritize those things that are most important to you and let fall away those that do not matter. Let that which seems to limit you, force you to be more creative. Take a step back and look at the landscape from a new angle.

Finally, you have the power and understanding to define for yourself the boundaries of the community you wish to serve. For some it could be their family, for others, the whole neighborhood. The only correct size is the one that is manageable for you, and, by the way, the field of engagement should be a bit bigger than just you alone. As David Bower (1912–2000), founder of Friends of the Earth and one of the world's leading environmentalists, once said, "Think globally, act locally."[591]

When you have done this planning, use the tools described here and think about the examples of leadership found within these pages. You can begin to lead by design today, creating an architecture of trust that will transform the world around you.

NOTES

Introduction

1   Nicolo Machiavelli, *The Prince* (1513; reprint, London: Wordsworth Editions Ltd., 1993), 41, 51.

2   Sidney Kaplan, "The Miscegenation Issue in the Election of 1864," *Journal of Negro History* 34, no. 3 (July 1949): 274–343, http://www.aaregistry.com/african_american_history/1483/Miscegenation_a_story_of_racial_intimacy.

3   I refer the reader to the latest harassment of Florida's black voters that apparently aimed to level the playing field, not by activating voters, but by taking more out of the process, as reported by Ford Fessenden, "Florida List for Purge of Voters Proves Flawed," *New York Times*, July 10, 2004, and Bob Herbert, "Suppress the Vote?" *New York Times* (op-ed page), August 16, 2004; "Voting While Black," *New York Times* (op-ed page), August 20, 2004; "A Chill in Florida," *New York Times* (op-ed page), August 23, 2004.

Chapter 1: Four Philosophical Cornerstones of the Architecture

4   Remember the Willie Horton ad in the 1988 presidential campaign? The Republicans vilified the Democratic candidate, Michael Dukakis, by implying in their ad that, if elected, Dukakis would free every murderer sitting on death row because he had released one in Massachusetts. But Democrats have been equally calculating. In his run for the U.S. Senate, Republican Mitt Romney (current governor of Massachusetts) was characterized as a cold-hearted businessman who fired employees as the means to turn a profit. The example cited was his handling of the turnaround of Staples, the office supply superstore in the early 1990s. It is true that jobs were eliminated, but the health of the company was restored, and its subsequent growth has meant that many more jobs have been created than were originally lost.

5   Larry C. Spears, *Reflections on Leadership: How Robert K. Greenleaf's Theory of Servant Leadership Influenced Today's Top Management Thinkers* (New York: John Wiley & Sons, 1995), 4–7.

6   Ronald A. Heifetz, *Leadership without Easy Answers* (Cambridge: Belknap Press of Harvard Press, 1994); William C. Taylor, "The Leader of the Future," interview with Ronald Heifetz, *Fast Company* (June 1999): 131–138, http://www.fastcompany.com/magazine/25/heifetz.html.

7   Bente Lange, "Krieger, Johan Cornelius—Court Master Builder, 1728," *The Colours of Copenhagen* (Copenhagen: Royal Danish Academy of Fine Arts, School of Architecture, Publishers, 1997), 25–26.

8   Haken Lund, Anne Lise Thygessen, *C. F. Hansen* (Copenhagen: Arkitektens Forlag, 1995); Jørgen Sestoft and Jørgen Hegner Christiansen, *Danish Architecture 1000–1960*, vol. 1 (Copenhagen: Arkitektens Forlag, 1991), 146–152.

Chapter 3: Georg Carstensen and the New York Crystal Palace

9   "The Crystal Palace, Opening of the Crystal Palace," *Scientific American* 8, no. 45 (July 23, 1853): 354, Making of America Database, Cornell University, http://library8.library.cornell.edu/moa/.

10   Robert W. Rydall, John E. Findling, and Kimberly D. Pelle, *Fair America: World's Fairs in the United States* (Washington, D.C.: Smithsonian Institution Press, 2000), 16–17.

11   "Our Crystal Palace," *Putnam's Monthly* 2, no. 8 (August 1853): 121–129, Making of America Database, Cornell University, http://library8.library.cornell.edu/moa/.

12   Ibid.

13   Martin Zerlang, "Urban Life as Entertainment, New York and Copenhagen in the Mid-Nineteenth Century," in *The Urban Lifeworld, Formation, Perception, Representation*, ed. Peter Madsen and Richard Plunz (London: Routledge, 2002), 316.

14   Ib Boye, *Georg Carstensen* (Copenhagen: Fiskers Forlag, 1988); *Dansk Biografisk Lexikon*, vol. 3, 409–410.

15   "Otto Boetticher," http://www.germanheritage.com/biographies.

16   *Appleton's Cyclopedia of American Biography* (1887–1889), s.v. "Christian Edward Detmold," http://famousamericans.net/williamludwigdetmold/.

17   "Our Crystal Palace," 123.

18   Ibid., 125.

19   Ibid.

20   "Editor's Easy Chair," *Harper's New Monthly Magazine* 7, no. 42 (November 1853): 844, Making of America Database, Cornell University, http://library8.library.cornell.edu/moa/.

21   "The Crystal Palace," *United States Democratic Review* 33, no. 7 (July 1853): 92–95, Making of America Database, Cornell University, http://library8.library.cornell.edu/moa/.

22   Zerlang, "Urban Life as Entertainment," 326.

23   "Our Crystal Palace," 125.

24   "Editor's Easy Chair," 844.

25   Zerlang, "Urban Life as Entertainment," 323.

26   Georg Carstensen & Chs. Gildemeister, *New York Crystal Palace: illustrated description of the building* (New York: Riker, Thorne & Co., 1854), Smithsonian Institution Library Catalogue, http://siris-libraries.si.edu.

27   "The so-called 'fireproof' building burned in 15 minutes on October 5, 1858," http://www.nypl.org/research/chss/spe/art/print/exhibits/movingup/labeliv.htm.

28   "The New York Crystal Palace: The End of an Era," World's Fair Collection, University of Maryland Library, http://www.lib.umd.edu/ARCH/honr219f/1853nyci.html.

29   *Scientific American* 12, no. 24 (February 21, 1857): 1, Making of America Database, Cornell University, http://library8.library.cornell.edu/moa/.

Chapter 4: Professional Leadership: Born on the Sharp Edge of the Sword

30   *Your Future Home, Architect-Designed Houses of the Early 1920s* (1923; reprint, with an introduction by Lisa D. Schrenk, Washington. D.C.: American Institute of Architects Press, 1992), xxii (note 5).

31   William H. Wisely and Virginia Fairchild, eds., *The American Civil Engineer 1852–2002* (Reston: American Society of Civil Engineers, 2002), 33, http://www.asce.org/150/150years.html.

32   Henry H. Saylor, *The AIA's First 100 Years* (Washington., D.C.: Journal of the American Institute of Architects, May 1957), 1–9.

33   Roger W. Moss, "Thomas Ustick Walter," Philadelphia Architects and Buildings Survey, http://www.philadelphiabuildings.org/pab/app/ar_display.cfm/21624.

34   "American Institute of Architects Certificate of Incorporation, April 13, 1857," Archives of AIA New York, New York City.

35   Robert H. Bremmer, "The Big Flat: History of a New York Tenement House," *American Historical Review* 64, no. 1 (October 1958): 54-62.

36   Biographical information from various resources: Paul R. Baker, *Richard Morris Hunt* (Cambridge: MIT Press, 1980); Brief Biographies of American Architects, Society of Architectural Historians, http://www.sah.org/oldsite06012004/aame/bioint.html; Philadelphia Architects and Buildings Project, http://www.philadelphiabuildings.org/; Royal Institute of British Architects Library Online Catalogue, www.architecture.com/go/Architecture/Reference/Library_897.html; "Architects, New Jersey Churchscape," http://66.92.127.80/architects.html; "Richard Upjohn and Richard Mitchell Upjohn Papers," New York Public Library, www.nyplorg/research/chss/spe/rbk/faids/upjohn.html; *Appleton's Cyclopedia of American Biography* (1887–1889), www.famousamericans.net; Charles Babcock, "125 Years of Achievement: The History of Cornell's College of Architecture, Art and Planning," http://rmc.library.cornell.edu/Aap-exhibit/; Ammi B. Philips: "US Post Office and Courthouse," http://members.valley.net/~connriver/VO9-18.htm; "Gothic Revival Library," Metropolitan Museum of Art, www.metmuseum.org/collections/vr_html/vr/temp_v_gothic_place.htm#withers; John Notman, John Welch: Kevin F. Decker, "Grand and Godly Proportions: Roman Catholic Cathedral Churches of the Northeast, 1840–1900" (Ph.D. diss., State University of New York, Albany, 2000), http://faculty.plattsburgh.edu/kevin.decker/Research%20Information/biographies.htm; Frederick Diaper, Henry Dudley: Walter Richard Wheeler, "Troy Architecture: The Quackenbush Stores," 1999, http://www.uncle-sams-house.com/tui/1999070320513607.html; John D. Hatch: St. Johnsbury Athenaeum, www.stjathenaeum.org/history.htm; John Welch: New Jersey Historic Trust, St. James A.M.E. Church, http://www.njht.org/

profiles/essex-st-james-african-methodist-episcopal-church.html; Henry Dudley: Park-McCullough House Association, Inc., www.parkmccullough.org/history.html; Joseph C. Wells: Henry Bischoff and T. Robins Brown, "The Hermitage, A History of the House," www.thehermitage.org/ArchitectureTextPage.html; Jacob Wrey Mould: Elizabeth Barlow Rogers, "Lectures, Definitions: Jacob Wrey Mould," http://www.elizabethbarlowrogers.com/lecture/definitions/def_mould.htm; George Snell: Robert A.M. Stern, "The Architecture of St. Paul's School and the Design of Ohrstrom Library," http://library.sps.edu/exhibits/stern/shattucksplan.shtml; Leopold Eidlitz: *Architectural Record*, http://archrecord.construction.com/intheCause/onTheState/eidelitz-bio.asp.

Chapter 5: Creating Architecture's System of Higher Education

37   "Jasper Francis Cropsey (1823–1900)," Newington Cropsey Foundation, Hastings-on-Hudson, N.Y., http://www.newingtoncropsey.com/jasper.htm.

38   Nathan C. Ricker Papers, 1875–1925, Archives, University of Illinois at Urbana-Champaign, http://web.library.uiuc.edu.

39   Allan Nevins, *The State Universities and Democracy* (Urbana: University of Illinois Press, 1962); Turpin C. Bannister, ed., *The Architect at Mid-Century*, vol. 1, *Evolution and Achievement* (New York: Reinhold, 1954), 93–104; "History of the Mechanics Institute," 2002 School Catalogue, www.generalsociety.org; Annual Reports of the Cooper Union, 1861–1888, Cooper Union Library (copies from microfilm), New York; "Backgrounder On The Morrill Act," http://usinfo.state.gov/usa/infousa/facts/democrac/27.htm; Marietta Pritchard, "Root & Branch: The Land-Grant Idea at UMASS," *UMass Magazine Amherst*, University of Massachusetts (summer 1999), http://www.umass.edu/umassmag/archives/1999/summer_99/summ99_root_branch.html; "About the Land-Grant System," West Virginia University Extension Service, NASULGC, 1995, http://www.wvu.edu/~exten/about/land.htm; "The Charter of the Massachusetts Institute of Technology," 1861–1977, http://web.mit.edu/corporation/charter.shtml; William R. Ware, "An Outline of a Course of Architectural Instruction," MIT, 1866, http://libraries.mit.edu/archives/mithistory/pdf/architecture.pdf; "UILC Architecture Program Report 2003, A3. Program description and history," University of Illinois at Urbana, https://www-s.arch.uiuc.edu/Admin/APR2003/APR2003A3.html; "Land Grant Mission," Cornell Infobase, http://cuinfo.cornell.edu/Campus/Infobase/index.phtml?kindex=462; "125 Years of Achievement: The History of Cornell's College of Architecture, Art and Planning," http://rmc.library.cornell.edu/Aap-exhibit/AAP1.html.

Chapter 6: Architect-Leaders during the Civil War Era

40 *Biographical Encyclopedia of Ohio of the Nineteenth Century* (Cincinnati: Galaxy Publishing Company, 1876), 368–369, Making of American Database, University of Michigan, http://www.hti.umich.edu/m/moagrp/.

41 Dankmar Adler (1844–1900) Collection, 1844–1941, Ryerson & Burnham Archives, Art Institute of Chicago, http://www.artic.edu/aic/libraries/rbarchives/html.

42 Charles E. Beveridge and David Schuyler, eds., *The Papers of Frederick Law Olmsted*, vol. 3, *Creating Central Park, 1857–1861* (Baltimore: Johns Hopkins University Press, 1983); Jane Turner Censer, ed., *The Papers of Frederick Law Olmsted*, vol. 4, *Defending the Union: The Civil War and the U.S. Sanitary Commission 1861–1863* (Baltimore: Johns Hopkins University Press, 1986); Will Irwin, Earl C. May, and Joseph Hotchkiss, *A History of the Union League Club of New York City* (New York: Dodd, Mead & Co., 1952); Henry W. Bellows, *Historical Sketch of the Union League Club of New York 1863–1879* (New York: Union League Club,1879); Iver Bernstein, *The New York City Draft Riots* (New York: Oxford University Press, 1990).

43 David T. Valentine, *A Compilation of the Laws of the State of New York, relating particularly to the city of New York. Prepared, at the request of the Common Council* (New York: E. Jones & Co., 1862), 1018, 1020, Making of America Database, University of Michigan, www.hti.umich.edu.

44 "Richard Morris Hunt," Howland Cultural Center, http://www.howland culturalcenter.org/Hunt.html#Top.

45 *Report of the Special Committee on Emigration* (New York: Union League Club, May 12, 1864), collection of Richard N. Swett; *Report of special committee on the passage by the House of Representatives of the constitutional amendment for the abolition of slavery. January 31st, 1865* (New York: Union League Club, 1865), African American Pamphlet Collection, Rare Book and Special Collections Division, Library of Congress, Washington, D.C., http://memory.loc.gov.; The American Presidency Project, "1864 Republican Party Platform," http://www.presidency.ucsb.edu; "1860 Republican Party Platform," http://teachingamericanhistory.org/library/index.asp?document=149; John C. Waugh, *Reelecting Lincoln, The Battle for the 1864 Presidency* (New York: Crown Publishers, 1997), 182–202.

46 Baker, *Richard Morris Hunt*, 192.

47 M.F. Armstrong and Helen W. Ludlow, *Hampton and Its Students* (New York, G.P. Putnam's Sons, 1874), 145, Making of America Database, University of Michigan, http://www.hti.umich.edu.

48 Ibid., 134–136, 145, 170.

49 Booker T. Washington, "The Struggle for an Education," chap. 3 in *Up From Slavery: An Autobiography* (Tuskegee: Tuskegee Institute, 1900), University of Virginia, American Studies, Hypertexts, http://xroads.virginia.edu/~HYPER/WASHINGTON/cho3.html.

50   Research drawn from the following sources: Baker, *Richard Morris Hunt*; Saylor,
      AIA's First 100 Years; Irwin, May, and Hotchkiss, *History of the Union League Club*; Bel-
      lows, *Historical Sketch of the Union League Club*; Bernstein, *New York City Draft Riots*;
      The Metropolitan Fair Ladies Executive Committee, New York, 1864, Library of Congress,
      Washington, D.C., Three Centuries of Broadsides and Printed Ephemera, http:
      memory.loc.gov; Mitchell J. Hunt, Sanford B. Hunt III, *Manuscript on Early Hunt His-
      tory*, http://freepages.genealogy.rootsweb.com/~hunt/archive/mnscript/mitchell.txt;
      Biographical Directory of the U.S. Congress, s.v. "Hunt, Jonathan,"
      http://bioguide.congress.gov; Carter B. Horsely, "The Tenth Street Studio Building,"
      The City Review, www.thecityreview.com/tenth.htm; Helen W. Ludlow, "The Hamp-
      ton Normal and Agricultural Institute," *Harper's New Monthly Magazine* 47, no. 281
      (October 1873): 672–685, Making of America Database, Cornell University,
      http://library8.library.cornell.edu/moa/; "Hampton's Heritage," Hampton Univer-
      sity, www.hampton.edu/hampton_facts/hampt_heritage.htm; "Virginia Hall, Hamp-
      ton Institute," Mary Ann Sullivan, Digital Imaging Project, Bluffton University,
      www.bluffton.edu/~sullivanm/virginia/hampton/hampton.html.

51   Michael J. Lewis, *Frank Furness, Architecture and the Violent Mind* (New York: W.W.
      Norton, 2001). Research drawn from the following sources: "Frank Furness," Philadel-
      phia Architects and Buildings, http://www.philadelphiabuildings.org; Eric J. Witten-
      berg, "Captain Frank Furness: Brilliant Architect and Medal of Honor Winner," 2000,
      http://www.rushlancers.com/furness.html; Robert Wojtowicz, "Waging Architec-
      ture: How the Civil War—and his own rage—shaped Frank Furness," Off the Shelf,
      May/June 2003, University of Pennsylvania, ww.upenn.edu/gazette/0503books.html;
      Lawrence Biemiller, "Penn Restores a Masterpiece by One of America's Most
      Idiosyncratic Architects," *Chronicle of Higher Education*, May 8, 1991, http://www
      .iceandcoal.org/nfa/furness.html; "Furness Library, University of Pennsylvania," nom-
      ination form, http://uchs.net/HistoricDistricts/furness.html; Furness-Hewitt Build-
      ing of the Pennsylvania Academy of the Fine Arts, http://www.pafa.org/the
      Buildings.isp; First Unitarian Church of Philadelphia, http://www.firstuu-philly.org.

52   Lewis, *Frank Furness*, 48–49.

53   Ibid., 47–48, 241–243.

54   Ibid., 89–91.

55   Martin H. Martin, "Judicial Restraints on Professional Self-Regulation," *Perspectives
      on the Professions* (Center for the Study of Ethics in Professions, Illinois Institute of
      Technology, Chicago) 1, no.1 (March 1981), http://www.iit.edu/departments/csep/
      perspective/pers1_1mar81_5.html; Robert Gutman, *Architectural Practice, A Critical View*
      (New York: Princeton Architectural Press, 1988), 75–77.

56   Tim Harrison, "General Grant's Report of the Battle of Shiloh," The American Civil
      War, Stroudsburg, 1999–2003, http://www.swcivilwar.com/GrantReportShiloh.html;
      http://americancivilwar.com/statepic/ms/ms002.html; http://www.shilohbattlefield.org.

57   Memorials to: the Commanders at Vicksburg, William L. B. Jenney, Captain, Vicksburg National Military Park, http://www.nps.gov/vick/us_cmnd/jenny.htm; Illinois State Memorial, Vicksburg National Military Park, http://www.nps.gov/vick/il/il_stm.htm.

58   Censer, *Papers of Frederick Law Olmsted*, vol. 4, 573.

59   Ibid., 609.

60   Ibid., 572–573, 577, 609–612.

61   "New Publications," *Scientific American* (June 5, 1869), 363, Making of America Database, Cornell University, http://library8.library.cornell.edu/moa/.

62   Ibid.

63   Beveridge, *Papers of Frederick Law Olmsted*, vol. 3, 577; Erik Haden, "William LeBaron Jenney," Structural Engineers Association of Texas, Austin Chapter SEAoT, www.seat.org/chapters/austin/eor/jenney; Wells I. Bennet, "William LeBaron Jenney, Pioneer of the Steel Frame Structure," *Michigan Quarterly Review* 3, no. 1 (winter 1964): 50–45, www.hti.umich.edu; "William LeBaron Jenney," Chicago Landmarks, www.ci.chi.il.us/Landmarks/Architects/Jenney.html; Society of Architectural Historians, American Architects' Biographies, s.v. "Jenney, William Le Baron," http://www.sah.org/oldsite0601200/4/aame/bioj.html#10.

64   Christian Frederik Hansen, Architect (1756–1845), Guide to the Danish Golden Age, http://www.guldalder.dk/show.asp?id=245.

65   "Denmark History—The Schleswig Issue," The Royal Danish Ministry of Foreign Affairs http//www.um/dk/english/danmarksbog/kap6/6-8.asp; "Schleswig-Holstein," http:www.wikipedia.org/wiki/Schleswig-Holstein; Adolpus L. Koeppen, "Wars between the Danes and Germans, for the Possession of Schleswig," *American Whig Review* 8, no. 5 (November 1848): 453–470, Making of America Database, Cornell University, http://library8.library.cornell.edu/moa/; "Denmark, Austria, and Prussia," *The Living Age* 26, no. 332 (September 28, 1850): 617–618, Making of America Database, Cornell University, http://library8.library.cornell.edu/moa/.

66   Research sources: Ellen W. Kramer, "The Domestic Architecture of Detlef Lienau: A Conservative Victorian" (Ph.D. diss., New York University, 1957); Saylor, *AIA's First Hundred Years*; Nina Gray, "Leon Marcotte: Cabinetmaker and Interior Decorator," *American Furniture* (1994), http://www.chipstone.org; Lawrence O'Kane, "Victorian-Era Mansion Will Become a Museum," *New York Times*, August 28, 1966; "Bech Family History," Marist College, Poughkeepsie, N.Y., http://library.marist.edu/archives/MHP/bechfamily/architect.html; "Detlef Lienau: Architect of the Sugar House," http://www.sugar-house.com/lienau; "Grace Van Vorst Church," Jersey City Past & Present, http://www.njcu.edu; "Vault #182 & 224-Booraem," The Marble Cemetery, http://home.attbi.com/nycmc/vault182.html; "Moorerege Estate," www.moorrege.de.

67   Kramer, "Domestic Architecture of Detlef Lienau," 4.

68   Robert A. M. Stern et al., introduction to *New York 1880: Architecture and Urbanism in the Gilded Age* (New York: Monacelli Press, 1999), 18.

69   Kramer, "Domestic Architecture of Detlef Lienau," 256 (note 3), 245.

70   *Annual Report of the General Society of Mechanics and Tradesmen of the City of New York, 1887*, 23, Making of America Database, Cornell University, http://library8.library .cornell.edu/moa/.

71   Kramer, "Domestic Architecture of Detlef Lienau," 258–259.

72   Cynthia R. Field, Ph.D., and Sabina Dugan, "Cluss Timeline" (8/8/2000), unpublished research provided by Field, September 8, 2004, 4; Cynthia R. Field, Ph.D., e-mail correspondence with Colleen Thornton, October 6, 2004.

73   Field, "Cluss Timeline," 4.

74   Ibid., 1–4.

75   Ibid.; Sabina Dugan (architectural history specialist, Smithsonian Institution), e-mail correspondence with Colleen Thornton, October 4, 2004; "Establishing German Organizations in America," http://www.germanheritage.com/Essays/1848/forty-eighters_part2.html.

76   Field, "Cluss Timeline," 3; "David Shribman, The Marxist Who Left His Mark on the Capital," *New York Times*, February. 18, 1984.

77   Dugan, e-mail correspondence with Thornton.

78   Friedrich Engels to Jenny Marx, May 11, 1858, Marx-Engels Correspondence, http://www.marxists.org/archive/marx/works/1859/letters/58_05_11.htm.

79   Karl Marx to Joseph Weydemeyer, February 1, 1859, Marx-Engels Correspondence, http://www.marxists.org/archive/marx/works/1859/letters/59_02_01.htm.

80   Michael A. Peake, "A History of the 1st German, 32nd Regiment Indiana Volunteer Infantry," 1–2, Max Kade German-American Center, http://www.ulib.iupui.edu/kade/peake/title_page.html; *Appleton's Cyclopedia of American Biography* (1887–1889), s.v. "August Willich," http://www.virtualology.com/augustwillich/; Don Heitman, "The 32nd Indiana Volunteer Infantry Regiment," http://www.germanheritage.com/Essays/1848/germanarmy.html.; "August Willich," Indiana in the Civil War, http://www.indianainthecivilwar.com/hoosier/willich.htm; "August Willich," International Institute of Social History, Amsterdam, The Netherlands, Online Archive, http://www.iisg.nl/archives/gias/w/10777118.html.

81   Cynthia R. Field, Ph.D. (chair, Architectural History and Historic Preservation, Smithsonian Institution, Washington, D.C.), e-mail correspondence with Colleen Thornton, September 30, 2004.

82   Stan Phipps, "Joseph Weydemeyer: Pioneer Advocate for a U.S. Labor Party," *The Early History of Labor Parties in the United States: 1827–1921*, The Socialist Organizer, http://www.theorganizer.org/LP/USHistory/Weydemeyer.html; "The Volunteer Army," http://www.germanheritage.com/Essays/1848/civil_war_part2.html.

83   Biographical Directory of the United States Congress, s.v. Sumner, Charles (1811–1874), http://bioguide.congress.gov/scripts/biodisplay.pl?index=S001068.

84   Field, "Cluss Timeline"; "The Charles Sumner School," National Register of Historic Places Travel Itinerary, Washington, D.C., http://www.cr.nps.gov/nr/travel/wash/dc58.htm; "Most Endangered Places for 2004, Franklin School," D.C. Preservation League, http://www.dcpreservation.org/endangered/2004/franklin.html.

85   Dugan, e-mail correspondence with Thornton.

86   A. Cluss, "A New Tumbrel Car," *Scientific American* (October 17, 1863): 256, Making of America Database, Cornell University, http://library8.library.cornell.edu/moa/.

87   "Smithsonian Institution Building," Histories of the Smithsonian Institution's Museums and Research Centers, http://www.si.edu/archives/historic/history.htm.

88   Field, "Cluss Timeline," 16.

89   Saylor, *AIA's First 100 Years*, 8–9.

90   Bushong, *Centennial History*, 114; Field, "Cluss Timeline," 6, 16.

91   Antoinette J. Lee, *Architects to the Nation: The Rise and Decline of the Supervising Architect's Office* (New York: Oxford University Press, 2000), 100–101.

92   Ibid., 97–98.

93   Field, "Cluss Timeline," 15; Bushong, *Centennial History*, 114; Field, e-mail correspondence with Thornton, October 6, 2004.

94   Bushong, *Centennial History*, 114.

95   Joseph L. Browne, "Hold the Mothballs," *Washington Post*, November 30, 2003; Benjamin Forgey, "Naked Splendor: The Old Patent Office was designed by dueling geniuses, then buried under 100 years of misguided 'improvements,'" *Washington Post*, July 24, 2003, http//:hnn.us/comments/15633.html; Cynthia R. Field, Ph.D., "Adolf Cluss Buildings (list)," unpublished research provided by Field, September 8, 2004.

96   Bushong, *Centennial History*, 1–4, 12, 114; "Notes on Adolf Cluss," Adolf Cluss Exhibition Project, Goethe Institute, Washington, D.C., http://www.goethe.de/uk/was/vtour/dc1/clussbio.htm.

97   Field, "Cluss Timeline," 15; "The Architects' Council," *New York Times*, November 18, 1869.

98   Adolf Cluss Exhibition Project, Goethe Institute, http://www.goethe.de/uk/was/pdf/Clussletterheadfinala.pdf; "Transnational Adolf Cluss Exhibit Slated for City Museum in Fall of 2005," *Heritage Matters*, National Park Service (December 2003), http://www.cr.nps.gov/crdi/publications/HM8_PartnersInitiatives.pdf.

99   Maria Kolanczyk and Michall Karzynski, "Flood Hazard in the Gdansk Area," Sustainable Community Development Course, Technical University of Gdansk, videoconference transcript, January 11, 2001, www.pg.gda.pl/cerso/scd/html/SCD_videoconf02.html.

100   "The Hero of the Dykes. Colonel Peterson—His Strange Adventures—Fact more Interesting than Fiction," *Daily Graphic* (New York), May 22, 1885.

101   Ibid.

102   Ibid.

103   Eric Dorn Brose, *The Politics of Technical Change in Prussia: Out of the Shadow of Antiquity 1809–1848* (New York: Princeton University Press, 1992), 109–132.

104   David E. Barclay, *Frederik William IV and the Prussian Monarchy 1840–1861* (Oxford: Clarendon Press, 1995), 104; W. O. Henderson, *The State and the Industrial Revolution in Prussia 1740–1870* (Liverpool: Liverpool University Press, 1958), 163.

105   "Hero of the Dykes."

106   Henderson, *State and the Industrial Revolution*, 161–162; Greg Martin, "On Track: Robert Stephenson, Locomotives for Germany," http://saxoncourtbooks.co.uk/ontrack/germany.htm.

107   Colleen A. Dunlavy, *Politics and Industrialization: Early Railroads in the United States and Prussia* (New York: Princeton University Press, 1994), 63–69, 153; Brose, *Politics of Technical Change*, 209–240.

108   *Handbuch über den königlichen Preussischen Hof und Staat für das Jahr 1841, 1843–44*, Royal Danish Library, Rare Book collection (1843–1844), 377, 382.

109   Dunlavy, *Politics and Industrialization*, 30.

110   Karl Marx, "Decision of the Berlin National Assembly," Neue Rheinische Zeitung no. 141 (special edition), November 11, 1848, http://www.marxists.org/archive/marx/works/1848/11/12a.htm.

111   James G. Chastain, ed., *Encyclopedia of Revolutions of 1848*, http://www.ohiou.edu/~chastain/contents.htm, updated October 26, 2000; University of Ohio—Articles sourced: David Barclay, "Frederick William IV," Kalamazoo College; Donald J. Mattheisen, "Prussia," University of Lowell; Konrad Canis, "Prussia, Coup d'Etat," Humboldt University; Rolf Weber, "March Revolutions (Germany)," Institute of Historical Research, Berlin; Konrad Canis, "Court Clique (Camarilla)," Donald J. Mattheisen, "Prussian Assembly," Helmut Bleiber, "Germany, September Crisis 1848," Institute of Historical Research, Berlin; Arnold Price, "Schleswig-Holstein," U.S. Library of Congress; Timothy M. Roberts, "United States and the 1848 Revolutions," Santa Fe Community College, Gainesville.

112   Jay Shockley and Susan Tunick, "The Cooper Union Building and Architectural Terra Cotta," unpublished paper (September 2001), 6; Jay Shockley (New York City Landmarks Preservation Commission), e-mail correspondence with Colleen Thornton, May 12, 2003.

113   Johan Georg Heck and Spencer F. Baird, eds., *Iconographic Encyclopedia of Science, Literature and Art* (New York: D. Appleton & Co., 1860), Making of America Database, University of Michigan, http://www.hti.umich.edu/m/moagrp/.

114   Jay Shockley, e-mail correspondence with Colleen Thornton, September 1, 2004; "The
      New Washington Market (from Petersen's Design)," *NY Illustrated News*, March 26,
      1853, New York Public Library Picture Collection; Kramer, "Domestic Architecture
      of Detlef Lienau," 3.
115   "Hero of the Dykes"; Kramer, "Domestic Architecture of Detlef Lienau," 3–4.
116   "Hero of the Dykes."
117   Jay Shockley, e-mail correspondence with Colleen Thornton, August 31, 2004.
118   Ibid.; Charles H. Haswell, *Reminiscences of New York by an Octogenarian (1816–1860)*,
      chap. 24 (New York, 1896), www.earlyrepublic.net/octo/octo-24.htm.
119   "Cooper Union for the Advancement of Science and Art," 1971–1975, Historic Amer-
      ican Buildings Survey/Historic American Engineering Record, Library of Con-
      gress, 48–49, http://memory.loc.gov.
120   Augustine E. Costello, *Our Firemen, The History of the New York Fire Departments from
      1609–1887*, chap. 11, part 2 (New York: 1887), New York History and Genealogy,
      http://www.usgennet.org/usa/ny/state/fire/11-20/ch11pt2.html; Haswell, *Reminiscences*.
121   Saylor, *AIA's First 100 Years*, 4.
122   Baker, *Richard Morris Hunt*, 85.
123   *New York State Business Directory and Gazetteer* (Syracuse, N.Y., 1870), advertise-
      ment, 500, Making of America Database, Cornell University, http://library8.library
      .cornell.edu/moa/.
124   Frederick A. Petersen obituary, *Orange Journal*, Orange, New Jersey, April 25, 1885.
125   Frederick A. Petersen: obituary, death certificate, probate records, cemetery location,
      U.S. Census Records (1860, 1870, 1880), New Jersey State Archives, Trenton.
126   Petersen obituary, *Orange Journal*.
127   "Hero of the Dykes."

Chapter 7: The Military and Political Writings of Frederick A. Petersen
128   [Frederick A. Petersen], *Major-General George B. McClellan from August 1st, 1861 to
      August 1st, 1862* (New York: H. Dexter, 1862), 16 pages, referred to and extensively quot-
      ed in text.
129   Richard L. Baker (Department of the Army, U.S. Army Heritage and Education Cen-
      ter, Carlisle, Pa.), e-mail correspondence with Colleen Thornton, December 12, 2003;
      Gabriel Furman (bibliography by Henry Onderdonk Jr.), *Antiquities of Long Island*
      (New York, 1874), 459, Making of America Database, Cornell University,
      http://library8.library.cornell.edu/moa/.
130   "Antietam," *McClellan and Fremont: a reply to "Fremont and McClellan, Their Political
      and Military Careers Reviewed* (New York: Sinclair Tousey Wholesale Agent, Septem-
      ber 30, 1862), referred to and quoted in text. Making of America Database, Univer-
      sity of Michigan, http://www.hti.umich.edu/cgi/t/text/text-idx?c=moa;idno
      =ADH1520.

131   Van Buren Denslow (1834–1902), *Fremont and McClellan: their political and military careers reviewed*, (Yonkers, N.Y., Semiweekly Clarion, 1862), Washburn University Library, http://lib.wuacc.edu/search/o?17061052.

132   "Antietam," 14.

133   F.A. Petersen, *Military Review of the Campaigns in Virginia & Maryland under Generals John C. Fremont, N.P. Banks, Irwin McDowell, Franz Sigel, John Pope, James S. Wadsworth, Wm. H. Halleck and George B. McClellan in 1862* (New York: Sinclair Tousey and H. Dexter, 1862); F. A. Petersen, *Military Review of the Campaigns in Virginia & Maryland under Generals J. C. Fremont, N.P. Banks, Irwin McDowell, Franz Sigel, John Pope, James S. Wadsworth, Wm. H. Halleck, George B. McClellan and Ambrose Burnside in 1862, Part II* (New York: Sinclair Tousey and H. Dexter, 1863); both pamphlets referred to and extensively quoted in text.

134   *The Life, Campaigns and Public Services of General McClellan, the Hero of Western Virginia! South Mountain! and Antietam!* (Philadelphia: T.B. Peterson & Brothers, 1864), 185–186, Making of America Database, University of Michigan, http://www.hti.umich.edu/.

135   Wolfgang Hochbruch, "'Forty-Eighters' in the Union Armies: A Preliminary Checklist," Geschichtstheatergesellschaft 1848 e.V., http://www.gtg1848.de/check.htm; "Civil War and Reconstruction, Parts 2 & 3," http://www.germanheritage.com; "NY Civil War Infantry Regiments," New York State Military Museum and Veterans Research Center, http://www.dmna.ny.us.

136   Waugh, *Reelecting Lincoln*, 301.

137   Irwin, May, and Hotchkiss, *History of the Union League Club*, 46.

Chapter 8: The Union League Club: How Architectural Thinking Created a Powerful Political Organization

138   Bellows, *Historical Sketch of the Union League Club*, 8–9.

139   "The official warrant creating the commission was issued by the War Department on June 9, 1861, though not signed by the President until June 18. It named as President of the Commission, Rev. Henry W. Bellows, D.D., New York. Put in charge of the central office as General Secretary of the Commission was Mr. Frederick Law Olmstead. It is to Mr. Olmstead's powers of organization that a large share of the success of the commission must be attributed." Jan P. Romanovich, *The Beginnings, United States Sanitary Commission*, 1997–2001, http://www.netwalk.com/~jpr/index.htm.

140   Bellows, *Historical Sketch of the Union League Club*, 5–31; Censer, *Papers of Frederick Law Olmsted*, vol. 4, 39–42.

141   "Cooper Union's Chronology 1859–1876," The Cooper Union, http://www.cooper.edu/history/extended/hi00002.htm.

142   "Let us have faith that right makes might; and in that faith let us to the end, dare to do our duty as we understand it." Abraham Lincoln (1809–1865), address, Cooper Union, New York City, February 27, 1860, in John Bartlett, *Familiar Quotations*, 10th ed. (1919), no. 6668.

143   "To The Women Of New York, And Especially To Those Already Engaged In Preparing Against The Time Of Wounds And Sickness In The Army," newspaper advertisement, April 29, 1861, U.S. Sanitary Commission Web site, Jan P. Romanovich, 1997–2001, http://www.netwalk.com/~jpr/ad42961.htm.

144   *Proceedings at the Mass Meeting of Loyal Citizens, On Union Square, New York, 15th day of July, 1862*, compiled by John Austin Stevens Jr., secretary (New York: G.F. Nesbitt & Co, Printers, 1862), Making of America Database, University of Michigan, http://www.hti.umich.edu/cgi/t/text/text-idx?c=moa;idno=ACR6040.0001.001.

145   Bellows, *Historical Sketch of the Union League Club*, 90; "Political Writing Since 1850, Opposition to the Administration," *Cambridge History of English and American Literature* (18 vols., 1907–1921), vol. 17, *Later National Literature, Part II*, http://www.bartleby.com/227/1415.html; Loyal Publication Society, 14 Pamphlets (New York: Edward O. Jenkins, W. C. Bryant & Co., C. S. Westcott & Co., Holman Book and Job Printers, 1863–64), http://www.clements.umich.edu/dup/indx5.html; *Loyal Publication Society—Documents for the South*, broadside (undated, circa 1865–1866), http://www.horsesoldier.com/catalog/337-80.JPEG.

146   "Immorality in Politics," *North American Review* 98, no. 202 (January 1864): 105–128, http://cdl.library.cornell.edu/cgi-bin/moa/moa-cgi?notisid=ABQ7578-0098-7; "Political Writing Since 1850"; Antony Dugdale et al., "Morse College" (New Haven: The Amistad Committee, 2001), http://www.yaleslavery.org/WhoYaleHonors/morse.html.

147   Albon P. Man Jr., "The Church and the New York Draft Riots of 1863," *Records of the American Catholic Historical Society of Philadelphia* 62, no.1 (March 1951): 42–44, http://lachlan.bluehaze.com.au/books/albon_man/church_ny_irish/.

148   Albon P. Man Jr., "Labor Competition and the New York Draft Riots of 1863," *Journal of Negro History* 36, no. 4 (October 1951): 375–405, http://lachlan.bluehaze.com.au/books/albon_man/labor_ny_draft_riots_1863/.

149   "Governor Seymour declared the Emancipation Proclamation unconstitutional....His speech in New York City on the occasion of the draft riots (July,1863) played into Republican hands and was a factor in his defeat (1864). He was the Democratic presidential candidate in 1868, and after his defeat by Ulysses S. Grant he assumed the role of elder statesman in his party." *Columbia Encyclopedia* (6th ed., 2001), http://www.bartleby.com/65/se/SeymourH.html.

150   Bellows, *Historical Sketch of the Union League Club*, 10.

151   Ibid., 11.

152   Ibid., 12.

153 Bernstein, *New York City Draft Riots*, 151.
154 Bellows, *Historical Sketch of the Union League Club*, 13.
155 Ibid., 13–14.
156 Ibid., 14.
157 Ibid.
158 Ibid.
159 Ibid., 15.
160 Ibid., 28.
161 Ibid., 30.
162 Irwin, May, and Hotchkiss, *History of the Union League Club*, 27; "House for Daniel Parish," Royal Institute of British Architects, library archive, record control no. P234967, http://195.171.22.30/uhtbin/cgisirsi.exe/abc/0/49; "Clubs and Club Life," *Galaxy Magazine* 22, no. 2 (August 1876): 235, Making of America Database, Cornell University, http://cdl.library.cornell.edu/cgi-bin/moa/sgml/moa-idx?notisid=ACB8727-0022-31.
163 Bernstein, *New York City Draft Riots*, 159, 272–276.
164 Ibid., 148–161.
165 F.L. Olmsted to Dr. Gibbs, January. 31, 1863, in Bellows, *Historical Sketch of the Union League Club*, 30.
166 Bernstein, *New York City Draft Riots*, appendix H; "The Twelve Society Founders," American Society of Civil Engineers, http://www.asce.org/150/founders.html; "The New York Rapid Transit Railway Extensions, Ch. II," *Engineering News* 72, no. 15 (October 8, 1914), http://www.nycsubway.org/dual/en_ch2.html; "Recent Acquisitions, portrait bust of Mayor Ambrose C. Kingsland," Museum of the City of New York, http://www.mcnyc.org/recentac.htm; "Mayors of New York," http://politicalgraveyard.com/geo/NY/ofc/newyork.htm.
167 Bernstein, *New York City Draft Riots*, appendix H; Beveridge, *Papers of Frederick Law Olmsted*, vol. 3, 1–54, 63–68, 78, 81–82, 91 201, 267, 270, 276, 321, 326–327; Censer, *Papers of Frederick Law Olmsted*, vol. 4, 215–216, 256, 259, 378, 463–471, 477–478, 505–508, 636–637, 694–701, 713–715; Bellows, *Historical Sketch of the Union League Club*, 86–87; Irwin, May, and Hotchkiss, *History of the Union League Club*, 23, 35, 62, 295–297.
168 Censer, *Papers of Frederick Law Olmsted*, vol. 3, 694–701, 713–715.
169 "The Mob in New York," *New York Times*, v. 12, July 15, 1863, nos. 3680–3685, Yale Center for International and Area Studies, Gilder Lehrman Center for the Study of Slavery, Resistance, and Abolition, www.yale.edu/glc/archive/964.htm.
170 Ibid.
171 "The Archbishop and his Flock," *New York Times*, v. 12, July 18, 1863, nos. 3680–3685, Yale Center for International and Area Studies, Gilder Lehrman Center for the Study of Slavery, Resistance, and Abolition, www.yale.edu/glc/archive/968.htm.

172   "Reports of Mr. Edward S. Sanford, U.S. Military Telegraph Service, July 13–18, 1863, Draft Riots in New York City," Official Records of the War of the Rebellion, Troy and Boston O.R., series 1, vol. 27/2 [S#44], http://www.civilwarhome.com/essanfordor.htm.

173   Man, "Labor Competition and the New York Draft Riots," 375 (note 3); Theodore Roosevelt (Jr.), *New York, A Sketch of the City's Social, Political, and Commercial Progress from the First Dutch Settlement to Recent Times*, chap. 14 (New York: Charles Scribner's Sons, 1906), http://www.bartleby.com/171.

174   Irwin, May, and Hotchkiss, *History of the Union League Club*, 30–31.

175   Henry O'Rielly, secretary, *First organization of colored troops in the state of New York, to aid in suppressing the slave-holders' rebellion. Statements concerning the origin, difficulties and success of the movement: including official documents, military testimonials, proceedings of the "Union League club," etc., collated for the "New York association for colored volunteers"* (New York: Baker & Godwin, printers, 1864), From Slavery to Freedom: African-American Pamphlet Collection, 1824–1909, Library of Congress, http://memory.loc.gov.

176   Ibid.; Liana D. Martino, *United States Colored Troops and their Normal School Officers*, http://www.albany.edu/nystatehistory/44/USCT.html; Irwin, May, and Hotchkiss, *History of the Union League Club*, 31–36.

177   Emmett J. Scott, *Scott's Official History of the American Negro in the World War*, chap. 13 (1919), Harold B. Lee Library, Brigham Young University, http://www.lib.byu.edu/~rdh/wwi/comment/Scott/SCh13.htm.

178   Irwin, May, and Hotchkiss, *History of the Union League Club*, 31–36, 90; Bernstein, *New York City Draft Riots*, 66, 67, 68.

179   Bernstein, *New York City Draft Riots*, 67; "Miscegenation or the Millennium of Absolution," political caricature, no. 2; "The Miscegenation Ball," political caricature, no. 4, Bromley series (1864), HarpWeek, LLC 1998–2000, http://loc.harpweek.com.

180   Bernstein, *New York City Draft Riots*, 234.

181   "Metropolitan Fair for the U.S. Sanitary Commission," Broadsides and Printed Ephemera Collection, Library of Congress, http://memory.loc.gov/cgi-bin/query/f?rbpebib:o:./temp/~ammem_e7Q4.

182   Bellows, *Historical Sketch of the Union League Club*, 87; "Education of the Freedmen," editorial, *Harpers Weekly*, February 10, 1866, 83, http://www.impeach-andrewjohnson.com/05AJFirstVetoes/iiia-3.htm.

183   Bellows, *Historical Sketch of the Union League Club*, 90.

184   *Appleton's Cyclopedia of American Biography*, s.v. "Willard Parker," http://www.famousamericans.net/willardparker, and s.v. "John Ostood Stone," http://famousamericans.net/johnostoodstone/.

185   Bellows, *Historical Sketch of the Union League Club*, 87.

186   Ibid., 88.

187 Ibid., 92.

188 "Table Talk: Lincoln Monument," *Appleton's Journal: a magazine of general literature*, October 15, 1870, 475, Making of America Database, University of Michigan, http://www.hti.umich.edu/.

189 Sarah Bradford Landau, "Coming to Terms: Architectural Competitions in America and the Emerging Profession, 1789 to 1922," in *The Experimental Tradition: Essays on Competitions in Architecture*, ed. Hélène Lipstadt (New York: The Architectural League of New York, Princeton Architectural Press, 1989), 63 (note 30), 76.

190 "Proceedings of the Second Annual Convention of the American Institute of Architects," *Manufacturer and Builder* 1, no. 7 (July 1869): 214, Making of America Database, Cornell University, http://cdl.library.cornell.edu/cgi-bin/moa/moa-cgi?notisid =ABS1821-0001-400; "Proceedings of the Third Annual Convention of the American Institute of Architects, held in New York, November 16th and 17th, 1869," *Manufacturer and Builder* 2, no. 3 (March 1870): 86, Making of America Database, Cornell University, http://cdl.library.cornell.edu/cgi-bin/moa/moa-cgi?notisid=ABS1821-0002-205.

191 J.C.M., FAIA, "Real Estate—What is the Chief Element of its Value?" *Manufacturer and Builder* 1, no. 8 (August 1869): 238, Making of America Database, Cornell University, http://cdl.library.cornell.edu/cgi-bin/moa/moa-cgi?notisid=ABS1821-0001-466.

192 Alfred Stone, ed., *Proceedings of the Twenty Seventh Annual Convention of the American Institute of Architects*, (Chicago: Inland Architect Press, 1893), 48, 115–117, AIA Archives, Washington, D.C.

193 Bernstein, *New York City Draft Riots*, 263.

194 Roosevelt, *New York*, chap. 14, 257, http://www.bartleby.com/171.

195 Bellows, *Historical Sketch of the Union League Club*, 10.

Chapter 9: Architectural Leadership During the Progressive Era

196 David Valentine, *A Compilation of the Laws of the State of New York Relating Particularly to the City of New York* (New York: Edward Jones & Co.,1862), sec. 30, 41, 42, 47, Making of America Database, University of Michigan, www.hti.umich.edu.

197 "Prize Tenements," *New York Times*, March 16, 1879.

198 Olive Hoogenboom, "Alfred T. White," Dictionary of Unitarian and Universalist Biography, Unitarian Universalist Historical Society, http://www.uua.org/uuhs/duub/articles/alfredwhite.html.

199 "Sir Sydney H. Waterlow," www.waterlow.stamps.org.uk/sirsydney.htm; Victoria Street Walk, London Footprints, www.london-footprints.co.uk; Hampstead Garden Trust, www.hgs.org.uk/tour; "George Peabody—Philanthropist 1795–1869," London People, www.london-footprints.co.uk/peabody.htm.

200 Matt Pacenza, "Warren Place, Brooklyn: history of a NYC landmark" (graduate student home page, School of Journalism, New York University, 2000), http://pages.nyu.edu/~mp458/warren.htm; "Photographic Reproductions of Work of Graduates," *Rensselaer Polytechnic Institute Bulletin* 30, no. ix (March 1931), http://www.lib.rpi.edu/cgi-bin/bulletin.pl?vol=30&iss=ix&pg=33; Adam Raphael, "Philanthropic Architecture: Alfred Tredway White" (March 1998), Bryn Mawr College, http://www.brynmawr.edu/Acads/Cities/98-city245/p1/p1ara.html.

201 "The Independent Republicans," *New York Times*, March 5, 1884; "The Plain Duty of Voters," outlined by Mr. Carl Schurz, *New York Times*, September 19, 1892.

202 Jacob A. Riis, "How the Case Stands," chap. 25 in *How the Other Half Lives, Studies Among the Tenements of New York* (New York: Charles Scribner's Sons, 1890), http://www.bartleby.com/208/.

203 "Commissioner White Explains," *New York Times*, February 11, 1894.

204 "Brooklyn's Sewer System: Commissioner A.T. White reports that he has completed 81.26 miles of sewers in two years," *New York Times*, October 22, 1895; "What Alfred T. White has spent: Mayor Schieren learns how one man he appointed has saved Brooklyn Money without penury," *New York Times*, October 25, 1895; "Charles A. Schieren," http://ftp.rootsweb.com/pub/usgenweb/ny/kings/bios/1902/schieren-charlesa.txt.

205 "Mr. Schieren's Final No: Positively declines to run again for the mayoralty of Brooklyn. Republicans have a conference. Franklin Woodruff names Alfred T. White...," *New York Times*, September 26, 1895

206 "Alfred T. White's Clock Tower," *New York Times*, June 19, 1896; Kris Sherer, "Farm Fresh," *Quarterly Williamsburg Arts Review* (Brooklyn, N.Y.), http://wburg.com/0101/context/farmersmarkets.html.

207 "Health and Profit," *New York Times*, November 29, 1896.

208 "City and Suburban Homes Company," *New York Times*, June 5, 1898.

209 Ernest Flagg, "The New York Tenement-House Evil and Its Cure," *Scribner's Magazine* 16, no. 1 (July 1894): 108–117, Making of America Database, Cornell University, http://library8.library.cornell.edu/moa/.

210 Francis Morrone, "The Ghost of Monsieur Stokes," *City Journal* (Autumn 1997), http://www.city-journal.org/html/7_4_urbanities-the_ghost.html.; I. N. Phelps Stokes, *The Iconography of Manhattan Island 1498–1909: Compiled from Original Sources and Illustrated by Photo-intaglio Reproductions of Important Maps, Plans, Views and Documents in Public and Private Collections*, 6 vols. (New York: Robert H. Dodd, 1915–1926); R. Waddell, "I.N. Phelps Stokes Collection of American Historical Prints," February 1998, New York Public Library, http://www.nypl.org/research/chss/spe/art/print/collections/stokes/stokes.htm.

211 "Tenement Improvers Report," *New York Times*, November 25, 1899

212 "The Tenement Commission," *New York Times*, April 17, 1900.

213 "Defects of Tenements," *New York Times*, May 3, 1900; "Model Tenement Homes," *New York Times*, May 17, 1900.

214 "Tenement Commission Makes Its Report," *New York Times*, February 26, 1901.

215 "Commissioner of Tenements Chosen," *New York Times*, December 7, 1901.

216 "There will be No More Flats If This Movement Wins," *New York Times*, September 17, 1911.

217 Hoogenboom, "Alfred T. White"; "A. T. White Drowns in Forest Lake," *New York Times*, January 31, 1921; "Alfred T. White, Brooklyn Philanthropist Leaves $15,000,000 Estate to Daughter," *New York Times*, February 20, 1921; "A Noble Life," *New York Times*, February 21, 1921.

218 "Hon. William J. Fryer," obituary, *Real Estate Record and Guide*, June 8, 1907, 1109 (Science, Business and Industry Division, New York Public Library, microfilm).

219 Patent Claims, #41,498, *Scientific American*, February 27, 1864, 138–139, Making of America Database, Cornell University, http://library8.library.cornell.edu/moa/.

220 Patent Claims, #52,986, *Scientific American*, March 17, 1866, 184; Patent Claims, #88,958, *Scientific American*, May 1, 1869, 285, Ibid.; Wm. J. Fryer Jr., "Compensating Railroad Car Wheel" (New York, Jackson Iron Works, 1866), An American Time Capsule: Three Centuries of Broadsides and Other Printed Ephemera, Library of Congress, http://memory.loc.gov/cgi-bin/query/r?ammem/rbpebib:@field(NUMBER+@band(rbpe+1270090a)).

221 Stern et al., *New York 1880*, 708 (note: Fryer, with Messers James L. Jackson, "Iron Store Fronts").

222 William J. Fryer Jr., *Architectural Iron Work: a practical work for iron workers, architects, and engineers, and all whose trade, profession, or business connects them with architectural iron work, showing the organization and mechanical and financial management of a foundry and shops for the manufacturer of iron work for buildings, with specifications of iron work, useful tables, and valuable suggestions for the successful conduct of the business* (New York: John Wiley & Sons, 1876), New York Public Library, Research Libraries Online Catalogue, http://catnyp.nypl.org/; Sarah Bradford Landau and Carl W. Condit, *Rise of the New York Skyscraper 1865–1913* (New Haven: Yale University Press, 1996), 106.

223 Margot Gayle and Carol Gayle, *Cast-Iron Architecture in America: The Significance of James Bogardus* (New York: W.W. Norton, 1998), 74.

224 William J. Fryer, Jr., *A proposed new city park for the extreme eastern portion of New York* (New York, 1879), New York Public Library, Humanities-History & Gen, IRH p. v. 6, no. 3, http://catnyp.nypl.org/search/aFryer/afryer/85,96,190,B/frameset&FF=afryer+william&1,1,

225 "Fryer," obituary; 1880 United States Census and National Index, FHL film 1254880, Nat. Archives Film T9-0880, p. 412C; The Church of the Latter Day Saints, CD-ROM, 2001.

226   Thomas Edison Papers, online archive, http://edison.rutgers.edu/; Schenectady
      County Clerk Office, Certificate of Changing Place of Business of the Edison
      Machine Works, November 23, 1887, http://www.schenectadycountyclerk.com/
      modules.php?op=modload&name=News&file=article&sid=3&mode=thread&order=0
      &thold=0; History of Delaware County, City of Chester, John Roach, www.delco
      history.org/ashmead_pg389.htm.

227   "Mr. Esterbrook gives a curious account…," *American Architect and Building News*,
      March 26, 1892 (Humanities and Social Sciences Division, New York Public Library,
      microfilm).

228   Costello, *Our Firemen*, chap. 50, part III, http://www.usgennet.org/state/fire/41-
      50/ch50pt3.html.

229   "Mr. Esterbrook gives a curious account…"

230   "Some Soho Addresses: 500 Broome Street, 93 Grand Street," www.paulrush
      walks.com/history2.htm.

231   Matthias Bloodgood obituary, *New York Times*, January 6, 1890, 5.

232   "A Better Building Law," *New York Times*, April 17, 1892, 20.

233   Costello, *Our Firemen*, chap. 50, part V, http://www.usgennet.org/usa/ny/state/fire/41-
      50/ch50pt5.html; "Albert D'Oench (1852–1918)," http://www.archinform.net/arch/
      28653.htm?ID=XC1ouq6ITGTjArvr; "D'Oench, Albert F.," American Architects'
      Biographies, Society of Architectural Historians, http://www.sah.org/old-
      site06012004/aame/biod.html#40; "New York Tribune Building," Skyscrapers.com,
      http://www.skyscrapers.com/re/en/wm/bu/102532.

234   "Daniel Manning Married, The Democratic Leader Takes to Himself a Wife," *New
      York Times*, November 20, 1884, 1; "Fryer," obituary.

235   Daniel Manning (1885–1887), Office of the Curator, U.S. Department of the Treasury,
      http://www.ustreas.gov/offices/management/curator/collection/secretary/manning.htm;
      Columbia Encyclopedia (6th ed., 2001), s.v. "Manning, Daniel," www.bartleby.com/65/
      e-/E-ManningD.html.

236   William J. Fryer Jr., Superintendent of Repairs, *U.S. Public buildings in the city of New
      York, A report to Colonel W. A. Freret, supervising architect…, Feb. 8, 1888* (New York: W.
      McDonald & Co., 1888), Research Libraries Online Catalogue, New York Public
      Library, http://catnyp.nypl.org/.

237   "For New Public Buildings," *New York Times*, September 6, 1888, 8.

238   *To the Honorable the Senate and House of Representatives of the United States, in Congress
      assembled: Regarding the removal of the Custom-house in the city of new York to the Bat-
      tery . . .*, New York, May 10, 1872, American Memory: Broadsides and other printed
      ephemera, Library of Congress, http://memory.loc.gov; Lee, *Architects to the Nation*,
      86–89, 142–147.

239	*Report of a special committee of the Chamber of Commerce of the State of New York: on a suitable location in the city of New York for a new customs building* (New York: New York Chamber of Commerce, Press of the Chamber of Commerce, 1888), Research Libraries Online Catalogue, New York Public Library, http://catnyp.nypl.org/.

240	"New Customs Building," *New York Times*, April 10, 1890, 8.

241	"To Check the Syndicate," *New York Times*, August 5, 1890, 8.

242	"Fryer," obituary.

243	William J. Fryer, ed., *Laws Related to buildings, in the city of New York* (Real Estate Record and Guide, N.Y., 1886 and 1892), Research Libraries Online Catalogue, New York Public Library, http://catnyp.nypl.org/.

244	"LeBrun, Napoleon (1821–1901)," Philadelphia Architects and Buildings, www.philadelphiabuildings.org; "Fire Engine Company 39 and Ladder Company 16 Station House, 157–159 East 67th Street, Manhattan," New York City Landmarks Commission, Designation Process Summaries, http://home.nyc.gov; Costello, *Our Firemen*, chap. 57, part II, http://www.usgennet.org/state/fire/51-58/ch57pt2.html.

245	Fryer, *Laws Related to buildings, in the city of New York*, 1886 and 1892.

246	"An Inn on the National Register of Historic Places, History of the Normandy Inn, Spring Lake, N.J.," www.normandyinn.com.

247	"Architect Robinson Against Law," *New York Times*, November 28, 1889, 9.

248	"Suggestions for Buildings," *New York Times*, April. 4, 1891, 8.

249	*Real Estate Record & Building Guide*, March 19 and March 26, 1892, Science, Industry and Business Division, New York Public Library; *American Architect and Building News*, March 19, 1892 (Humanities and Social Sciences Division, New York Public Library, microfilm); "A Better Building Law."

250	"The Hotel Royal Fire and the Laws Relating to Buildings," *Real Estate Record & Building Guide*, February 13, 1892 (Science, Industry and Business Division, New York Public Library, microfilm); "Hotel Fires," www.emergency-management.net/hotel_fire.htm.

251	"A Better Building Law."

252	"The Hotel Royal Fire and the Laws Relating to Buildings."

253	*Real Estate Record & Building Guide*, March 12, 1892 (Science, Industry and Business Division, New York Public Library, microfilm).

254	"A Better Building Law."

255	*Real Estate Record & Building Guide*, March. 12, March. 19, March. 26, April. 2, 1892 (Science, Industry and Business Division, New York Public Library, microfilm); *American Architect and Building News*, March 19, 1892, (Science, Industry and Business Division, New York Public Library, microfilm).

256	"A Better Building Law."

257   "What's the Matter with the Institute?" *Real Estate Record & Building Guide*, March 26, 1892 (Science, Industry and Business Division, New York Public Library, microfilm).

258   *Real Estate Record & Building Guide*, April 2, 1892 (Science, Industry and Business Division, New York Public Library, microfilm).

259   "A Better Building Law."

260   *Real Estate Record & Building Guide*, April 16, 1892 (Science, Industry and Business Division, New York Public Library, microfilm).

261   "For Safety in Tenements," *New York Times*, May 29, 1892, 5.

262   Landau and Condit, *Rise of the New York Skyscraper*, 120–122, 413 (note 28), 181–184, 419 (note 30).

263   "A Better Building Law"; *Real Estate Record & Building Guide*, April 30, 1892, June 25, 1892 (Science, Industry and Business Division, New York Public Library, microfilm).

264   William J. Fryer Jr., ed., *Laws Relating to Buildings, in the City of New York, passed June 9, 1885: with marginal notes, a complex index, colored engravings and answers to questions arising under the law; Law limiting the height of dwelling houses, passed June 9, 1885; Mechanic lien law for the city and state of New York, passed May 27, 1885; also a complete directory of architects in New York City, Brooklyn, Jersey City, Newark and Yonkers* (New York: The Record and Guide, 1886); William J. Fryer Jr., ed., *Laws Relating to Buildings, in the City of New York, with headings and marginal notes, full indexes, and colored engravings, Also a complete directory of architects in New York City, Brooklyn, Jersey City and Newark* (New York: The Record and Guide, 1892), Research Libraries Online Catalogue, New York Public Library, http://catnyp.nypl.org/.

265   William J. Fryer, ed., *The Tenement House Law and the Lodging House Law of the city of New York* (New York: The Record and Guide, 1902); William J. Fryer, ed., *The New York Laws relating to apartment and tenement houses* (New York: C.W. Sweet Co., 1903), Research Libraries Online Catalogue, New York Public Library, http://catnyp.nypl.org/.

266   *Real Estate Record & Building Guide*, April 16, 1892.

267   *Real Estate Record & Building Guide*, April 9, 1892 (Science, Industry and Business Division, New York Public Library, microfilm).

268   *Real Estate Record & Building Guide*, June 11, 1892, Ibid.; "Fryer," obituary; biographical sketches of John T. Hoffman and Allan C. Beach…, Cornell Library Historical Monographs, http://historical.library.cornell.edu.

269   "For Honesty in Politics," *New York Times*, April 6, 1892, 9.

270   "Samuel McMillan For Mayor," *New York Times*, September 26, 1894, 5; Biographical Directory of the United States Congress, s.v. "McMillan, Samuel, 1850–1924," http://bioguide.congress.gov.

271 "Fusion Mayor Reformed DOC&C," New York City Department of Corrections Centennial Issue; http://www.correctionhistory.org/html/chronicl/nycdoc/html/100years.html.

272 "Moss Arraigns the Rule of Tammany," *New York Times*, December 25, 1899, 1.

273 "Mazet Witnesses Warned," *New York Times*, April 23, 1899, 3.

274 "Moss Arraigns the Rule of Tammany."

275 "Mazet Witnesses Warned."

276 "Mazet Committee's Work," *New York Times*, September 23, 1899, 4.

277 "Status of Building Laws," *New York Times*, May 29, 1899, 4.

278 Ibid.; Dennis Steadman Francis, *Architects in Practice in New York City, 1840–1900* (New York: Committee for the Preservation of Architectural Records, 1979).

279 *Report of the Charter Revision Commission to the Governor of the State of New York*, December 1, 1900, Making of America Database, University of Michigan, www.hti.umich.edu.

280 *American Architect and Building News*, June 15, 1907, 229.

281 "Fryer," obituary.

282 Ibid.

Chapter 10: Political Defeat That Could Have Been Avoided: The Real Story of the Defeat of the 1892 Architects' Licensing Law

283 John Haddock, "Biography of Roswell Pettibone Flower (1853–1899)—Watertown, New York," excerpted from *A Biographical Sketch of Roswell P. Flower, The Centennial History of Jefferson County New York* (Philadelphia: Sherman & Co., 1894), http://www.gegoux.com/gov_flow.htm; Biographical Directory of the United States Congress, s.v. "Flower, Roswell Pettibone," http://bioguide.congress.gov/scripts/biodisplay.pl?index=F000217.

284 "In Opposition to Assembly Bill No. 451, Entitled 'An Act to Regulate the Practice of Architecture,' New York, April 4, 1892, Wm. J. Fryer, et al," Chapter Reports, Annual Report of the Western New York Chapter A.I.A., Elmira, N.Y., September 1892, *Proceedings of the Twenty-sixth Annual Convention of the American Institute of Architects*, Chicago, October 20–22, 1892 (Chicago: Inland Architect Press, 1892), 68–70, extensively quoted in text.

285 "Grant's Tomb: History, Construction and Dedication," http://www.grantstomb.org/history.html.

286 "Cornelius O'Reilly is Fatally Hurt in Church," *New York Times*, April 30, 1903; Francis, *Architects in Practice in New York City*; "Mr. Cornelius O'Reilly," obituary, *American Architect and Building News*, May 9, 1903; "Obituary Note," *Real Estate Record and Guide*, May 1903, 861 (Science, Industry and Business Division, New York Public Library, microfilm); Norval White and Elliot Willensky, AIA *Guide to New York City*, 4th ed. (New York: Three Rivers Press, 2000), 484; Christopher Gray, "A Marvel of

Fancy Brickwork Awaits the Dawn of a New Day," *New York Times*, February 12, 1989, R12; classified advertisement for Lexington Central Storage Warehouse, *The City of New York, A complete Guide* (New York: Taintor Brothers, Merrill & Co., 1876), Making of America Database, Cornell University, http://library8.library.cornell.edu/moa/.

287 "O'Reilly," obituary.

288 "Chas. Graham & Sons," *New York's Great Industries. Exchange and Commercial Review* (New York: Historical Publishing Company, 1885), 238, Making of America Database, Cornell University, http://library8.library.cornell.edu/moa.

289 Ibid., *New York's Great Industries*; Francis, *Architects in Practice New York City*; *Real Estate Record and Guide*, February 6, 1892 (Science, Industry and Business Division, New York Public Library, microfilm); White and Willensky, *AIA Guide to New York City*, 338, 427; "Presbyterian Church, 1869–71, Newton, NJ," www.newtonnj.net; Frank Greenagel, "Simpson Methodist Episcopal Church, Perth Amboy," *New Jersey Churchscape* no. 6 (September 2001), http://66.92.127.80: Northampton County Courthouse, http://www.easton-pa.com/ History/HistoricEaston.htm#courthouse; http://www.nccpa.org/geninfo/history.html; The Borough of Easton, Davis's 1877 History of Northampton County, PA, 161–162, http://www.rootsweb.com/ ~usgenweb/pa/northampton/davistoc.htm.

290 "For Honesty in Politics."

291 "Vassar Center for Drama and Film," http://centerfordramaandfilm.vassar.edu/ project/index.html; "Vassar History 1861–1870," http://faculty.vassar.edu/daniels/1861 _1870.html.

292 Annon Adams, "John A. Wood Architecture Inventory," unpublished research, April 26, 2003, Poughkeepsie, New York; Raymond C. Heun, "Ponckhockie Union Chapel—1870," *Concrete International*, October 1, 1993, http://www.concreteinternational.com; "Ponckhockie Union Chapel, Kingston, NY," National Register of Historic Places, http://www.nationalregisterofhistoricplaces.com/NY/Ulster/state3.html; "Ponckhockie Union Congregational Church," Kingston, New York, National Park Service, http://www.cr.nps.gov/nr/travel/kingston/k19.htm.

293 Adams, "John A. Wood Architecture Inventory"; Annon Adams, "Assisting in Building a New City," unpublished paper, April 24, 2003, Poughkeepsie, New York; Manufacturer and Builder (August, September, October 1879; March, June, September, December 1882; June, February 1883), Making of America Database, Cornell University, http://library8.library.cornell.edu/moa; University of Tampa, www.ut.edu/ aboutut/history-museum.html; Plant Museum, www.plantmuseum.com/history/ index.shtm.

294 Landau and Condit, *Rise of the New York Skyscraper*, 218, 222.

295 Ibid., 423 (notes 40 and 41).

296   Research drawn from following sources: "Francis H. Kimball," obituary, *New York Times*, December 1919; Henry F. Withey & Elsie Rathburn Withey, *Biographical Dictionary of American Architects* (Deceased) (New Age Publishing: Los Angeles, 1956); Kimball, Francis H[atch], Grove Artists Biographies, www.artnet.com/library/04/0465/T046575.asp; "A Brief History of Planning at Trinity," http://www.trincoll.edu/proj/masterplan/history2.htm; William Morrison, *Broadway Theatres, History & Architecture* (Mineola, N.Y.: Dover Publications, 1999), 1–5, 12–13; Mary C. Henderson, *The City and the Theatre* (Clifton, N.J.: James T. White & Co., 1973), 219; Nicholas Van Hoogstraten, *Lost Broadway Theatres* (New York: Princeton Architectural Press, 1991), 15–18; "New York on the Rise," Museum of the City of New York, www.mcy.org/plate19.htm, www.mcy.org/plate24.html; "The Catholic Apostolic Church," New York City Landmarks Commission, http://www.ci.nyc.ny.us/html/lpc/html/designation/summaries/aposto.html, "A.T. Demarest & Co and Peerless Motor Car Company Buildings," New York City Landmarks Commission, http://www.ci.nyc.ny.us/html/lpc/html/designation/summaries/a_t_demarest.html; "The Montauk Club," Victorian Society of America, www.preserve.org/vsametro/embellishments.htm; "The Day House," Harriet Beecher Stowe Center, www.harrietbeecherstowecenter.org/visit/dayhouse.shtml; "Proposed Johns Street/Maiden Lane Historic District," www.hdc.org/johnstmaidenlnhistory.htm; Andrew S. Dolkart, "The Architecture and Development of New York City, Key Figures," Columbia University, http://nycarchitecture.columbia.edu/global/0242_2_key_figures.html; www.nyc-architecture.com/LM/LM054.htm.

297   Landau and Condit, *Rise of the New York Skyscraper*, 148.

298   "In Opposition to Assembly Bill No. 451."

299   "Licenses for Architects. Superintendent D'Oench's Suggestions to the Profession," *New York Times*, May 8, 1888, 5.

300   Ibid.

301   "Western New-York Architects," *New York Times*, November 21, 1890, 9.

302   "Meeting of the AIA Board of Directors on January 9, 1892 at #18 Broadway, NYC," *American Architect and Building News*, January 30, 1892 (Humanities and Social Sciences Division, New York Public Library, microfilm).

303   "To License Architects," *Real-Estate Record and Building Guide*, February 6, 1892 (Science, Industry and Business Division, New York Public Library, microfilm).

304   Tuthill, William Burnet (1845–1929), American Architects' Biographies, Society of Architectural Historians, http://www.sah.org/oldsite06012004/aame/biot.html.

305   "Annual Report of the Western New York Chapter AIA, September, 1892," *Proceedings of the Twenty-sixth Annual Convention of the AIA*, 65–67.

306   Ibid.

307   *Real-Estate Record and Building Guide*, April 16, 1892 (Science, Industry and Business Division, New York Public Library, microfilm).

308 "Annual Report of the New York Chapter AIA, August 25, 1892," *Proceedings of the Twenty-sixth Annual Convention of the AIA*, 71–72.

309 *Real-Estate Record and Building Guide*, April 23, 1892 (Science, Industry and Business Division, New York Public Library, microfilm).

310 "Gov. Flower's Work Done," *New York Times*, May 22, 1892.

311 "Report of the Commission for the Survey of Education and Registration of AIA," in Bannister, *Architect at Mid-Century* (vol. 1), tables 54, 56.

312 Edward H. Kendall, "President's Address," *Proceedings of the Twenty-sixth Annual Convention of the AIA*, 9–11.

313 "Report of the Board of Directors," *Proceedings of the Twenty-sixth Annual Convention of the AIA*, 16.

314 "Annual Report of the Western New York Chapter A.I.A., September, 1892," *Proceedings of the Twenty-sixth Annual Convention of the AIA*, 67.

Chapter 11: Architectural Leadership at the End of the Gilded Age

315 Bannister, *Architect at Mid-Century*, 73.

316 Saylor, *AIA's First 100 Years*, 16–20; The American Institute of Architects: A History, www.aia.org/about/history/default.asp; Texas Society of Architects, The Handbook of Texas Online, www.tsha.utexas.edu/handbook/nline/articles/view/TT/catgm.html; Adriana Barbasch, "The AIA Accepts Its First Woman Member," in *Architecture: A Place for Women*, ed. Ellen Perry Berkeley (Washington, D.C.: Smithsonian Institution Press, 1990), http://ah.bfn.org/a/archs/beth/bethberk.html.

317 Bannister, *Architect at Mid-Century*, 73.

318 Saylor, *AIA's First 100 Years*, 16–20; AIA: A History.

319 W. W. Carlin, "Statutory Regulations," World's Congress of Architects, *Journal of the Proceedings of the Twenty-seventh Annual Convention of the American Institute of Architects*, Chicago, July 31–August 1, 1893, 313–317.

320 Ibid.

321 C. H. Blackall, "Influence of Building Laws on Architecture," World's Congress of Architects, *Journal of the Proceedings of the Twenty-seventh Annual Convention of the American Institute of Architects*, 346–347.

322 Ibid., 348.

323 Ibid, 343.

324 Edward H. Kendall, "President's Address," *Journal of the Proceedings of the Twenty-seventh Annual Convention of the American Institute of Architects*, 8.

325 Lee, *Architects to the Nation*, 141.

326 Alfred Stone, Secretary, letter to the membership, American Institute of Architects, Providence, R.I., March 6, 1893, AIA Archives, Washington, D.C.

327 *Proceedings of the Twenty-seventh Annual Convention of the American Institute of Architects*, 14.

328 Lee, *Architects to the Nation*, 168–169; Biographical Directory of the United States Congress, s.v. "Carlisle, John Griffin, 1834-1910," http://bioguide.congress.gov; "Secretary of the Treasury—John G. Carlisle (1893–1897)," Office of the Curator, Department of the Treasury, www.ustreas.gov/offices/management/curator/collection/secretary/carlisle.htm.

329 *Proceedings of the Twenty-seventh Annual Convention of the American Institute of Architects*, 10.

330 Lee, *Architects to the Nation*, 145–159; Kevin F. Decker, "Grand and Godly Proportions: Roman Catholic Cathedral Churches of the Northeast, 1840–1900, Jeremiah O'Rourke (1833–1915)," (Ph.D. diss., Albany, State University of New York, 2000), http://faculty.plattsburgh.edu/kevin.decker/Research%20information/O'Rourke.htm.

331 Jeremiah O'Rourke, "On Architectural Practice of the United States Government," World's Congress of Architects, *Journal of the Proceedings of the Twenty-seventh Annual Convention of the American Institute of Architects*, 274–280.

332 "Mr. Carlisle and the Architects, A New View of the Controversy over Public Buildings," *New York Times*, March 19, 1894, 4.

333 Lee, *Architects to the Nation*, 171.

334 Ibid., 173–174.

335 Ibid., 176–187.

336 Richard Foy, "Architects of the Payne Estate, Carrère and Hastings and Burroughs," Marist Brothers in Esopus, 3rd ed. (New York: Chappaqua, April 2004), http://ecommerce.marist.edu/foy/esopus/esop05.htm.

337 Lee, *Architects to the Nation*, 185 (note 70).

338 Ibid., 203 (note 44).

339 Geoffrey Blodgett, *Cass Gilbert, The Early Years* (St. Paul: Minnesota Historical Society Press, 2001), 3–8; Patricia Anne Murphy, "Architectural Education and Minnesota Career," in *Cass Gilbert, Life and Work: Architect of the Public Domain*, ed. Barbara S. Christen and Steven Flanders (New York: W.W. Norton, 2001); "The West Virginia Capital, A Commemorative History," Legislature of West Virginia, June 20, 1982, http://www.legis.state.wv.us/General/Commemorative/cap.html.

340 Alexander Hamilton U.S. Custom House, Statement of Significance, Historic Federal Buildings Program, U.S. General Services Administration, http://w3.gsa.gov/web/p/interaia_save.nsf/0/5b0419befb670b9c852565d90053a011?OpenDocument

341 Cass Gilbert to Julia Gilbert, September 20, 1899, Cass Gilbert Papers, General Correspondence Box 6 445 H, Library of Congress, Washington, D.C.

342 Ibid.

343 "Custom House Plans Chosen," *New York Times*, September 24, 1899, 11.

344 Cass Gilbert to Julia Gilbert, September 24, 1899, Gilbert Papers.

345 Ibid.

346 Ibid.

347 Ibid.
348 Samuel Gilbert to Cass Gilbert, September 25, 1899, Ibid.
349 Cass Gilbert to Julia Gilbert, September 27, 1899, Ibid.
350 Ibid.
351 "New York's Custom House," *New York Times*, September 29, 1899, 11.
352 Letter to Julia Gilbert, October 4, 1899, Ibid.
353 Ibid.
354 Cass Gilbert to Julia Gilbert, October 8, 1899, Ibid.
355 Ibid.
356 Ibid.
357 "The Custom House Architect," *New York Times*, October 24, 1899, 1.
358 Cass Gilbert to Julia Gilbert, October 24, 1899, Gilbert Papers.
359 "The Custom House Plans," *New York Times*, October 25, 1899, 7.
360 Ibid.
361 Ibid.
362 "Kimball, Thomas R., FAIA," American Architects' Biographies, Society of Architectural Historians, http://www.sah.org/oldsite06012004/aame/biok.html#29.
363 "The Custom House Plans, Protest to Mr. McKinley," *New York Times*, November 2, 1899, 2.
364 "Architects for Gilbert," *New York Times*, November 3, 1899, 6.
365 Custom House Architect, Secretary Gage Accepts The Plans of Cass Gilbert, *New York Times*, November 4, 1899, 1.
366 Ibid.
367 "New Custom House Plans," *New York Times*, December 1, 1899, 12
368 Saylor, *AIA's First 100 Years*, 131, 142.
369 Lee, *Architects to the Nation*, 208–209.

Chapter 12: Seeking Power: An Unvarnished View of the Golden Era of Influence

370 "Thomas Jefferson on Politics & Government," University of Virginia, in *The Writings of Thomas Jefferson*, Memorial Edition, ed. Lipscomb and Bergh, 20 vols. (Washington, D.C., 1903–04), http://etext.virginia.edu/jefferson/quotations/jeff1290.htm.
371 Sibel Bozdogan Dostoglu, "Towards Professional Legitimacy and Power: An Inquiry into the Struggle, Achievements and Dilemma of the Architectural Profession Through an Analysis of Chicago 1871–1909" (Ph.D. diss., University of Pennsylvania, 1982), 63.
372 Ibid., 65.
373 Ibid., 70.
374 Tony P. Wrenn, "The Eye of Guardianship: Theodore Roosevelt and the American Institute of Architects," *White House History Journal*, no. 11 (Summer 2002), http://www.whitehousehistory.org/08/subs/08_b11.html.

375   Glenn Brown, "A Bill for the Creation of a Proposed Bureau of Buildings and Grounds," presented to the 47th AIA Convention by the Washington, D.C., Chapter (December 1913), AIA Archives, Washington, D.C.

376   Lee, *Architects to the Nation*, 235.

377   Ibid., 236.

378   Bannister, *Architect at Mid-Century*, 73.

379   A.B. Jennings to Glenn Brown, July 22, 1909, AIA Archives, Washington, D.C.

380   John M. Harris to Glenn Brown, July 15, 1909, Ibid.

381   Robert W. Gibson to Glenn Brown, July 15, 1909, Ibid.

382   Henry Lord Gay, FAIA, to Glenn Brown, July 21, 1909, Ibid.

383   Saylor, *AIA's First 100 Years*, 121–125.

384   Bushong et al., *Centennial History of the Washington Chapter*, 38 (note 7).

385   Ibid., 22.

386   Bannister, *Architect at Mid-Century*, table 56.

387   Ibid., table 54.

388   *Proceedings of the Forty-eighth Annual Convention of the A.I.A*, December 3–5, 1914 (Washington, D.C.: AIA, 1914), 21, AIA Archives, Washington, D.C.

389   Jacob A. Riis, "Theodore Roosevelt's Father," chap. 18 in *Theodore Roosevelt, the Citizen* (New York: The Outlook Co., 1904), http://www.bartleby.com/206/18.html; Josh Cracraft, "1858–1880: Early Life," *SparkNote on Theodore Roosevelt* (September 29, 2004), http://www.sparknotes.com/biography/troosevelt/section1.html

390   Lewis, *Frank Furness*, 104–105.

391   Wrenn, "Eye of Guardianship."

392   Glenn Brown, "Roosevelt and the Fine Arts," *The American Architect*, part 2, no. 2295 (December 17, 1919), 741–745, AIA Archives, Washington, D.C.

393   Edgar S. Yergason Papers, White House Historical Association, Research Archives, http://www.whitehousehistory.org/08/subs/08_b09.html.

394   Joseph Purtell, *The Tiffany Touch* (New York: Random House, 1971), 118; White House Historical Association, Timeline—Decorative Arts, 1880s, http://www.whitehousehistory.org/05/subs/05_g10.html, Timeline—Architecture, 1880s, http://www.whitehousehistory.org/05/subs/05_f10.html.

395   President Theodore Roosevelt, "Art and the Republic," *Addresses at the Annual Dinner of The American Institute of Architects*, January 11, 1905, Washington, D.C., AIA Archives, Washington, D.C.

396   William B. Bushong, "Glenn Brown, The American Institute of Architects and the Development of the Civic Core of Washington, D.C." (Ph.D. diss., George Washington University, Washington, D.C., 1988), 156, 166.

397   Ibid., 161.

398   Ibid., 175–204; "Amicus curiae," or "friend of the court," refers to "someone who is not a party to the litigation, but who believes that the court's decision may affect its interest." *Tech Law Journal*, http://www.techlawjournal.com/glossary/legal/amicus.htm.

399   "House Artists Hurt, Hostile to Council of Fine Arts," *New York Tribune*, January 22, 1909, 1 (clipping), AIA Archives, Washington, D.C.

400   "In Creating a 'Council of Fine Arts,'" *New York Sun*, January 22, 1909 (clipping), Ibid.

401   President Theodore Roosevelt, "Memorandum To Accompany Sundry Civil Bill, 1909, White House, March 4, 1909," George Peabody Wetmore Papers, General Correspondence, Fine Art Commission 1910, Box 1, Library of Congress, Washington, D.C.

402   J.M. Dickerson, Secretary of War, to President William Taft, April 17, 1909, Wetmore Papers.

403   Bushong, "Glenn Brown," 188.

404   Bureau of Arts Council of Arts, 60th Congress, 2nd session, Document No. 665, Government Printing Office, 1909, AIA Archives, Washington, D.C.

405   Biographical Directory of the United States Congress, s.v. "Wetmore, George Peabody (1846–1921)," http://bioguide.congress.gov/scripts/biodisplay.pl?index=W000312.

406   Glenn Brown to President Theodore Roosevelt, January 16, 1909, AIA Archives, Washington, D.C.

407   Bushong, "Glenn Brown," 191.

408   Ibid., 192.

409   Biographical Directory of the United States Congress, s.v. "Mann, James Robert (1856–1922)," http://bioguide.gov; Chicago Public Library, http://www.chipublib.org/digital/lake/CFDNewCity.html; Reviving the Vision of the Great South Park, http://www.uchicago.edu/docs/mp-site/plaisanceplan/2revive.html.

410   Daniel H. Burnham to Senator George P. Wetmore, May 19, 1910, Wetmore Papers.

411   Carolyn Kinder Carr et al., *Revisiting the White City: American Art at the 1893 World's Fair*, exhibition catalogue, (Washington, D.C.: National Museum of American Art and National Portrait Gallery, Smithsonian Institution, 1993), 26.

412   Bushong et al., *Centennial History of the Washington Chapter*, 42.

413   Isabelle Gournay, "From New York to Paris, the Leadership and Prestige of American Beaux-Arts Architects" (paper presented at the symposium, "Architectural Culture by 1900. Critical Reappraisal and Heritage Preservation," Buenos Aires, Argentina, September 1999), 6.

414   A Change in the Schedule of Charges, December 15, 1908, AIA Archives, Washington, D.C.

415   Bushong, "Glenn Brown," 218–220.

416   Biographical Directory of the United States Congress, s.v. "Brown, Bedford (1795–1870)," http://bioguide.congress.gov; "Historic Buildings in Halifax County, Virginia, South of the Dan Driving Tour, The Original Bloomsburg," http://www.halifax.com/county/SouthoftheDanTour4.htm

417   "Brown, Bedford Jr. papers," Narvarro College Archives, Cosicana, Texas, www
      .narvarrocollege.edu/library/civilwar/finding_aids/a_f/brown.htm.

418   "Joint Committee on Reconstruction, Senator Bedford Brown, Washington, D.C.,
      March 28, 1866," www.adena.com/adena/usa/cw/cw191.htm.

419   Bushong, "Glenn Brown," 236 (note 11): "Brown was not placed on the committee on
      government architecture [1914] because a strong faction within the organization
      wished to secure the political support of Superintendent of the Capital Elliot Woods
      who refused to work with Brown because of past differences concerning architec-
      tural and landscape treatment of the Capitol building and its grounds."

420   Saylor, *AIA's First 100 Years*, 43–45; Bushong, "Glenn Brown," 214–239; *Proceedings of the
      Forty-seventh Annual Convention of the A.I.A.*, December 2–4, 1913 (Harrisburg: J.
      Horace McFarland Co., 1913), 73–81, 101–102, AIA Archives, Washington, D.C.

421   *Congressional Record*, August 27, 1911, 13142, AIA Archives, Washington, D.C.

422   *The Architectural Review* 2, no. 10 (October 1913): 259, AIA Archives, Washington. D.C.

423   Richard Michael Levy, "The Professionalization of American Architects and Civil
      Engineers, 1865–1917" (Ph.D. diss., University of California, Berkeley, 1980), 280.

424   Ibid, 277–281; Saylor, *AIA's First 100 Years*, 174-175; Bushong, "Glenn Brown," 228.

Chapter 13: The 1919 AIA Convention: Postwar Reform for the 20th Century

425   *Proceedings of the Fifty-second Annual Convention of the American Institute of Architects*,
      April 30–May 2, 1919, Nashville, Tennessee (Washington, D.C.: AIA, 1919), 48, AIA
      Archive, Washington, D.C.

426   Ibid., 50–51.

427   Ibid., 52.

428   Ibid., 53–54.

429   Ibid., 78–79, 81–82.

430   Ibid., 107.

431   Ibid., 51.

432   Robert D. Kohn, quote cited in "80 years of service to New York City and the con-
      struction industry," New York Building Congress, Annual Report 2001,
      http://www.buildingcongress.com/code/annual/2001/80years.htm.

433   "Frederick Lee Ackerman, FAIA (1878–1950)," "Robert D. Kohn, FAIA (1870–1953),"
      Philadelphia Architects and Buildings Project, www.phildelphiabuildings.org; Fred-
      erick L. Ackerman, "The Architectural Side of City Planning," *Proceedings of the Sev-
      enth National Conference on City Planning, 1915*, 107–128; John Waring with Lois M.
      Scheel, "The Technical Alliance Profiles," Section 3 Newsletter, no. 91 (March 1991),
      Technocracy Incorporated, http://www.technocracyinc.org/history.htm; "House and
      Yard, the Design of the Suburban Home, Part 3," National Register Bulletin, U.S.
      Department of the Interior, National Park Service, www.cr.nps.gov; Elizabeth
      Edwards Harris, "Housing the War-Time Workers: Experimenting with an Ideal,"

Architronic 4, no. 1 (May 1995); Chronology of the Ethical Culture Movement, 1876–1988, http://www.ethicalsociety.org/Chronology.asp.

434 "The History of NCARB," The Regulation of Architecture in the United States, National Council of Architectural Registration Boards, Washington, D.C., 1999, www.ncarb.org/forms/history.pdf.; Bannister, *Architect at Mid-Century*, vol. 1, 371.

435 *Your Future Home*, 7, and introduction by Schrenk, xxii (notes 10, 12).

436 "Gordon, James Riely (1863–1937)," Alexander Architectural Archive, University of Texas at Austin, www.lib.utexas.edu; The Handbook of Texas, www.tsha.utexas.edu; New York Society of Architects, www.nysarch.com; "James Riely Gordon," www.rootsweb.com~~txecm/james_riely_gordon.htm; "A3027. material related to Commission proposals to Consolidate Building Inspection Agencies in New York City, 1912–1914," New York State Archives, http://iarchives.nysed.gov.

437 Saylor, *AIA's First 100 Years*, 30.

Chapter 14: Leadership through the Great Depression: Henry K. Holsman and Mutual-Ownership Housing in Chicago

438 Virginia Holsman (granddaughter of Henry K. Holsman), e-mail correspondence with Colleen M. Thornton, regarding her grandfather's life, June 9, 2004.

439 Grinnell College History, www.grinnell.edu/aboutinfo/history/; Application to the National Register of Historic Places, Maharishi International University, May 1983, Henry K. Holsman Family Papers, Northbrook, Illinois (access provided by J. Peter Holsman, licensed architect, son of John Holsman and grandson of Henry K. Holsman).

440 Henry K. Holsman curriculum vitae, Holsman Papers.

441 "Henry K. Holsman," *Who's Who* (undated copy), 345, Holsman Papers.

442 "History of College Buildings," Grinnell College, http://lib.grin.edu/Collections/Archives/album/History ofCollegeBuildings/.

443 Cooper W. Norman (Prairie Architects Inc., Fairfield, Iowa), e-mail correspondence with Colleen M. Thornton, May 26, 2004; Maharishi University of Management, Reconstruction Plan, Demolition (Henry K. Holsman National Historic District), http://mum.edu/reconstruction/demolition.html; Application to National Register of Historic Places.

444 Franklin B. Tucker, *Holsman History 1901–1910, A History of the Holsman High Wheel Automobile* (Decorah, Iowa: Anundsen Publishing Co., 1994), 5–7, Holsman Papers.

445 Don Gunning, "Oak Park House Database," http://www.dgunning.org; Beverly Area Planning Association, http://www.bapa.org/historichomes.htm; Chicago Landmarks Historic Resources Survey, http://w16.cityofchicago.org/landmark/SilverStream/Pages/landmarks.html.

446 "Background History of the Holsman Plan of Mutual Ownership," 1–3, Holsman Papers.

447 Henry K. Holsman, FAIA, "A Résumé of Thirty Five Years' Successful Experience & Discovery," June 22, 1957, 10, Holsman Papers.

448 Ralph Bennett, AIA, and Isabelle Gournay, Ph.D. (curators), "Affordable Housing: Designing an American Asset," National Building Museum, Washington, D.C., February 28–August 8, 2004, exhibition script, 7, http://www.nbm.org/Exhibits/current/Affordable_Housing_Exhibition_Script.pdf.

449 Ibid.

450 Parker-Holsman Company History, http://ww.parkerholsman.com/phc/history.htm.

451 Holsman curriculum vitae; Henry K. Holsman, president, Illinois Chapter, American Institute of Architects Inaugural Address, June 10, 1919, Holsman Papers.

452 "Architects Award Two Gold Medals," *New York Times*, May 14, 1927, 9.

453 Henry K. Holsman, "Rehabilitating Blighted Areas, Report of the Committee on Blighted Area Housing," The Architects Club of Chicago, 1932, 34, Holsman Papers.

454 "High Apartment Record, Eight Chicago Cooperatives Fully Occupied for Many Years," *New York Times*, November 22, 1931, 34.

455 "Henry K. Holsman, "Blighted Area Housing and Cooperation," transcript, Armour Institute Radio Program, Station WJJD, Chicago, May 7, 1933, Holsman Papers.

456 "Rebuilding Slum Areas, Low Cost Construction at Low Ebb, Says Architect," *New York Times*, October 22, 1933, RE, 12.

457 Holsman & Holsman, "The Construction of the Country Home Model Farm House at the Century of Progress," undated memo, Holsman Papers; *Country Home Model Farm House* (Cromwell Publishing Co., 1934), Century of Progress Collection, Burnham Library, Art Institute of Chicago, call # 00.18, series 1, box FF, 2.7.

458 Edo J. Belli (1918–2003), interview by Betty J. Blum, in *Chicago Architects Oral History Project*, November 3, 1983, Burnham Library, Art Institute of Chicago, 3–20.

459 Lawrence Bradford Perkins (1907–1997), interview by Betty J. Blum, in *Chicago Architects Oral History Project*, November 8, 9, 10, 17, 1985, Burnham Library, Art Institute of Chicago, 50, 99; memo and notes, Holsman Papers.

460 Belli, interview, 7–8.

461 Henry K. Holsman, "Adverse Gossip and Tort Liability," January 11, 1954, 2, Holsman Papers.

462 Perkins, interview, 80.

463 D. Coder Taylor (1913-2000), interview by Betty J. Blum, in *Chicago Architects Oral History Project*, Burnham Library, Art Institute of Chicago, June 4, 5, 6, 1985, 139.

464 Jackson-Laramie Garden Homes Prospectus, Winchester & Hood Garden Apartments Extension B Prospectus, Community Development Trust, 1950, Holsman Papers.

465 Holsman, "Adverse Gossip," 1–2.

466   Charles Booher Genther (1907–1987), interview by Betty J. Blum, in *Chicago Architects Oral History Project*, Burnham Library, Art Institute of Chicago, September 30, 1983, 33.

467   Taylor, interview, 135–136.

468   Ibid., 144–145.

469   Bennett and Gournay, "Affordable Housing," 18.

470   Holsman, "Adverse Gossip," 3.

471   Ibid., 1–4; "The Powerhouse," report provided via e-mail by the Chicago Housing Authority, May 3, 2004, 176–178.

472   "The Powerhouse," 178.

473   Genther, interview, 22.

474   "Pioneering Construction Ideas," *Architectural Forum* (January 1950), 79; "The Financing of the Promontory," *Architectural Forum* (January 1950), 124, Holsman Papers.

475   "Financing of the Promontory," 124.

476   John T. Holsman, "Community Trust," *Architectural Forum* (January 1950), 78.

477   Bennett and Gournay, "Affordable Housing," 15.

478   Holsman, "Adverse Gossip," 1–4.

479   Taylor, interview, 172.

480   Ibid., 171.

481   "Convict Father 90, Son in Mail Fraud," undated Chicago newspaper clipping; Holsman, "Résumé."

482   Taylor, interview, 175–177.

483   Holsman, "Résumé," 3.

484   Frank Hughes, "Clews [sic] in Marcus Killing Dead End in Cuff Links," newspaper clipping, dated by hand, November 22, 1959, Holsman Papers.

485   Holsman, "Résumé," 3–4, 9, 11.

486   Henry K. Holsman, "Economic, Architectural & Sociological Aspects of Parkway Garden Homes and Other Projects Sponsored by The Community Development Trust," September 30, 1950, Holsman Papers.

Chapter 15: 20th-Century Leadership: Appraising the Past and Future Promise

487   Saylor, *AIA's First 100 Years*, 144.

488   Bannister, *The Architect at Mid-Century*, vol. 1, *Evolution and Achievement*, Report of the Commission for the Survey of Education and Registration of the American Institute of Architects, vol. 2, *Conversations Across the Nation*, ed. Francis R. Bellamy (New York: Reinhold, 1954).

489   Bannister, *Architect at Mid-Century*, vol. 1, 483.

490   Maisah B. Robinson, Ph.D., "Norma Sklarek: The First African American Woman Architect," Suite University, www.suite101.com/article.cfm/harlem_renaissance/80270; "Norma Merrick Sklarek," http://africanpubs.com/Apps/bios/1151SklarekNorma.asp?pic=none.

491   Barbasch, "AIA Accepts Its First Woman Member"; Austin M. Fox, "Louise Blanchard Bethune: Buffalo Feminist and America's First Woman Architect," Buffalo Spree (Summer 1986), http://ah.bfn.org; "Louise Blanchard Bethune," http://www.distinguishedwomen.com/biographies/bethune1.html.

492   "Sophia Hayden," http://www.distinguishedwomen.com; "Sophia Hayden Bennett," MIT Museum Archive, http://w3.mit.edu/museum/chicago/bennett.html.

493   "Florence Hope Luscomb: A Radical Foremother," Notable American Unitarians, www.harvardsquarelibrary.org/unitarians/luscomb.html; "Florence H. Luscomb," MIT Archive, http://web.mit.edu/museum/fun/equality/html; Massachusetts State House Women's Leadership Project, www.mfh.org; Margaret Foley Papers, Radcliffe College, http://oasis.harvard.edu/html/sch00004.html.

494   Ida Annah Ryan, International Archive of Women in Architecture (IAWA) Database, http://lumiere.lib.vt.edu/iawa_db/browse_by_last_name.php3?last_name=r; Orlando Lake Ivanhoe Trail, http.att.net/~orlandohistory/1922.htm; *The TEC* 27, no.3 (October 7, 1907) and 28, no. 42 (January 11, 1909), http://kurzweil.mit.edu/.

495   Biographical Directory of the United States Congress, s.v. "Knox, Samuel (1815–1905)," http://bioguide.congress.gov/scripts/biodisplay.pl?index=K000297.

496   "'Hear Us' recalls influential words of six women," *Yale Bulletin & Calendar* 28, no 11 (November 1–8, 1999).

497   Clarence G. Williams, "From 'Tech' to Tuskegee: The Life of Robert Robinson Taylor, 1868–1942," http//libraries.mit.edu/archives/mithistory/blacks-at-mit/taylor.html.

498   William E. King, "Julian Abele, Architect: Hidden in the Shadows," Duke University Libraries, www.lib.duke.edu/archives/history/julian_abele.html; History of Wilson Hall, Monmouth University, www.monmouth.edu/about/history/Wilson.asp; Deborah Bolling, "Truly Abele," Philadelphia Citypaper.net, February 20–26, 2003, http:citypaper.net/articles/2003-02-20/cityspace.shtml; Max Bond, "Still Here: Three Architects of Afro-America: Julian Francis Abele, Hilyard Robinson and Paul R. Williams," *Harvard Design Magazine* no. 2 (Summer 1997).

499   Robert Fox (director), *Flash of a Dream*, documentary film on the life of Jacob Riis (Copenhagen: Zentropa Studios, Danish Film Institute, 2002), screening with film director and the author, April 10, 2002.

500   Jacob A. Riis, "Roosevelt Comes—Mulberry Street's Golden Age," chap. 13 of *The Making of an American* (New York: Macmillan, 1901), http://www.bartleby.com/207/13.html.

501   Ibid.

502   Theodore Roosevelt Jr., "Practical Politics" (chap. 3) and "The New York Police" (chap. 6), in *Theodore Roosevelt, An Autobiography* (New York: Macmillan, 1913), http://www.bartleby.com/45/6.html.

503   "Landscapes by Jens Jensen," Henry Ford Estate National Historic Landmark, http://www.henryfordestate.com/jensen.htm.

504   "About the Clearing," http://www.theclearing.org/about.php.

505   Julia Sniderman Bachrach, "Jens Jensen: Friend of the Native Landscape," *Chicago Wilderness Magazine* (Spring 2001), http://chicagowildernessmag.org/issues/spring2001/jensjensen.html; "Jens Jensen," The Clearing, http://www.theclearing.org/jens.php; "Jens Jensen," Forest Preserve District of Cook County, Illinois; www.newton.dep.anl.gov/natbitn/600-699/nb608.htm;"Chicago's Columbus Park—Setting the Stage," National Park Service, www.cr.nps.gov/nr/twhp/wwwlps/lessons/81columbus/81setting.htm; Alf Siewers, "Chicago Wilderness, Chicago Renaissance?" *Chicago Wilderness Magazine* (Fall 1977), http://chicago wildernessmag.org/issues/fall1977/renaissance.html; Mary Beth Klatt, "Divided Landscapes," Preservation Online, May 16, 2003, National Trust for Historic Preservation, http://www.nationaltrust.org/magazine/archives/arch_story/051603.htm.

506   Hans Helge Madsen, *Chicago-København, Alfred Råvads Univers* (Copenhagen: Gyldendal, 1990), translation and synopsis by Peter Wedell-Wedellsberg, MAA, 2003.

507   Alfred J. Roewade, "How Copenhagen Was Fortified," *Professional Memoirs* 3, no. 12 (October-November 1911): 648–662.

508   Various articles by Alfred J. Råvad published in *Arkitekten* (Copenhagen) between 1908–1929, trans. Kenneth Krabat.

509   A.J. Råvad's letters and private papers, Royal Danish Library, Manuscripts and Letters Archive.

510   Ivar Bentsen, "Alfred J. Råvad og hans Byplanværk Borgmesterbogen," Steen Eiler Rasmussen, ed., *Arkitekten* (Copenhagen, 1929), 15–16 (trans. Kenneth Krabat).

511   Alfred J. Råvad, *The Mayor's Book* (Copenhagen: Arkitekten Forlag, 1929), 138 (trans. Kenneth Krabat).

512   Katherine Russell, "Canberra: An Ideal City, the 46 Plans," Australian National University, Canberra, 1995, http://rubens.anu.edu.au/student.projects/idealcity/46plans.html.

513   Madsen, *Chicago-København*, 163; Arne Gaardmand, Dansk Byplanlægning 1938–1992 (Copenhagen: Arkitektens Forlag, 1993), introduction.

514   Råvad, *Mayor's Book*, 10.

515   Raoul Wallenberg, *Letters and Dispatches, 1924–1944*, trans. Kjersti Board (New York: Arcade Publishers, with the U.S. Holocaust Museum, 1995), quoted in "I Come to America," *Michigan Today* (Spring 1999), University of Michigan, www.umich.edu/~newsinfo/MT/99/Spr99/mt12s99.html.

516   Ibid.

517   Jan Larsson, "Raoul Wallenberg," www.raoul-wallenberg.org.ar/english/wallening.htm; Zachary M. Raimi, "Wallenberg leaves historical legacy at 'U'," Michigan Daily Online, April 19, 1997, http://www.pub.umich.edu/daily/1997/apr/04-10-97/arts/arts1.html.

518   Wallenberg Studio, Taubman School of Architecture and Urban Planning, University of Michigan, www.tcaup.umich.edu/.

Chapter 16: From Superstar to Star Citizen: Speaking Truth to Power

519   Daniel Kemmis, *Community and the Politics of Place* (Norman: University of Oklahoma Press, 1990), 46.

520   Ibid., 73.

521   Ibid., 33.

522   Ibid., 22–23.

Chapter 17: Building Community through Community Engagement

523   Elsebeth Gerner Nielsen, remarks delivered at the AIA 's international conference, "Design Diplomacy: Public Policy and the Practice of Architecture," September 7, 2000, Copenhagen, Denmark,.

524   Fred Kent, letter to the *New York Times*, June 24, 2004; Marin Gottlieb, "One Who Would Like to See Most Architects Hit the Road," *New York Times*, March 28, 1993; Andrea Oppenheimer Dean, interview with Fred Kent (executive director, Project for Public Spaces, Inc.), *Architectural Record* (April 2000); Susan Hines, "Preaching the Gospel of Place," *Landscape Architecture* (March 2002); Project for Public Spaces, www.pps.org.

525   Fred Kent, interviewed by Richard N. Swett, January 30, 2001, New York City.

526   Fred Kent, letter to the *New York Times*, June 24, 2004.

527   Fred Kent, interview.

528   Ibid.

529   Greg Tung, interviewed by Richard N. Swett, June 14, 2002.

530   Ibid.

531   Plan New Hampshire Mission Statement, http://www.plannh.com/index.php?option=com_frontpage&Itemid=1.

532   Jeff Taylor (Plan NH board member), interviewed by Richard N. Swett, September 10, 2002.

533   Ibid.

534   Ibid.

535   Scholarships and Fellowships, Plan New Hampshire Web site, http://www.plannh.com/index.php?option=content&task=view&id=15&Itemid=39.

536 Merit Awards, Plan New Hampshire, http://www.plannh.com/index.php?option= content&task=view&id=17&Itemid=40.

537 James Howard Kunstler, *Home From Nowhere* (New York: Simon & Schuster, 1996), 147–148; e-mail correspondence between Kunstler and Colleen Thornton, 2003–2004.

538 Andrea Oppenheimer Dean, "Samuel Mockbee: A Life's Work," *Architectural Record*, June 4, 2004, 186.

539 Brian Libby, "Interview with Samuel Mockbee," Salon.com, August 9, 2001, http://dir.salon.com/people/conv/2001/08/09/mockbee/index.html.

540 Ibid.

541 "Mission Statement and History," The Rural Studio, http://www.ruralstudio.com/ mission.htm.

542 Dean, "Samuel Mockbee," 186.

543 Ibid., 187.

544 Ibid., 189.

545 Ibid., 186.

546 Douglas R. Parker, "Growing Value Through New Integration Models"; "Focus on the Future," *Design Intelligence* (January 2004), 2.

547 Ibid.

548 Phil Bernstein, interviewed by Richard N. Swett, February 1, 2001.

549 Scott Simpson, interviewed by Richard N. Swett, February 1, 2001.

550 Franklin MacVeagh, Office of the Curator, Department of the Treasury, www.ustreas.gov/offices/management/curator/collection/secretary/macveagh.htm.

551 "NBBJ, Who We Are," http://www.nbbj.com/whoweare/history/.

552 "Gensler, What Makes Us Different," http://www.gensler.com/about/index.html.

553 Marc Grossman, "Are We Ready for 21st Century Diplomacy," remarks delivered at "A New American Diplomacy: Requirements for the 21st Century" conference, Belmont Conference Center, Elkridge, Md., October 2, 2000.

Chapter 18: Issues to Lead By

554 Steve Gunderson (senior manager, The Greystone Group), "The Relationship between Design and Public Policy," remarks delivered at the AIA international conference, "Design Diplomacy: Public Policy and the Practice of Architecture," September 8, 2000, Copenhagen, Denmark, 3.

555 Richard N. Swett, "Next Generation Policy Making: The Challenge of Federal/Local Partnerships," in *A Nation Reconstructed, A Quest for the Cities That Can Be*, ed. Roger D. Hart (Milwaukee: ASQC Quality Press, 1997), 11–25.

556 Congressman Earl Blumenauer (3rd district, Oregon) and Robert E. Stacey (congressional aide), interviewed by the authors, June 25, 2002.

557 "Our Team: Douglas Wright," Smith, Dawson & Andrews, http://www.sda-inc.com/team.php#19.

558   Blumenauer, interview.

559   Ibid.

560   Ibid.

561   Edward Feiner, "The GSA and Design Excellence," remarks delivered at the AIA international conference, "Design Diplomacy: Public Policy and the Practice of Architecture," September 8, 2000, Copenhagen, Denmark.

562   Ibid.

563   Robert Peck, interviewed by the authors, June 26, 2002, Washington, D.C.

564   Ibid.

565   Feiner, "GSA and Design Excellence."

566   "The Honorable Harvey B. Gantt—Architect & Politician," South Carolina African American History Online, February 1994, http://scaftricanamericanhistory.com.

567   Harvey B. Gantt, Official City of Charlotte & Mecklenburg County Government Web site, www.charmeck.org

568   Gary Orren and Pamela Varly, "Jesse Helms v. Harvey Gantt: Race, Culture, and Campaign Strategy in the 1990 Senate Battle," abstract (1/1/91), Case Studies in Public Policy and Management, John F. Kennedy School of Government, Harvard University, http://www.ksgcase.harvard.edu/case.htm?PID=1099.

569   "The Honorable Harvey Gantt's Speech Before the Democratic National Convention, Thursday, July 29, 2004," http://news.findlaw.com/prnewswire/20040729/29jul2004184401.html.

570   Harvey B. Gantt, McColl Graduate School of Business, http://mccoll.queens.edu/Leaders_In_Action/harvey_gantt.htm.

571   Harvey Gantt, remarks delivered at the AIA international conference, "Design Diplomacy: Public Policy and the Practice of Architecture," September 8, 2000, Copenhagen, Denmark, 1–4.

572   Cameron Sinclair, interviewed by the authors, May 24, 2004.

573   Ibid.

574   Fredric Bell, interviewed by the authors, July 9, 2002, New York City; Jean Phifer, interviewed by the authors, July 10, 2002, New York City; Fredric Bell and Jean Phifer, interviewed by Richard N. Swett, Yale Club, New York City, June 14, 2001.

575   http://www.alexander-garvin.com/biography/index.htm.

576   Alexander Garvin, interviewed by the authors, June 14, 2002.

577   Joseph Giovannini, "The 'X' Men," New York Magazine, January 15, 2001, http://newyorkmetro.com/nymetro/arts/art/reviews/4261/.

578   Garvin, interview.

579   NYC 2012 Olympic Committee, www.nyc2012.com.

580   Giovannini, "The 'X' Men."

581   Garvin, interview with Richard N. Swett, May 10, 2004.

Epilogue: Back to the Question of the Future: Draw Up Your Personal Plan!

582 Jean Phifer, interviewed by Richard N. Swett, July 22, 2002, New York City. Note: Since this interview, lawyers for New York City have determined that the parts of the street grid that are proposed to be restored to the World Trade Center site should be considered city property, opening the likelihood of Art Commission review of at least street furniture, sidewalks, lighting, etc.

583 Ibid.

584 Jerry Howard, interviewed by the authors, July 8, 2002, New York City.

585 Bente Beedholm, interviewed by Richard N. Swett, May 3, 2001, Copenhagen.

586 Pat Natale, interviewed by Richard N. Swett, January 31, 2001, Washington, D.C.

587 Jeff Soule and Peter Hawley, interviewed by Richard N. Swett, January 31, 2001, Washington. D.C.

588 Tom Peters, "Design Matters," electronic presentation, "Design Mindfulness," electronic booklet, http://www.tompeters.com

589 Ernest L. Boyer and Lee D. Mitgang, *Building Community: A New Future for Architecture Education and Practice* (Princeton: Carnegie Foundation for the Advancement of Teaching, 1996); AIA Wisconsin, Leadership Institute 2004 fall workshop, http://www.aiaw.org/members/news/documents/fallworkshop.shtml.

590 Gunderson, "Relationship between Design and Public Policy," 4.

591 "FoE mourns founder's death," Friends of the Earth, http://www.foe.co.uk/pubsinfo/infoteam/pressrel/2000/20001107132336.html.

SUGGESTED READINGS

Historical Documents (19th and early 20th centuries)

Ackerman, Frederick L. "The Architectural Side of City Planning." In *Proceedings of the Seventh National Conference on City Planning*, Boston, 1915.

Antietam [pseud.]. *McClellan and Fremont: a reply to "Fremont and McClellan, Their Political and Military Careers Reviewed*. New York: Sinclair Tousey Wholesale Agent, September 30, 1862.

Bellows, Henry W. *Historical Sketch of the Union League Club of New York, Its Origin, Organization and Work 1863–1879*. New York: Union League Club, 1879.

Eidlitz, Leopold. "Competitions—The Vicissitudes of Architecture." *The Architectural Record*, fall 1894.

Flagg, Ernest. "The New York Tenement-House Evil and Its Cure." *Scribner's Magazine* 16, no. 1 (July 1894).

Fryer, William J., Jr. *U.S. Public buildings in the city of New York, A report to Colonel W.A. Freret, supervising architect . . . , Feb. 8, 1888*. New York: W. McDonald, 1888.

Fryer, William J., Jr., ed. *Laws Related to buildings, in the city of New York . . .* New York: Real Estate Record and Building Guide, 1886, 1892, 1898, 1903.

Howard, Ebenezer. *Garden Cities of Tomorrow* (originally published as *Tomorrow, A Peaceful Path to Real Reform*, 1898). ATC Books, Builth Wells, 1989.

Olmsted, Frederick Law. *A Journey in the Seaboard Slave States; With Remarks on Their Economy*. New York: Dix and Edwards; London: Sampson Low, Son & Co., 1856.

———. "Chicago in Distress." *The Nation*, November 9, 1871.

Petersen, Frederick A. *Major-General George B. McClellan, From August 1, 1861 to August 1, 1862*. New York: H. Dexter, 1862.

———. *Military Review of the Campaign in Virginia & Maryland, under Generals John C. Fremont, N.P. Banks, Irwin McDowell, Franz Sigel, John Pope, James S. Wadsworth, Wm. H. Halleck and George B. McClellan in 1862*. New York: Sinclair Tousey & H. Dexter, 1862.

———. *Military Review of the Campaign in Virginia & Maryland, under Generals J.C. Fremont, N.P. Banks, Irwin McDowell, Franz Sigel, John Pope, James S. Wadsworth, Wm. H. Halleck , George B. McClellan and Ambrose Burnside in 1862*. Part II. New York: Sinclair Tousey & H. Dexter, 1863.

Riis, Jacob A. *How the Other Half Lives.* New York: Charles Scribner's Sons, 1890.

Råvad, Alfred J. *Borgmesterbog, En Bog om Dansk Byplanægning.* Copenhagen: Arketekten Akademisk Arkitektfoening, 1929.

Roewade (Råvad), Alfred J. "How Copenhagen Was Fortified." *Professional Memoirs* (Corps of Engineers, U.S. Army & Engineering Department at Large) 3, no. 12 (Fall 1911).

Roosevelt, Theodore, Jr. *New York.* New York: Charles Scribner's Sons, 1906.

Union League Club of New York. *Report of the Special Committee on Emigration.* May 12, 1864.

Van Rensselaer, Mrs. Schuyler. "Client and Architect." *North American Review* 151, no. 406 (September 1890).

Van Rensselaer, Mrs. Schuyler. "Frederick Law Olmsted." *The Century* 46, no. 6 (October 1893).

Veiller, Lawrence. *Housing Reform, A Hand-book for Practical Use in American Cities.* New York: Russell Sage Foundation, 1910.

Washington, Booker T. *Up From Slavery: An Autobiography.* Tuskegee, Ala.: Tuskegee Institute, 1901.

Books

Altshuler, Alan A. *The City Planning Process: A Political Analysis in Large American Cities.* Ithaca, N.Y.: Cornell University Press, 1966.

Altshuler, Alan A., and Robert D. Behn, eds. *Innovation in American Government: Challenges, Opportunities, and Dilemmas.* Washington, D.C.: Brookings Institution Press, 1997.

Baker, Paul R. *Richard Morris Hunt.* Cambridge: MIT Press, 1980.

Bannister, Turpin, ed. *The Architect at Mid-Century, Evolution and Achievement,* vol. 1, Report of the Commission for the Survey of Education and Registration of the American Institute of Architects; Bellamy, Francis R., ed., *Conversations Across the Nation,* vol. 2, New York: Reinhold, 1954.

Bauman, John F., ed. *From Tenements to the Taylor Homes: In Search of an Urban Housing Policy in Twentieth-Century America.* University Park, Pa.: Pennsylvania State University Press, 2000.

Berkeley, Ellen Perry, ed. *Architecture: A Place for Women.* Washington, D.C.: Smithsonian Institution Press, 1989.

Bernstein, Iver. *The New York City Draft Riots, Their Significance for American Society and Politics in the Age of the Civil War.* New York: Oxford University Press, 1990.

Beveridge, Charles E., and David Schuyler, eds. *Creating Central Park 1857–1861.* Vol. 3 of *The Papers of Frederick Law Olmsted.* Baltimore: Johns Hopkins University Press, 1983.

Blodgett, Geoffrey. *Cass Gilbert: The Early Years.* St. Paul: Minnesota Historical Society Press, 2001.

Borins, Sandford F. *Innovating with Integrity: How Local Heroes Are Transforming American Government.* Washington, D.C.: Georgetown University Press, 1998.

Boyer, Ernest L., and Lee D. Mitgang. *Building Community: A New Future for Architecture Education and Practice.* Princeton: Carnegie Foundation for the Advancement of Teaching, 1996.

———. *Building Connections: Enriching Learning Through the Power of Architecture and Design.* Princeton: Carnegie Foundation for the Advancement of Teaching and the American Architectural Foundation, 1999.

Bushong, William, Judith Helm Robinson, Julie Mueller, and Don Myer. *A Centennial History of the Washington Chapter, The American Institute of Architects.* Washington, D.C.: Washington Architectural Foundation Press, 1987.

Censer, Jane Turner, ed. *Defending the Union: The Civil War and the U.S. Sanitary Commission 1861–1863.* Vol. 4 of *The Papers of Frederick Law Olmsted.* Baltimore: Johns Hopkins University Press, 1986.

Coleman, A.D. *The Digital Evolution.* Tucson: Nazraeli Press, 1998.

Craig, Lois. *The Federal Presence: Architecture, Politics, and Symbols in United States Government Building.* Cambridge: MIT Press, 1984.

Cramer, James P. *Design Plus Enterprise: Seeking a New Reality in Architecture.* Washington, D.C.: American Institute of Architects Press, 1994.

Cuff, Dana. *Architecture: The Story of Practice.* Cambridge: MIT Press, 1992.

De Bono, Edward. *New Thinking for the New Millennium.* London: Penguin Books, 2000.

DePree, Max. *Leadership Is an Art.* New York: Dell Publishing, 1989.

———. *Leadership Jazz.* New York: Dell Publishing, 1992.

———. *Leading Without Power.* San Francisco: Jossey-Bass, 1997.

Dirckinck-Holmfeld, Kim, ed. *Copenhagen Spaces.* Copenhagen: Arkitektens Forlag, 1996.

Edwards, Trystan. *Good and Bad Manners in Architecture: An Essay on the Social Aspects of Civic Design.* London: John Tirani Ltd., 1924.

Faber, Tobias. *A History of Danish Architecture.* Copenhagen: American-Scandinavian Foundation, 1978.

Fishman, Robert. *Urban Utopias in the Twentieth Century.* Cambridge: MIT Press, 1989.

Fitch, James Marston. *American Building: The Historical Forces That Shaped It.* New York: Schocken Books, 1973.

Friedman, Thomas L. *The Lexus and the Olive Tree.* New York: Random House, Anchor Books, 2000.

Garvin, Alexander. *The American City: What Works, What Doesn't.* New York: McGraw-Hill, 1996.

Gehl, Jan, and Lars Gemzøe. *Public Spaces—Public Life.* 2nd ed. Copenhagen: Danish Architectural Press and the Royal Danish Academy of Fine Arts School of Architecture, 1999.

Gehl, Jan, and Lars Gemzøe. *New City Spaces.* Copenhagen: Danish Architectural Press, 2000.

Gutman, Robert. *Architectural Practice A Critical View.* New York: Princeton Architectural Press, 1988.

Hall, Peter. *Cities of Tomorrow: An Intellectual History of Urban Planning and Design in the Twentieth Century.* Oxford: Basil Blackwell, 1988.

Harries, Karsten. *The Ethical Function of Architecture.* Cambridge: MIT Press, 1997.

Hart, Roger D., ed. *A Nation Reconstructed: A Quest for the Cities That Can Be.* Milwaukee: ASQC Quality Press, 1977.

Hemple, Jan. *Building Connections: Enriching Learning Through the Power of Architecture and Design.* Washington, D.C.: American Architectural Foundation, 1999.

Heifetz, Ronald A. *Leadership Without Easy Answers.* Cambridge: Harvard University Press, Belknap Press, 1994.

Hill, Jonathan, ed. *Occupying Architecture.* London: Routledge, 1998.

Holsman, Henry K. *Rehabilitating Blighted Areas: Report of the Committee on Blighted Area Housing.* Chicago: Architects Club of Chicago, 1932.

Jensen, Jens. *Siftings.* 1939. Reprint, Baltimore: Johns Hopkins University Press, 1990.

Juel-Christiansen, Carsten. *Monument & the Niche: The Architecture of the New City.* Copenhagen: Rhodos, 1985.

Kemmis, Daniel. *Community and the Politics of Place*. Norman: University of Oklahoma Press, 1990.

Kunstler, James Howard. *Home From Nowhere: Remaking our Everyday World for the Twenty-First Century*. New York: Simon & Schuster, 1996.

———. *The Geography of Nowhere: The Rise and Decline of America's Man-Made Landscape*. New York: Simon & Schuster, 1994.

Leadbeater, Charles. *Living on Thin Air—the New Economy*. London: Viking Press, 1999.

Lee, Antoinette J. *Architects to the Nation: The Rise and Decline of the Supervising Architect's Office*. New York: Oxford University Press, 2000.

Lewis, Michael J. *Frank Furness: Architecture and the Violent Mind*. New York: W.W. Norton, 2001.

Loeffler, Jane C. *The Architecture of Diplomacy: Building America's Embassies*. New York: Princeton Architectural Press, 1998.

Longo, Gionni. *Great American Public Places*. New York: Urban Initiatives, 1996.

Machiavelli, Nicolo. *The Prince*. 1513. Reprint, London: Wordsworth Editions, 1993.

Madden, Kathleen. *How to Turn a Place Around: A Handbook for Creating Successful Public Spaces*. New York: Project for Public Spaces, 2001.

McCormick, Richard L. *From Realignment to Reform: Political Change in New York State 1893–1910*. Ithaca: Cornell University Press, 1981.

Moe, Richard, and Carter Wilkie. *Changing Places: Rebuilding Community in the Age of Sprawl*. New York: Henry Holt, 1997.

Norquist, John O. *The Wealth of Cities: Revitalizing the Centers of American Life*. New York: Basic Books, Perseus Books Group, 2000.

Pelletier, L., and A. Pérez-Gómez, eds. *Architecture, Ethics and Technology*. Montréal: McGill-Queen's University Press, 1994.

Pérouse de Montclos, Jean-Marie. "Jefferson and Architecture in the Second Half of the Eighteenth Century." In *The Eye of Thomas Jefferson*, edited by William Howard Adams. Washington, D.C.: Thomas Jefferson Memorial Foundation, Inc., 1976.

Rand, Ayn. *The Fountainhead*. New York: Signet, 1943.

Robin, Ron. *Enclaves of America: The Rhetoric of American Political Architecture Abroad 1900–1965*. Princeton: Princeton University Press, 1992.

Rodgers, Johannah, ed. *Memorials Process Team Briefing Book*. New York: New York New Visions, 2002.

Rogers, Richard (Lord). *Towards an Urban Renaissance: Final Report of the Urban Task Force.* London: Department of the Environment, Transport and the Regions, 1999.

Roper, Laura Wood. *Flo: A Biography of Frederick Law Olmsted.* Baltimore: Johns Hopkins University Press, 1974.

Rubin, Hilary. *The Princessa: Machiavelli for Women.* London: Bloomsbury, 1997.

Saylor, Henry H. *The AIA's First Hundred Years.* Washington, D.C.: Journal of the American Institute of Architects, 1957.

Schaer, Roland, ed. *Utopia: The Search for the Ideal Society in the Western World.* New York: New York Public Library/Oxford University Press, 2000.

Spears, Larry C. *Reflections on Leadership: How Robert K. Greenleaf's Theory of Servant Leadership Influenced Today's Top Management Thinkers.* New York: John Wiley & Sons, 1995.

Spector, Tony. *The Ethical Architect: The Dilemma of Contemporary Practice.* New York: Princeton Architectural Press, 2001.

Stern, Robert A.M., Thomas Mellins, and David Fishman. *New York 1880: Architecture and Urbanism in the Gilded Age.* New York: Monacelli Press, 1999.

Strom, Sharon Hartman. *Political Woman: Florence Luscomb and the Legacy of Radical Reform.* Philadelphia: Temple University Press, 2001.

Tinniswood, Adrian. *Visions of Power: Ambition and Architecture from Ancient Times to the Present.* London: Reed Consumer Books, Mitchell Beazley, 1998.

Trachtenberg, Alan. *The Incorporation of America: Culture and Society in the Gilded Age.* New York: Hill & Wang, 1982.

Vale, Lawrence J. *Architecture, Power and National Identity.* New Haven: Yale University Press, 1992.

Wallenberg, Raoul. *Letters and Dispatches, 1924–1944.* Translated by Kjersti Board. New York: Arcade Publishers, with the U.S. Holocaust Museum, 1995.

Wolfe, Tom. *From Bauhaus to Our House.* New York: Farrar, Straus and Giroux, 1981.

Articles

Bodner, Paul. "Balancing Security and Openess: State Sponsors Forum to Begin Dialogue on Terrorism, Public Buildings." *State Magazine,* February-March 2000.

Bond, Max. "Still Here, Three Architects of Afro-America: Julian Francis Abele, Hilyard Robinson, and Paul R. Williams." *Harvard Design Magazine,* no. 2 (summer 1997).

Bremner, Robert H. "The Big Flat: History of a New York Tenement House." *American Historical Review* 64, no. 1 (October 1958).

Dixon, John Morris. "A White Gentleman's Profession?" *Progressive Architecture*, November 1994.

Dolkart, Andrew S. "The Tenement House Act." Lower East Side Tenement Museum, New York, 2001.

———. "The Biography of a Lower East Side Tenement; 97 Orchard Street, Tenement Design, and Tenement Reform in New York City." Lower East Side Tenement Museum, New York, 2001.

Duany, Andrés. "Principles Essential to the Renewal of Architecture." *Planetizen*, September 15, 2003.

Forgey, Benjamin. "Senator of Design." *Metropolis*, December 5, 2000.

Galbraith, John Kenneth. "For Public and Potent Building." *New York Times Magazine*, October 9, 1960.

Harvard Magazine Roundtable: "Cities and Suburbs." *Harvard Magazine*, January–February 2000.

Livingston, J. Sterling. "Myth of the Well-Educated Manager." *Harvard Business Review*, January 1971.

Polk, William M. "Public Service and Community Outreach." *Public Life*, May 2000.

Scott, Janny. "The State of the City: Packed Like Sardines." *New York Times*, November 26, 2000.

Simon, Arthur R. "New Yorkers without a Voice: A Tragedy of Urban Renewal." *Atlantic Monthly*, April 1966.

Taylor, William C. "The Leader of the Future." Interview with Ronald Heifetz. *Fast Company*, June 1999.

Tolson, Jay. "Putting the Brakes on Suburban Sprawl." *U.S. News & World Report*, March 20, 2000.

AIA and Other Professional Association and Industry Documents and Publications

American Institute of Architects. "Code of Ethics and Professional Conduct." AIA, Washington, D.C.

———. *Proceedings of the Annual Convention of the American Institute of Architects.* 1892, 1893, 1904, 1905, 1913, 1914, 1919.

American Planning Association. *Millennium Survey.* Washington, D.C., December 2000.

Baker, Kermit. "Alternative Career Paths Provide Vast Differences in Compensation for Architects." *AIArchitect*, October 2000.

Brown, Glenn. "A Bill for the Creation of a Proposed Bureau of Buildings and Grounds" (presented to the 47th AIA convention by the Washington, D.C., chapter). December 1913.

"Design Diplomacy: Public Policy and the Practice of Architecture." Transcripts of the AIA International Conference, September 6–9, 2000, Copenhagen, Denmark.

Geddes, Robert. "Toward a Discourse on Architectural Ethics." *AIArchitect*, September 2000.

Holsman, Henry K. (president, Illinois chapter, AIA). "Inaugural Address." June 10, 1919.

Lower Manhattan Development Corporation. "Plans in Progress, Innovative Designs for the World Trade Center Site." New York, LMDC, December 18, 2002.

Moore, Charles, ed. *The Promise of American Architecture: Addresses at the Annual Dinner of the American Institute of Architects*. Washington, D.C.: AIA, 1905.

Simpson, John. "The Legacy of Whitney M. Young Jr." *AIArchitect*, May 2000.

Skaggs, Ronald L. "For the Next Generation." *AIArchitect*, September 2000.

Steinberg, Harris. "Models of Civic Engagement: A Call to Action." AIA National Convention, Dallas, 1999.

Walker, Ralph. "The Education Necessary to the Professional Practice of Architecture." *Journal of the American Institute of Architects* 15 (February 1951) and 16 (March 1951).

Wrenn, Tony P. " AIA Convention of the Century—Washington, D.C., 1900." *AIArchitect*, May 2000.

Government Documents and Publications

Moynihan, Senator Daniel Patrick. *Guiding Principles for Federal Architecture, Ad Hoc Committee on Federal Office Space*. 1962–1963 (Kennedy administration).

U.S. General Services Administration, Public Buildings Service, Office of the Chief Architect. "The Design Excellence Program: Building a Legacy: Architect/Engineer Selection and Design Review." Washington, D.C., August 2000.

U.S. General Services Administration, Public Buildings Service. "Architecture of the Great Society: Assessing the GSA Portfolio of Buildings Constructed during the 1960s and 1970s." Summary of Comments and Issues from a Forum Convened at Yale University's Center for British Art, December 5, 2000.

ABOUT THE AUTHOR

RICHARD N. SWETT, FAIA, is the only architect to serve in the U.S. Congress during the 20th century and one of very few architect-ambassadors in the nation's history. While serving in Congress, he authored the Transportation for Livable Communities Act, coauthored the landmark Congressional Accountability Act, and introduced bills on energy conservation and use of renewable energy. He also served as a member of the Public Works and Transportation Committee; the Committee on Science, Space and Technology; the U.S. Congressional Delegation for Relations with the European Parliament; and the Congressional Human Rights Caucus. In the private sector, his experience includes architectural design, project and corporate management, and development. Swett was also a contributing author for the book *A Nation Reconstructed: A Quest for the Cities That Can Be.* Twice he has been awarded the Presidential citation by the AIA, in addition to numerous other awards and honorary degrees.

ABOUT THE CHIEF RESEARCHER

COLLEEN M. THORNTON, an independent art historian, writer/researcher and visual artist, began her career thirty years ago with the cofounding of the artist-led cultural institution City Without Walls Gallery in Newark, New Jersey. After more than a decade of activist work in the New York-New Jersey artists' community, Thornton decided to fulfill her dream of studying European Art firsthand and moved to London for that purpose. Since then, Thornton has pursued an expertise in Danish Art for which she moved to Copenhagen in 1993. Thornton's professional objectives as a cultural emissary and her personal goal to facilitate a deeper understanding of the critical social role of the arts and creative professionals in society has made her contribution to Richard Swett's design diplomacy project a particularly fruitful collaboration.

AVAILABLE FROM GREENWAY...

How Firms Succeed: A Field Guide to Design Management,
James P. Cramer and Scott Simpson.

A hands-on guide to running any design-related business—from a two-person graphics team to middle-management to CEOs of multinational firms—offering advice on specific problems and situations and providing insight into the art of inspirational management and strategic thinking.

"*How Firms Succeed* is a fountainhead of great ideas for firms looking to not just survive, but thrive in today's challenging marketplace.
—Thompson E. Penney, FAIA
President/CEO, LS3P Architecture, Interior Architecture, Land Planning and President, The American Institute of Architects, 2003

Communication by Design, Joan Capelin

How to communicate—and, especially why—to clients, prospects, staff, and the public is the basis of this powerful book. It is targeted to business principals as well as anyone who aspires to a leadership position in a firm, association, or business joint venture.

"Joan Capelin offers thought-provoking practical lessons in marketing leadership—illustrated by interesting insights and implementable ideas. Read this book, put her advice into action, and your firm will flourish."
—Howard J. Wolff
Senior Vice President/Wimberly Allison Tong & Goo

Almanac of Architecture & Design, James P. Cramer and Jennifer Evans Yankopolus, editors.

The only complete annual reference for rankings, records, and facts about architecture, interior design, landscape architecture, industrial design, and historic preservation.

"The reader who uses this book well will come away with a richer sense of the texture of the profession and of the architecture it produces."
—Paul Goldberger, *The New Yorker*

DesignIntelligence

The Design Futures Council's monthly "Report on the Future" provides access to key trends and issues on the cutting edge of the design professions. Each month it offers indispensable insight into management practices that will make any firm a better managed and more financially successful business.

"We read every issue with new enthusiasm because the information always proves so timely. No other publication in our industry provides as much useful strategy information."
—Davis Brody Bond LLP

—Order form on back—

ORDER FORM

How Firms Succeed: A Field Guide to Design Management: $39

Communication by Design: $34.95

Almanac of Architecture & Design: $49.50

***DesignIntelligence* (including a one-year membership to the Design Futures Council): $289 annually**

Shipping: $4.95
(add $1.50 per additional title)

NOTE: Shipping is included with *DesignIntelligence*—there is
NO additional charge

Title	Quantity	Price:
	Shipping	

❑ Check   ❑ Credit card   Order Total

Card #   Expiration   Signature

Contact/Shipping Information

Name   Company

Address

City   State   Zip

Telephone   Fax

Email

Please fax this form to Greenway Communications: (770) 209-3778
or mail: Greenway Communications, 30 Technology Parkway South, Suite 200, Norcross, GA
30092. For additional information call (800) 726-8603.

östberg™

Library of Design Management

Every relationship of value requires constant care and commitment. At Östberg, we are relentless in our desire to create and bring forward only the best ideas in design, architecture, interiors, and design management. Using diverse mediums of communications, including books and the Internet, we are constantly searching for thoughtful ideas that are erudite, witty, and of lasting importance to the quality of life. Inspired by the architecture of Ragnar Östberg and the best of Scandinavian design and civility, the Östberg Library of Design Management seeks to restore the passion for creativity that makes better products, spaces, and communities. The essence of Östberg can be summed up in our quality charter to you: "Communicating concepts of leadership and design excellence."